Value Sets for EQ-5D-5L

Nancy Devlin • Bram Roudijk • Kristina Ludwig
Editors

Value Sets for EQ-5D-5L

A Compendium, Comparative Review
& User Guide

 Springer

Editors
Nancy Devlin
Centre for Health Policy
University of Melbourne
Melbourne, VIC, Australia

Bram Roudijk
EuroQol Research Foundation
Rotterdam, The Netherlands

Kristina Ludwig
Department of Health Economics and
Health Care Management, School of
Public Health
Bielefeld University
Bielefeld, Germany

ISBN 978-3-030-89288-3   ISBN 978-3-030-89289-0   (eBook)
https://doi.org/10.1007/978-3-030-89289-0

Cover illustration: agsandrew/shutterstock.com

This Springer imprint is published by the registered company Springer Nature Switzerland AG
The registered company address is: Gewerbestrasse 11, 6330 Cham, Switzerland

Foreword by Michael Drummond

Since its development by the EuroQol Group in 1990, the EQ-5D instrument has probably become the most widely used measure of health-related quality of life in economic evaluations of healthcare treatment and programmes. It is also frequently used in health technology assessments (HTAs), which are a key element in technology adoption decisions in several countries. Reasons for its success include it being generic, concise – and it being accompanied by the value sets that are required to support economic evaluation. This prominence of the EQ-5D means that it is important that the users of the instrument fully understand the attributes and limitations of these value sets. This is the aim of the book *Value Sets for EQ-5D-5L: A Compendium, Comparative Review & User Guide* by Devlin, Roudijk and Ludwig. The primary 'users' in this case are those using EQ-5D data in economic evaluation or other applications, and decision makers interpreting economic evaluations or HTAs as part of their decision-making processes.

The main impetus for the book is the development of the new '5L' version of the EQ-5D instrument. The original version had only three levels on each of the 5 dimensions of health-related quality of life, which in some dimensions resulted in a rather large or 'abrupt' change between levels. For example, in the dimension of 'mobility', a change from level two to level three is expressed as moving from 'some problems in walking about' to being 'confined to bed'. By moving from 3 to 5 levels on each of the dimensions, it is possible to characterise a more gradual change between health states, which is arguably more realistic.

The main implication of the decision to move from 3 to 5 levels was the need to develop a new series of value sets for the EQ-5D-5L. These represent the value of each of the 3125 health states defined by the instrument (i.e. individual combinations of the 5 levels and 5 dimensions) and are critical to the calculation of the quality-adjusted life years (QALYs) gained by healthcare treatments and programmes. This is no mean task, especially as there is no reason to believe that the preferences for health states of the general public would be the same in different jurisdictions. Indeed, more than 35 distinct value sets have been developed for the original 3L instrument, and decision makers in several jurisdictions require that the value set used in HTAs should be representative of the preferences of the population of the country concerned.

To undertake this task, the EuroQol Group embarked on an extensive programme of methodological and empirical research which is reported in the book. Rather than just replicate the approaches used in the development of value sets for the original instrument, the group took the opportunity to develop and strengthen the methods of valuing health states, with a view to specifying a common protocol. (This programme of research is discussed in Chaps. 2 and 3 of the book.)

Users of the new instrument will probably be most interested in the value sets themselves. These are described and classified in the country-by-country overview given in Chap. 4. Looking at the classification given, it is hard to think of any critical information that is not given about the precise methods used to generate the value set for each country, the sample of individuals whose preferences were measured, and the main results obtained. I find this chapter useful both in providing information about each country, and for understanding the results for each country in the overall context of all the research conducted.

The comparisons between the various country value sets and issues of which value set to use are discussed in Chaps. 5 and 6. These choices can be quite complicated, especially during the period while value sets for the new instrument are still being developed. For example, if a value set is not currently available for EQ-5D-5L in my country, should I use a value set from a country I perceive to be similar to my own, or an earlier value set for my country from the 3L instrument, using the mapping/crosswalk algorithm that has been developed? What should I do if no value set for either instrument exists for my country?

The final chapter discusses the future for value sets. My take from it is that there will be continuing debate about the different results produced by different versions of the EQ-5D, what the change from 3 to 5 levels does to the sensitivity of the instrument, and the conditions under which it makes sense to develop a new value set for a particular jurisdiction. Being based in 'God's Own Country' (Yorkshire), I often wonder whether we should develop our own value set or continue to use those available for the UK! Some of these big questions will probably never be answered. But in the meantime, I have reached a simple conclusion. If you are a decision maker or researcher using the EQ-5D-5L, you should read this book.

Professor of Health Economics   Michael Drummond
University of York, York, UK

Foreword by Kim Rand

The EuroQol Group started small, and made a concise instrument. After a short detour down the track towards a 6-dimension questionnaire, the EQ-5D was born in a form we easily recognize today, covering "no", "some", and "extreme" problems in mobility, self-care, usual activities, pain/discomfort, and anxiety/depression. A visual analogue scale reminiscent of a thermometer completed the questionnaire, which took all of two pages. That's it.

Today, the EQ-5D is the most used instrument worldwide for measuring quality-adjusted life years (QALYs) for health-economic analyses, even though such use constitutes merely a fraction of publications using the instrument.

The brevity and simplicity of the EQ-5D is also its primary strength, and driver behind its apparent success. It is also the instrument's greatest weakness, and has spurned debates that continue unabated today: which dimensions of health should be included, how should they be described, and what levels of functioning should be provided?

The first large-scale time trade-off (TTO) based national value set for the EQ-5D, from the seminal UK Measuring and Valuing Health (MVH) study, was published in 1997, initiating a flurry of research and costly valuation studies for the 3-level version of the EQ-5D (EQ-5D-3L). In just a few years, the number of studies had risen to the point where potential users could easily lose track as to which value sets were available, and for what jurisdictions. The question as to which value set to use became a real issue. The 2007 book *EQ-5D Value Sets: Inventory, Comparative Review and User Guide* by Szende, Oppe, and Devlin came to the rescue, describing 8 TTO-based and 9 VAS-based national EQ-5D-3L value sets. Around the same time, the development of the new and current 5-level version of the EQ-5D was underway; after years of intense debates, it was decided that three levels of problems were impractically large grained as a descriptive tool. A new, five level tool was developed: the EQ-5D-5L.

While the EQ-5D-5L remains the briefest of instruments in its class, and still takes up just two pages, the additional levels provided great challenges in terms of how the instrument should be valued. Over the past decade, the primary focus of the EuroQol Group has been a massive effort around the methods, logistics, tools, and decisions necessary to produce high-quality preference-based values for the instrument. As a consequence, 25 national value sets have been produced, and more are underway. While this is great news from a scientific perspective, the co-existence of value sets for the 3L and 5L versions of the instrument has further complicated the question as to which value set to use.

This book, I am happy to say, does not provide a definite answer. It does, however, provide insightful discussions around the topic, as well as simple and useful guidance as to how users of the EQ-5D worldwide can identify the value set best suited for their purposes.

The EQ-5D and associated value sets are powerful tools to guide decision-making in the health sector and beyond. However, value sets are derived in a particular setting, conventionally designed to reflect the health preferences of the adult general population in a particular country. For use in public decision making, where legitimacy and transparency are increasingly required, decisions around what constitutes the best reference value set is a decision best placed at a national jurisdictional level. For any reader of this book who happens to be a decision maker in a country contemplating the use of the EQ-5D, I hope that this book will provide inspiration and insight to help develop national guidelines. We would, of course, be happy to be of assistance in this process.

For non-economic use, and for research involving international comparison, different reasoning may come into play. Regardless of the purpose for which value sets are used, this book, which will be updated with new value sets in the future, provides an excellent source of structured information on available EQ-5D-5L value sets, including methods and other details around the studies from which they derive.

While I appreciate having such books in hardback format, to be retrieved from my bookshelf at need, I am delighted and proud that this book is also available online and for free as an open-source e-book. In the spirit of transparency, *Value Sets for EQ-5D-5L: A Compendium, Comparative Review & User Guide* by Devlin, Roudijk, and Ludwig presents to the world what the EuroQol Group has produced over the last decade, and highlights the important challenges we are currently facing. This book is not intended to stop the debates around the EQ-5D. Rather, it provides an overview of where we currently stand in terms of value sets, which should be of interest to end users, researchers, and decision makers. In the meantime, the EuroQol Group is funding an unprecedented volume of research in a wide range of areas, including a strong push forward for the youth version of the instrument. New books will be needed in just a few years.

In the meantime, enjoy!

Chair of the EuroQol Executive Committee,   Kim Rand
EuroQol Research Foundation, Rotterdam, The Netherlands
Co-founder and Principal, Maths in Health B.V.,
Rotterdam, The Netherlands
Senior Researcher, Health Services Research Unit, Akershus University Hospital,
Lørenskog, Norway

Preface

The aim of this book is to collate information about and provide guidance on the use of EQ-5D-5L value sets, providing an easy-to-use resource for users of the EQ-5D-5L instrument. By creating this compendium of value sets, our hope is not just to increase the accessibility of this material, but to also encourage users to be aware of how these value sets were created, the characteristics of value sets, their differences and similarities, and the implications for their use in analysing of EQ-5D-5L data.

The availability of value sets is one of the reasons the EQ-5D instruments are widely used in economic evaluations in healthcare and in population studies around the world. However, these value sets are generally published in peer-reviewed scientific journals largely aimed at other researchers. The information presented about these studies differs somewhat between journals, authors, and studies. Furthermore, not all value sets are published Open Access, making it more difficult for some (especially non-academic) users to access the value sets. This creates a place for a book pulling together all the relevant information into a single source and similar format, allowing for an easier comparison.

Our focus in this book is on value sets for the EQ-5D-5L. The development of a standardised international protocol for conducting such studies, and the related training and quality control processes that nowadays accompany it, now constitutes a 'mature technology' that was successfully employed to generate a considerable number of value sets since the first wave of studies commenced in 2012. The timing therefore seems appropriate to produce this compendium of these value sets. In doing so, we build on the precedent set by Szende, Oppe, and Devlin's 2007 book on EQ-5D-3L value sets, which continues to be widely used and cited as a resource on value sets for that instrument.

We are grateful to the EuroQol Research Foundation for their support of our work and in particular for their commitment to Open Access publication of this book. We would also like to express our gratitude to the principal investigators of the value set studies reported in this book for their support and input, and to all those who contributed to the authorship of chapters. This was a team effort and a credit to the collegiality and common purpose of the EuroQol Group in promoting the measurement and valuation of health.

We hope you find this book useful!

Melbourne, VIC, Australia,   Nancy Devlin
London, UK

Rotterdam, The Netherlands   Bram Roudijk

Bielefeld, Germany   Kristina Ludwig
Rotterdam, The Netherlands

Acknowledgements

We acknowledge with gratitude the EQ-5D-5L value set principal investigators, and their research teams in each country, for giving us permission to include their studies in this book, allowing us access to their valuation data, and for their input to and clarifications on the summaries presented in Chap. 4. Without their efforts in conducting these studies, this book would not have been possible. We are also grateful to Kim Rand, chair of the Executive Committee, and to Elly Stolk, scientific team leader, for their careful reviews of the chapters and thoughtful comments and suggestions, and to Rosalind Rabin and KMHO for helpful edits. Lastly, we would like to thank Gerben Bakker for his support with legal and copyright matters.

Funding for this book was provided by the EuroQol Research Foundation EQ169-2020RA. Views expressed in this book are not necessarily those of the EuroQol Group.

Contents

About the Editors

Nancy Devlin is Professor of Health Economics at the University of Melbourne, Australia, and senior visiting fellow at the Office of Health Economics, London. She was 2019–2020 president of ISPOR and a past president of the EuroQol Group. Her principal areas of research are the measurement and valuation of health-related quality of life, priority setting in healthcare, and the cost effectiveness thresholds used in making judgements about value for money in healthcare. Her previous books include *Methods for Analysing and Reporting EQ-5D Data* (with Bas Janssen and David Parkin), *Using Patient Reported Outcomes to Improve Health Care* (with John Appleby and David Parkin), and *Economic Analysis in Health Care* (with Stephen Morris, David Parkin, and Anne Spencer). She was also a co-author (with Agota Szende and Mark Oppe) of the book on EQ-5D-3L values, *EQ-5D Valuation Sets: An Inventory, Comparative Review and User Guide.* Nancy contributed to methodological work underpinning the EQ-VT protocol and to the development of EQ-5D-5L value sets in Mexico, Ireland, and England.

Bram Roudijk works as a scientist at the business office of the EuroQol Research Foundation in Rotterdam, the Netherlands. His main research interests are valuation of health-related quality of life, modelling health-related quality of life valuation data, and differences in preferences for health-related quality of life between countries and cultures. Bram is involved in supporting valuation studies for the EQ-5D family of instruments, including the EQ-5D-5L. Furthermore, Bram is a member of EuroQol's Valuation Working Group.

Kristina Ludwig works as a senior scientist in the Department of Health Economics and Health Care Management at Bielefeld University, Germany, and as a freelance senior scientist for the business office of the EuroQol Research Foundation in Rotterdam, the Netherlands. Her main research area is the measurement and valuation of health-related quality of life in the context of economic evaluation and measuring patient preferences. During her position at the EuroQol office, she provided support to various valuation studies for the EQ-5D-5L. She contributed methodological work for the refinement of the EQ-VT protocol and was significantly involved in the development of the value sets for the EQ-5D instruments, including EQ-5D-5L in Germany.

Contributors

Jan Busschbach Section of Medical Psychology, Department of Psychiatry, Erasmus MC, Rotterdam, The Netherlands

Nancy Devlin Centre for Health Policy, University of Melbourne, Melbourne, VIC, Australia

Aureliano Paolo Finch EuroQol Research Foundation, Rotterdam, The Netherlands

Bas Janssen EuroQol Research Foundation, Rotterdam, The Netherlands
Section of Medical Psychology, Department of Psychiatry, Erasmus MC, Rotterdam, The Netherlands

Kristina Ludwig Department of Health Economics and Health Care Management, School of Public Health, Bielefeld University, Bielefeld, Germany
EuroQol Research Foundation, Rotterdam, The Netherlands

Richard Norman School of Population Health, Curtin University, Bentley, Australia

Jan Abel Olsen Department of Community Medicine, University of Tromsø – The Arctic University of Norway, Tromsø, Norway
Division of Health Services, Norwegian Institute of Public Health, Oslo, Norway

Mark Oppe Maths in Health B.V., Rotterdam, The Netherlands

David Parkin Office of Health Economics, University of London, London, UK

Simon Pickard Department of Pharmacy Systems, Outcomes and Policy, College of Pharmacy, University of Illinois at Chicago, Chicago, IL, USA

Juan Manuel Ramos-Goñi Maths in Health B.V., Rotterdam, The Netherlands

Bram Roudijk EuroQol Research Foundation, Rotterdam, The Netherlands

Elly Stolk EuroQol Research Foundation, Rotterdam, The Netherlands

Ben van Hout School of Health and Related Research, University of Sheffield, Sheffield, UK
Pharmerit International, York, UK

Zhihao Yang Health Services Management Department, Guizhou Medical University, Gui'an, People's Republic of China

Chapter 1
The Development of the EQ-5D-5L and its Value Sets

Nancy Devlin, Simon Pickard, and Jan Busschbach

Abstract This chapter introduces the EQ-5D-5L questionnaire and its development by the EuroQol Group. The availability of the EQ-5D-5L, and the growing evidence of its pivotal role as a measurement system, generated a demand for 'values' to accompany it that would enable the use of EQ-5D-5L data in the estimation of quality-adjusted life-years (QALYs) and other applications where EQ-5D-5L profile data needs to be summarised by a single number. Chapter 1 sets out the main aim of the book: to provide an accessible source of information and guidance to support users of EQ-5D-5L and its value sets. Specifically, the book aims to improve users' understanding of how EQ-5D-5L value sets are generated using the internationally standardised EQ-VT protocol; to raise awareness of the characteristics and properties of value sets; and to inform users' choice of which value set to select for which purpose, and how that choice may affect analysis. The chapter concludes with an overview of the content of the book.

1.1 The EQ-5D as an Instrument for Measuring and Valuing Health

Since the 1990s, the EQ-5D instrument has held a pivotal role in the measurement of self-reported health status and health-related quality of life (HRQoL) (Devlin and Brooks 2017). The availability of a *concise* generic instrument for measuring

N. Devlin (✉)
Centre for Health Policy, University of Melbourne, Melbourne, VIC, Australia
e-mail: nancy.devlin@unimelb.edu.au

S. Pickard
Department of Pharmacy Systems, Outcomes and Policy, College of Pharmacy, University of Illinois at Chicago, Chicago, IL, USA

J. Busschbach
Section of Medical Psychology, Department of Psychiatry, Erasmus MC, Rotterdam, The Netherlands

© The Author(s) 2022
N. Devlin et al. (eds.), *Value Sets for EQ-5D-5L*,
https://doi.org/10.1007/978-3-030-89289-0_1

1

patients' and population self-reported health[1] meant that it could be included, with minimal responder burden, in clinical trials, observational studies, and population health surveys. More recently, it has become the cornerstone of routine outcomes measurement in health care systems such as the English NHS PROMs programme and Sweden's national quality registers. The ability of the EQ-5D to measure HRQoL in a *generic* manner has the important advantage of yielding data that can readily be compared across disease areas and between patient and population sub-groups, and against population norms. This broad comparability of EQ-5D data is particularly crucial in providing evidence that quantifies health benefits in a standardised and transparent manner to inform decisions regarding alternative ways of using health care resources.

The EQ-5D was developed by the EuroQol Group, then a small group of academics which has now grown into an international network of multidisciplinary researchers with more than 100 members worldwide (Devlin and Brooks 2017). The development of the EQ-5D was motivated in part by the specific goal of providing evidence on the outcomes of health care programmes in a manner that would facilitate economic evaluation. One of the considerations underpinning the development of the instrument was that it would be accompanied by the 'values' (sometimes also referred to as 'utilities', 'quality of life weights', the 'EQ-5D Index' or 'EQ Index weights') that would enable the quality adjustment of life years as required for the estimation of quality-adjusted life-years (QALYs) used in cost effectiveness analysis (Drummond et al. 2015). The availability of value sets for this purpose has been a notable part of the success and uptake of EQ-5D instruments.

The value sets that accompany EQ-5D instruments provide a means of summarising, via a single number, how good or bad health status is as described by the EQ-5D. The responses to the EQ-5D instrument – that is, the particular combination of levels which are indicated on each of the five dimensions (mobility, self-care, usual activities, pain/discomfort, and anxiety/depression), by those completing it – can be described as EQ-5D 'profiles' (see Box 1.1). The original version of the EQ-5D, the EQ-5D-3L, has three response levels for each of the five dimensions, describing a total of $3^5 = 243$ possible profiles (Brooks 1996). The focus of this book is on the later five level version, the EQ-5D-5L, development of which is described in more detail in the following section – which describes a total of $5^5 = 3125$ profiles (Herdman et al. 2011).

The value sets for these instruments provide a single value for each of the possible profiles described by them. These values lie on a scale anchored at 1 (full health) and 0 (dead), as is required for the estimation of QALYs. The values are built up from a set of sub-weights which represent the relative importance of each level of problem in each dimension, and indicate how good or bad these are overall, when combined in EQ-5D-5L profiles. The term *value set* refers to a set of values

---

[1] There is ongoing debate about the term health-related quality of life (HRQoL) and whether EQ-5D measures HRQoL or self-perceived health status (Brazier and Karimi 2016). For simplicity, in the remainder of this book, we refer to the EQ-5D-5L value sets as providing values for health states or health as described by the EQ-5D-5L.

Box 1.1: EQ-5D Questionnaires, EQ-5D Profiles and Values
EQ-5D questionnaires comprise two key parts:

(i) the EQ-5D descriptive system, as shown below for the EQ-5D-5L. Respondents are asked to indicate the level of problem they experience on each of the five dimensions today. The combination of these ticks describes that person's EQ-5D self-reported health state, referred to as an 'EQ-5D profile'

(ii) the EQ VAS, a vertical visual analogue scale capturing respondents' overall assessment of their health on a scale from 0 (worst possible health you can imagine) to 100 (best possible health you can imagine) (not shown here).

The EQ-5D-5L questionnaire

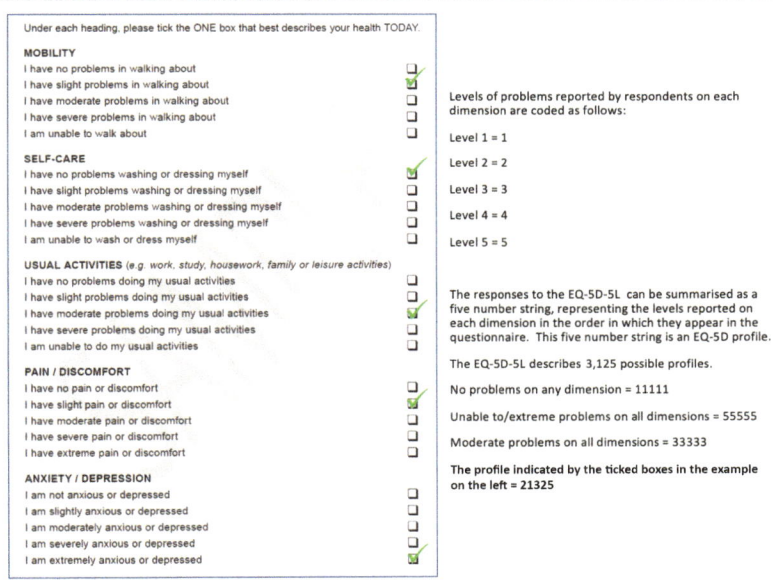

© EuroQol Research Foundation. EQ-5D™ is a trademark of the EuroQol Research Foundation. Reproduced by permission of EuroQol Research Foundation. Reproduction of this version is not allowed. For reproduction, use or modification of the EQ-5D (any version), please register your study by using the online EQ registration page: www.euroqol.org.

The EQ VAS is an important part of the questionnaire and provides the patients' overall assessment of their own health on a visual analogue scale. However, many applications of EQ-5D data, including the estimation of QALYs for economic evaluation, focus instead on the use of EQ-5D profile

(continued)

Box 1.1 (continued)

data. The profile data, and the use of value sets to summarise those data, is the focus of this book, and therefore the EQ VAS is not discussed further. There are in fact many ways of analysing EQ-5D profile data, as detailed in Devlin et al. (2020). One of these ways is by weighting the profile using values sets. This is the most common way of using EQ-5D data in cost effectiveness analysis. This book focuses on the value sets available for the EQ-5D-5L and their use in weighting EQ-5D-5L profile data.

The value sets provide a way of converting the profiles into a single number that reflects how good or bad people think they are. The values are usually obtained using stated preference methods, and yield values that lie on a scale anchored by the value of 1 for full health, and 0 for dead. EQ-5D values cannot be higher than 1, but values <0 are possible, and indicate health states considered on average to be worse than dead (WTD). Value sets are generally intended to represent the average preferences of local/national populations – so EQ-5D value sets differ between countries. See Chap. 4 for a summary of the available value sets for EQ-5D-5L, and Chap. 6 for information about the differences and similarities between them.

for all possible profiles defined by a particular EQ-5D instrument, and is occasionally also referred to by other names, such as an EQ-5D 'tariff' or 'social values.' For the purposes of this book, we will use the terms value and value set.

These values are usually based on the average preferences of the relevant adult general population, obtained using stated preference methods such as the Time Trade-Off (TTO). These stated preference methods aim to elicit values which have the desired properties for estimating QALYs (see Box 5.1 in Chap. 5). Indeed, the availability of EQ-5D values which are suitable for this purpose has led to the EQ-5D being the most widely recommended questionnaire for use in the cost effectiveness evidence submitted to Health Technology Appraisal (HTA) bodies. The EQ-5D is recommended in 85% of HTA guidelines (Kennedy-Martin et al. 2020), including those of the UK's National Institute for Health and Care Excellence (NICE 2013).

The EuroQol Group was and continues to be a pioneer in the development of local/national value sets. The development of EQ-5D-3L value sets was, as an international research effort, unparalleled in the availability of country-specific values (Szende et al. 2007). There are currently EQ-5D-3L value sets available for 35 countries and, for the EQ-5D-5L, 25 countries, with still further value set studies underway or planned. Both the EQ-5D-3L and the EQ-5D-5L, and the value sets which accompany them, continue to be used next to each other in many countries. The value sets facilitated the use of data from EQ-5D instruments in the estimation of QALYs based on local preferences, as well as in other, 'non-economic' applications where EQ-5D profile data are summarised in a way that reflects the relative importance of the different dimensions.

1.2   The Development of the EQ-5D-5L

In 2005 the EuroQol Group initiated efforts to develop an expanded-level version of the EQ-5D-3L. This was motivated by concerns by some stakeholders about limitations of the original instrument, particularly ceiling effects and changes in health that were too small to be detected by the three-level version. Studies which had been undertaken by EuroQol Group members prior to 2005 had shown that various experimental five-level versions of EQ-5D could reduce ceiling effects while at the same increasing reliability and sensitivity (discriminatory power) and maintaining feasibility (Janssen et al. 2008a, b; Pickard et al. 2007a, b).

The development and testing of the EQ-5D-5L is reported in Herdman et al. (2011). A decision was made early in the new instrument's development to retain the same five dimensions as the EQ-5D-3L, but to expand the number of response levels. This could in principle have been achieved simply by adding two 'unlabelled' intermediate levels between the existing three. However, in order to arrive at values for the EQ-5D-5L profiles, each health state to be evaluated by respondents needed to be capable of being described by five sentences. This in turn required a label for each level. An example of an EQ-5D-5L health state, displayed in the manner it might be presented in a stated preference task, is shown in Fig. 1.1. The state described in Fig. 1.1 is the same combination of levels and dimensions as the example in Box 1.1 i.e., it is EQ-5D-5L profile 21325.

Herdman et al. (2011) describe the process by which these labels were established, using both English and Spanish as root languages in order to support further translation and adaptation of the new instrument. Severity labels for 5 levels in each dimension were identified using response scaling. Selecting labels at approximately the 25th, 50th, and 75th centiles produced two alternative 5-level versions. Focus groups were used to investigate the face and content validity of the two versions, including hypothetical health states generated from those versions. This showed evidence in favour of the wording 'slight-moderate-severe' problems, with level one described as 'no problems' in each dimension, and level five being 'unable to' in the EQ-5D functional dimensions (mobility, self-care, usual activities) and 'extreme problems' in the pain/discomfort and anxiety/depression dimensions.

- Slight problems in walking about
- No problems washing or dressing myself
- Moderate problems doing my usual activities
- Slight pain or discomfort
- Extremely anxious or depressed

Fig. 1.1 An example of an EQ-5D-5L health 'state' described by five sentences

The final version of the five-level instrument which emerged from this work is described in the EQ-5D-5L User Guide (EuroQol Group 2019). Beside the increased number of levels of the dimensions, the 5-level version of the EQ-5D has other notable features which represent improvements on the EQ-5D-3L. Most importantly, the wording of the mobility dimension is improved: the most severe level of the mobility dimension of the EQ-5D-3L is 'confined to bed', which means that it cannot capture severe problems with mobility that do not involve being confined to bed. This acts to limit its usefulness both in detecting problems with mobility and in capturing improvements in mobility resulting from treatment (Oppe et al. 2011). In the EQ-5D-5L, the most severe level of mobility has been changed to 'unable to walk about'.

These improvements have yielded a number of advantages for the EQ-5D-5L over the EQ-5D-3L. These are summarised by Devlin et al. (2018) and include:

(a) A reduction in the ceiling effect: Using the EQ-5D-5L, compared to the EQ-5D-3L, fewer respondents report no problems on any dimension (e.g., see Feng et al. 2015 and Craig et al. 2014).

(b) Reduced clustering on just a few states: The lack of granularity in the EQ-5D-3L descriptive system imposes constraints on the self-report of health. Observations tend to cluster on a few health states (Devlin et al. 2020). The EQ-5D-5L consistently produces considerably more unique health states than the EQ-5D-3L, as shown by Buchholz et al. (2018).

(c) Improved ability to discriminate between patient groups/subgroups: The EQ-5D-5L has better discriminative ability, as demonstrated by improved ability to detect differences between subgroups defined by severity at a given sample size (Janssen et al. 2018). EQ-5D-5L users thus benefit from lower sample size requirements within samples of patients (Pickard et al. 2007b). The EQ-5D-5L has improved ability to measure health accurately at the top of the scale and therefore captures finer differences between mild states of ill health and full health at the top of the scale, whereas the EQ-5D-3L has much larger steps between levels 2 and 1.

(d) Improvements in the EQ-5D-5L with respect to problems with mobility: As noted above, changing the EQ-5D-3L level 3 descriptor 'confined to bed' constitutes an important improvement in the EQ-5D-5L. Level 3 problems on mobility are rarely observed in EQ-5D-3L data. For example, among patients about to receive hip replacement surgery in the English National Health Service, *none* reported a level 3 problem (Devlin et al. 2010). In effect, in most settings, the EQ-5D-3L only has two levels on mobility: no and some problems. Consequently, the EQ-5D-3L will underestimate benefits of treatments that improve severe problems with mobility (Oppe et al. 2011).

Overall, the evidence suggests that the EQ-5D-5L retains the principal benefits of EQ-5D-3L—its brevity and validity in a wide range of conditions—and produces a more accurate measurement of patient health than the EQ-5D-3L (Devlin et al. 2018). These advantages have been recognised by users and use of the EQ-5D-5L has rapidly increased. There are now more than 130 language versions of the EQ-5D-5L available.

1.3 The need for EQ-5D-5L Values

The availability of the EQ-5D-5L, and the supporting evidence of its improved measurement system, generated a demand for values to accompany it, to allow use of its data in the estimation of QALYs and any other applications where EQ-5D-5L profile data need to be summarised by a preference-weighted single number.

In anticipation of the need to provide EQ-5D-5L value sets, the EuroQol Group initiated an ambitious programme of methodological research, running in parallel with the development of the EQ-5D-5L instrument, and aimed at producing an internationally standardised state-of-the-art valuation protocol. This was timely, as most of the EQ-5D-3L value sets were based on the so called 'MVH-protocol' developed in the early 1990s (Dolan 1997). There was a lack of consistency in the design and implementation of that protocol between value sets studies. Furthermore, limitations of the MVH protocol had been recognised, suggesting improved methods were required for valuation of the EQ-5D-5L.

The aim was therefore not just to improve on the instrument, but to also ensure that the valuation of EQ-5D-5L profiles would be based on the best possible stated preference methods – and to provide a well-described, standard valuation study protocol which could be fielded in a consistent way across different countries. This would ensure that the value sets generated for the new instrument would, as far as possible, be comparable across countries. That is, that differences between the EQ-5D-5L value sets which are observed would reflect the local variations in preferences and opinions which they are intended to capture, rather than being confounded by differences in methods.

As it was anticipated that value sets would take several years to be developed and disseminated, an interim solution was to map EQ-5D-5L data to the EQ-5D-3L instrument by linking descriptive systems, and to use the value sets that already existed for the EQ-5D-3L (van Hout et al. 2011) (further explanation of mapping is provided in Chap. 5). While this provided a practical stop-gap means of summarising EQ-5D-5L data, these mapped values were recognised to be suitable only as a temporary solution as these indirect methods introduce additional error variance, and would still rely upon old and non-standardised value sets. Further, one might question whether values sets for the EQ-5D-3L, developed in the 1990s, would be an adequate representation of the average preferences of today's societies. There are numerous reasons to consider the need to update value sets, including changes in the underlying preferences of populations, improvements in the methods available to value health; changes in the distribution of population demographics; and concerns about potential bias in previous studies (Pickard 2015) – these issues are discussed further in Chap. 7.

In order to arrive at an improved and standardised valuation protocol, the EuroQol Group therefore commissioned a substantial programme of research to develop and test methods suitable for creating new value sets for the EQ-5D-5L that was initiated while the descriptive system was under development. The program of research – which is detailed in Chap. 2 – was started with the intention of providing investigators around the world with the tools to conduct a valuation study that would follow a standardised protocol and produce high quality data based on validated methods that supported comparisons between countries. These efforts culminated in an international protocol for conducting EQ-5D-5L valuation studies, which has been used to produce the 25 country-specific value sets which are summarised in Chap. 4 of this book (Fig. 1.2).

This endeavour is unique in scale and ambition in the field of HRQoL valuation and represents a significant body of work with direct relevance to decision makers and impact on health care policy internationally.

1.4   The Aims of this Book

The book draws together and summarises, for the first time, the body of evidence on EQ-5D-5L value sets that has been produced internationally from the EuroQol Group's programme of research and protocol development.

The primary aim of the book is to provide an accessible source of information and guidance to support users of EQ-5D-5L and its value sets. Specifically, we aim to improve users' understanding of how value sets are generated; raise awareness of the characteristics and properties of value sets; and inform users' choice of which value set to select for particular application, and how that choice may affect their analysis and conclusions. Moreover, the book will also be useful to health economics and outcomes researchers specialising in HRQoL who want to obtain information on the research practises and protocols developed by the EuroQol Group to support EQ-5D-5L valuation.

We begin in Chap. 2 by detailing the process of developing the research protocol underpinning EQ-5D-5L valuation studies. This included a methodological programme of work and international pilot testing; development of a protocol; the first wave of studies and the conclusions drawn from those early studies; modification and strengthening of the protocol and quality assurance processes; and use of the revised protocol in subsequent waves of value set studies. The chapter indicates the considerable learning and progress that was made through this journey of designing and refining the protocol.

Chapter 3 sets out the various aspects of the study design and the basis on which methodological choices were made with respect to the stated preference methods to use; the sub-set of states to value using these methods; and minimum sample size needed.

Chapter 4 provides a reference source and 'thumbnail overview' of the characteristics of the value set in each of 25 countries. In each case, we provide a summary of the value set itself and its characteristics, a worked example of the calculation of values from it; information on the sample from which values were obtained; the methods used in analysing the data and modelling the value set; and the uptake by local HTA bodies and other health care decision makers.

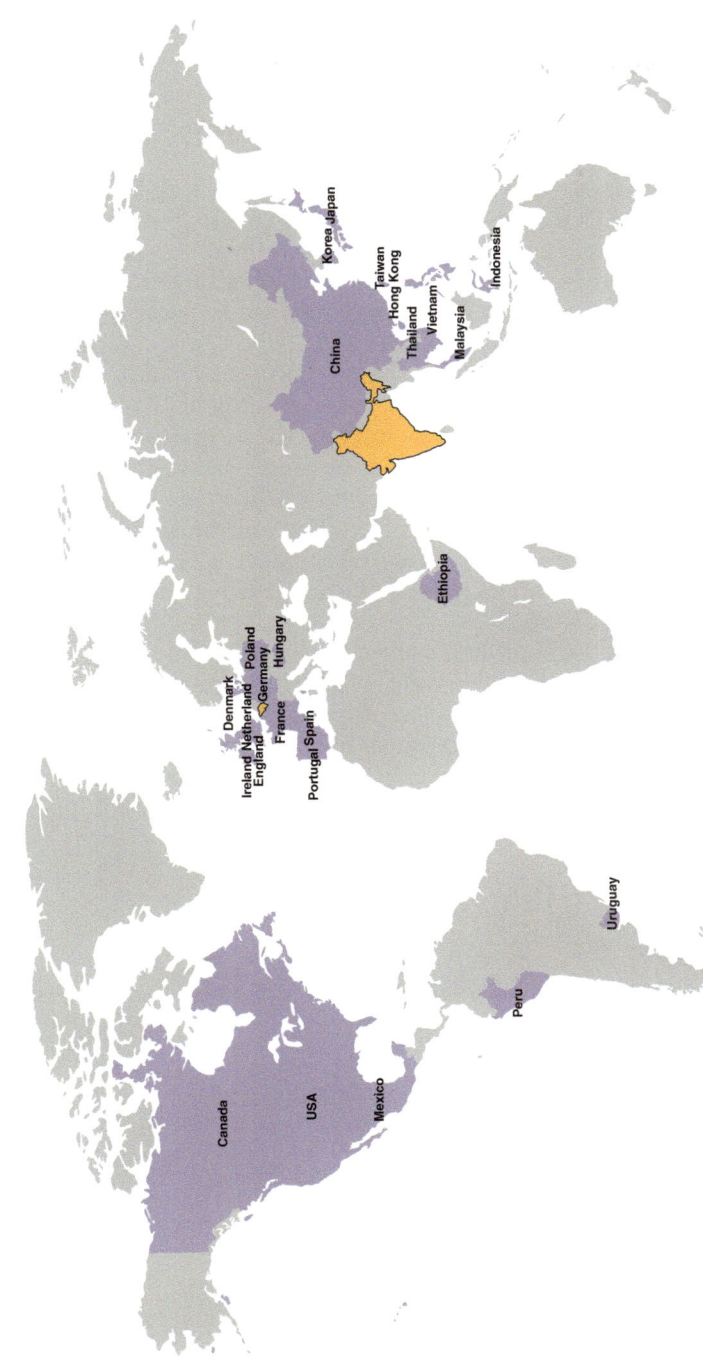

Fig. 1.2 Countries/regions that have currently published their EQ-5D-5L value set study in a peer reviewed journal (Other valuation studies for the EQ-5D-5L were not yet published at the time of writing this book (Belgium and India). Furthermore, other countries/regions have completed the data collection for their valuation study for the EQ-5D-5L, and may publish their value set in a peer reviewed journal in the future)

Chapter 5 provides guidance to those who have collected EQ-5D-5L data and want to know how to choose between the value sets reported in Chap. 4. This includes consideration of the purpose of using value sets, how to proceed when there is no value set for a specific country of interest or where there is more than one value set for a given country; and when it is appropriate to use mapping to obtain EQ-5D-5L values.

Chapter 6 draws together the value sets summarised in Chap. 4, and compares and contrasts their characteristics, reporting original comparative analysis undertaken specifically for this book. To what extent are there similarities between EQ-5D-5L value sets across countries – and are there important differences between them? Our intention in Chap. 6 is to encourage users to be aware of the specific properties of the value sets they select to use.

We conclude in Chap. 7 by reflecting on the value sets produced to date and considering a number of questions about future directions for this body of work. For example, what is the 'shelf-life' of a value set – and what factors should prompt an update, in order to ensure that value sets represent an adequate representation of the average preferences of a society? What methodological questions remain – and how are improvements or variations in methods reconciled with the need for consistency in the evidence presented to HTA bodies and other users?

The book includes a glossary of terms for those unfamiliar with the EQ-5D and the valuation of the EQ-5D-5L.

The stated vision of the EuroQol Group is the aim "to improve decisions about health and health care throughout the world by developing, promoting and supporting the use of instruments with the widest possible applicability for the measurement and valuation of health" (EuroQol Group 2021). We hope this book contributes to that aim, and that it supports your use of EQ-5D-5L to provide evidence for better health care decision making.

References

Brazier J, Karimi M (2016) Health, health-related quality of life, and quality of life: what is the difference? Pharmacoeconomics 34(7):645–649

Brooks R, on behalf of the EuroQol Group (1996) EuroQol: the current state of play. Health Policy 37(1):53–72

Buchholz I, Janssen B, Kohlman T, Feng Y-S (2018) A systematic review on studies comparing the measurement properties of the three-level and the five-level version of the EQ-5D. Pharmacoeconomics 36(6):645–661

Craig BM, Pickard AS, Lubetkin EI (2014) Health problems are more common, but less severe when measured using newer EQ-5D versions. J Clin Epidemiol 67(1):93–99

Devlin N, Brooks R (2017) EQ-5D and the EuroQol group: past, present and future. Appl Health Econ Health Policy 15(2):127–137

Devlin N, Parkin D, Browne J (2010) Patient-reported outcome measures in the NHS: new methods for analysing and reporting EQ-5D data. Health Econ 19(8):886–905

Devlin N, Brazier J, Pickard AS, Stolk E (2018) 3L, 5L, what the L? A nice conundrum. Pharmacoeconomics 36(6):637–640

Devlin N, Parkin D, Janssen B (2020) Methods for analysing and reporting EQ-5D data. Springer, Cham

Dolan P (1997) Modelling valuations of EuroQol health states. Med Care 35(11):1095–1108

Drummond M, Sculpher M, Claxton K, Stoddart G, Torrance G (2015) Methods for the economic evaluation of health care programmes, 4th edn. Oxford University Press, Oxford

EuroQol Research Foundation (2019) EQ-5D-5L User Guide. Version 3.0. EuroQol Research Foundation: Rotterdam. https://euroqol.org/publications/user-guides. Accessed 25 June 2021

EuroQol Research Foundation (2021). https://euroqol.org/euroqol/vision-and-mission/. Accessed 23 July 2021

Feng Y, Devlin N, Herdman M (2015) Assessing the health of the general population in England: how do the three- and five-level versions of EQ-5D compare? Health Qual Life Outcomes 13:171. https://doi.org/10.1186/s12955-015-0356-8

Herdman M, Gudex C, Lloyd A, Janssen MF, Kind P, Parkin D, Bonsel G, Badia X (2011) Development and preliminary testing of the new five-level version of EQ-5D (EQ-5D-5L). Qual Life Res 20(10):1727–1736

Janssen M, Birnie E, Bonsel G (2008a) Quantification of the level descriptors for the standard EQ-5D three level system and a five level version according to 2 methods. Quality Life Res 17(3):463–473

Janssen M, Birnie E, Haagsma J, Bonsel G (2008b) Comparing the standard EQ-5D three level system with a five level version. Value Health 11(2):275–284

Janssen MF, Bonsel G, Luo N (2018) Is EQ-5D-5L better than EQ-5D-3L? A head-to-head comparison of descriptive systems and value sets from seven countries. Pharmacoeconomics 36(6):675–697

Kennedy-Martin M, Slaap B, Herdman M, van Reenen M, Kennedy-Martin T, Greiner W, Busschbach J, Boye KS (2020) Which multi-attribute utility instruments are recommended for use in cost-utility analysis? A review of national health technology assessment (HTA) guidelines. Eur J Health Econ 21(8):1245–1257

National Institute for Health and Care Excellence (2013) Guide to the methods of technology appraisal 2013. https://www.nice.org.uk/process/pmg9/chapter/foreword. Accessed 17 July 2021

Oppe M, Devlin N, Black N (2011) Comparison of the underlying constructs of the EQ-5D and Oxford Hip Score: implications for mapping. Value Health 14(6):884–891

Pickard AS (2015) Is it time to update societal value sets for preference-based measures of health? Pharmacoeconomics 33(3):191–192

Pickard AS, Kohlmann T, Janssen M, Bonsel G, Rosenbloom S, Cella D (2007a) Evaluating equivalency between response systems: Application of the Rasch model to a 3-level and 5-level EQ-5D. Med Care 45(9):812–819

Pickard AS, de Leon M, Kohlmann T, Cella D, Rosenbloom S (2007b) Psychometric comparison of the standard EQ-5D to a 5 level version in cancer patients. Med Care 45(3):259–263

Szende A, Oppe M, Devlin N (2007) EQ-5D value sets: inventory, comparative review and user guide. Springer, Dordrecht

van Hout B, Janssen MF, Feng YS, Kohlmann T, Busschbach J, Golicki D, Lloyd A, Scalone L, Kind P, Pickard AS (2011) Interim scoring for the EQ-5D-5L: mapping the EQ-5D-5L to EQ-5D-3L value sets. Value Health 15(5):708–715

Chapter 2
The Development and Strengthening of Methods for Valuing EQ-5D-5L – An Overview

Elly Stolk, Juan Manuel Ramos-Goñi, Kristina Ludwig, Mark Oppe, and Richard Norman

Abstract The introduction of the EQ-5D-5L offered an opportunity to develop a standardised valuation protocol, the EQ-VT protocol, with improved methods for health state valuation that enables comparison of the resulting value sets between countries. This chapter summarises the process of developing and strengthening the methods for valuing EQ-5D-5L in the EQ-VT protocol which underpins the valuation studies reported in this book. This includes an overview of the methodological research programme that informed the initial EQ-VT protocol and a description of the key elements of the protocol and the included valuation techniques, i.e. composite time trade-off and discrete choice experiments. This chapter also discusses the first wave of EQ-5D-5L valuation studies which used the protocol and the resulting conclusions; the subsequent modification and strengthening of the EQ-VT protocol including a quality control procedure; and experience with use of the improved EQ-VT protocol in the subsequent waves of EQ-5D-5L valuation studies. The chapter concludes with an overview of the lessons learned during this journey of evidence-based refinement of the EQ-VT protocol from version 1.0 to the current version 2.1.

E. Stolk
EuroQol Research Foundation, Rotterdam, The Netherlands

J. M. Ramos-Goñi · M. Oppe
Maths In Health B.V., Rotterdam, The Netherlands

K. Ludwig (✉)
Department of Health Economics and Health Care Management, School of Public Health, Bielefeld University, Bielefeld, Germany

EuroQol Research Foundation, Rotterdam, The Netherlands
e-mail: kristina.ludwig@uni-bielefeld.de

R. Norman
School of Population Health, Curtin University, Bentley, Australia

© The Author(s) 2022
N. Devlin et al. (eds.), *Value Sets for EQ-5D-5L*,
https://doi.org/10.1007/978-3-030-89289-0_2

13

2.1 Development of the EQ-VT Protocol

Over the past 25 years, approaches taken to the valuation of EQ-5D-3L have not changed much from those used in Dolan (1997). While issues had been noted in regard to valuing the EQ-5D-3L, the desire to produce new EQ-5D-3L value sets using the same approaches as previously lessened the impetus for change. The introduction of the EQ-5D-5L offered an opportunity to explore how methods for health state valuation could be improved to produce an updated valuation protocol (Oppe et al. 2014). To arrive at a protocol that could be supported broadly, the initial development – and later refinement – of that protocol coincided with an extensive programme of methodological research within the EuroQol Group. This chapter summarises the research that was undertaken, the results that underpinned the initial version of the EQ-5D-5L valuation protocol and later modifications, and the main lessons learned from the international EQ-5D-5L valuation work.

While the research programme had a broader scope, the focus was on two different methods to elicit preferences for health states, time trade-off (TTO) and discrete choice experiments (DCEs). TTO had emerged as the first method of choice in earlier valuation studies, and the introduction of the EQ-5D-5L did not change that. Yet, concerns had been expressed about extremely low values that could be produced for states worse than dead (WTD), requiring arbitrary rescaling (Janssen et al. 2013) and therefore refinement of the TTO method was pursued within the research programme. Lead time TTO (LT-TTO) had been identified as a possible TTO approach that could mitigate issues valuing states WTD (Robinson and Spencer 2006; Tilling et al. 2010; Devlin et al. 2011) and therefore the relative merits of that approach were explored (Attema and Versteegh 2013; Devlin et al. 2013; Versteegh et al. 2013). DCE was at that time recognised as a promising new method for health state valuation (e.g. Salomon 2003; McCabe et al. 2006), and having become more widely used in other aspects of health economics (Ryan 2004). DCE was, therefore the second focus of the research programme and was studied both as a potential alternative to TTO and as a complement. DCE has the benefit of having a generally simpler task compared with TTO, requiring simple choices rather than completion of an iterative process, with potential significant benefits for data collection. Questions around the way to collect and model DCE-data therefore also were addressed. Based on the desire to replace the props used in TTO interviews (e.g. TTO board) by computers and develop a computerised TTO procedure, all tasks were integrated into a digital aid (the EuroQol-Valuation Technology, EQ-VT), which was developed in conjunction with the protocol. As a result, the protocol is commonly referred to as the EQ-VT protocol.

We will not cover all findings of the research programme in this chapter. However, several findings require particular highlighting:

1. while the conducted research on LT-TTO produced ample proof of concept for the use of LT-TTO in health state valuation, values for states better than dead (BTD) seemed to be subject to a downward bias. Therefore, composite TTO

(cTTO) was introduced (Janssen et al. 2013), which uses conventional TTO for the valuation of states BTD, and LT-TTO for states WTD;
2. while implementation of the protocol in EQ-VT software allows, in theory, for the tasks to be self-completed, such an approach to administration leads to significant data quality issues; therefore, computer-assisted personal interviews (CAPI) remained the preferred mode of administration (Shah et al. 2013);
3. DCE tasks that produce values on a latent scale are straightforward to generate, but many open questions remain regarding tasks that can produce DCE values anchored at the full health-dead scale (Norman et al. 2016).

Further results obtained in the methodological research programme have been documented in 19 journal articles. Oppe et al. (2014) described how those results supported the development of the EQ-VT protocol version 1.0.

2.2   Description of the EQ-VT Protocol

2.2.1   Contents of the Protocol

From its origins in 2012, some elements of the EQ-VT protocol have evolved but the overall structure has been retained, comprising the following six parts:

1. general welcome,
2. self-reported health using EQ-5D-5L and background questions,
3. introduction to the cTTO valuation task,
4. health state valuation using cTTO,
5. health state valuation using DCE,
6. general thank you and goodbye.

After a general welcome and explanation of the purpose of the study, self-reported health as measured by the EQ-5D-5L including EQ VAS and background questions regarding age, gender and experience with illness are asked. The third section then introduces respondents to the cTTO valuation tasks (see Figs. 2.1a and 2.1b). The interviewer uses the example health state "being in a wheelchair" to explain how to interpret and carry out the cTTO tasks. After cTTO task understanding is confirmed, respondents move on to value ten EQ-5D-5L health states and answer three debriefing questions regarding the cTTO tasks. In the next part of the interview, the interviewer explains how to carry out the DCE. The respondents are asked to complete seven forced-choice paired comparisons of EQ-5D-5L health states without a "duration" attribute (see Fig. 2.2), meaning the choice is simply between two EQ-5D-5L health states independent of time. Following this, respondents answer three debriefing questions regarding the DCE tasks. In the concluding part of the interview, the respondents can leave feedback and are thanked for their participation.

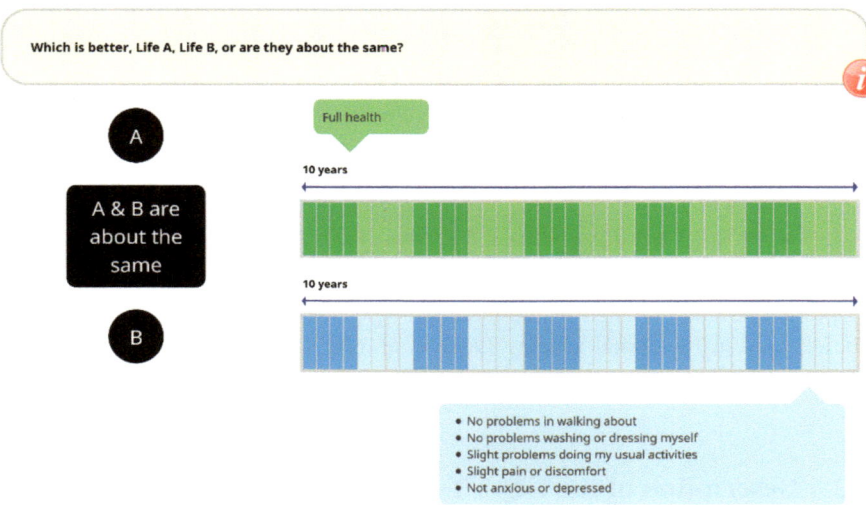

Fig. 2.1a Presentation of the composite time trade-off used in the EQ-VT protocol: better than dead task. (© 2021 EuroQol Research Foundation. Reprinted with permission)

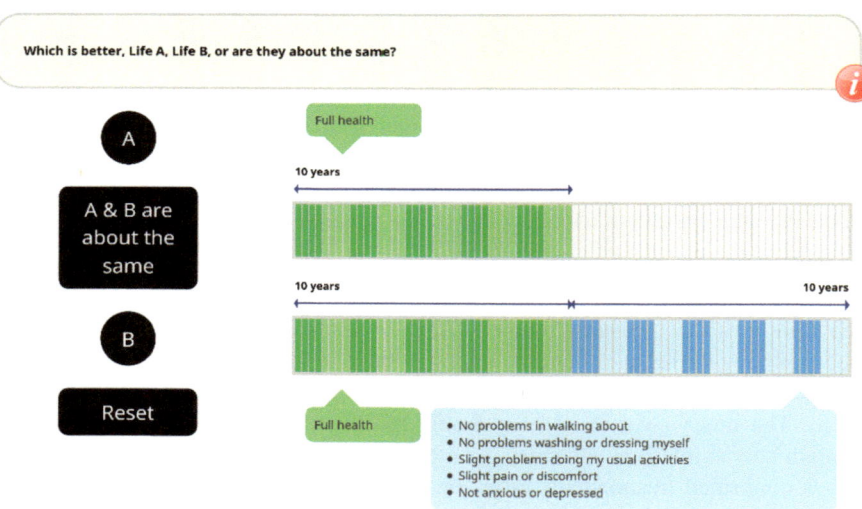

Fig. 2.1b Presentation of the composite time trade-off used in the EQ-VT protocol: worse than dead task. (© 2021 EuroQol Research Foundation. Reprinted with permission)

The cTTO approach begins with the 'conventional' TTO with the first question being ten years in the health state being valued versus ten years in full health (see Fig. 2.1a), and only shifts to an LT-TTO when the respondent considers the health state to be WTD. In that case, the following LT-TTO task involves a twenty-year time frame: ten years of lead time followed by ten years in the EQ-5D-5L health

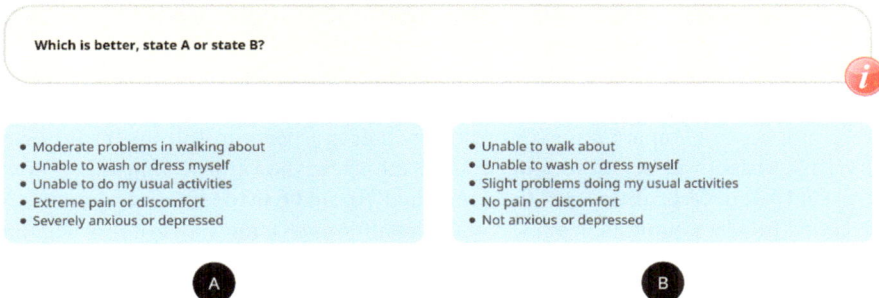

Fig. 2.2 Presentation of a discrete choice experiment task used in the EQ-VT protocol. (© 2021 EuroQol Research Foundation. Reprinted with permission)

state being valued (see Fig. 2.1b). The resulting cTTO values range from −1 (trading all of the lead time) to 1 (trading no years in full health) in 0.05 increments. The exact iteration scheme is reported elsewhere (Oppe et al. 2016). The underlying experimental design including the health state selection for both the cTTO and DCE tasks, and other study design considerations such as sample size requirements, is addressed in Chap. 3.

To ensure that respondents can give valid and meaningful responses during the cTTO task, they first get the opportunity to experience the cTTO task by completing the wheelchair example and are made aware that they will be asked to evaluate a set of other health states in the same way. After that – still in the wheelchair example – they learn, amongst other things, how their responses will be interpreted, what the range of possible answers is, how the task proceeds in a slightly different way when a state WTD is encountered, and how they need to interpret the health states. Delivering these instructions is challenging for the interviewer, as most are not prompted on screen, the task is difficult for some respondents, and the interview needs to be completed in a standardised and neutral way. Furthermore, a high level of task engagement is expected from the respondent, and this depends on the level of engagement demonstrated by the interviewer and the quality of interactions with the respondent. Since the wheelchair example is the point in the interview where all of this needs to be discussed, this section is the key to the successful implementation of the EQ-VT protocol; especially the cTTO part.

2.2.2 Why the cTTO Task was Adopted

Concern with the way in which values for states WTD were produced in EQ-5D-3L value sets motivated much of the research carried out to develop the new protocol. It is well known that a standard TTO task, by contrasting a ten-year life in a disease state to a shorter life of t years in full health, can only produce positive values. In this task the value x of the disease state is given by t/10 at the point where the respondent is indifferent between the options. Since lifespans cannot have a negative value, t cannot be negative and so only values for x in the [0, 1] range can be observed. If respondents indicated that they preferred immediate death over living for ten years in the disease state, a modified task was offered inviting the respondents to compare a health profile including t years in full health followed by 10−t years in ill health to immediate death. Here the value x of health is given by −t/(10−t). As the difference between t and 10 can be made infinitely small (e.g. counted in years, months, weeks, days or smaller units), the value of this negative ratio statistic can become extremely large. To counteract the effect on mean values, an arbitrary transformation was applied to bound the negative values at −1. Various options to transform the data have been proposed, however, the choice between them remained arbitrary but could affect the results substantially.

LT-TTO offers – in theory – a unified approach for the valuation of states BTD and WTD. As in standard TTO, respondents consider how good or bad it would be to spend ten years in a state of impaired health. However, the period of impaired health does not start now, but starts ten years from now so that the total remaining lifespan is 20 years. This is compared to a life that has t years in full health and the duration t is varied between 0 and 20 to identify indifference. The value x of the disease state can be computed by solving 10+10x=t which gives a positive value for all t>10 and a negative value for all t<10.[1] However, due to presence of a bias, described below, the cTTO approach was preferred over LT-TTO.

Regarding LT-TTO, larger lead times *ceteris paribus* extend the range of negative values that can be observed, but higher bounds on the maximum hypothetical lifespan and lower bounds on the size of the trade-off unit also need to be considered. Key findings were that values for states BTD seemed to be affected by a downward bias in the LT-TTO task, and larger ratios of lead time to disease time amplified this problem. A possible explanation is that respondents considered what portion of their remaining years to trade off without recognising that trading into the lead time implied a WTD response. Therefore, the decision was made to use standard TTO in the valuation of states BTD and only adopt LT-TTO for the valuation of WTD states. Consistent with previous valuation studies, the standard TTO was again specified with a ten-year time frame and in the LT-TTO frame a lead time of ten years was offered to even out the changes in value associated with the trade-off unit (years) in the BTD and WTD size of the scale. The name 'composite' TTO was adopted as the name for the TTO protocol adopting standard TTO for the valuation of states BTD and lead time TTO for states WTD.

---

[1] For example: if t=16, the formula 10+10x=t will read 10+10x=16, thus 10x=6, which solves to x=0.6. If t=6, the same formula reads 10+10x=6, thus 10x=−4, and x=−0.4.

2.2.3   Why the DCE Task was Adopted

In most EQ-5D-3L valuation studies, respondents received multiple valuation tasks, of increasing complexity and from the start it was assumed that the EQ-VT protocol would also include at least two types of stated preference tasks. But which tasks?

The non-standardised protocols for EQ-5D-3L valuation (see Chap. 1) supplied researchers with rank, VAS (visual analogue scale) valuation and TTO responses. At the discretion of the study teams, the collected data were used in various ways. In the early years, both VAS- and TTO-based value sets were developed while the ranking task was seen as a useful precursor. Gradually, however, the views on these methods started to shift. TTO became the method of first choice and the use of VAS valuation started to decline. Alternatives to VAS valuation were considered for the EQ-VT protocol. At the same time, the underused potential of rank data started to be recognised (e.g. Salomon 2003; Craig and Busschbach 2009; Craig et al. 2009). In the EQ-VT protocol, the ranking and VAS valuation tasks eventually were displaced by DCE. This method is akin to a ranking task.

There were several reasons to choose DCE. For example, one reason for including DCE was because of the different nature of the instrument being valued, i.e., the EQ-5D-5L, rather than the EQ-5D-3L. The subtler differences between levels – especially at the mild end of the descriptive system – meant some people might not be willing to trade off any life years; whereas the DCE could still obtain preferences between mild states. Furthermore, DCEs were widely recognised as a promising new method for valuing health and shown to be feasible for EQ-5D (Stolk et al. 2010). Lastly, a DCE task can be set up in different ways and depending on the chosen configuration, it can produce values (a) on a latent scale or (b) values directly anchored on the QALY (Quality Adjusted Life Year) scale if either the attribute "duration" or the alternative "dead" is included in the DCE (Norman et al. 2016). In the latter case, DCEs yield values that can have the same cardinal measurement properties as TTO, but with a more straightforward and less costly data collection process. Anticipating future developments, it was also considered important to include DCE (instead of VAS or rank) now, to familiarise more researchers with the DCE method and promote learning.

The DCE task included in the EQ-5D-5L was a basic one, comparing two EQ-5D-5L health states without reference to lifespan, i.e., number of years lived in each state. Methodological research that guided this decision had suggested that this basic approach produces robust results, whereas the approaches that could produce values on the QALY scale initially suffered from unexplained high variability in the results, and researchers had different ideas about how to make these advanced tasks work. Therefore, it seemed unwise to push for a harmonised method when the protocol for EQ-5D-5L valuation was introduced. However, it was agreed to continue research about other DCE approaches and see if issues with those approaches could be resolved (for further discussion on this, see Chap. 7).

2.2.4   Value Set Generation

Subsequent to completion of the EQ-VT data collection protocol, value set generation can be based on either hybrid models that draw on both types of data at the
same time (i.e., cTTO and DCE), or on cTTO data only. The DCE data cannot be
used independently as a basis for value set generation because DCE values are estimated on a latent scale and lack the interpretation of health state values that are
anchored at 0 (dead) and 1 (full health). The option to generate a value set based on
two types of data has the benefit of providing extra assurance about the ability to
construct a value set based on data collected in the valuation study.

While cTTO and DCE results provide two measures of the same construct, preferences for health, perfect agreement of cTTO and DCE results is not to be expected
due to the differences between the methods:

- results are derived from two different tasks that may evoke different respondent
  behaviour and can be subject to different biases;
- the theoretical models used to infer health state values from observable
  responses differ;
- values are estimated on a different scale.

Choices between methods for value set generation must reflect judgments about
the relative merits of each method, given theoretical considerations and/or the properties of the empirical data. If the two data sources agree, that could be an argument
to include all data deriving a value set with greater precision. Conversely, if there
are discrepancies, it might be questioned which is the "correct" one and it might be
considered problematic to combine the two data sources. However, the latter might
be considered a fallacious argument, because there exists no gold standard against
which the values derived from cTTO or DCE can be judged. Discrepancies therefore can also be looked at as providing complementary information.

As neither line of reasoning will be universally accepted, the EQ-VT protocol
sets the frame for eliciting health state preferences and the local research team
makes the decision about the way of value set generation (e.g. type of data included
and modelling).

2.3   How the EQ-VT Protocol Updates Evolved

After the first wave of EQ-5D-5L valuation studies (Canada, China, England,
Netherlands, and Spain) were completed using the new EQ-VT protocol, it became
apparent that there was scope to improve on the first version of the protocol, especially by strengthening it on the implementation side. In some of those initial studies, issues with the cTTO data were observed such as strong clustering effects,

limited coverage of the value range, and high number of inconsistencies.[2] The data issues seemed to reflect low levels of task engagement of the respondents and/or the interviewers, leading to detrimental effects on quality of cTTO valuations. It was recognised that these issues clustered in interviewers and were not universally present, leading to the hypothesis that the data issues represented interviewer effects. This motivated the development and integration of a procedure that would allow the data to be monitored in real time to detect the presence of any issue and to enable timely interventions: a quality control (QC) procedure (Ramos-Goñi et al. 2017). In addition, the introduction of three practice cTTO tasks following the wheelchair example and the inclusion of confirmatory pop-ups for each cTTO task to validate answers before storing led to EQ-VT version 1.1 (see Table 2.1).

In addition, a comprehensive EQ-VT research programme was launched to test a range of suggestions for strategies that could help to prevent the data quality issues and interviewer effects from occurring. Shah et al. (2015) described the studies (N=7) that were done aimed at remedying cTTO data issues and improving EQ-VT. All studies were set up as experiments with at least two arms, allowing results obtained from a modified version of the protocol (experimental arm) to be compared to the EQ-VT version 1.1 (control arm). The battery of tests included:

- introduction of a ranking task for warm-up purposes,
- comparison of whether the definition of the comparator state matters for the results ('full health' or state 11111, i.e., no problems on any dimension),
- modified iteration procedures,
- separation of the BTD and WTD task in cTTO,
- presenting respondents with rank ordering implied by cTTO valuations (feedback module).

Table 2.1 Overview of EQ-VT elements by protocol versions

EQ-VT protocol version	Self-reported health	Back-ground questions	cTTO	DCE	Practice states	Confirmatory pop-ups	QC monitoring	Feedback module[a]	Dynamic question after wheelchair example
1.0	X	X	X	X					
1.1	X	X	X	X	X	X	X		
2.0	X	X	X	X	X	X	X	X	
2.1	X	X	X	X	X	X	X	X	X

Note: The cross mark shows that an element was included in the protocol version
cTTO composite time trade-off, *DCE* discrete choice experiment, *EQ-VT* EuroQol-Valuation Technology, *QC* quality control
[a]Sometimes used as optional element

---

[2] There were spikes (i.e., clustering of values at −1, −0.5, 0, 0.5, 1), lower than expected values for mild health states (i.e., a big gap to 1) and a low number of negative values (i.e., few WTD values). Moreover, there was a high number of inconsistencies overall and with regard to the worst possible health state 55555 (i.e., valuing less severe health states lower than the value for 55555).

The collected data provided strong support for integration of a QC module, as it improved data quality markedly. It also supported implementation of the feedback module (see Fig. 2.3), since respondents frequently appreciated having the option to review and reconsider their own responses if needed. The other tested modifications did not produce clear benefits (Shah et al. 2015). Interviewer effects, clustering of cTTO values, and inconsistencies were strongly reduced in valuation studies that applied the updated EQ-VT protocol (Ramos-Goñi et al. 2017; Stolk et al. 2019). Guided by results obtained in this work, the EQ-VT has received two updates in 2013 (EQ-VT 1.1) and 2014 (EQ-VT 2.0). Later on, in 2017 one more update was implemented (EQ-VT 2.1), which altered the flow of the wheelchair example to include more prompts for interviewers (Stolk et al. 2019). Box 2.1 provides further details on the QC procedure, as implemented from protocol version 1.1 onwards.

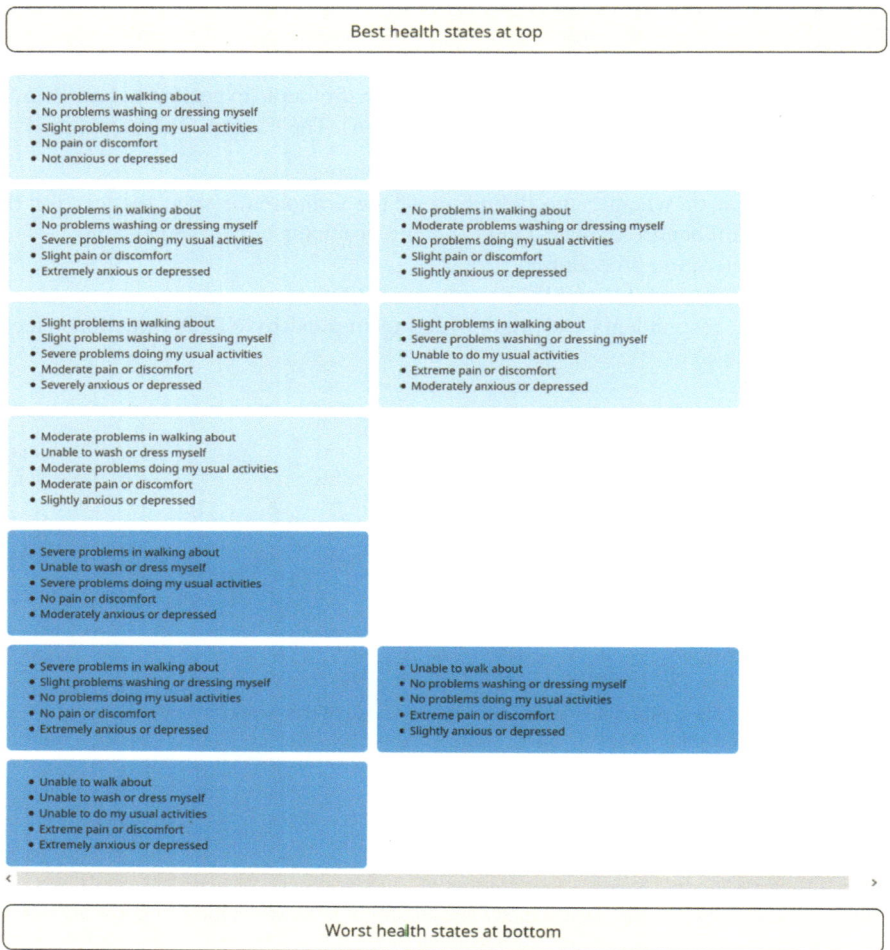

Fig. 2.3 Example of the feedback module used in the EQ-VT protocol since version 2.0. (© 2021 EuroQol Research Foundation. Reprinted with permission)

Box 2.1: QC Procedure Since EQ-VT Protocol 1.1
A QC procedure was introduced to monitor the interviewer's protocol compliance and interviewer effects as well as the face validity of the data. By looking at four QC criteria it is possible to determine whether an individual interview is of "suspect" quality. If any of the four following criteria is met for an individual interview, it is flagged:

1. no explanation of the WTD task (LT-TTO) during the wheelchair example;
2. too short time period spent on the wheelchair example (i.e., less than three minutes);
3. clear inconsistency in the cTTO ratings (the worst possible health state 55555 is not the lowest and at least 0.5 higher than the state with the lowest value);
4. too short time period for the cTTO task (i.e., total time for the ten cTTO tasks less than five minutes).

Initial QC reports are used to evaluate whether interviewers met the minimum quality requirements. If 40% out of the ten interviews are flagged as being of *suspect* quality by using the QC tool provided by the EuroQol Executive Office, all interviews thus far conducted by that interviewer will be removed and the interviewer will be retrained. After further ten interviews, interviewer's performance and compliance are re-evaluated. If again 40% or more interviews are flagged, these interviews will also be removed and the interviewer is removed from the interviewer team. A threshold value of 40% was selected because flagged interviews could hold genuine responses (e.g., respondents who quickly build their opinion and perform the cTTO tasks). Additionally, this allows interviewers to grow into their roles when they built up experience with valuation interviews following the EQ-VT protocol.

During the entire study, the local study team continuously monitors data quality. Later QC reports allow to reflect on interviewers' performance, discuss possible improvements and intervene when the performance of an interviewer worsens.

2.4 Lessons Learned

The evidence from the valuation studies and the comprehensive EQ-VT research programme (Shah et al. 2015) led to increased awareness of how challenging the interview is, both for the respondent and the interviewer. Data issues driven by interviewer effects showed that the interviewer and his/her skills are pivotal in the success of the interview, especially for the cTTO tasks. The amount of guidance to respondents affects their engagement and task understanding, and thereby accuracy and reliability of responses. The DCE task may be more robust to interviewer effects, but it may also be that data issues are simply relatively more transparent in cTTO data. While technical aspects of the tasks were the key focus before the first valuation studies were launched, focus shifted to the human interaction side of the task after the first wave, which is equally important and clearly needed more attention.

The changes made to the protocol can be categorised into (a) monitoring of and providing support to the interviewers and (b) supporting the respondents. As outlined above, the introduction of the QC procedure since version 1.1 with accompanying QC tool enables monitoring of the protocol compliance of the *interviewers* and interviewer effects. Moreover, it facilitates the support of the interviewer by providing data-based feedback. The items measured are reported elsewhere (Ramos-Goñi et al. 2017). In order to support the *respondents*, it was realised that an extended introduction and practising cTTO is necessary before the valuation tasks can be carried out in the intended way: three additional practice states and a dynamic question after the wheelchair example were added as EQ-VT elements. Depending on the respondent's response for the wheelchair task, in the dynamic question the respondent is asked to imagine a health state that is much better or much worse than being in a wheelchair in order to move to the other part of the evaluation space in the cTTO. Moreover, as mistakes and/or learning effects can still occur, confirmatory pop-ups after each task and the feedback module presented in Fig. 2.3 were additionally included. The latter presents respondents with the rank ordering implied by their cTTO valuations and provide the opportunity to flag problematic valuations for removal from the data. Further details on the EQ-VT elements and its changes are provided elsewhere (Stolk et al. 2019).

To prepare interviewers for their role in the execution of a study, the EuroQol Executive Office started to work more closely with study teams. Besides making available an interviewer script and EQ-VT software tailored to the needs of each team, the EuroQol Executive Office now also offers training for the local research team, who in turn train their interviewers (a 'train the trainer' approach). While this training helps, due to the complexity of the interview and because the topics taught are abstract until the interviewers start doing interviews, it will not prevent all issues. Learning on the job – as supported by the QC process – therefore has a big additional impact to promote performance of interviewers, using information on the behaviour of an interviewer to tailor and deliver a personalised set of additional instructions. The initial training addresses therefore a mix of topics related to content and process, to build up interviewer skills and to discuss collaboration when the study is ongoing.

Related topics that need consideration are the selection of interviewers, the logistics of data collection, and, more broadly, how investigators and interviewers can work together most effectively. This part of the study is not standardised, but the EuroQol Executive Office can offer recommendations. To date, working with a small team of dedicated students, who travel together with a data coordinator throughout the country, and collect data in weekly round of ten interviews per interviewer, serves as an example of good practice (e.g. Pickard et al. 2019; Shafie et al. 2019; Welie et al. 2020). Students have relevant background knowledge, are familiar with the concepts validity and bias, are keen to learn, want to do well, and do not mind having their performance assessed. Working as a group allows the data coordinator to deliver effective feedback, and individuals are likely to be receptive to it, since they see other interviewers work on similar issues. Undertaking the work as a group makes everyone more focused on the goal of the study.

2.5   Concluding Remarks

Over the last ten years the accumulation of extensive multinational evidence supported the development and the subsequent refinement of a standardised EQ-VT protocol for conducting national EQ-5D-5L valuation studies. A multinational research programme examined alternative approaches for eliciting health state preferences, developed methods to improve data quality and demonstrated the robustness of these approaches across languages and countries.

The EQ-VT protocol was developed in a way that evidence-based refinements are anticipated. Across the different versions of the protocol, EQ-VT 1.0 to the current version 2.1, the valuation tasks have remained the same, but later versions pay more attention to the optimal implementation of these tasks combined with a QC procedure. The refinements of the EQ-VT protocol have been shown to improve data quality and minimize interviewer effects.

The EQ-VT protocol has to date successfully been applied in about 30 countries worldwide and, at time of writing, 25 of these have been published. These 25 value sets are summarised in Chap. 4, and their similarities and differences are described in Chap. 6. Even though the improved valuation protocol with its QC process provides a solid basis for estimating national EQ-5D-5L value sets, there remain methodological questions that can be addressed in future research (see Chap. 7). This might further improve the EQ-VT protocol.

References

Attema AE, Versteegh MM (2013) Would you rather be ill now, or later? Health Econ 22(12):1496–1506

Craig BM, Busschbach JJ (2009) The episodic random utility model unifies time trade-off and discrete choice approaches in health state valuation. Popul Health Metr 13(7):3. https://doi.org/10.1186/1478-7954-7-3

Craig BM, Busschbach JJ, Salomon JA (2009) Keep it simple: ranking health states yields values similar to cardinal measurement approaches. J Clin Epidemiol 62(3):296–305

Devlin NJ, Tsuchiya A, Buckingham K, Tilling C (2011) A uniform time trade off method for states better and worse than dead: feasibility study of the 'lead time' approach. Health Econ 20(3):348–361

Devlin N, Buckingham K, Shah K, Tsuchiya A, Tilling C, Wilkinson G, van Hout B (2013) A comparison of alternative variants of the lead and lag time TTO. Health Econ 22(5):517–532

Dolan P (1997) Modeling valuations for EuroQol health states. Med Care 35(11):1095–1108

Janssen BMF, Oppe M, Versteegh MM, Stolk EA (2013) Introducing the composite time trade-off: a test of feasibility and face validity. Eur J Health Econ 14(Suppl 1):S5–S13

McCabe C, Brazier J, Gilks P, Tsuchiya A, Roberts J, O'Hagan A, Stevens K (2006) Using rank data to estimate health state utility models. J Health Econ 25(3):418–431

Norman R, Mulhern B, Viney R (2016) The impact of different DCE-based approaches when anchoring utility scores. PharmacoEconomics 34(8):805–814

Oppe M, Devlin NJ, van Hout B, Krabbe PFM, de Charro F (2014) A program of methodological research to arrive at the new international EQ-5D-5L valuation protocol. Value Health 17(4):445–453

Oppe M, Rand-Hendriksen K, Shah K, Ramos-Goñi JM, Luo N (2016) EuroQol protocols for time trade-off valuation of health outcomes. PharmacoEconomics 34(10):993–1004

Pickard AS, Law EH, Jiang R, Pullenayegum E, Shaw JW, Xie F, Oppe M, Boye K, Chapman RH, Gong CL, Balch A, Busschbach JJV (2019) United States valuation of EQ-5D-5L health states using an international protocol. Value Health 22(8):931–941

Ramos-Goñi JM, Oppe M, Slaap B, Busschbach JJV, Stolk E (2017) Quality control process for EQ-5D-5L valuation studies. Value Health 20(3):466–473

Robinson A, Spencer A (2006) Exploring challenges to TTO utilities: valuing states worse than dead. Health Econ 15(4):393–402

Ryan M (2004) Discrete choice experiments in health care. BMJ 328(7436):360–361

Salomon JA (2003) Reconsidering the use of rankings in the valuation of health states: a model for estimating cardinal values from ordinal data. Popul Health Metr 1(1):12. https://doi.org/10.1186/1478-7954-1-12

Shafie AA, Thakumar AV, Lim CJ, Luo N, Rand-Hendriksen K, Yusof FAM (2019) EQ-5D-5L valuation for the Malaysian population. PharmacoEconomics 37(5):715–725

Shah KK, Lloyd A, Oppe M, Devlin NJ (2013) One-to-one versus group setting for conducting computer-assisted TTO studies: findings from pilot studies in England and the Netherlands. Eur J Health Econ 14(Suppl 1):S65–S73

Shah K, Rand-Hendriksen K, Ramos-Goñi JM, Prause AJ, Stolk E (2015) Improving the quality of data collected in EQ-5D-5L valuation studies: a summary of the EQ-VT research methodology programme. In: Proceedings of the 31st Scientific Plenary Meeting of the EuroQol Group, Stockholm, Sweden, 25–26 September 2014. http://eq-5dpublications.euroqol.org/download?id=0_53918&fileId=54332. Accessed 22 June 2021

Stolk EA, Oppe M, Scalone L, Krabbe PFM (2010) Discrete choice modeling for the quantification of health states: the case of the EQ-5D. Value Health 13(8):1005–1013

Stolk E, Ludwig K, Rand K, van Hout B, Ramos-Goñi JM (2019) Overview, update and lessons learned from the international EQ-5D-5L valuation work: version 2 of the EQ-5D-5L valuation protocol. Value Health 22(1):23–30

Tilling C, Devlin N, Tsuchiya A, Buckingham K (2010) Protocols for time tradeoff valuations of health states worse than dead: a literature review. Med Decis Making 30(5):610–619

Versteegh MM, Attema AE, Oppe M, Devlin NJ, Stolk EA (2013) Time to tweak the TTO: results from a comparison of alternative specifications of the TTO. Eur J Health Econ 14(Suppl 1):S43–S51

Welie AG, Gebretekle GB, Stolk E, Mukuria C, Krahn MD, Enquoselassie F, Fenta TG (2020) Valuing health state: an EQ-5D-5L value set for Ethiopians. Value Health Reg Issues 22:7–14

Chapter 3
Experimental Design for the Valuation of the EQ-5D-5L

Mark Oppe, Richard Norman, Zhihao Yang, and Ben van Hout

Abstract The EQ-VT protocol for valuing the EQ-5D-5L offered the opportunity to develop a standardised experimental design to elicit EQ-5D-5L values. This chapter sets out the various aspects of the EQ-VT design and the basis on which methodological choices were made in regard to the stated preference methods used, i.e., composite time trade-off (cTTO) and discrete choice experiments (DCE). These choices include the sub-set of EQ-5D-5L health states to value using these methods; the number of cTTO and DCE valuation tasks per respondent; the minimum sample size needed; and the randomisation schema. This chapter also summarises the research studies developing and testing alternative experimental designs aimed at generating a "Lite" version of the EQ-VT design. This "Lite" version aimed to reduce the number of health states in the design, and thus the sample size, to increase the feasibility of undertaking valuation studies in countries with limited resources or recruitment possibilities. Finally, this chapter outlines remaining methodological issues to be addressed in future research, focusing on refinement of current design strategies, and identification of new designs for novel valuation approaches.

M. Oppe (✉)
Maths in Health B.V., Rotterdam, The Netherlands
e-mail: moppe@mathsinhealth.com

R. Norman
School of Population Health, Curtin University, Bentley, Australia

Z. Yang
Health Services Management Department, Guizhou Medical University,
Gui'an, People's Republic of China

B. van Hout
School of Health and Related Research, University of Sheffield, Sheffield, UK

Pharmerit International, York, UK

© The Author(s) 2022
N. Devlin et al. (eds.), *Value Sets for EQ-5D-5L*,
https://doi.org/10.1007/978-3-030-89289-0_3

29

3.1 Introduction

As explained in Chap. 2, having decided that the protocol for valuing EQ-5D-5L would include both composite time trade-off (cTTO) and discrete choice experiment (DCE) as elicitation techniques, the next step was to provide a study design that would enable the researchers to identify a model that would appropriately predict values for all 3125 potential health states. For this, choices needed to be made about:

1. the selection of health states in the cTTO part of the study,
2. the selection of pairs of health states in the DCE tasks,
3. the number of respondents and
4. the number of tasks per respondent.

It was envisaged that not all respondents needed to value the same health states and that respondents could be randomised over different blocks of health states. The aim of this chapter is to describe the basis for the protocol designs and the factors that were considered in developing them. In addition, alternative designs and directions for future research with respect to designs will be addressed.

Valuation studies do not test hypotheses, and as such there is no classic power calculation as with randomised clinical trials. Generally, the more subjects and the more data per health state decreases the standard errors around the value for each health state, decreases the standard errors around the model estimates and one would expect it to decrease the probability of misspecification. A traditional method to test different designs is by simulating experiments (i.e., simulate respondents' answers to the tasks – informed by prior evidence on how people respond) and compare the simulated means with the means one would expect. The simulated experiments are analysed to determine whether the model that is being estimated corresponds with the model which underlies the simulations (the true model) and what the width is of the confidence intervals surrounding the estimates.

Within the above considerations it was also decided that both the cTTO task and the DCE task needed to be designed such that the data would allow for estimating separate models without the need for data from the other part of the study. This would leave room for the scientists conducting such studies to estimate models using only cTTO data, or only DCE data, or hybrid models combining the two sets of data. The EQ-VT designs were developed using a staged approach. Designs were created for the pilot studies that informed the development of the EQ-VT protocol. These pilot studies also informed refinements with respect to the experimental design.

As described in Chap. 1, for EQ-5D-3L valuation studies, the study protocols and experimental designs were not standardised, although most studies followed some or all of the protocol used in the first time trade-off (TTO) study for EQ-5D-3L: the Measurement and Valuation of Health (MVH) study conducted in the United Kingdom (Dolan 1997). In the end, different countries produced EQ-5D-3L value sets based on different elicitation tasks. Some used a visual analogue scale (VAS) based elicitation technique, while others used TTO. In addition, different numbers of health states were used (e.g., 43 health states in total for MVH, while others used e.g., 17 states or 24 states, or a more saturated 196 health state approach), and a different selection of health states. These methodological differences between studies hampered comparison between countries: it is unknown to what extent differences in results obtained between countries were due to differences in the preferences of the study populations or due to differences in the study protocol and experimental design. Therefore, for the valuation of the EQ-5D-5L, the EuroQol Group decided to create a standardised study protocol including an experimental design (see Chap. 2 for more details on this standardisation).

3.2 EQ-VT Designs

3.2.1 cTTO Design

The states selected for the design of the cTTO need to be optimised for model estimation. This means the objective is to avoid introducing a bias in the model that originates from the selection of the health states included in the design. For example, if mild or moderate states are highly overrepresented in the design, this could lead to a bias in the model estimation. In addition, there should be enough states included, so that the model can be specified. For example, since there are 20 main effect parameters (i.e., the four dummy parameters for each of the five EQ-5D dimensions) the theoretical minimum number of health states to be included would be 21 (20 main effects +1 error term). For the main pilot study, also referred to as the core multinational pilot study (Oppe et al. 2014), the number of states that would be required for estimating an EQ-5D-5L value set was expected to be around 100. It was considered that a main effects model would have 21 parameters (5*4 dummy variables for the main effects + intercept) leaving 79 degrees of freedom. Such a number of states would allow estimation of random coefficient models, and inclusion of different kinds of interactions and/or the effects of background variables.

When regarding the number of observations per EQ-5D-5L health state included in the cTTO tasks, we found that in the cTTO pilot study with 121 observations per state, the standard errors for the severe states were around 0.056, while those for the mild states were around 0.01 (Janssen et al. 2013). This suggested we would achieve adequate average precision of the mean observed values with 100 observations per cTTO state. This was based on the assumption that with the standard errors at those levels, a repetition of the sample would result in observed mean values that would very likely fall within the bounds provided by these standard errors.

From the pilot studies, as well as the valuation studies undertaken for the EQ-5D-3L, it was clear that respondents would be able to complete at least 17 cTTO tasks each without negatively impacting on data quality (Tsuchiya et al. 2002; Lamers et al. 2006). However, since we also wanted to include a DCE task for the same respondents, it was decided that we should limit the number of cTTO tasks per respondent to ten (excluding warm-up and practice tasks). In order to counteract biases due to framing effects, a blocked design was chosen to achieve a balanced mix of states with respect to where they are expected to lie on the overall value scale. That is to say, each respondent should complete a good balance of health states, covering the entire range from mild to severe. Therefore, each block was designed to include one of the five very mild states (i.e., states 21111, 12111, 11211, 11121, 11112) and the worst state (i.e., state 55555, sometimes referred to as the "pits" state). It was decided to include ten blocks with two fixed states in each block such that eight states per block would need to be generated, i.e. 80 states. This implied that we would have (10*8 + 5 + 1=) 86 states in total, which is a little less than in the main pilot study, but still more than four times the number of parameters for a typical main effects model.

Putting the above together, ten blocks of ten EQ-5D-5L states each, with 100 observations per block lead to a required sample size of 1000 respondents. This leaves the final part of the design for the cTTO part of the EQ-VT: selecting the set of 80 EQ-5D-5L states to be included.

We selected the 80 states from the total set of 3119 (i.e., the 3125 states in the EQ-5D-5L, minus the six states that were already included in the design, namely the five mildest states and the "pits" state) using Monte Carlo simulation (see Box 3.1). First, values for all 3125 states for a sample of n=1000 respondents were simulated using a simulation programme implemented in R. Details of the simulation programme can be found in (Oppe and van Hout 2010). For the simulation as well as the optimisation algorithm, a main effects model (without constant) was used. This was decided based on the pilot studies and on two previous studies using the EQ-5D-3L. In the first EQ-5D-3L study, OLS models including main effects and the N3 term (an interaction parameter which takes the value of 1 if any dimension is at level 3, or 0 otherwise) were estimated on the full data set of the MVH study, which resulted in an adjusted R^2 of 0.43, and on a data set that included only the mean observed values of the 42 states included in the MVH study (thereby removing the within state variance), which resulted in an adjusted R^2 of 0.97 (Oppe et al. 2013). These results indicate that the main contributor to the uncertainty is the within state variance, not the between state variance; that there is very little to gain by adding interaction terms (i.e., R^2 can only increase marginally from 0.97); that you run the risk of overfitting if interactions are added. The EQ-5D-5L pilot valuation studies showed that interactions similar to N3 or D1 (a parameter which corresponds to the number of impaired dimensions beyond the first) from the EQ-5D-3L models did not improve the EQ-5D-5L models. Lastly, in a DCE study for EQ-5D-3L using a design optimised for main effects plus all two-way interactions the (pseudo) R^2 increased from 0.266 for main effects to 0.277 for a model including interactions. In total there were 12 model parameters, but three of the main effects were no longer included (Stolk et al. 2010). Therefore, it becomes an issue of parsimony: Is adding interactions – consequently making the model less interpretable – worth a small increase in model fit?

Box 3.1: Algorithm for Selection of cTTO Health States Used for the EQ-VT Design

start	
step 1	simulate dataset with 1000 respondents and all 3125 states
step 2	split the data set into six "fixed states" and 3119 "selection states"
step 3	randomly select 80 health states from the "selection states" of the simulated data set and add the six states
step 4	calculate level balance
step 5	calculate main effects OLS regression model
step 6	calculate difference with parameter estimates used to create simulated data
step 7	repeat steps 3 to 6 10,000 times and keep the design with best level balance, and smallest difference of parameter estimates
step 8	block the design of 80 states found in step 7 into ten blocks of eight health states
step 9	add the worst state and one of the five mildest states to each block
end	

A random design of 80 states was generated from the simulated data. An OLS main effects regression model (without constant) was estimated on the simulated set of cTTO data comprising the 80 states and 1000 respondents. Next, the sum of the mean squared errors (MSE) was calculated between the parameters that were used to create the simulated preference data and the parameters resulting from the OLS model. The difference between perfect level balance and achieved level balance of the 80 generated states was also calculated. The construction of the level balance criterion can be found in Appendix A. The regression procedure was repeated 10,000 times and an iterative procedure was used where designs that had either worse level balance or worse MSE were discarded.

The "optimal" set of 80 states was divided over the ten blocks using the blocking algorithm included in the "AlgDesign" package in R (Wheeler 2004). The blocking algorithm divides the states over the blocks in such a way that the within block variance is maximised (i.e., the full severity range is more or less covered within a block), while the between block variance is minimised (i.e., all blocks are more or less the same with respect to the mean severity per block).

In summary, the design of the cTTO experiment consists of 86 states divided over ten blocks with 100 observations per block, leading to about 10,000 observations in total, where the five very mild states and state 55555 were oversampled compared to the other 80 states. For a main effects model this means that there will be about 400 observations per model parameter (8000 observations/20 parameters). The required sample size was determined to be 1000 (i.e., 10 blocks * 100 observations per block). The 86 states of the cTTO design can be found in Appendix B.

3.2.2 DCE Design

A Bayesian efficient design algorithm was used to select the pairs for the DCE. The priors were based on the results of a main effects model (without intercept) estimated on the data of an EQ-5D-3L DCE study (Stolk et al. 2010). We assumed that the levels 1, 2 and 3 from the EQ-5D-3L study corresponded to the levels 1, 3 and 5 for the EQ-5D-5L, while the levels 2 and 4 were assumed to be the mid-points between the levels 1 and 3, and 3 and 5 respectively. The standard errors of the parameters of the model we estimated on the EQ-5D-3L DCE data varied between 0.06 and 0.08. Conservatively, these were increased to 0.10 for the priors. The priors that were used can be found in Table 3.1.

Similar to the cTTO design there was an interest in making sure that at least some pairs of health states containing only mild states would be included in the DCE design. Therefore, ten such pairs were created manually. Pilot studies showed that the sample size of 1000 respondents determined for the cTTO would also be sufficient for estimating a DCE model (Krabbe et al. 2014; Oppe et al. 2014). In order to put limits on respondent burden, the number of DCE pairs per respondent was set to seven. The minimum number of observations needed per pair was deemed to be 35. This was based on being slightly more conservative than Hensher and colleagues, who refer to a minimum of 30 responses per set, based on the law of large numbers as stated by Bernoulli (Hensher et al. 2005). Putting these numbers together, a 196 pair design divided over 28 blocks of seven pairs was created using a Bayesian D-efficient design algorithm (see Box 3.2).

First, the set of ten mild pairs was manually selected. Next, a set of 186 pairs was randomly generated. For this set of 186 pairs, the Bayesian D-error of the design was determined using 1000 randomly drawn sets of priors. This process was repeated 10,000 times and the 186 pair design with the best D-error was kept. The ten mild pairs were added to this design, and the total set of 196 pairs was then blocked into 28 blocks of seven pairs each.

The Bayesian D-efficient design algorithm was implemented in R and we used the blocking algorithm included in the "AlgDesign" package in R (Wheeler 2004).

In summary, the DCE designs consists of 196 pairs divided over 28 blocks of seven pairs each. With the same sample size as the cTTO, this leads to a total of 7000 observations, meaning about 350 observations per parameter for a main effects model. The 196 pair DCE design can be found in Appendix C.

Table 3.1 Priors used for the DCE design

	Level 2	Level 3	Level 4	Level 5
Mobility	−0.122	−0.245	−0.892	−1.539
Self-care	−0.285	−0.570	−0.895	−1.220
Usual activities	−0.153	−0.305	−0.670	−1.035
Pain/discomfort	−0.104	−0.208	−0.853	−1.499
Anxiety/depression	−0.250	−0.500	−1.054	−1.609

Reproduced from Oppe and van Hout (2017)

Box 3.2: Algorithm for Selection of DCE Pairs of Health States Used for the EQ-VT Design

start	
start outer loop	
step 1	a set of 186 pairs of states is randomly generated
	start inner loop
step 2	a set of priors is drawn
step 3	the D-error of the design is computed
step 4	steps 2 and 3 are repeated
	end inner loop
step 5	the overall D error is calculated (i.e., the combined D error from the inner loops)
step 6	repeat steps 1 to 5 10,000 times and keep the design with the best overall D error
end outer loop	
step 7	add the ten fixed pairs of mild health states to the set of 186 pairs from step 7
step 8	block the design from step 7 into 28 blocks of seven pairs each
end	

3.2.3 Other Considerations

Apart from the sample size, and the selection of the set of health states for the cTTO and pairs for the DCE, another consideration for the experimental design of the EQ-VT was the randomisation schema needed. This is important, as a proper randomisation schema can counteract potential biases. For the cTTO, each respondent is randomly allocated one block of ten health states. The order in which the ten health states appear for each respondent is also randomised. For the DCE, each respondent is randomly assigned to one of the 28 blocks of pairs. The order of appearance of the seven pairs allocated to each respondent is also randomised, and for each pair of health states the order of appearance on the screen of the two health states comprising a pair (i.e., left versus right) is randomised. The order of appearance of the dimensions was not randomised, because the EQ-5D-5L instrument itself has a fixed order of appearance with respect to the dimensions (see Chap. 1).

3.3 Alternative cTTO Designs

As noted above, the cTTO design of the EQ-VT protocol includes the selection of 86 different EQ-5D-5L health states and a minimal sample size of 1000. While this sample size is considered sufficient and achievable for most countries, reducing the number of states in the design, and thus the sample size, has the appeal that it could increase the feasibility of a valuaticn study in countries with limited resources or difficulty recruiting such a large number of respondents.

An important criterion for using a small design is that the accuracy of the estimated health state values should not be compromised (i.e., bias should be minimized). Following the study design established by Yang et al. in comparing EQ-5D-3L designs in a saturated VAS study (Yang et al. 2018), this process was replicated for the EQ-5D-5L. First, an EQ-5D-5L saturated VAS dataset was collected from a Chinese university student sample, with 100 VAS values for all 3125 EQ-5D-5L health states. Next, 100 variants of an orthogonal design[1] with 25 health states were created and modelled. Their predictive performances were quantified by calculating the Root Mean Squared Error (RMSE) against the observed VAS values from the saturated dataset. 25 health states were chosen as it is the minimal number for an orthogonal design in a five-dimension five-level classification system. For comparison, 100 variants of a random design and 100 variants of a D-efficient design were created, also with 25 states in each design. The EQ-VT design was also included as a reference (Yang et al. 2019a). The results showed that the RMSE was 3.44 for the EQ-VT design and 3.40 for the orthogonal design on the VAS scale (from 0 to 100). Little variance is observed among the 100 variants of the orthogonal design. Nevertheless, the inclusion of 11111 in the orthogonal design degraded the overall prediction performance. When extending the orthogonal design with the five mildest states and the "pits" state (to counteract biases due to framing effects), the RMSE was 3.87. These results showed that the orthogonal design extended with five mildest and the "pits" state could allow robust and precise estimations of EQ-5D-5L VAS values, as the RMSE was only slightly increased compared with the RMSE of 3.44 for EQ-VT design (i.e., the difference was 0.43 on VAS scale).

Considering the data distribution characteristics of the cTTO values from EQ-5D-5L valuation studies using the EQ-VT (e.g., they are not normally distributed, their distribution was separated by death into two parts, they displayed large heterogeneity etc.), a second study was performed validating the performance of orthogonal designs using cTTO data (Yang et al. 2019b). Following the EQ-VT protocol version 1.1 (as described in Chap. 2) cTTO data were collected from a sample of Chinese university students. In total, three designs were included in the study, i.e., (1) the EQ-VT design; (2) the best performing orthogonal design variant from the VAS saturated study; (3) a D-efficient design with 25 states. In total, 100 observations per health state were collected for the three designs of a total 136 health states (i.e., 86 + 25 + 25). Next, the value sets were modelled by design and their prediction accuracy was evaluated for the 136 states. The RMSEs of the (1) EQ-VT, (2) orthogonal + five mildest states + the "pits" state and (3) D-efficient designs + five mildest states + the "pits" state were 0.053, 0.066 and 0.063 on the value scale (0-1) respectively. Based on the findings of these two studies, the use of

---

[1] An orthogonal design satisfies the criterion that all severity levels and all severity level combinations are equally prevalent and therefore balanced.

the EQ-VT design was confirmed as a default design choice for EQ-5D-5L valuation studies. However, the orthogonal design with 25 states + five mildest states + one "pits" state can be used in some specific contexts, e.g., when resources are not available for a standard EQ-VT study. Peru is the first country to use the orthogonal design + five mildest states + one "pits" state (referred as 'Lite' protocol; see Appendix D) for establishing its EQ-5D-5L value set (see Chap. 4). In that study, the modelling results suggested the 'Lite' protocol could produce logical consistent coefficients, but some coefficients were not significant. Additionally, the DCE coefficients and cTTO coefficients were found to be inequivalent in that study and a hybrid model of combining both responses was not used for the final Peruvian EQ-5D-5L value set. For the above-mentioned reasons, the authors suggest more research is needed to further explore the feasibility of such 'Lite' protocol (Augustovski et al. 2020).

3.4 Future Research

Regarding design principles employed in EQ-5D-5L valuation studies, ongoing work focuses on refinement of current design strategies, and identification of new designs for emerging valuation approaches. Regarding the design used in the EQ-VT, evidence to date suggests that the design is fit for purpose. Across the range of studies already conducted with the EQ-VT (see Chap. 1 for details), the design has allowed precise estimation of health state values. However, there are a number of issues that require addressing in future.

First, it is apparent that the ten pairs of relatively mild health states appended to the DCE design are potentially problematic, and may cause bias in the parameter estimates. One plausible explanation for this is that the values for these health states are likely to be similar (as they are all close to full health and to each other), but the choice probabilities are not necessarily close to 50/50 since there may be a small but consistent preference for accepting a particular dimension at level two over another. Second, it may be that using a broader set of EQ-5D-5L health states yields a more accurate value set as the value of health states not directly observed in the data are more likely to have a near neighbour health state valued. For instance, the ongoing Indian EQ-5D-5L valuation study is exploring the use of an expanded set of 150 health states as part of the cTTO (Jyani et al. 2020). Third, the number of DCE choice pairs typically asked in the standard EQ-VT (i.e., seven) is limiting in terms of the models we might seek to estimate using the resultant data. For example, if we are interested in preference heterogeneity of the DCE data, then only having a small amount of DCE data precludes reliable estimation of more sophisticated latent class, mixed logit or generalised multinomial logit models (Fiebig et al. 2010), particularly if we are concerned with estimating correlations.

One more novel valuation approach that is under consideration currently is the use of DCE as a stand-alone task, a concept which has been growing in popularity in the health preference literature more generally (Mulhern et al.

2019). There are a range of potential advantages of a stand-alone DCE. Most importantly, the task can be undertaken without an interviewer (hence reducing the cost significantly) (Mulhern et al. 2013). Further, as it does not require interviewer travel, a smoother geographical distribution of respondents can be achieved (assuming that the surveying approach is equally accessible across regions). However, if we are reliant on the DCE alone (rather than as a component of the EQ-VT alongside cTTO tasks), then there is a need for more than seven choice observations per person, particularly if we want to move beyond estimation of population mean preferences, which is useful if we want to identify population sub-groups with specific views. Further, there is a need to anchor the data so they can be used to populate cost-utility analysis, for instance through including one or more of a duration attribute, a 'dead' health state, or some other external anchor. Regarding design strategy for a stand-alone DCE, there has been particular focus on generator-type approaches and efficient designs. The relative merits of each have been widely discussed in the literature. For example, EuroQol-funded work has conducted a large DCE in Peru looking at different composite approaches to anchoring and design; these results have been reported as part of a larger study including cTTO and latent DCE tasks (Augustovski et al. 2020). Ongoing analysis of these data, and similar data collected in Denmark (Jensen et al. 2021), will explore whether there is clear enough evidence of superiority of one or the other design approach for this specific purpose, and then to identify a design (or design approach) which can be used across countries conducting such a valuation survey.

This chapter has described the design strategies that have been used in existing EQ-5D-5L valuation projects, and their relative advances on those used for the EQ-5D-3L. The designs have been selected to balance statistical efficiency with respondent ease (and hence data quality), and the current approach appears to reflect a good trade-off between the two, with good completion rates, precise model estimates, and face validity of the final value sets across a number of languages, countries and cultures. The approaches used to this point are flexible, and can be adapted to meet the challenge of novel valuation approaches which may become more prominent in future years, and give policy makers confidence that the valuation surveys have accurately captured the attitudes of the general public without bias.

Appendices

Appendix A: Construction for Level Balance Optimisation Criterion

Step 1: A matrix (labelled "EQ lvl mat") with the counts for each level-domain combination is constructed (note that the example tables below contain hypothetical data using ten EQ-5D-5L states for illustrative purposes):

	MO	SC	UA	PD	AD
lvl 1	2	2	1	3	1
lvl 2	1	2	2	2	3
lvl 3	3	2	2	1	2
lvl 4	2	2	3	1	1
lvl 5	2	2	2	3	3

Reproduced from Oppe and van Hout (2017)
AD anxiety/depression, *MO* mobility, *PD* pain/discomfort, *SC* self-care, *UA* usual activities

Step 2: Using the data from "EQ lvl mat" a second matrix, containing the squares of the differences between the presence of levels per dimension is created (labelled "lvl dist mat"):

	MO	SC	UA	PD	AD
(lvl 1 - lvl 2)^2	1	0	1	1	4
(lvl 1 - lvl 3)^2	1	0	1	4	1
(lvl 1 - lvl 4)^2	0	0	4	4	0
(lvl 1 - lvl 5)^2	0	0	1	0	4
(lvl 2 - lvl 3)^2	4	0	0	1	1
(lvl 2 - lvl 4)^2	1	0	1	1	4
(lvl 2 - lvl 5)^2	1	0	0	1	0
(lvl 3 - lvl 4)^2	1	0	1	0	1
(lvl 3 - lvl 5)^2	1	0	0	4	1
(lvl 4 - lvl 5)^2	0	0	1	4	4

Reproduced from Oppe and van Hout (2017)
AD anxiety/depression, *MO* mobility, *PD* pain/discomfort, *SC* self-care, *UA* usual activities

Step 3: The elements of "lvl dist mat" are summed and the square root is taken over the sum to obtain the optimisation parameter (labelled "lvl bal check"):

"lvl bal check" = square root (sum ("lvl dist mat")) = 7.75
A value for "lvl bal check" = 0 indicates perfect level balance (i.e. each level-domain combination occurs twice).
A value for "lvl bal check" = 44.72 indicates the worst possible level balance: for each domain only 1 level is included. In this case "EQ lvl mat" contains one 10 and four 0's for each domain; "lvl dist mat" contains four 100's and six 0's, and the sum of "lvl dist mat" = 2000, with a square root = 44.72.
Note that perfect level balance is not a requirement (and might actually be undesirable in some cases). Small deviations can be allowed by e.g., setting a maximum allowable value for "lvl bal check" and letting the algorithm sample designs until it finds one for which "lvl bal. check" is lower than this preset maximum.

Appendix B: The cTTO design of the EQ-VT

Table 3.2 The 86 EQ-5D-5L health states included in the composite TTO task of the EQ-VT

block nr	state nr	MO	SC	UA	PD	AD	block nr	state nr	MO	SC	UA	PD	AD
1	1	1	1	2	2	1	6	41	1	2	1	1	2
1	2	1	1	2	3	5	6	42	1	1	2	1	2
1	3	5	4	2	3	1	6	43	4	4	5	5	3
1	4	5	1	4	5	1	6	44	2	1	3	4	5
1	5	3	4	5	1	5	6	45	3	4	2	4	4
1	6	3	5	2	4	5	6	46	2	3	1	5	2
1	7	1	2	5	1	4	6	47	4	3	5	1	4
1	8	4	5	1	4	4	6	48	5	5	4	2	4
1	86	5	5	5	5	5	6	86	5	5	5	5	5
1	82	1	2	1	1	1	6	81	2	1	1	1	1
2	9	1	2	5	4	3	7	49	1	3	1	2	2
2	10	1	2	1	2	1	7	50	2	4	5	5	3
2	11	4	3	5	4	2	7	51	5	1	1	5	2
2	12	3	4	1	5	5	7	52	1	1	4	2	5
2	13	5	2	2	1	5	7	53	2	2	4	3	4
2	14	4	5	1	3	3	7	54	4	2	1	1	5
2	15	3	2	4	4	3	7	55	3	5	3	3	2
2	16	2	3	5	1	4	7	56	4	5	4	1	3
2	86	5	5	5	5	5	7	86	5	5	5	5	5
2	83	1	1	2	1	1	7	83	1	1	2	1	1
3	17	4	5	2	3	3	8	57	3	3	2	5	3
3	18	5	5	2	3	3	8	58	2	3	2	4	2
3	19	3	1	5	2	5	8	59	2	4	3	4	2
3	20	5	2	4	5	5	8	60	3	2	3	1	4
3	21	1	2	2	4	4	8	61	1	2	3	3	4
3	22	1	3	3	1	3	8	62	2	1	3	3	4
3	23	2	5	1	2	2	8	63	5	5	2	2	5
3	24	1	1	4	2	1	8	64	5	3	4	1	2
3	86	5	5	5	5	5	8	86	5	5	5	5	5
3	81	2	1	1	1	1	8	85	1	1	1	1	2
4	25	2	1	1	1	2	9	65	1	1	4	1	4
4	26	1	4	5	5	4	9	66	2	5	3	3	1
4	27	1	2	5	1	3	9	67	2	5	2	2	2
4	28	4	4	3	4	5	9	68	2	1	4	4	4
4	29	1	2	3	4	4	9	69	3	1	5	1	4
4	30	5	3	2	2	1	9	70	5	3	2	4	3
4	31	5	4	3	4	2	9	71	5	3	2	4	4
4	32	4	4	1	2	5	9	72	3	5	1	4	3
4	86	5	5	5	5	5	9	86	5	5	5	5	5
4	84	1	1	1	2	1	9	84	1	1	1	2	1

(continued)

Table 3.2 (continued)

block nr	state nr	MO	SC	UA	PD	AD	block nr	state nr	MO	SC	UA	PD	AD
5	33	4	3	3	1	5	10	73	1	1	1	2	2
5	34	5	4	1	5	3	10	74	5	2	3	3	5
5	35	5	2	4	3	1	10	75	3	5	3	1	1
5	36	2	4	4	4	3	10	76	4	3	5	5	5
5	37	1	4	1	1	3	10	77	2	4	4	4	5
5	38	3	1	5	2	4	10	78	1	3	2	2	4
5	39	1	5	1	5	1	10	79	3	4	2	3	2
5	40	2	1	3	1	5	10	80	4	2	3	2	1
5	86	5	5	5	5	5	10	86	5	5	5	5	5
5	85	1	1	1	1	2	10	82	1	2	1	1	1

Reproduced from Oppe and van Hout (2017)
AD anxiety/depression, *MO* mobility, *PD* pain/discomfort, *SC* self-care, *UA* usual activities

Appendix C: The DCE design of the EQ-VT

Table 3.3 The 196 pairs of EQ-5D-5L health states included in the DCE task of the EQ-VT

block nr	pair nr	MO	SC	UA	PD	AD	MO	SC	UA	PD	AD
1	16	3	5	5	5	4	5	5	2	1	1
1	64	4	3	1	4	1	2	5	5	5	4
1	69	3	1	1	3	5	1	1	4	4	4
1	95	2	5	5	1	5	2	2	2	5	1
1	120	4	2	4	4	1	2	1	4	1	5
1	143	2	2	4	1	1	4	3	1	3	3
1	170	3	3	2	2	5	5	3	3	1	4
2	21	5	2	1	3	2	2	1	5	3	4
2	41	3	1	3	3	1	3	5	1	2	4
2	68	4	2	2	5	5	5	5	5	2	4
2	79	2	3	2	3	5	1	1	1	4	1
2	98	3	4	4	1	2	5	4	2	5	3
2	149	3	5	3	1	2	1	4	4	2	2
2	181	1	3	5	5	3	3	1	2	3	4
3	31	5	1	3	1	1	3	2	1	5	4
3	70	3	4	3	5	5	4	3	3	4	2
3	80	1	4	3	3	3	2	4	4	2	4
3	115	2	2	4	5	3	1	3	4	4	2
3	136	4	1	5	5	2	2	2	4	2	2
3	150	4	5	1	1	5	5	4	2	2	5
3	194	1	2	1	1	2	2	2	2	1	1
4	3	4	4	1	1	5	2	1	4	5	5
4	28	2	3	4	4	3	2	5	1	1	3

(continued)

Table 3.3 (continued)

block nr	pair nr	MO	SC	UA	PD	AD	MO	SC	UA	PD	AD
4	67	3	1	4	5	1	4	5	4	3	1
4	97	4	5	5	5	2	3	2	4	1	3
4	134	2	5	3	3	2	5	1	5	4	4
4	156	4	1	1	1	4	2	4	1	4	2
4	193	1	1	2	1	2	2	2	1	1	2
5	7	1	2	1	4	5	1	5	3	4	4
5	24	3	3	4	2	4	4	1	5	4	2
5	81	3	5	5	2	1	4	3	3	5	5
5	88	4	4	3	2	3	2	1	5	2	5
5	152	5	2	1	5	5	4	5	2	3	1
5	166	3	3	4	4	3	5	4	1	3	3
5	189	1	1	2	1	1	2	2	1	1	1
6	19	1	3	4	3	2	1	3	2	4	5
6	66	2	4	3	1	4	4	3	2	2	2
6	72	5	1	3	5	4	4	1	3	3	5
6	73	4	3	2	4	4	2	5	5	2	2
6	82	1	2	2	5	3	1	2	5	5	1
6	131	2	3	5	1	3	5	2	2	5	4
6	173	5	4	1	2	1	4	4	3	2	2
7	26	2	3	5	5	1	4	3	1	3	5
7	30	5	1	2	5	5	3	1	3	4	3
7	77	1	1	3	5	2	3	1	4	1	3
7	114	2	5	2	1	2	3	2	4	4	3
7	132	4	3	4	1	2	1	3	3	4	2
7	168	5	4	4	2	4	1	5	3	2	1
7	185	3	4	1	3	4	4	5	3	2	5
8	37	1	4	5	5	2	5	5	3	2	5
8	58	5	1	1	1	4	4	1	2	5	3
8	59	2	5	2	3	5	1	3	4	1	3
8	110	2	5	1	4	5	5	2	2	4	4
8	117	4	5	5	3	3	1	4	4	4	4
8	154	5	1	5	5	2	3	5	5	1	3
8	187	2	1	1	1	1	1	2	1	2	1
9	43	2	5	3	1	2	4	1	5	3	2
9	48	4	1	3	1	5	1	5	1	2	1
9	85	4	4	3	5	1	2	4	4	1	5
9	90	2	4	1	4	5	3	2	2	5	3
9	133	5	1	4	2	4	3	5	5	2	5
9	137	2	3	5	5	2	3	2	2	4	4
9	176	1	3	2	2	2	3	1	1	3	1
10	46	3	5	3	2	1	5	3	2	1	5
10	47	2	4	4	5	3	4	1	3	3	1
10	51	2	1	4	2	3	1	3	1	1	4

(continued)

Table 3.3 (continued)

block nr	pair nr	MO	SC	UA	PD	AD	MO	SC	UA	PD	AD
10	52	5	1	3	3	1	2	2	4	2	1
10	103	3	5	2	3	5	4	2	3	2	5
10	171	2	2	5	4	4	3	5	4	5	2
10	182	5	1	1	3	1	3	5	3	5	3
11	6	1	5	2	4	4	4	4	2	4	1
11	32	4	4	1	5	1	5	3	2	4	2
11	78	2	2	4	1	3	2	2	3	3	1
11	126	4	1	4	2	4	3	5	5	3	3
11	162	4	2	4	5	2	2	3	1	4	4
11	165	5	3	4	2	2	4	2	5	2	5
11	177	2	3	1	2	2	1	2	4	1	5
12	2	4	3	5	3	4	3	2	1	2	5
12	12	2	4	1	5	5	3	2	5	3	4
12	91	2	2	4	3	3	1	2	4	4	3
12	123	5	2	4	2	2	5	5	2	5	4
12	148	5	5	2	4	4	5	3	5	3	1
12	157	2	2	2	2	2	2	5	5	1	4
12	188	1	2	1	1	1	2	1	1	2	1
13	29	4	4	1	3	4	2	2	3	5	2
13	60	4	2	2	4	3	3	5	4	3	3
13	94	2	2	5	1	2	5	5	3	1	3
13	102	1	5	5	3	4	4	3	4	5	4
13	119	5	5	1	5	3	2	2	5	2	1
13	125	2	1	2	3	5	1	2	2	4	3
13	158	1	2	5	2	1	4	1	1	1	5
14	10	1	1	2	1	4	4	5	3	1	2
14	25	2	5	3	4	2	5	1	1	5	2
14	39	3	4	4	4	2	1	5	2	1	4
14	121	2	1	1	1	4	5	2	4	3	2
14	124	3	5	2	5	2	3	2	2	5	4
14	138	4	2	5	1	2	2	3	5	4	4
14	184	5	4	3	4	4	1	5	4	1	1
15	35	5	5	3	3	5	5	3	4	4	2
15	40	4	5	5	4	2	4	2	1	3	3
15	56	1	2	1	5	1	3	5	5	4	3
15	84	4	3	2	4	5	3	4	3	2	4
15	139	1	3	5	1	5	1	1	3	2	4
15	161	4	1	3	1	2	2	4	2	5	3
15	190	1	1	1	2	1	2	1	2	1	1
16	54	2	3	4	4	2	2	5	4	1	4
16	61	5	2	5	4	4	3	4	2	2	2
16	65	5	2	2	1	1	1	1	3	2	5
16	92	3	3	2	2	4	4	2	1	1	3

(continued)

Table 3.3 (continued)

block nr	pair nr	MO	SC	UA	PD	AD	MO	SC	UA	PD	AD
16	107	5	1	1	2	3	4	3	4	5	1
16	109	1	5	2	4	1	1	2	3	5	2
16	116	1	4	3	4	4	5	2	4	5	4
17	57	5	2	5	2	3	5	4	1	4	2
17	63	2	3	4	5	1	3	4	3	5	4
17	96	5	3	5	5	1	2	1	2	2	4
17	101	5	3	1	2	5	3	1	4	1	5
17	104	1	5	1	1	3	1	4	4	3	4
17	130	1	3	3	3	4	4	5	4	4	1
17	192	1	1	1	2	2	2	3	1	1	1
18	5	3	3	2	2	3	2	1	2	3	2
18	45	3	1	5	2	1	4	3	1	5	2
18	50	4	4	1	2	3	5	1	2	3	2
18	74	1	4	4	5	5	1	5	5	1	4
18	100	2	5	5	4	5	3	5	2	2	5
18	141	3	3	1	1	1	3	2	5	4	5
18	186	4	1	4	3	1	2	4	2	1	2
19	1	3	5	2	3	1	5	3	5	5	4
19	20	4	2	4	2	1	5	4	2	5	5
19	38	5	4	4	2	3	3	2	3	1	4
19	99	2	3	2	3	3	1	2	4	1	1
19	153	2	2	1	2	3	1	1	1	5	5
19	159	2	1	4	4	5	5	5	1	4	1
19	178	5	4	4	5	4	2	4	5	1	1
20	11	3	5	2	1	1	4	2	5	5	1
20	27	3	4	1	3	2	2	4	4	4	5
20	105	2	4	5	2	3	4	5	1	2	5
20	113	5	2	1	1	1	1	1	4	3	1
20	122	2	1	3	5	4	4	1	3	2	1
20	135	5	4	5	5	5	3	5	5	3	5
20	169	1	1	4	4	5	3	2	1	1	5
21	4	1	3	1	1	1	1	1	2	1	5
21	15	1	3	2	5	1	5	3	3	1	3
21	83	4	4	2	3	4	3	3	4	4	1
21	118	2	1	5	2	2	2	5	3	2	4
21	128	4	5	5	1	5	3	4	4	3	3
21	145	4	3	5	2	5	2	3	4	4	4
21	175	4	2	1	5	3	5	3	1	5	1
22	13	2	2	3	4	1	4	5	1	4	5
22	44	3	2	3	3	4	2	2	2	5	4
22	89	4	1	5	4	5	3	3	5	3	1
22	108	5	5	2	3	5	2	2	5	3	3
22	111	1	5	4	2	4	3	3	3	2	2
22	140	3	2	2	4	1	5	1	5	2	5

(continued)

Table 3.3 (continued)

block nr	pair nr	MO	SC	UA	PD	AD	MO	SC	UA	PD	AD
22	146	3	2	2	1	1	1	4	2	1	1
23	36	1	1	5	1	2	2	2	2	4	1
23	53	3	4	3	4	5	5	1	3	2	5
23	55	4	2	1	2	2	3	1	3	2	5
23	71	4	5	5	3	1	1	4	3	3	4
23	144	5	1	2	1	4	4	5	1	5	3
23	174	1	5	3	5	1	1	4	3	1	2
23	183	2	1	3	3	5	4	4	5	5	1
24	8	3	2	4	4	2	5	4	4	4	1
24	62	1	1	5	4	5	1	4	1	1	3
24	86	5	2	2	2	3	5	4	1	3	2
24	87	1	1	2	3	4	2	1	5	3	2
24	112	3	5	3	2	2	4	1	5	3	5
24	151	1	3	1	3	1	2	3	1	1	3
24	172	5	5	5	3	4	3	3	3	5	5
25	14	3	3	4	3	2	1	5	5	5	1
25	34	1	4	1	2	2	5	4	2	3	1
25	49	5	1	3	2	4	3	4	5	4	3
25	93	3	3	2	4	3	1	1	1	1	5
25	106	3	4	2	3	4	1	3	5	3	3
25	155	2	3	5	3	1	5	3	1	3	3
25	179	5	3	5	4	3	4	1	2	1	5
26	9	4	4	5	2	1	4	1	1	5	3
26	23	5	4	4	5	5	5	5	2	3	4
26	142	4	4	2	3	1	2	5	5	3	3
26	163	1	5	5	5	5	5	3	4	5	5
26	164	2	2	3	4	3	3	4	5	1	3
26	191	1	1	1	1	2	1	2	2	2	1
26	195	2	1	1	1	2	1	2	2	1	1
27	18	1	4	5	3	3	2	1	5	4	2
27	42	2	3	1	3	4	1	4	3	1	4
27	75	5	3	4	3	1	5	2	2	5	5
27	76	5	1	5	2	2	4	5	2	4	4
27	127	1	4	2	2	4	3	2	3	2	2
27	180	4	4	1	4	5	4	5	4	3	2
27	196	1	1	2	2	1	2	2	1	2	2
28	17	4	2	3	2	3	5	5	2	2	3
28	22	4	1	3	2	5	1	3	4	4	5
28	33	3	4	3	3	3	3	3	1	4	2
28	129	2	3	2	3	1	2	5	3	2	3
28	147	3	1	4	4	4	1	1	3	5	3
28	160	1	5	3	3	5	4	3	5	3	2
28	167	3	5	4	3	1	5	1	3	2	3

Reproduced from Oppe and van Hout (2017)
AD anxiety/depression, *MO* mobility, *PD* pain/discomfort, *SC* self-care, *UA* usual activities

Appendix D: The Design Used in the Peruvian EQ-5D-5L Valuation Study

Table 3.4 The 31 EQ-5D-5L health states included in the composite TTO task in the EQ-VT in the Peruvian valuation study (Augustovski et al. 2020)

block nr	state nr[a]	MO	SC	UA	PD	AD
1	3	2	4	1	1	3
1	4	1	2	3	2	4
1	5	3	2	5	1	1
1	7	1	5	1	5	1
1	13	3	1	4	5	2
1	15	5	1	1	4	4
1	24	4	4	3	5	5
1	25	5	5	5	3	5
1	28	1	1	2	1	1
1	30	2	1	1	1	1
1	31	5	5	5	5	5
2	2	2	1	3	3	1
2	8	2	5	2	2	2
2	14	4	1	5	2	3
2	17	3	4	2	3	4
2	19	2	2	4	4	5
2	20	5	2	2	5	3
2	21	3	5	3	4	3
2	22	4	5	4	1	4
2	27	1	1	1	2	1
2	29	1	2	1	1	1
2	31	5	5	5	5	5
3	1	1	1	2	1	5
3	6	4	2	1	3	2
3	9	1	3	4	3	3
3	10	3	3	1	2	5
3	11	4	3	2	4	1
3	12	5	3	3	1	2
3	16	1	4	5	4	2
3	18	5	4	4	2	1
3	23	2	3	5	5	4
3	26	1	1	1	1	2
3	31	5	5	5	5	5

[a]Health states numbers 1 to 25 are based on the orthogonal design, 26 to 30 are the five mildest states and 31 is the "pits" state

AD anxiety/depression, *MO* mobility, *PD* pain/discomfort, *SC* self-care, *UA* usual activities

Table 3.5 The 80 pairs of EQ-5D-5L health states included in the DCE task of the EQ-VT in the Peruvian valuation study (Augustovski et al. 2020)

block nr	MO	SC	UA	PD	AD	MO	SC	UA	PD	AD
1	3	2	2	5	3	4	1	5	3	5
1	4	3	2	1	1	4	1	1	5	1
1	1	5	2	4	3	5	4	4	3	4
1	4	5	1	1	1	4	1	4	2	4
1	5	3	1	5	4	4	5	2	4	5
1	4	3	4	5	2	3	1	3	1	5
1	2	4	5	5	1	1	1	3	2	3
1	2	1	5	1	2	1	5	4	2	5
2	4	5	1	2	2	1	5	4	5	5
2	1	1	5	1	2	3	5	3	3	3
2	5	4	3	3	2	3	4	5	4	4
2	1	4	4	1	3	2	3	2	5	4
2	2	2	4	3	3	4	5	4	1	5
2	5	5	1	3	1	5	1	4	2	4
2	3	2	3	1	1	3	3	1	2	1
2	2	3	4	2	1	3	1	3	4	5
3	2	5	1	5	3	1	3	5	4	3
3	4	3	2	3	2	1	5	1	4	2
3	4	3	2	2	4	4	1	3	4	5
3	2	1	3	5	3	4	4	3	2	5
3	2	1	1	5	3	5	3	1	5	3
3	3	5	4	2	1	1	2	2	4	5
3	3	4	1	3	2	4	1	2	5	4
3	4	5	3	3	2	5	2	5	3	2
5	1	2	1	3	1	1	4	5	2	2
5	1	4	1	1	2	4	3	4	2	5
5	3	2	4	2	5	2	2	3	4	5
5	4	4	2	3	2	5	2	2	4	4
5	3	3	1	4	2	4	1	5	2	3
5	2	5	2	3	1	1	3	2	5	1
5	5	1	5	3	2	2	3	5	2	5
5	5	5	5	3	1	4	4	1	5	4
6	4	1	3	5	2	4	5	2	2	5
6	3	2	3	3	3	1	1	2	2	4
6	5	4	3	2	3	3	3	5	2	5
6	1	5	1	4	1	5	3	4	1	4
6	3	1	5	1	1	5	1	2	5	3
6	5	4	2	2	2	2	1	2	5	4
6	3	5	4	2	3	2	3	2	3	3
6	3	4	2	1	1	2	3	1	1	5
7	2	3	3	3	5	3	4	4	4	5
7	3	2	2	4	2	4	4	4	2	4
7	3	1	3	4	3	4	4	5	2	5
7	4	2	2	4	1	1	4	4	5	1
7	4	3	3	3	3	5	1	2	5	5
7	4	2	3	2	1	5	5	5	4	1
7	2	5	2	4	2	1	4	1	4	3
7	3	3	4	3	4	1	2	3	5	4

(continued)

Table 3.5 (continued)

block nr	MO	SC	UA	PD	AD	MO	SC	UA	PD	AD	block nr	MO	SC	UA	PD	AD	MO	SC	UA	PD	AD
3	5	3	1	1	1	2	3	4	5	3	7	3	4	1	2	2	3	5	4	1	3
3	1	1	5	5	1	2	5	5	3	4	7	1	5	3	3	1	1	2	4	2	4
3	5	5	4	1	5	2	5	1	2	5	7	2	4	1	4	1	3	3	3	1	5
3	4	2	4	1	3	2	1	4	1	5	7	3	2	3	5	1	5	4	5	4	4
3	3	5	5	5	2	1	5	2	1	3	7	5	2	3	2	5	4	2	4	3	5
3	1	1	1	4	1	5	3	4	3	2	7	5	1	3	1	2	2	2	1	1	4
4	5	4	3	1	2	3	5	1	5	2	8	1	3	4	1	2	2	2	3	4	3
4	4	4	1	5	1	3	4	3	4	4	8	2	4	4	5	2	4	5	3	3	3
4	2	4	2	4	2	5	4	4	2	4	8	3	1	5	1	4	2	1	2	3	4
4	2	3	3	4	4	1	2	4	5	5	8	4	2	1	3	4	1	4	1	4	5
4	1	1	5	5	3	3	3	1	1	5	8	2	3	4	5	1	2	4	2	1	4
4	5	3	5	3	1	5	4	1	1	3	8	5	2	3	4	4	2	2	5	5	5
4	5	3	2	3	2	2	2	5	5	4	8	4	2	2	3	1	4	2	5	2	4
4	3	4	2	1	3	2	2	4	3	5	8	1	2	2	2	2	2	3	2	4	3
4	1	2	1	1	1	2	1	5	1	2	8	5	5	3	2	1	5	3	3	1	2
4	3	3	4	3	2	2	2	3	5	3	8	2	5	1	2	1	5	4	4	5	5

AD anxiety/depression, MO mobility, PD pain/discomfort, SC self-care, UA usual activities

Table 3.6 The 180 pairs of EQ-5D-5L health states included in the DCE task of the DCE-only interviews in the Peruvian valuation study (Augustovski et al. 2020)

block nr	MO	SC	UA	PD	AD	MO	SC	UA	PD	AD	block nr	MO	SC	UA	PD	AD	MO	SC	UA	PD	AD
1	3	3	2	2	3	2	1	2	3	2	10	4	5	5	5	2	3	2	4	1	3
1	2	5	3	1	2	4	1	5	3	2	10	2	1	1	1	4	5	2	4	3	2
1	2	2	5	4	4	3	5	4	5	2	10	4	4	1	3	4	2	2	3	5	2
1	5	2	1	3	2	2	1	5	3	4	10	5	5	5	3	4	3	3	3	5	5
1	5	2	1	5	5	4	5	2	3	1	10	2	3	1	2	2	1	2	4	1	5
1	1	5	5	5	5	5	3	4	5	5	10	1	4	5	5	2	5	5	3	2	5
1	1	2	5	2	1	4	1	1	1	5	10	2	3	1	3	4	1	4	3	1	4
1	4	3	1	4	1	2	5	5	5	4	10	5	2	2	2	3	5	4	1	3	2
1	3	5	3	2	1	5	3	2	1	5	10	3	1	5	2	1	4	3	1	5	2
1	4	1	3	1	5	1	5	1	2	1	10	2	2	4	5	3	1	3	4	4	2
2	4	3	2	4	5	3	4	3	2	4	11	4	5	5	1	5	3	4	4	3	3
2	3	5	5	5	4	5	5	2	1	1	11	2	2	3	4	3	3	4	5	1	3
2	1	2	1	4	5	1	5	3	4	4	11	2	4	4	2	3	1	3	1	1	4
2	2	1	3	3	5	4	4	5	5	1	11	4	2	4	2	1	5	4	2	5	5
2	5	1	3	1	1	3	2	1	5	4	11	4	4	1	2	3	5	1	2	3	2
2	3	5	3	2	2	4	1	5	3	5	11	1	5	2	4	1	1	2	3	5	2
2	5	3	4	3	1	5	2	2	5	5	11	5	5	2	4	4	5	3	5	3	1
2	1	5	3	5	1	1	4	3	1	2	11	3	2	3	3	5	2	2	2	5	4
2	1	2	5	1	5	1	1	3	2	4	11	2	4	1	5	5	3	2	5	3	4
2	5	2	1	1	1	5	1	4	3	1	11	4	1	4	3	1	2	4	2	1	2
3	2	2	3	4	1	2	5	1	4	5	12	1	3	5	5	3	3	1	2	3	4
3	1	5	5	3	4	1	3	4	5	4	12	5	1	4	2	4	3	5	5	2	5
3	4	5	1	1	5	4	4	2	2	5	12	2	3	4	4	3	2	5	1	1	3

(continued)

Table 3.6 (continued)

block nr	MO	SC	UA	PD	AD	MO	SC	UA	PD	AD	block nr	MO	SC	UA	PD	AD	MO	SC	UA	PD	AD
3	4	1	3	2	5	1	3	4	4	5	12	2	1	3	5	4	4	3	3	2	1
3	1	1	5	1	2	2	2	2	4	2	12	4	1	1	1	4	2	4	1	4	2
3	2	3	2	3	3	1	2	4	1	3	12	3	5	5	2	1	4	3	3	5	5
3	5	4	1	2	1	4	4	3	2	1	12	1	3	1	1	1	1	1	2	1	5
3	5	1	5	5	2	3	5	5	1	2	12	4	5	5	3	1	1	4	3	3	4
3	3	5	2	5	2	3	2	2	5	2	12	3	4	3	5	5	4	3	3	4	2
3	2	4	4	5	3	4	1	3	3	3	12	5	1	1	2	3	5	3	4	5	1
4	3	1	4	5	1	4	5	4	3	1	13	4	2	4	5	2	4	3	1	4	4
4	3	5	4	3	5	5	1	3	2	1	13	1	3	3	3	1	2	3	1	1	3
4	3	1	1	3	2	1	1	4	4	3	13	4	2	2	2	3	5	5	3	2	3
4	2	5	2	1	4	3	2	4	4	4	13	2	3	5	3	5	1	1	2	3	5
4	5	1	3	2	5	3	4	5	4	3	13	4	5	4	3	3	1	4	5	2	3
4	1	1	5	4	4	1	4	1	1	5	13	3	3	2	2	4	5	2	3	3	4
4	4	3	5	3	3	3	2	1	2	4	13	3	3	5	3	2	5	2	5	5	2
4	5	1	1	3	1	3	5	3	5	3	13	3	2	2	4	5	5	3	2	3	1
4	3	5	3	1	2	1	4	4	2	2	13	3	5	5	3	2	5	2	2	3	5
5	2	2	5	4	5	5	2	2	4	4	14	3	3	3	4	4	5	3	2	1	1
5	4	3	5	3	4	4	3	3	5	3	14	2	3	2	2	1	3	5	5	5	4
5	5	2	1	5	4	5	5	1	2	5	14	5	4	5	4	3	3	3	3	4	4
5	2	3	2	3	3	4	5	5	3	3	14	3	3	3	3	4	2	2	2	4	3
5	3	2	5	2	3	4	3	2	3	3	14	2	2	2	3	5	5	3	3	4	3
5	3	3	2	2	3	3	3	3	3	4	14	5	1	5	3	2	3	1	5	4	4

4	1	2	5	1	2	4	4	4	3	14	2	2	2	4	3	4	4	5	2	5	5
2	1	3	5	4	4	1	2	1	1	14	2	3	5	3	4	5	3	3	5	1	5
2	4	1	3	3	3	3	3	4	3	15	2	5	1	1	5	2	4	3	5	2	6
2	4	1	4	5	3	2	5	2	5	15	3	4	4	2	1	3	3	4	2	2	6
4	1	5	5	2	2	2	2	2	2	15	4	4	5	3	2	2	1	5	2	4	6
2	3	5	1	2	4	3	2	1	1	15	2	2	2	3	4	4	1	3	4	2	6
3	3	5	5	2	1	3	2	4	4	15	5	2	3	5	4	4	3	1	4	3	6
5	1	2	1	4	3	4	5	3	5	15	1	2	3	5	1	4	2	4	4	5	6
1	4	4	3	3	4	3	2	4	4	15	2	4	2	3	5	1	5	1	4	4	6
4	5	3	4	3	1	5	4	3	2	15	3	1	4	1	3	2	5	3	1	1	6
5	4	2	3	1	2	3	4	3	1	15	4	1	5	5	1	5	5	4	4	1	6
4	1	3	3	5	5	2	2	3	3	16	3	5	2	1	4	4	1	1	1	5	6
2	2	4	2	2	2	5	5	1	4	16	2	4	4	3	5	5	3	3	5	5	7
5	1	4	4	2	1	5	3	4	4	16	4	1	4	5	2	2	4	4	3	2	7
2	3	4	5	4	5	4	1	4	4	16	4	5	4	2	5	4	4	3	4	1	7
1	3	2	4	5	2	2	1	4	1	16	5	1	1	2	3	5	4	4	1	1	7
5	1	4	1	2	1	4	4	2	4	16	2	4	3	3	1	2	1	4	3	4	7
3	5	2	4	5	2	1	4	4	3	16	5	4	4	4	2	2	3	1	4	3	7
5	5	4	1	2	5	1	1	4	4	16	3	3	1	3	4	1	1	4	2	2	7
4	2	3	5	2	2	2	5	1	2	17	1	2	5	2	2	3	5	1	5	5	7
1	3	3	2	2	3	1	4	2	2	17	5	2	3	1	1	1	1	2	2	5	7
3	5	2	2	3	5	4	1	4	2	17	1	4	1	5	5	5	4	4	1	2	8
2	2	3	3	3	4	2	4	5	1	17	3	3	5	5	3	4	2	4	1	4	8
3	5	3	1	1	4	4	4	1	3		2	2	3	2	3	4	2	2	4	1	8
5	2	2	5	3	5	4	5	5	2		4	2	5	5	5	5	5	2	2	4	8
5	5	1	1	1	3	2	1	2	2		1	5	5	2	4	1	1	2	5	3	

(continued)

Table 3.6 (continued)

block nr	MO	SC	UA	PD	AD	MO	SC	UA	PD	AD	block nr	MO	SC	UA	PD	AD	MO	SC	UA	PD	AD
8	5	1	5	2	2	4	5	2	4	4	17	5	1	3	3	1	2	2	4	2	1
8	1	4	3	3	3	2	4	4	2	4	17	1	5	2	4	4	4	4	2	4	1
8	4	2	1	5	3	5	3	1	5	1	17	5	3	4	2	2	4	2	5	2	5
8	3	3	2	4	3	1	1	1	1	5	17	1	3	2	5	1	5	3	3	1	3
8	5	3	5	5	1	2	1	2	2	4	17	4	4	3	2	3	2	1	5	2	5
8	2	5	5	1	5	2	2	2	5	1	17	5	2	4	2	2	5	5	2	5	4
9	4	5	5	4	2	4	2	1	3	3	18	1	5	1	1	3	1	4	4	3	4
9	2	5	2	3	5	1	3	4	1	4	18	2	3	5	5	1	4	3	1	3	5
9	3	1	3	3	1	3	5	1	2	5	18	3	2	4	4	2	5	4	4	4	1
9	3	3	1	1	1	3	2	5	4	1	18	5	3	1	2	5	3	1	4	4	5
9	1	3	3	3	4	4	5	4	4	3	18	5	4	4	5	4	2	4	5	5	1
9	3	3	4	4	3	5	4	1	3	3	18	2	4	5	2	3	4	5	1	2	5
9	4	1	3	1	2	2	4	2	5	3	18	1	4	5	3	3	2	1	5	4	2
9	3	4	3	3	5	5	1	3	2	5											

AD anxiety/depression, *MO* mobility, *PD* pain/discomfort, *SC* self-care, *UA* usual activities

References

Augustovski F, Belizán M, Gibbons L, Reyes N, Stolk E, Craig BM, Tejada RA (2020) Peruvian valuation of the EQ-5D-5L: a direct comparison of time trade-off and discrete choice experiments. Value Health 23(7):880–888

Dolan P (1997) Modeling valuations for EuroQol health states. Med Care 35(11):1095–1108

Fiebig DG, Keane MP, Louviere J, Wasi N (2010) The generalized multinomial logit model: accounting for scale and coefficient heterogeneity. Mark Sci 29(3):393–421

Hensher DA, Rose JM, Greene WH (2005) Applied choice analysis: a primer. Cambridge University Press, New York

Janssen BM, Oppe M, Versteegh MM, Stolk EA (2013) Introducing the composite time trade-off: a test of feasibility and face validity. Eur J Health Econ 14(Suppl 1):S5–S13

Jensen CE, Sørensen SS, Gudex C, Jensen MB, Pedersen KM, Ehlers LH (2021) The Danish EQ-5D-5L value set: a hybrid model using cTTO and DCE data. Appl Health Econ Health Policy. https://doi.org/10.1007/s40258-021-00639-3

Jyani G, Prinja S, Kar SS, Trivedi M, Patro B, Purba F, Pala S, Raman S, Sharma A, Jain S, Kaur M (2020) Valuing health-related quality of life among the Indian population: a protocol for the development of an EQ-5D value set for India using an extended design (DEVINE) study. BMJ Open 10(11):e039517. https://doi.org/10.1136/bmjopen-2020-039517

Krabbe PFM, Devlin NJ, Stolk EA, Shah KK, Oppe M, van Hout B, Quik EH, Pickard AS, Xie F (2014) Multinational evidence of the applicability and robustness of discrete choice modeling for deriving EQ-5D-5L health-state values. Med Care 52(11):935–943

Lamers LM, McDonnell J, Stalmeier PFM, Krabbe PFM, Busschbach JJ (2006) The Dutch tariff: results and arguments for an effective design for national EQ-5D valuation studies. Health Econ 15(10):1121–1132

Mulhern B, Longworth L, Brazier J, Rowen J, Rowen D, Bansback N, Devlin N, Tsuchiya A (2013) Binary choice health state valuation and mode of administration: head-to-head comparison of online and CAPI. Value Health 16(1):104–113

Mulhern B, Norman R, Street DJ, Viney R (2019) One method, many methodological choices: a structured review of discrete-choice experiments for health state valuation. PharmacoEconomics 37(1):29–43

Oppe M, van Hout B (2010) The optimal hybrid: Experimental design and modelling of a combination of TTO and DCE. In: Proceedings of the 27th Scientific Plenary Meeting of the EuroQol Group, Athens, Greece, September 2010. https://eq-5dpublications.euroqol.org/download?id=0_53738&fileId=54152. Accessed 26 June 2021

Oppe M, van Hout B (2017) The "power" of eliciting EQ-5D-5L values: the experimental design of the EQ-VT. EuroQol Working paper 17003. https://euroqol.org/wp-content/uploads/2016/10/EuroQol-Working-Paper-Series-Manuscript-17003-Mark-Oppe.pdf Accessed 12 July 2021

Oppe M, Oppe S, de Charro F (2013) Statistical uncertainty in TTO derived utility values. In: Oppe M. Mathematical approaches in economic evaluations. Dissertation, Erasmus University Rotterdam. https://repub.eur.nl/pub/41260. Accessed 26 Jun 2021

Oppe M, Devlin NJ, van Hout B, Krabbe PF, de Charro F (2014) A program of methodological research to arrive at the new international EQ-5D-5L valuation protocol. Value Health 17(4):445–453

Stolk EA, Oppe M, Scalone L, Krabbe PFM (2010) Discrete choice modeling for the quantification of health states: the case of the EQ-5D. Value Health 13(8):1005–1013

Tsuchiya A, Ikeda S, Ikegami N, Nishimura S, Sakai I, Fukuda T, Hamashima C, Hisashige A, Tamura M (2002) Estimating an EQ-5D population value set: the case of Japan. Health Econ 11(4):341–353

Wheeler RE (2004) AlgDesign: algorithmic experimental design. The R project for statistical computing. https://CRAN.R-project.org/package=AlgDesign. Accessed 26 Jun 2021

Yang Z, Luo N, Bonsel G, Busschbach J, Stolk E (2018) Selecting health states for EQ-5D-3L valuation studies: statistical considerations matter. Value Health 21(4):456–461

Yang Z, Luo N, Bonsel G, Busschbach J, Stolk E (2019a) Effect of health state sampling methods on model predictions of EQ-5D-5L values: small designs can suffice. Value Health 22(1):38–44

Yang Z, Luo N, Oppe M, Bonsel G, Busschbach J, Stolk E (2019b) Toward a smaller design for EQ-5D-5L valuation studies. Value Health 22(11):1295–1302

Chapter 4
EQ-5D-5L Value Set Summaries

Bram Roudijk, Kristina Ludwig, and Nancy Devlin

Abstract This chapter provides structured summaries of all 25 currently published national EQ-5D-5L value sets. The summaries were developed by extracting information from the published manuscripts of each value set and conducting secondary data analyses of the original valuation data generated in each country/region. The summaries include the mathematical formula for the preferred model for each national value set; information on the representativeness of the samples that were used to generate the value set; the mean values observed for each health state valued using composite time trade-off, the distribution of responses in the discrete choice experiment; information on the number of interviewers and whether any interviewer effects were present in the valuation data; key characteristics of the predicted values and relative importance of the EQ-5D-5L dimensions; and information on the uptake of the value set by local decision makers and health technology assessment bodies. This chapter serves as a compendium of EQ-5D-5L value sets, which may inform users of these value sets about the characteristics of all published EQ-5D-5L value sets.

4.1 Introduction

This chapter provides summary-level information on the currently published EQ-5D-5L value sets. The countries/regions are reported alphabetically, by study wave. This means that the oldest studies are reported first, and the newest studies are reported last. Figure 4.1 provides an overview of the 25 studies which are included, by wave and protocol version.

B. Roudijk (✉)
EuroQol Research Foundation, Rotterdam, The Netherlands
e-mail: roudijk@euroqol.org

K. Ludwig
Department of Health Economics and Health Care Management, School of Public Health, Bielefeld University, Bielefeld, Germany

EuroQol Research Foundation, Rotterdam, The Netherlands

N. Devlin
Centre for Health Policy, University of Melbourne, Melbourne, VIC, Australia

© The Author(s) 2022
N. Devlin et al. (eds.), *Value Sets for EQ-5D-5L*,
https://doi.org/10.1007/978-3-030-89289-0_4

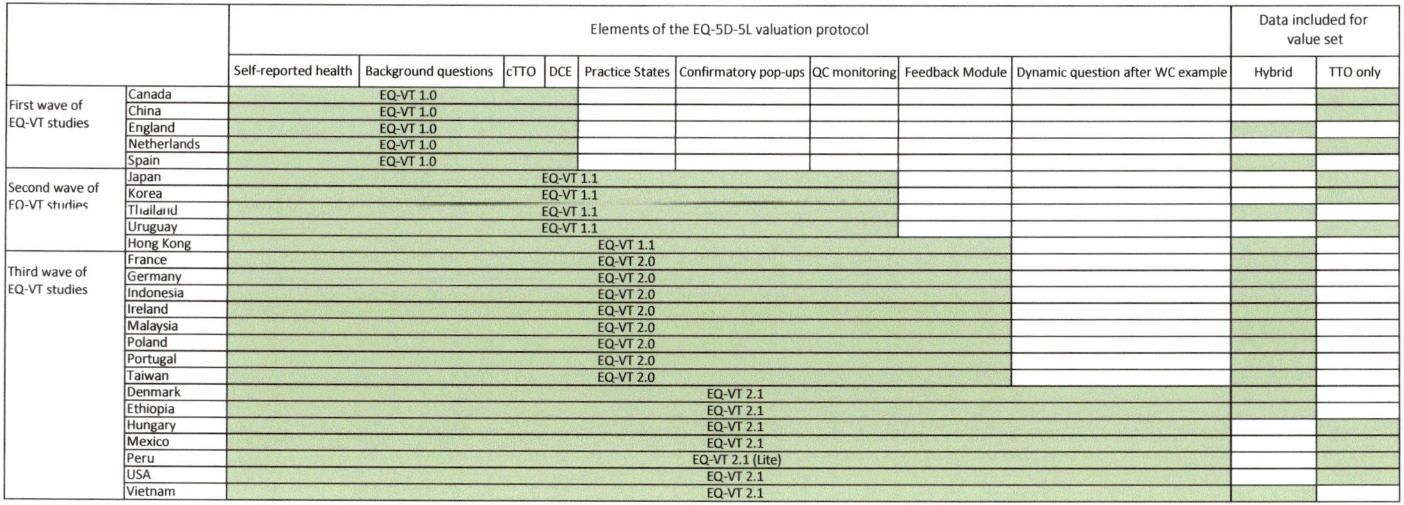

		Elements of the EQ-5D-5L valuation protocol									Data included for value set	
		Self-reported health	Background questions	cTTO	DCE	Practice States	Confirmatory pop-ups	QC monitoring	Feedback Module	Dynamic question after WC example	Hybrid	TTO only
First wave of EQ-VT studies	Canada		EQ-VT 1.0									
	China		EQ-VT 1.0									
	England		EQ-VT 1.0									
	Netherlands		EQ-VT 1.0									
	Spain		EQ-VT 1.0									
Second wave of EQ-VT studies	Japan			EQ-VT 1.1								
	Korea			EQ-VT 1.1								
	Thailand			EQ-VT 1.1								
	Uruguay			EQ-VT 1.1								
	Hong Kong					EQ-VT 1.1						
Third wave of EQ-VT studies	France					EQ-VT 2.0						
	Germany					EQ-VT 2.0						
	Indonesia					EQ-VT 2.0						
	Ireland					EQ-VT 2.0						
	Malaysia					EQ-VT 2.0						
	Poland					EQ-VT 2.0						
	Portugal					EQ-VT 2.0						
	Taiwan					EQ-VT 2.0						
	Denmark						EQ-VT 2.1					
	Ethiopia						EQ-VT 2.1					
	Hungary						EQ-VT 2.1					
	Mexico						EQ-VT 2.1					
	Peru						EQ-VT 2.1 (lite)					
	USA						EQ-VT 2.1					
	Vietnam						EQ-VT 2.1					

Fig. 4.1 Overview of EQ-VT studies by study wave and protocol version

Most of the information reported in this chapter was extracted from the manuscripts in which these value sets were published. However, in some cases, some of the relevant information was not included in the published papers. In these cases, we have undertaken secondary analyses of the data sets, with permissions from the study authors, using the methods reported below.

From each value set, we have extracted the mathematical formula for the preferred model for the value set, presented as $V(x)$ and present the relative weights for each of the different dimension levels (20 parameters). The parameter therefore represents the decrement from level 1 to the respective level. We also present some other key characteristics of the value sets, such as the order of importance of each of the 5 dimensions of the EQ-5D-5L, the value for the worst and best health states, as well as the value for the best suboptimal health state. Lastly, we report key aspects of the study, such as the time frame in which the valuation data was collected, the sample size, sampling frame and sample characteristics.

4.2 Methods

As each study has valued the same 86 health states using cTTO using the study design discussed in Chap. 3,[1] we report the arithmetic means and standard errors for each of these 86 health states in each country/region. The means are calculated for the same sample used in modelling the value set in each case i.e., following any exclusions which may have been made, which we describe. For studies in which the feedback module was used, as discussed in Chap. 2, the arithmetic means are calculated after the exclusion of any flagged responses.

For the DCE data, we report the proportion of respondents choosing EQ-5D-5L state A by the difference in level sum score between the two states included in the pair. Here, the level sum score is merely the sum of the levels of an EQ-5D-5L health state to give a broad indication of the severity of the state. For example, for state 12312, the level sum score would be 1+2+3+1+2=9. For example, the difference in level sum scores within a DCE choice pair with alternative A being 12341 and alternative B being 22335 is then $11 - 15 = -4$. We then report the percentage of responses choosing A when the difference in level sum scores equals -4. This will be a mix of choice pairs, as various choice pairs will have a level sum score difference of -4.

The modelling and other data analysis strategies used by the value set research team in each country/region differ somewhat. Therefore, we report the following for

---

[1] With the exception of Peru, where a different health state design for the cTTO was used, as this study was conducted using an EQ-VT 'Lite' protocol. A health state design including 31 unique health states was used instead of the 86-state design. For Peru, we therefore report the means of 31 health states.

each study: (1) data exclusion criteria and the number of excluded responses/respondents; (2) interviewer effects; and (3) a description of modelling choices. To determine whether there are any interviewer effects, we partition the variance in the valuation data into variance related to interviewers i, respondents j and responses k, and determine the relative share of variance attributed to differences between interviewers. This is done by employing a mixed model in the form of equation 4.1 to each of the valuation datasets:

$$U_{ijk} = \beta_0 + \gamma_i + \mu_{ij} + \varepsilon_{ijk} \qquad (4.1)$$

This model assumes there is a mean value β_0 for all health states, which varies by interviewer (γ_i), respondent (μ_{ij}) and health state valued (ε_{ijk}). Here, β_0 is a fixed effects parameter, while all others are random effects parameters. We then assume that $\gamma_i \sim N\left(0, \sigma_\gamma^2\right)$, $\mu_{ij} \sim N\left(0, \sigma_\mu^2\right)$ and $\varepsilon_{ij} \sim N\left(0, \sigma_\varepsilon^2\right)$.[2]

To determine the share of variance attributed to differences between interviewers, we then calculate the Intra Class Correlation (ICC) coefficient as in Eq. 4.2[3]:

$$ICC = \frac{\sigma_\gamma^2}{\sigma_\gamma^2 + \sigma_\mu^2 + \sigma_\varepsilon^2} \qquad (4.2)$$

The relative importance of the EQ-5D-5L dimensions was determined by taking the sum of the coefficients for one dimension, and dividing this by the sum of the coefficients for all coefficients. This measure can be seen as the size of the share of the total weight assigned to all dimension levels, and takes into account the relative importance for each dimension at all levels.

Finally, depending on the availability of the relevant information, we report the uptake of the value set by local HTA agencies, as reported in the manuscript or drawing on information provided by the principal investigators of the valuation studies to the authors of this book.

For each value set, we include full reference details and any other relevant literature directly related to the value set. Permission to reproduce these value sets and related information have been granted by the journals in which they are published, and access to the data to facilitate secondary analyses reported in this chapter was granted by the principal investigators, on behalf of the study teams in each case.

---

[2] We did not consider correlation between the variance in responses between interviewers, respondents and responses, which is a limitation. However, accounting for correlation between variance in random slopes for interviewers and respondents may be challenging, as not every study may use a number of interviewers that is sufficiently large to be able to compute these correlations reliably.

[3] The ICC partitions variance into shares attributed to interviewers, respondents and responses. This is a way of operationalising interviewer effects, as it measures the share of variance caused by differences between interviewers. Small differences in distributions reflect good agreement between interviewers, and therefore small interviewer effects. However, they do not necessarily reflect good data quality only, as other factors, such as clustering of values and inconsistent responses are not captured by this measure.

4.3   Country-by-Country Overview of Value Sets

4.3.1   Wave 1

4.3.1.1 Country/Region: Canada (Table 4.1)

Table 4.1 Overview of EQ-5D-5L value set for Canada[a]

Canadian EQ-5D-5L value set		Example: the value for health state 21232	
Intercept	1.1351	Intercept	=1.1351
Mobility	0.0389	Minus MO (level 2)	−0.0389[a]2
Mobility level 4/5	0.051	Minus if MO is level 4 or 5	−0.000
Self-care	0.0458	Minus SC level 1	−0.0458
Self-care level 4/5	0.0584	Minus if SC is level 4 or 5	−0.000
Usual activities	0.0195	Minus UA (level 2)	−0.0195[a]2
Usual activities level 4/5	0.1103	Minus if UA is level 4 or 5	−0.000
Pain/discomfort	0.0444	Minus PD (level 3)	−0.0444[a]3
Pain/discomfort level 4/5	0.1409	Minus if PD is level 4 or 5	−0.000
Anxiety/depression	0.0376	Minus AD (level 2)	−0.0376[a]2
Anxiety/depression level 4/5	0.1277	Minus if AD is level 4 or 5	−0.000
Num45sq	0.0085	Plus the number of level 4 and 5 problems beyond the first, squared	+0.0085[a]0
		State 21232	=0.764

AD anxiety/depression, *MO* mobility, *PD* pain/discomfort, *SC* self-care, *UA* usual activities
[a]We report the value set up to four decimals instead of the 3 decimal structure seen in other value set summaries in this chapter, due to the different modelling strategy that was applied to the Canadian data

The mathematical representation of the model for health state X is[4]:

$$V(x) = 1.1351 - 0.0389\,MO * Level - 0.0458\,SC * Level - 0.0195\,UA$$
$$* Level - 0.0444\,PD * Level - 0.0376\,AD * Level$$
$$- 0.051\,MO45 - 0.0584\,SC45 - 0.1103\,UA45$$
$$- 0.1409\,PD45 - 0.1277\,AD45 + 0.0085\,Num45sq$$

(i) **Date/wave of study**

Data were collected in the first wave of EQ-5D-5L valuation studies using the EQ-5D-5L valuation protocol 1.0. Additionally, traditional TTO was used as elicitation technique to supplement the EQ-VT. Interviews were conducted in 2012.

(ii) **Sample size; sample frame**

1209 interviews with the general population were conducted in three English speaking metropolitan areas: Vancouver, Hamilton and Edmonton, and French speaking respondents were recruited in Montreal. Quota sampling with respect

---

[4]MO45, SC45, UA45, PD45 and AD45 are dummy variables that equal 1 when level 4 or 5 problems are reported in that dimension, and 0 otherwise. For example, SC45 will equal 1 in state 14111, but 0 in state 12111. Num45sq is a variable that represents the square of the number of level 4 or 5 problems in a health state, beyond the first.

to age, gender, and education was applied. Of the 1073 respondents included in the final value set, 55.5% were female and 44.5% were male. The age distribution of the respondents was:

18–24 years	12.5%
25–29 years	8.0%
30–39 years	14.6%
40–49 years	14.8%
50–64 years	31.6%
65–74 years	13.1%
75+ years	5.4%

(iii) **Representativeness of achieved sample**

The study sample was representative for the Canadian population in terms of age (over 18 years), gender, marital status, born in Canada and language spoken at home. The sample was more educated, but had lower incomes compared to the general population in Canada (Table 4.2).

Table 4.2 Representativeness of the sample in the Canadian valuation study

		Study sample (N=1073)	Canadian general population[a]
Sampling characteristics			
Age, n (%)	18–39	392 (36.5%)	35.5%
	40–59	382 (35.6%)	38.0%
	60–89	299 (27.9%)	25.4%
Gender, n (%)	Female	595 (55.5%)	51.5%
	Male	478 (44.5%)	48.5%
Education, n (%)	High school or lower	374 (34.9%)	45.7%
	College diploma	337 (31.4%)	29.1%
	University or higher	358 (33.4%)	25.3%
Marital status, n (%)	Married/common law partner	574 (53.5%)	53.4%
	Single	319 (29.7%)	28.0%
	Separated	28 (2.6%)	3.0%
	Divorced	108 (10.1%)	8.5%
	Widowed	40 (3.7%)	6.0%
Language spoken at home, n (%)	English	729 (67.9%)	64.8%
	Other	344 (32.1%)	35.2%
Annual household income, n (%)	<$15,000	107 (10.0%)	3.5%
	$15,000–$45,000	278 (25.9%)	19.7%
	$45,000–$75,000	237 (22.1%)	23.5%
	>$75,000	334 (31.1%)	53.3%
Born in Canada, n (%)	Yes	806 (75.1%)	75.1%
	No	267 (24.9%)	24.9%

Reproduced from Xie et al. (2016)
[a]Statistics Canada 2006 and 2011

(iv) **Mean observed cTTO values of EQ-5D-5L states** (Table 4.3)

Table 4.3 Mean observed cTTO[a] values by health state

State	Mean	SE	State	Mean	SE	State	Mean	SE
11112	0.915	0.012	21345	0.380	0.036	43315	0.385	0.050
11121	0.933	0.011	21444	0.224	0.051	43514	0.395	0.035
11122	0.908	0.015	22434	0.311	0.049	43542	0.235	0.045
11211	0.944	0.008	23152	0.443	0.041	43555	0.092	0.050
11212	0.928	0.011	23242	0.500	0.039	44125	0.278	0.049
11221	0.925	0.014	23514	0.375	0.053	44345	0.124	0.052
11235	0.549	0.043	24342	0.445	0.037	44553	0.211	0.037
11414	0.541	0.047	24443	0.225	0.055	45133	0.389	0.050
11421	0.661	0.039	24445	0.099	0.048	45144	0.158	0.042
11425	0.340	0.053	24553	0.155	0.051	45233	0.365	0.048
12111	0.912	0.012	25122	0.571	0.045	45413	0.298	0.043
12112	0.887	0.019	25222	0.539	0.050	51152	0.248	0.050
12121	0.835	0.029	25331	0.510	0.041	51451	0.287	0.043
12244	0.350	0.043	31514	0.443	0.050	52215	0.368	0.056
12334	0.515	0.044	31524	0.364	0.051	52335	0.284	0.047
12344	0.307	0.044	31525	0.383	0.046	52431	0.435	0.052
12513	0.621	0.038	32314	0.529	0.045	52455	0.116	0.049
12514	0.485	0.044	32443	0.323	0.049	53221	0.584	0.042
12543	0.373	0.049	33253	0.385	0.045	53243	0.269	0.056
13122	0.734	0.034	34155	0.143	0.053	53244	0.187	0.053
13224	0.460	0.050	34232	0.492	0.043	53412	0.502	0.041
13313	0.720	0.035	34244	0.252	0.044	54153	0.228	0.053
14113	0.617	0.042	34515	0.299	0.043	54231	0.470	0.044
14554	0.191	0.045	35143	0.245	0.056	54342	0.259	0.043
15151	0.343	0.052	35245	0.197	0.043	55225	0.206	0.050
21111	0.931	0.010	35311	0.560	0.043	55233	0.376	0.046
21112	0.815	0.027	35332	0.444	0.042	55424	0.219	0.041
21315	0.456	0.050	42115	0.399	0.050	55555	−0.050	0.014
21334	0.529	0.041	42321	0.601	0.039			

SE standard error

[a]Conventional TTO data was collected alongside the cTTO data and was included in the modelling as well. Here, we report only the cTTO data for comparability with the other value sets reported in the book

(v)   **Proportions choosing A in the DCE based on relative severities of A and B** (Fig. 4.2)

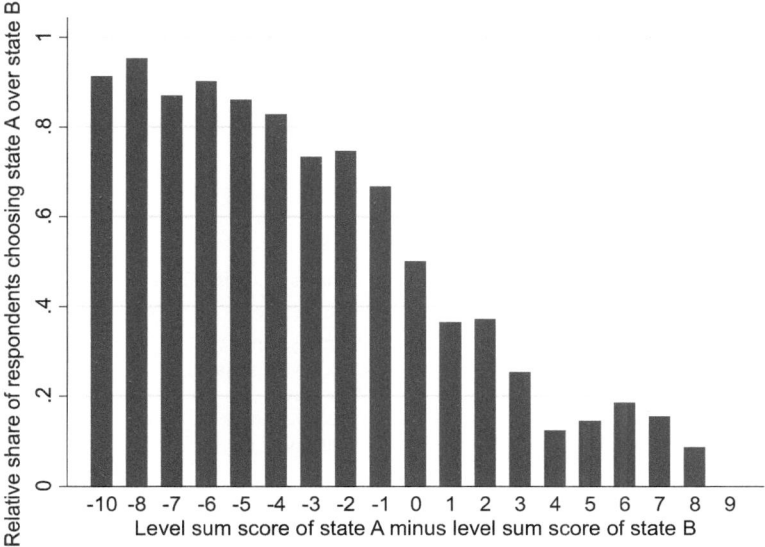

Fig. 4.2 Proportions choosing A based on relative severities of A and B. (DCE data were collected during the study, but not used in the modelling stage)

(vi)   **Exclusion criteria**
A share of respondents with inconsistent responses were excluded. Inconsistencies were defined as strict dominance (e.g., assigning a higher value to state 11411 compared to state 11311). For each respondent, the number of dominated states by the very mild health states (with just one deviation from full health, e.g., 11121) was counted. Respondents were excluded if they assigned (a) the same or a lower value to at least half of the states that were dominated or (b) the same or a lower value for the very mild health state compared with the pits state (55555). 136 respondents met these exclusion criteria.

(vii) **Number of interviewers; Interviewer effects**
In total, 1209 interviews were conducted by 8 interviewers. The variance of the responses included in the final value set can be partitioned into variance related to differences between interviewers (2.6%), respondents (35.8%) and responses (61.6%).

(viii) **Description of modelling choices**
The Canadian EQ-5D-5L value set was based on a combination of cTTO and conventional TTO data. The authors chose a final model that included a linear parameter for each dimension, with each dimension variables having levels 1,

2, 3, 4 and 5. Furthermore, the authors added dummy variables for each of the 5 dimensions, that equal 1 if that dimension reports level 4 or 5 problems, and 0 otherwise. Lastly, a term was added that represents the square of the number of dimensions reporting level 4 or 5 problems, beyond the first. The estimated model used a Tobit link function, assuming censoring at 0 for negative values and values equal to 0 in the cTTO, and assumed a random intercept for each respondent.

(ix)   **Value Set** (Table 4.4 and Fig. 4.3)

Table 4.4 Key characteristics of the Canadian value set

Characteristics	Canadian EQ-5D-5L value set
% states with negative values	1.86% (58 out of 3125)
Rank order of dimensions (from most to least relative importance)	Pain/discomfort Anxiety/depression Self-care Usual activities Mobility
Coefficient with highest weight	0.3629 (level 5 of pain/discomfort)
Range of values	Maximum value: 0.949 Minimum value: −0.148
Max value < 1:	0.949 (value of health state 11111)
Linearity/non-linearity of value decrements by level	Kink at level 3 for all dimensions (see Fig. 4.3). Reverse kink at level 4 for all dimensions.

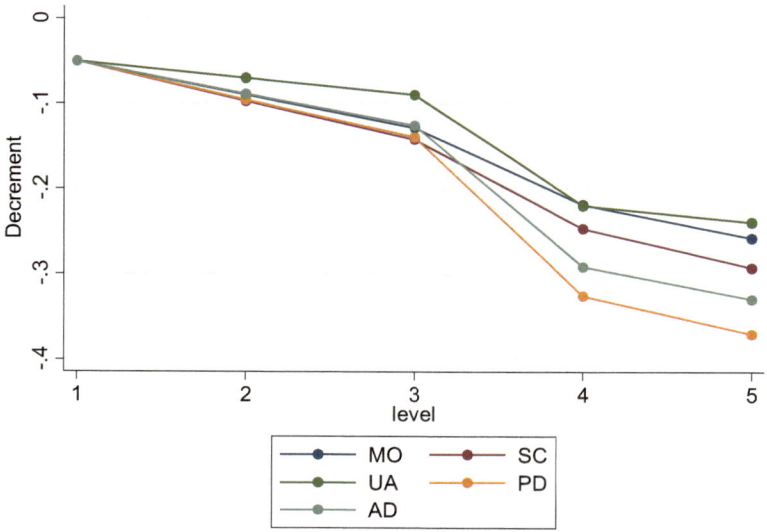

Fig. 4.3 Value decrements across dimensions (*AD* anxiety/depression, *MO* mobility, *PD* pain/ discomfort, *SC* self-care, *UA* usual activities)

(x)   **Uptake by local HTA/health care decision makers**

Canadian Agency for Drugs and Technologies in Health (CADTH) is the national HTA body that reviews and makes reimbursement recommendations to the public insurance programs across Canada. Cost-utility analysis (CUA) is a recommended type of economic evaluation for reimbursement applications. Validated generic health state classification systems with Canadian-specific value sets are recommended for the estimation of QALYs. Although there is no preference for any specific instrument, the EQ-5D-5L has become one of the commonly used instruments in clinical trials and economic evaluations.

(xi) **Reference(s) of value set**

Xie F, Pullenayegum E, Gaebel K, Bansback N, Bryan S, Ohinmaa A, Poissant L, Johnson JA (2016) A time trade-off-derived value set of the EQ-5D-5L for Canada. Med Care 54(1):98–105

Further Literature

Statistics Canada (2006) 2006 Census of Canada. https://www.statcan.gc.ca/. Accessed 14 July 2021

Statistics Canada (2011) https://www12.statcan.gc.ca/census-recensement/2011/dp-pd/tbt-tt/Index-eng.cfm. Accessed 28 July 2021

4.3.1.2 Country/Region: China (Table 4.5)

Table 4.5 Overview of EQ-5D-5L value set for China

Chinese EQ-5D-5L value set		Example: the value for health state 21232	
Full health (11111)	1	Full health	=1
Mobility = 2	0.066	Minus MO level 2	−0.066
Mobility = 3	0.158		
Mobility = 4	0.287		
Mobility = 5	0.345		
Self-care = 2	0.048	Minus SC level 1	−0.000
Self-care = 3	0.116		
Self-care = 4	0.210		
Self-care = 5	0.253		
Usual activities = 2	0.045	Minus UA level 2	−0.045
Usual activities = 3	0.107		
Usual activities = 4	0.194		
Usual activities = 5	0.233		
Pain/discomfort = 2	0.058		
Pain/discomfort = 3	0.138	Minus PD level 3	−0.138
Pain/discomfort = 4	0.252		
Pain/discomfort = 5	0.302		
Anxiety/depression = 2	0.049	Minus AD level 2	−0.049
Anxiety/depression = 3	0.118		
Anxiety/depression = 4	0.215		
Anxiety/depression = 5	0.258		
		State 21232	=0.702

AD anxiety/depression, *MO* mobility, *PD* pain/discomfort, *SC* self-care, *UA* usual activities

The mathematical representation of the model for health state X is:

$$V(X) = 1 - 0.066\,MO_2 - 0.158\,MO_3 - 0.287\,MO_4 - 0.345\,MO_5 - 0.048\,SC_2$$
$$- 0.116\,SC_3 - 0.210\,SC_4 - 0.253\,SC_5 - 0.045\,UA_2 - 0.107\,UA_3$$
$$- 0.194\,UA_4 - 0.233\,UA_5 - 0.058\,PD_2 - 0.138\,PD_3 - 0.252\,PD_4$$
$$- 0.302\,PD_5 - 0.049\,AD_2 - 0.118\,AD_3 - 0.215\,AD_4 - 0.258\,AD_5$$

(i)   **Date/wave of study**
       Data were collected in the first wave of EQ-5D-5L valuation studies using the
       EQ-5D-5L valuation protocol 1.0. Interviews were conducted in 2012.

(ii)   **Sample size; sample frame**
       1332 interviews with the general population were conducted in five urban areas
       in different parts of China: Beijing, Chengdu, Guiyang, Nanjing and Shenyang.
       Within these cities, respondents were sampled to represent these cities with

respect to age, gender and educational level using a nonprobability sampling strategy. Of the 1271 respondents included in the final value set, 49.9% were female and 50.1% were male. The age distribution of the respondents was:

18–24 years	16.5%
25–29 years	8.1%
30–39 years	19.2%
40–49 years	21.4%
50–64 years	25.9%
65–74 years	6.2%
75+ years	2.7%

(iii)   **Representativeness of achieved sample** (Table 4.6)

Table 4.6   Representativeness of the sample in the Chinese valuation study

		Study sample (N=1271)	Chinese adult general population (2011)[a]
Sampling characteristics			
Age, n (%)	18–29	313(24.6%)	25.3%
	30–39	244(19.2%)	19.7%
	40–49	272(21.4%)	22.9%
	50–59	220(17.3%)	14.7%
	≥ 60	222(17.5%)	17.3%
Gender, n (%)	Female	634 (49.9%)	49.4%
	Male	637 (50.1%)	50.6%
Education, n (%)	Primary or lower	138 (10.9%)	
	Junior high school	396 (31.2%)	
	Senior high school	446 (35.1%)	
	College or higher	291 (22.9%)	
Residence of origin	City	749 (58.9%)	
	Country	82 (6.5%)	
	Township or village	440 (34.6%)	
Employment status	Full time employee	378 (29.7%)	
	Temporary worker	301 (23.7%)	
	Individual freelancer	148 (11.6%)	
	Retired	240 (18.9%)	
	Student	115 (9.1%)	
	Unemployed	48 (3.8%)	
	Other	41 (3.2%)	

Reproduced from Luo et al. (2017)
[a]Chinese Statistical Yearbook 2011

(iv)   **Mean observed cTTO values of EQ-5D-5L states** (Table 4.7)

Table 4.7 Mean observed cTTO values by health state

State	Mean	SE	State	Mean	SE	State	Mean	SE
11112	0.871	0.014	21345	0.205	0.049	43315	0.173	0.042
11121	0.852	0.014	21444	0.153	0.049	43514	0.091	0.051
11122	0.821	0.016	22434	0.345	0.042	43542	0.047	0.049
11211	0.842	0.015	23152	0.387	0.045	43555	−0.144	0.051
11212	0.800	0.024	23242	0.424	0.045	44125	0.164	0.050
11221	0.837	0.014	23514	0.330	0.043	44345	−0.082	0.048
11235	0.502	0.044	24342	0.320	0.047	44553	−0.095	0.047
11414	0.488	0.039	24443	0.132	0.044	45133	0.201	0.045
11421	0.640	0.031	24445	−0.018	0.051	45144	0.089	0.054
11425	0.458	0.040	24553	0.078	0.054	45233	0.179	0.042
12111	0.871	0.010	25122	0.575	0.035	45413	0.157	0.051
12112	0.817	0.020	25222	0.426	0.043	51152	0.210	0.051
12121	0.765	0.025	25331	0.340	0.045	51451	0.191	0.051
12244	0.408	0.040	31514	0.305	0.044	52215	0.267	0.045
12334	0.487	0.043	31524	0.313	0.041	52335	0.051	0.052
12344	0.296	0.045	31525	0.338	0.043	52431	0.199	0.044
12513	0.433	0.043	32314	0.421	0.044	52455	−0.049	0.049
12514	0.425	0.049	32443	0.229	0.045	53221	0.351	0.045
12543	0.283	0.045	33253	0.274	0.051	53243	−0.008	0.053
13122	0.675	0.031	34155	0.068	0.048	53244	−0.073	0.055
13224	0.457	0.041	34232	0.323	0.046	53412	0.257	0.050
13313	0.608	0.032	34244	0.059	0.048	54153	0.067	0.043
14113	0.521	0.035	34515	0.248	0.051	54231	0.273	0.053
14554	0.027	0.049	35143	0.110	0.053	54342	0.051	0.045
15151	0.308	0.043	35245	0.112	0.054	55225	0.008	0.051
21111	0.852	0.013	35311	0.377	0.045	55233	0.088	0.047
21112	0.758	0.026	35332	0.319	0.047	55424	−0.102	0.050
21315	0.483	0.035	42115	0.361	0.046	55555	−0.341	0.015
21334	0.460	0.042	42321	0.425	0.044			

SE standard error

(v)   **Proportions choosing A in the DCE based on relative severities of A and B** (Fig. 4.4)

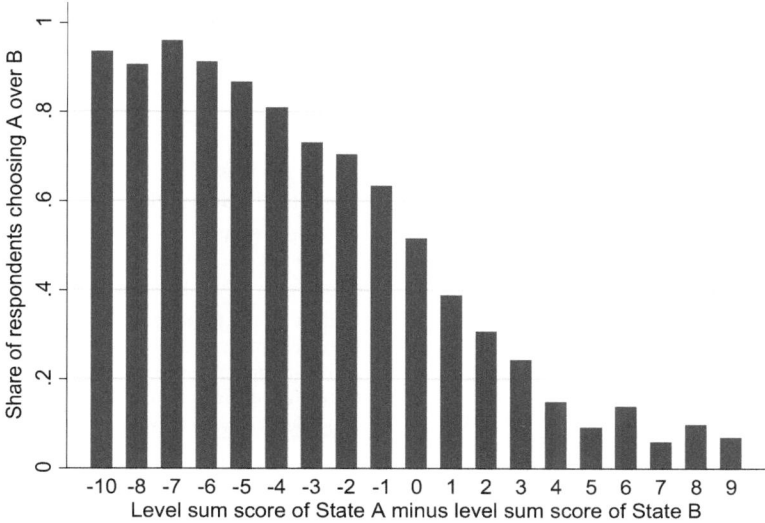

Fig. 4.4 Proportions choosing A based on relative severities of A and B

(vi) **Exclusion criteria**
Respondents that were younger than 18 years old were excluded (n=25). Another 36 respondents were excluded as they did not finish the interview.

(vii) **Number of interviewers; Interviewer effects**
In total, 1332 interviews were conducted by 20 interviewers. The variance of the responses included in the final value set can be partitioned into variance related to differences between interviewers (2.4%), respondents (28.8%) and responses (68.8%).

(viii) **Description of modelling choices**
The Chinese EQ-5D-5L value set was based on cTTO data only. The selected model was an 8-parameter multiplicative model with a random intercept, in which 5 coefficients are estimated for the EQ-5D-5L's 5 dimensions, and 3 coefficients are estimated for the 3 intermediate levels of the EQ-5D-5L (2,3 and 4), representing level weights. For levels 1 and 5, these are assumed to be 0 and 1, respectively. The predicted coefficients were rescaled by (1-intercept). The eight-parameter model can be converted to 20 parameters, as presented in Table 4.8 for consistency purposes in this chapter.

(ix)   **Value Set** (Table 4.8 and Fig. 4.5)

Table 4.8 Key characteristics of the Chinese value set

Characteristics	Chinese EQ-5D-5L value set
% states with negative values	10.11% (316 out of 3125)
Rank order of dimensions (from most to least relative importance)	Mobility Pain/discomfort Anxiety/depression Self-care Usual Activities
Coefficient with highest weight	0.345 (level 5 of mobility)
Range of values	Maximum value: 1 Minimum value: −0.391
Max value < 1:	0.955 (value of health state 11211)
Linearity/non-linearity of value decrements by level	Kink at level 3 for all dimensions (see Fig. 4.5). Reverse kink at level 4 for all dimensions. Due to the multiplicative model structure, there are no relative differences in distance between the dimensions over the levels.

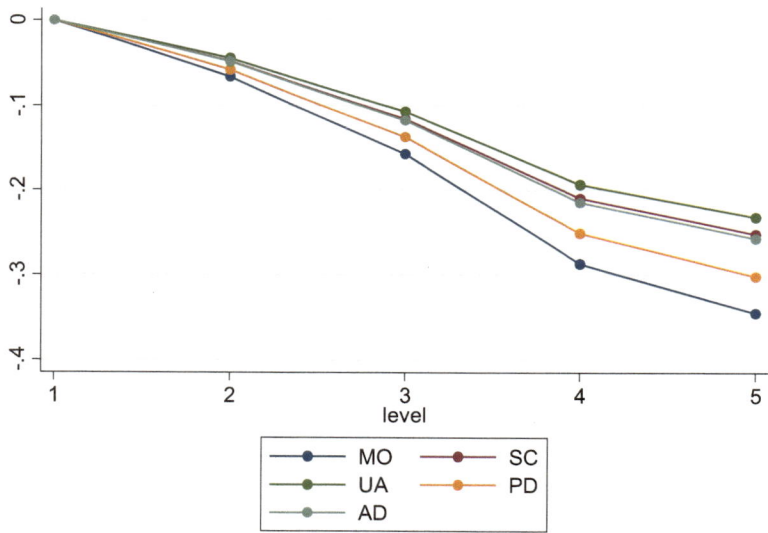

Fig. 4.5 Value decrements across dimensions (*AD* anxiety/depression, *MO* mobility, *PD* pain/discomfort, *SC* self-care, *UA* usual activities)

(x) **Uptake by local HTA/health care decision makers**

There is currently no HTA agency in China. There are only academic methodology Pharmacoeconomic/Health Technology Assessment guidelines, (China Guidelines for Pharmacoeconomic Evaluations Writing Group, 2019) but there are no recommendations about which specific health related quality of life instruments are preferred for use.

(xi) **Reference(s) of value set**

Luo N, Liu G, Li M, Guan H, Jin X, Rand-Hendriksen K (2017) Estimating an EQ-5D-5L value set for China. Value Health 20(4):662–669

Further Literature

Guidelines for Evaluation of Chinese Pharmacoeconomics (2019) China Guidelines for Pharmacoeconomic Evaluations Writing Group http://proa28198.pic40.websiteonline.cn/upload/0ikw.pdf. Accessed 14 July 2021

China Statistical Yearbook (2011) Population statistics. http://www.stats.gov.cn/tjsj/ndsj/2012/indexeh.htm. Accessed 15 July 21

4.3.1.3   Country/Region: England (Table 4.9)

Table 4.9 Overview of EQ-5D-5L value set for England

England EQ-5D-5L value set		Example: the value for health state 21232	
Full health (11111)	1	Full health	=1
Mobility = 2	0.058	Minus MO level 2	−0.058
Mobility = 3	0.076		
Mobility = 4	0.207		
Mobility = 5	0.274		
Self-care = 2	0.050	Minus SC level 1	−0.000
Self-care = 3	0.080		
Self-care = 4	0.164		
Self-care = 5	0.203		
Usual activities = 2	0.050	Minus UA level 2	−0.050
Usual activities = 3	0.063		
Usual activities = 4	0.162		
Usual activities = 5	0.184		
Pain/discomfort = 2	0.063		
Pain/discomfort = 3	0.084	Minus PD level 3	−0.084
Pain/discomfort = 4	0.276		
Pain/discomfort = 5	0.335		
Anxiety/depression = 2	0.078	Minus AD level 2	−0.078
Anxiety/depression = 3	0.104		
Anxiety/depression = 4	0.285		
Anxiety/depression = 5	0.289		
		State 21232	=0.730

AD anxiety/depression, *MO* mobility, *PD* pain/discomfort, *SC* self-care, *UA* usual activities

The mathematical representation of the model for health state X is:

$$V(X) = 1 - 0.058\,MO_2 - 0.076\,MO_3 - 0.207\,MO_4 - 0.274\,MO_5 - 0.050\,SC_2$$
$$- 0.080\,SC_3 - 0.164\,SC_4 - 0.203\,SC_5 - 0.050\,UA_2 - 0.063\,UA_3 - 0.162\,UA_4$$
$$- 0.184\,UA_5 - 0.063\,PD_2 - 0.084\,PD_3 - 0.276\,PD_4 - 0.335\,PD_5 - 0.078\,AD_2$$
$$- 0.104\,AD_3 - 0.285\,AD_4 - 0.289\,AD_5$$

(i)   **Date/wave of study**
Data were collected in the first wave of EQ-5D-5L valuation studies using the EQ-5D-5L valuation protocol 1.0. Interviews were conducted between November 2012 and May 2013.

(ii)   **Sample size; sample frame**
       1004 interviews were conducted (996 respondents completing the valuation
       tasks in full) with the general population. A sample of 2020 addresses from 66
       primary sampling units (based on postcode sectors) across England was ran-
       domly selected, using the Post Office small user Postcode Address File as the
       sampling frame. The sample was intended to be representative of adults aged
       18 years and over living in private residential accommodation in England.
       Of the 912 respondents included in the analysis, 59.3% were female and
       40.7% were male. The age distribution of the 912 respondents was:

18–24 years	5.37%
25–29 years	6.14%
30–39 years	18.75%
40–49 years	20.61%
50–64 years	23.14%
65–74 years	12.94%
75+ years	13.05%

(iii) **Representativeness of achieved sample**
       The study sample was broadly representative for the English population in
       terms of age (over 18 years), sex and employment status. However, compared
       to the general population, the sample included a larger proportion of those
       aged over 75 and retired and a smaller proportion of younger individuals and
       males (Office for National Statistics 2011) (Table 4.10).

Table 4.10 Representativeness of the sample in the England valuation study

		Study sample (N= 912)	English general population[a]
Sampling characteristics			
Age, n (%)	18–29	105 (11.5%)	20.7%
	30–44	270 (29.6%)	26.3%
	45–59	227 (24.9%)	24.7%
	60–74	191 (20.9%)	18.5%
	≥ 75	119 (13.0%)	9.9%
Gender, n (%)	Female	540 (59.2%)	50.8%
	Male	372 (40.8%)	49.2%
Employment status, n (%)	Employed or self-employed	463 (50.8%)	59.4%
	Retired	256 (28.1%)	13.1%
	Student	19 (2.1%)	8.8%
	Looking after home/ family	73 (8.0%)	4.2%
	Long-term sick/ disabled	42 (4.6%)	3.9%
	Other	47 (5.2%	10.6%

Reproduced from Devlin et al. (2018)
[a]Office for National Statistics 2011

(iv)   **Mean observed cTTO values by EQ-5D-5L state** (Table 4.11)

Table 4.11 Mean observed cTTO values by health state

State	Mean	SE	State	Mean	SE	State	Mean	SE
11112	0.853	0.017	21345	0.429	0.051	43315	0.415	0.049
11121	0.885	0.014	21444	0.153	0.050	43514	0.361	0.058
11122	0.788	0.029	22434	0.527	0.049	43542	0.227	0.051
11211	0.893	0.013	23152	0.395	0.047	43555	0.058	0.061
11212	0.820	0.028	23242	0.442	0.048	44125	0.318	0.060
11221	0.844	0.022	23514	0.399	0.052	44345	0.214	0.058
11235	0.526	0.044	24342	0.361	0.051	44553	0.094	0.058
11414	0.407	0.051	24443	0.332	0.052	45133	0.361	0.057
11421	0.648	0.037	24445	0.157	0.060	45144	0.172	0.046
11425	0.530	0.050	24553	0.330	0.052	45233	0.329	0.050
12111	0.867	0.015	25122	0.525	0.046	45413	0.345	0.059
12112	0.812	0.028	25222	0.595	0.037	51152	0.346	0.057
12121	0.811	0.033	25331	0.530	0.050	51451	0.257	0.046
12244	0.320	0.049	31514	0.386	0.051	52215	0.349	0.054
12334	0.443	0.049	31524	0.447	0.051	52335	0.329	0.053
12344	0.253	0.059	31525	0.429	0.044	52431	0.542	0.045
12513	0.612	0.049	32314	0.507	0.046	52455	0.074	0.055
12514	0.442	0.050	32443	0.290	0.055	53221	0.581	0.048
12543	0.321	0.058	33253	0.404	0.046	53243	0.232	0.056
13122	0.810	0.022	34155	0.243	0.058	53244	0.125	0.052
13224	0.492	0.050	34232	0.555	0.046	53412	0.438	0.046
13313	0.689	0.032	34244	0.255	0.052	54153	0.270	0.053
14113	0.687	0.037	34515	0.318	0.057	54231	0.404	0.049
14554	0.147	0.060	35143	0.265	0.053	54342	0.175	0.064
15151	0.417	0.050	35245	0.176	0.050	55225	0.170	0.058
21111	0.890	0.012	35311	0.511	0.052	55233	0.278	0.056
21112	0.828	0.025	35332	0.594	0.041	55424	0.249	0.057
21315	0.539	0.050	42115	0.414	0.050	55555	−0.080	0.017
21334	0.505	0.043	42321	0.544	0.046			

SE standard error

(v) **Proportions choosing A in the DCE based on relative severities of A and B** (Fig. 4.6)

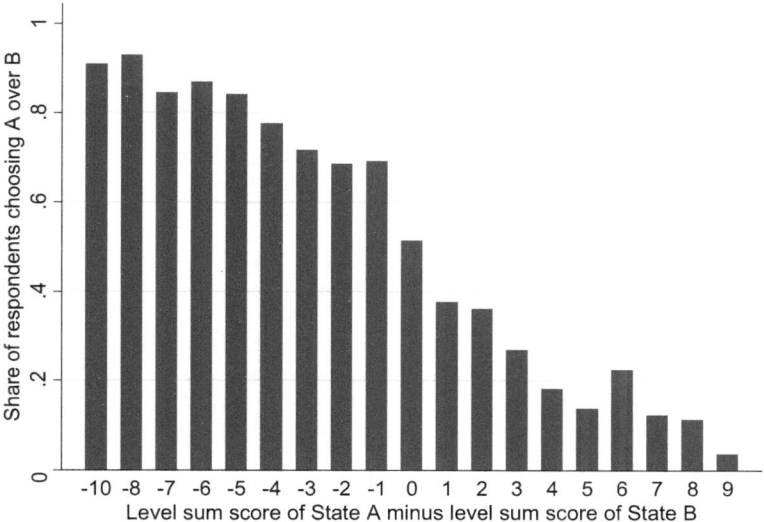

Fig. 4.6 Proportions choosing A based on relative severities of A and B

(vi) **Exclusion criteria**
Twenty-three participants (2.3%) gave all 10 health states the same value, and 61 participants (6.1%) valued 55555 no lower than the value they gave to the mildest health state. Excluding these participants gave a core modelling dataset of 912 participants (9120 cTTO observations). No DCE data were excluded.

(vii) **Number of interviewers; Interviewer effects**
In total, 1004 interviews were conducted by 48 interviewers. Primary data collection was carried out in England by the market research company Ipsos MORI. The valuation data were collected via face-to-face interviews in respondents' homes.
    The variance of the responses (following exclusions) can be partitioned into variance related to differences between interviewers (5.39%), respondents (32.46%), and responses (62.15%).

(viii) **Description of modelling choices**
The England EQ-5D-5L value set was based on 20-parameter hybrid model, combining both cTTO and DCE data. cTTO data were treated as being censored at -1 and at 1 (to account for asymmetry in the error distributions) and, for specific responses, at 0 (e.g., for respondents who gave a value of 0 for more than one health state, including 55555). Heterogeneity was addressed via three latent classes, accounting for different groups of respondents differing in their use of

the scale. The latent class coefficients act to apply an adjustment across all dimensions/level coefficients; the value set reported in Table 4.12 above simplifies the presentation of the value set by reporting the coefficients for dimensions/levels after the application of the latent class coefficients.

(ix)   **Value Set** (Table 4.12 and Fig. 4.7)

Table 4.12 Key characteristics of the English value set

Characteristics	English EQ-5D-5L value set
% states with negative values	5.1% (159 out of 3125)
Rank order of dimensions (from most to least relative importance)	Pain/discomfort Anxiety/depression Mobility Self-care Usual activities
Coefficient with highest weight	0.335 (level 5 of pain/discomfort)
Range of values	Maximum value: 1 Minimum value: −0.285
Max value < 1:	0.950 (value of health state 11211 & 12111)
Linearity/non-linearity of value decrements by level	Kink at level 3 for all dimensions (see Fig. 4.7). The largest change in value occurs between levels 3 and 4 for all dimensions. Between levels 4 and 5 there is only a very small change in value for anxiety/depression, in contrast to the other dimensions. Pain/discomfort has the largest value decrement at level 5.

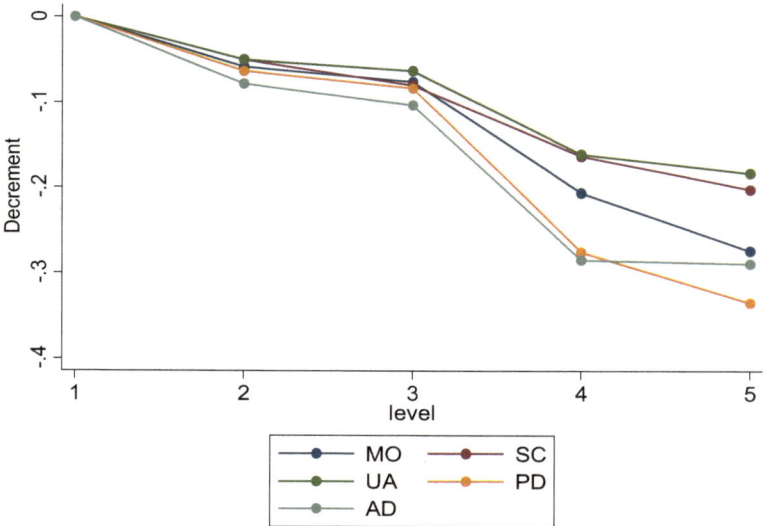

Fig. 4.7 Value decrements across dimensions (*AD* anxiety/depression, *MO* mobility, *PD* pain/discomfort, *SC* self-care, *UA* usual activities)

(x)   **Uptake by local HTA/health care decision makers**
The value set was subject to a 'quality assurance' commissioned by the Department of Health for England from the Economic Evaluation Policy Research Unit (EEPRU). EEPRU's critique is summarised in Hernandez-Alava et al. (2020) and a response from the authors is provided in van Hout et al. (2020). In response to concerns about data quality raised by EEPRU, NICE (2019) issued a position statement indicating it did not recommend use of the value set for England, recommending instead that EQ-5D-5L data be mapped to the EQ-5D-3L using the crosswalk published by van Hout et al. (2012) and the Dolan (1997) UK value set for the EQ-5D-3L be used. A new value set – for the UK, rather than for England – has been commissioned and NICE will review its policy once that study is complete (expected in 2022).

(xi) **Reference(s) for this value set**
Feng Y, Devlin N, Shah K, Mulhern B, van Hout B (2018) New methods for modelling EQ-5D-5L value sets: an application to English data. Health Econ 27(1):23–38
Devlin N, Shah K, Mulhern B, Feng Y, van Hout B (2018) Valuing health related quality of life: an EQ-5D-5L value set for England. Health Econ 27(1): 7–22.

Further Literature

Dolan P (1997) Modeling valuations for EuroQol health states. Med Care 35(11):1095–1108
Hernandez-Alava M, Pudney S, Wailoo A (2020) The EQ-5D-5L value set for England: findings of a quality assurance program. Value Health 23(5):642–648
National Institute for Health and Care Excellence (2019) Position statement on the use of the EQ-5D-5L valuation set for England. www.nice.org.uk/about/what-we-do/our-programmes/nice-guidance/technology-appraisal-guidance/eq-5d-5l. Accessed 14 June 2021
Office for National Statistics (2011) Census: Digitised boundary data (England and Wales) [computer file]. UK Data Service Census Support. http://edina.ac.uk/ukborders. Accessed 15 June 2021
van Hout B, Janssen M, Feng Y, Kohlmann T, Busschbach J, Golicki D, Lloyd A, Scalone L, Kind P, Pickard AS (2012) Interim Scoring for the EQ-5D-5L: Mapping the EQ-5D-5L to EQ-5D-3L Value Sets. Value Health 15(5):708–715.
van Hout B, Mulhern B, Feng Y, Shah K, Devlin N (2020) The EQ-5D-5L Value Set for England: Response to the "Quality Assurance". Value Health 23(5):649–655

4.3.1.4   Country/Region: Netherlands (Table 4.13)

Table 4.13 Overview of EQ-5D-5L value set for Netherlands

Dutch EQ-5D-5L value set		Example: the value for health state 21232	
Full health (11111)			
At least one 2, 3, 4 or 5	1	Full health	=1
(constant)	0.047	Minus constant	−0.047
Mobility = 2	0.035	Minus MO level 2	−0.035
Mobility = 3	0.057		
Mobility = 4	0.166		
Mobility = 5	0.203		
Self-care = 2	0.038	Minus SC level 1	−0.000
Self-care = 3	0.061		
Self-care = 4	0.168		
Self-care = 5	0.168		
Usual activities = 2	0.039	Minus UA level 2	−0.039
Usual activities = 3	0.087		
Usual activities = 4	0.192		
Usual activities = 5	0.192		
Pain/discomfort = 2	0.066		
Pain/discomfort = 3	0.092	Minus PD level 3	−0.092
Pain/discomfort = 4	0.360		
Pain/discomfort = 5	0.415		
Anxiety/depression = 2	0.070	Minus AD level 2	−0.070
Anxiety/depression = 3	0.145		
Anxiety/depression = 4	0.356		
Anxiety/depression = 5	0.421		
		State 21232	=0.717

AD anxiety/depression, *MO* mobility, *PD* pain/discomfort, *SC* self-care, *UA* usual activities

The mathematical representation of the model for health state X is:

$$V(X) = 1 - 0.047 - 0.035\,MO_2 - 0.057\,MO_3 - 0.166\,MO_4 - 0.203\,MO_5$$
$$- 0.038\,SC_2 - 0.061\,SC_3 - 0.168\,SC_4 - 0.168\,SC_5 - 0.039\,UA_2$$
$$- 0.087\,UA_3 - 0.192\,UA_4 - 0.192\,UA_5 - 0.066\,PD_2 - 0.092\,PD_3$$
$$- 0.360\,PD_4 - 0.415\,PD_5 - 0.070\,AD_2 - 0.145\,AD_3 - 0.356\,AD_4$$
$$- 0.421\,AD_5$$

(i) **Date/wave of study**

Data were collected in the first wave of EQ-5D-5L valuation studies using the EQ-5D-5L valuation protocol 1.0. Interviews were conducted in the fall of 2012.

(ii)   **Sample size; sample frame**
       1003 interviews with the general population were conducted in five cities and
       surrounds located in different parts of Netherlands: Utrecht, Rotterdam,
       Maastricht, Enschede and Groningen. Strata-based sampling with respect to
       age, gender and educational level as recorded by the by Statistics Netherlands
       (Centraal Bureau voor de Statistiek 2012). Of the 979 respondents included
       in the final value set, 50.85% were female and 49.15% were male. The age
       distribution of the respondents was:

18–24 years	11.91%
25–29 years	6.71%
30–39 years	13.71%
40–49 years	20.62%
50–64 years	28.53%
65–74 years	13.91%
75+ years	4.60%

(iii) **Representativeness of achieved sample**
       The study sample was representative for the Dutch population in terms of age
       (except for the age group 80 and older), gender, education, and employment
       status (Table 4.14).

Table 4.14 Representativeness of the sample in the Dutch valuation study

		Study sample (N=999[a])	Dutch general population[b]
Sampling characteristics			
Age, n (%)	18–19	26 (2.6%)	3.1%
	20–29	160 (16.0%)	15.7%
	30–39	137 (13.7%)	15.8%
	40–49	206 (20.6%)	19.7%
	50–59	189 (18.9%)	17.7%
	60–69	160 (16.0%)	14.8%
	70–79	113 (11.3%)	8.8%
	≥ 80	8 (0.8%)	4.4%
Gender, n (%)	Female	508 (50.9%)	50.7%
	Male	491 (49.1%)	49.3%
Education, n (%)	Lower education	385 (38.4%)	44.0%
	Middle education	322 (32.1%)	27.5%
	Higher education	292 (29.1%)	27.6%
	Unknown	4 (0.4%)	0.9%

Reproduced from Versteegh et al. (2016)
[a]This sample includes the recruited respondents where data on characteristics were available.
[b]Statistics Netherlands 2012

(iv) **Mean observed cTTO values of EQ-5D-5L states** (Table 4.15)

Table 4.15 Mean observed cTTO values by health state[a]

State	Mean	SE	State	Mean	SE	State	Mean	SE
11112	0.907	0.012	21345	0.113	0.068	43315	0.219	0.069
11121	0.900	0.017	21444	0.134	0.061	43514	0.165	0.064
11122	0.927	0.011	22434	0.314	0.054	43542	0.088	0.061
11211	0.925	0.012	23152	0.287	0.065	43555	−0.116	0.064
11212	0.879	0.025	23242	0.387	0.055	44125	0.121	0.064
11221	0.858	0.032	23514	0.315	0.059	44345	−0.183	0.064
11235	0.382	0.060	24342	0.236	0.059	44553	−0.089	0.070
11414	0.390	0.056	24443	0.067	0.068	45133	0.399	0.057
11421	0.635	0.046	24445	−0.143	0.062	45144	0.031	0.057
11425	0.244	0.061	24553	0.139	0.058	45233	0.314	0.067
12111	0.923	0.014	25122	0.591	0.054	45413	0.359	0.059
12112	0.830	0.035	25222	0.607	0.049	51152	0.217	0.060
12121	0.848	0.023	25331	0.601	0.049	51451	0.093	0.060
12244	0.222	0.069	31514	0.340	0.056	52215	0.212	0.060
12334	0.380	0.057	31524	0.286	0.065	52335	0.122	0.066
12344	0.199	0.064	31525	0.319	0.067	52431	0.474	0.056
12513	0.614	0.049	32314	0.426	0.057	52455	−0.129	0.069
12514	0.394	0.054	32443	0.161	0.062	53221	0.600	0.050
12543	0.130	0.063	33253	0.265	0.059	53243	0.182	0.062
13122	0.812	0.028	34155	−0.080	0.063	53244	0.057	0.060
13224	0.478	0.057	34232	0.606	0.048	53412	0.463	0.055
13313	0.749	0.036	34244	0.026	0.065	54153	0.050	0.073
14113	0.661	0.048	34515	0.100	0.064	54231	0.538	0.052
14554	−0.152	0.067	35143	0.320	0.054	54342	0.050	0.063
15151	0.216	0.073	35245	−0.044	0.063	55225	0.088	0.063
21111	0.922	0.011	35311	0.648	0.049	55233	0.267	0.068
21112	0.859	0.025	35332	0.585	0.050	55424	−0.036	0.068
21315	0.402	0.060	42115	0.323	0.060	55555	−0.298	0.019
21334	0.422	0.053	42321	0.692	0.040			

SE standard error

[a]In the Dutch EQ-5D-5L value set manuscript, slightly different means are reported. In this table, the means for the analytic sample are reported, which was used to generate the value set. Versteegh et al. (2016) report the means of the full sample, before excluding several respondents

(v)   **Proportions choosing A in the DCE based on relative severities of A and B** (Fig. 4.8)

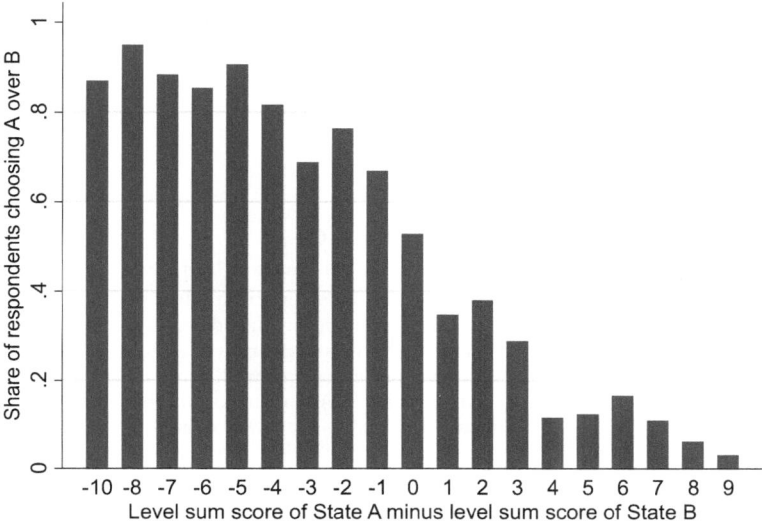

Fig. 4.8   Proportions choosing A based on relative severities of A and B

(vi)   **Exclusion criteria**
cTTO data were excluded when the task was not finished or when interviewers had indicated that the respondent had clearly not understood the task. Furthermore, respondents that gave the same value to all health states in the cTTO tasks were excluded. In total, 13 respondents were excluded from analysis of the cTTO data. In addition, no data were obtained from another 11 respondents, due to a loss of data caused by technical issues, respondents being unable to start the valuation tasks due to technical problems, the absence of an interviewer, unwillingness to participate after being informed about the topic of research and other and unknown reasons.

(vii)   **Number of interviewers; Interviewer effects**[5]
In total, 1003 interviews were conducted by 21 interviewers.

(viii)   **Description of modelling choices**
The Dutch EQ-5D-5L value set was based on the cTTO data only. The selected model was a Tobit model, that accounts for censoring at -1. Levels 4 and 5 were collapsed for the self-care and usual activities dimensions, as they were ordered inconsistently in other models.

---

[5] It was not possible to compute the variance attributed to differences between interviewers, as interviewers shared login information for the software used to conduct the interviews. Therefore, it is not possible to differentiate between interviewers.

(ix)   **Value Set** (Table 4.16 and Fig. 4.9)

Table 4.16 Key characteristics of the Dutch value set

Characteristics	Dutch EQ-5D-5L value set
% states with negative values	15.5% (485 out of 3125)
Rank order of dimensions (from most to least relative importance)	Anxiety/depression Pain/discomfort Usual activities Mobility Self-care
Range of values	Maximum value: 1 Minimum value: −0.446
Max value < 1:	0.918 (value of health state 21111)
Linearity/non-linearity of value decrements by level	Kink at level 3 for all dimensions (see Fig. 4.9). Value decrements in the functioning dimensions (mobility, self-care and usual activities) are similar to each other. The value decrements of the symptoms dimensions (pain/discomfort and anxiety/depression) were higher and similar to each other. In modelling, levels 4 and 5 were collapsed for the self-care and usual activities dimensions, which leads to these level-dimension combinations receiving the same weights.

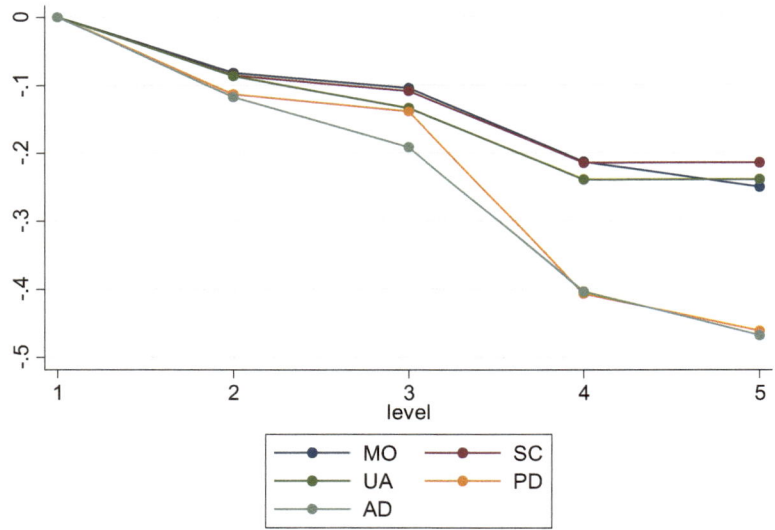

Fig. 4.9 Value decrements across dimensions. (*AD* anxiety/depression, *MO* mobility, *PD* pain/discomfort, *SC* self-care, *UA* usual activities)

(x)   **Uptake by local HTA/health care decision makers**
        Cost-utility analysis (CUA) is required by the Dutch regulatory body, Zorg
        Instituut Nederland (2016). For QALYs, the use of the EQ-5D-5L and the
        accompanying Dutch value set is recommended.

(xi)   **Reference(s) of value set**
        Versteegh MM, Vermeulen KM, Evers SMAA, De Wit GA, Prenger R, Stolk
        EA (2016) Dutch tariff for the five-level version of EQ-5D. Value Health
        19(4):343–352

Further Literature

Versteegh M, Knies S, Brouwer W (2016) From good to better: new Dutch guidelines
    for economic evaluations in healthcare. Pharmacoeconomics 34(11):1071–1074
Zorginstituut Nederland (2016) Guideline for economic evaluations in healthcare.
    https://english.zorginstituutnederland.nl/publications/reports/2016/06/16/
    guideline-for-economic-evaluations-in-healthcare. Accessed 12 May 2021
Statistics Netherlands (Centraal Bureau voor de Statistiek) (2012) Dutch Population
    data. https://www.cbs.nl. Accessed 14 July 2021

4.3.1.5 Country/Region: Spain (Table 4.17)

Table 4.17 Overview of EQ-5D-5L value set for Spain[a]

Spanish EQ-5D-5L value set		Example: the value for health state 21232	
Full health (11111)	1	Full health	=1
Mobility = 2	0.084	Minus MO level 2	−0.084
Mobility = 3	0.099		
Mobility = 4	0.249		
Mobility = 5	0.337		
Self-care = 2	0.050	Minus SC level 1	−0.000
Self-care = 3	0.053		
Self-care = 4	0.164		
Self-care = 5	0.196		
Usual activities = 2	0.044	Minus UA level 2	−0.044
Usual activities = 3	0.049		
Usual activities = 4	0.135		
Usual activities = 5	0.153		
Pain/discomfort = 2	0.078		
Pain/discomfort = 3	0.101	Minus PD level 3	−0.101
Pain/discomfort = 4	0.245		
Pain/discomfort = 5	0.382		
Anxiety/depression = 2	0.081	Minus AD level 2	−0.081
Anxiety/depression = 3	0.128		
Anxiety/depression = 4	0.270		
Anxiety/depression = 5	0.348		
		State 21232	=0.690

AD anxiety/depression, *MO* mobility, *PD* pain/discomfort, *SC* self-care, *UA* usual activities
[a]In the valuation study manuscript, the value set is reported as incremental dummies. For consistency, we report regular dummies here – see Sect. 4.2 for more information

The mathematical representation of the model for health state X is:

$$V(X) = 1 - 0.084\,MO_2 - 0.099\,MO_3 - 0.249\,MO_4 - 0.337\,MO_5 - 0.050\,SC_2$$
$$- 0.053\,SC_3 - 0.164\,SC_4 - 0.196\,SC_5 - 0.044\,UA_2 - 0.049\,UA_3$$
$$- 0.135\,UA_4 - 0.153\,UA_5 - 0.078\,PD_2 - 0.101\,PD_3 - 0.245\,PD_4$$
$$- 0.382\,PD_5 - 0.081\,AD_2 - 0.128\,AD_3 - 0.270\,AD_4 - 0.348\,AD_5$$

(i) **Date/wave of study**
Data were collected in the first wave of EQ-5D-5L valuation studies using the EQ-5D-5L valuation protocol 1.0. Interviews were conducted in June and July 2012.

(ii) **Sample size; sample frame**
1000 interviews with the general population were conducted, stratified over all provinces of Spain. Within these provinces, respondents were sampled to

represent the age and gender distribution of that province. Of the 973 respondents included in the final value set, 52.4% were female and 47.6% were male. The age distribution of the respondents was:

18–24 years	11.7%
25–29 years	15.1%
30–39 years	22.9%
40–49 years	14.8%
50–64 years	19.0%
65–74 years	11.1%
75+ years	5.3%

(iii) **Representativeness of achieved sample**
The study sample was representative for the Spanish population in terms of age (over 18 years) and gender (Table 4.18).

Table 4.18 Representativeness of the sample in the Spanish valuation study

		Study sample (N=973)	Spanish general population[a]
Sampling characteristics			
Age, n (%)	18–24	114 (11.7%)	9.0%
	25–34	270 (27.8%)	18.3%
	35–44	170 (17.5%)	19.6%
	45–54	148 (15.2%)	17.9%
	55–64	111 (11.4%)	13.5%
	65–74	108 (11.1%)	10.2%
	≥75	52 (5.3%)	11.0%
Gender, n (%)	Female	510 (52.4%)	50.7%
	Male	463 (47.6%)	49.3%
Education, n (%)	Missing	6 (0.6%)	-
	No studies	45 (4.7%)	2.1%
	Primary school	234 (24.2%)	26.3%
	High school	374 (38.7%)	53.9%
	Higher education	314 (32.5%)	17.7%
Employment status, n (%)	Housewife/ house husband	70 (7.2%)	10.5%
	Employed or freelance	529 (54.4%) 89 (9.1%)	45.0% 6.3%
	Student	132 (13.6%)	20.1%
	Retired	139 (14.3%)	15.0%
	Disabled	8 (0.8%)	3.0%
	Missing	6 (0.6%)	-

Reproduced from Ramos-Goñi et al. (2017)
[a]Spanish Ministry of Health 2012

(iv)   **Mean observed cTTO values of EQ-5D-5L states** (Table 4.19)

Table 4.19 Mean observed cTTO values by health state

State	Mean	SE	State	Mean	SE	State	Mean	SE
11112	0.899	0.013	21345	0.318	0.057	43315	0.329	0.054
11121	0.899	0.013	21444	0.337	0.046	43514	0.300	0.056
11122	0.838	0.025	22434	0.366	0.055	43542	0.306	0.048
11211	0.896	0.013	23152	0.423	0.057	43555	−0.059	0.062
11212	0.827	0.025	23242	0.595	0.038	44125	0.160	0.053
11221	0.839	0.025	23514	0.554	0.034	44345	0.047	0.053
11235	0.398	0.057	24342	0.484	0.042	44553	0.027	0.058
11414	0.558	0.040	24443	0.263	0.051	45133	0.369	0.049
11421	0.723	0.033	24445	0.096	0.064	45144	0.091	0.056
11425	0.370	0.057	24553	0.148	0.059	45233	0.307	0.055
12111	0.868	0.020	25122	0.566	0.046	45413	0.224	0.060
12112	0.806	0.028	25222	0.622	0.033	51152	0.167	0.062
12121	0.865	0.018	25331	0.540	0.043	51451	0.182	0.057
12244	0.327	0.055	31514	0.533	0.037	52215	0.367	0.049
12334	0.610	0.039	31524	0.427	0.048	52335	0.235	0.060
12344	0.347	0.053	31525	0.333	0.056	52431	0.359	0.052
12513	0.606	0.036	32314	0.559	0.046	52455	−0.013	0.053
12514	0.407	0.054	32443	0.398	0.041	53221	0.489	0.042
12543	0.447	0.043	33253	0.406	0.050	53243	0.315	0.048
13122	0.765	0.033	34155	0.218	0.056	53244	0.195	0.052
13224	0.508	0.057	34232	0.531	0.053	53412	0.414	0.053
13313	0.687	0.037	34244	0.274	0.057	54153	0.086	0.053
14113	0.670	0.035	34515	0.221	0.055	54231	0.322	0.055
14554	0.071	0.057	35143	0.382	0.045	54342	0.050	0.056
15151	0.365	0.051	35245	0.081	0.057	55225	0.194	0.056
21111	0.898	0.013	35311	0.497	0.058	55233	0.155	0.058
21112	0.819	0.026	35332	0.336	0.063	55424	0.026	0.056
21315	0.484	0.048	42115	0.271	0.063	55555	−0.166	0.017
21334	0.565	0.045	42321	0.499	0.058			

SE standard error

(v)   **Proportions choosing A in the DCE based on relative severities of A and B** (Fig. 4.10)

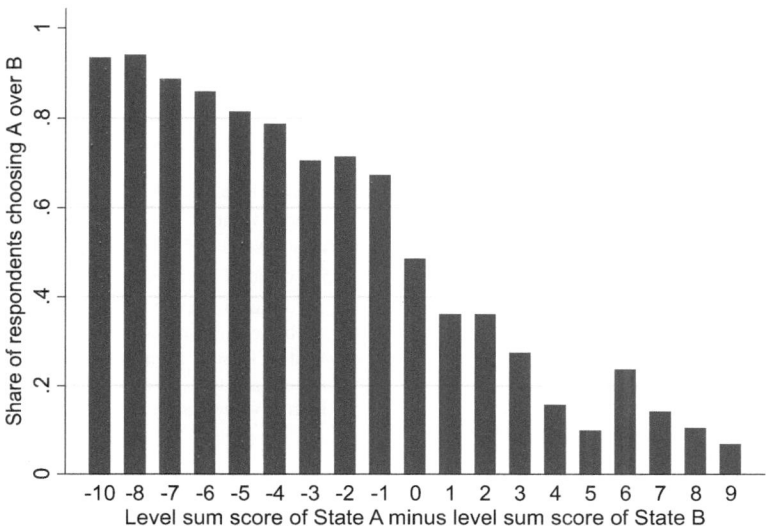

Fig. 4.10   Proportions choosing A based on relative severities of A and B

(vi)   **Exclusion criteria**

Respondents that valued all health states in the cTTO tasks as equal to dead were excluded. Furthermore, respondents that had a positive slope on the regression between respondent's cTTO values and level sum score were excluded. 27 out of 1000 respondents were excluded. No DCE data were excluded from the analysis.

(vii)   **Number of interviewers; Interviewer effects**

In total, 1000 interviews were conducted by 33 interviewers. The variance of the responses included in the final value set can be partitioned into variance related to differences between interviewers (7.3%), respondents (31.9%), and responses (60.8%).

(viii) **Description of modelling choices**

The Spanish EQ-5D-5L value set was based on a hybrid model combining a conditional logit model for the DCE data and a censored at -1 Tobit model for the cTTO data, correcting for heteroskedasticity. Furthermore, cTTO responses were treated as intervals rather than point responses. For respondents that were not shown the WTD task in the explanations (see Chap. 2 for more details), the data were considered to be censored at 0. The intercept was constrained in the final model, as it was not statistically significant.

(ix)   **Value Set** (Table 4.20 and Fig. 4.11)

Table 4.20 Key characteristics of the Spanish value set

Characteristics	Spanish EQ-5D-5L value set
% states with negative values	8.26% (258 out of 3125)
Rank order of dimensions (from most to least relative importance)	Anxiety/depression Pain/discomfort Mobility Self-care Usual activities
Range of values	Maximum value: 1 Minimum value: −0.416
Max value < 1:	0.956 (value of health state 11211)
Linearity/non-linearity of value decrements by level	For all dimensions, the largest change in value occurs between levels 3 and 4. For pain/discomfort there is a further large change in value between levels 4 and 5, such that it has the largest value decrement at level 5.

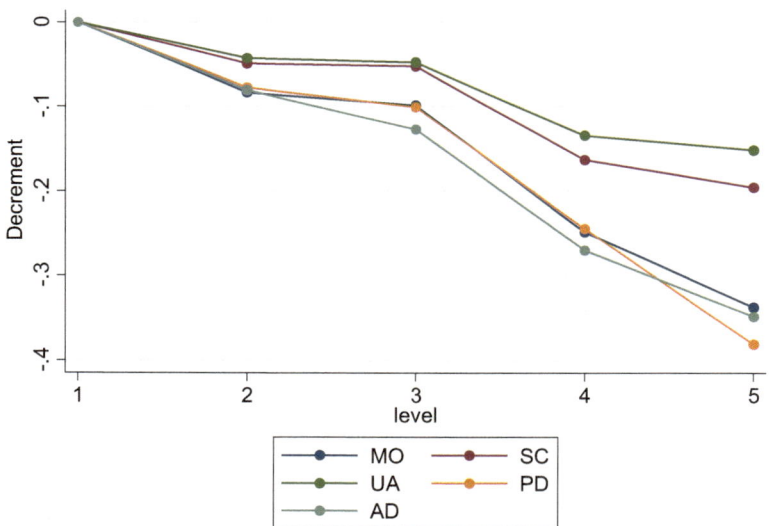

Fig. 4.11 Value decrements across dimensions (*AD* anxiety/depression, *MO* mobility, *PD* pain/discomfort, *SC* self-care, *UA* usual activities)

(x) **Uptake by local HTA/health care decision makers**

Cost-utility analysis (CUA) is currently not mandatory in pharmacoeconomics and health technology assessment reports either by AEMPS (Agencia Española de Medicamentos y Productos Sanitarios), or RedETS (Red Española de Agencias de Evaluación de Tecnologías Sanitarias y Prestaciones del Sistema Nacional de Salud); the agencies that provide evidence for reimbursement decisions on drugs and technical devices, respectively, in Spain. However, use of CUA is demanded by the State Health Authority in the assessment process of national Public Health programs such as Population Screening or Vaccination programs.

(xi) **Reference(s) of value set**

Ramos-Goñi JM, Craig BM, Oppe M, Ramallo-Fariña Y, Pinto-Prades JL, Luo N, Rivero-Arias O (2018) Handling data quality issues to estimate the Spanish EQ-5D-5L value set using a hybrid interval regression approach. Value Health 21(5):596–604

Further Literature

Ramos-Goñi JM, Pinto-Prades JL, Oppe M, Cabasés JM, Serrano-Aguilar P, Rivero-Arias O (2017) Valuation and modeling of EQ-5D-5L health states using a hybrid approach. Med Care 55(7):e51–e58

Spanish Ministry of Health (2012) Spanish national health survey 2011/2012. https://www.mscbs.gob.es/estadEstudios/estadisticas/encuestaNacional/encuesta2011.htm. Accessed 13 July 2021

4.3.2 Wave 2

4.3.2.1 Country/Region: Japan (Table 4.21)

Table 4.21 Overview of EQ-5D-5L value set for Japan

Japan EQ-5D-5L value set		Example: the value for health state 21232	
Full health (11111)	1	Full health	=1
Constant	0.0609	Minus constant	−0.0609
Mobility = 2	0.0639	Minus MO level 2	−0.0639
Mobility = 3	0.1126		
Mobility = 4	0.1790		
Mobility = 5	0.2429		
Self-care = 2	0.0436	Minus SC level 1	−0.000
Self-care = 3	0.0767		
Self-care = 4	0.1243		
Self-care = 5	0.1597		
Usual activities = 2	0.0504	Minus UA level 2	−0.0504
Usual activities = 3	0.0911		
Usual activities = 4	0.1479		
Usual activities = 5	0.1748		
Pain/discomfort = 2	0.0445		
Pain/discomfort = 3	0.0682	Minus PD level 3	−0.0682
Pain/discomfort = 4	0.1314		
Pain/discomfort = 5	0.1912		
Anxiety/depression = 2	0.0718	Minus AD level 2	−0.0718
Anxiety/depression = 3	0.1105		
Anxiety/depression = 4	0.1682		
Anxiety/depression = 5	0.1960		
		State 21232	=0.6848

AD anxiety/depression, *MO* mobility, *PD* pain/discomfort, *SC* self-care, *UA* usual activities

The mathematical representation of the model for health state X is:

$$V(X) = 1 - 0.0609 - 0.0639\,MO_2 - 0.1126\,MO_3 - 0.1790\,MO_4 - 0.2429\,MO_5$$
$$- 0.0436\,SC_2 - 0.0767\,SC_3 - 0.1243\,SC_4 - 0.1597\,SC_5 - 0.0504\,UA_2$$
$$- 0.0911\,UA_3 - 0.1479\,UA_4 - 0.1748\,UA_5 - 0.0445\,PD_2 - 0.0682\,PD_3$$
$$- 0.1314\,PD_4 - 0.1912\,PD_5 - 0.0718\,AD_2 - 0.1105\,AD_3 - 0.1682\,AD_4$$
$$- 0.1960\,AD_5$$

(i) **Date/wave of study**
   Data were collected in the second wave of EQ-5D-5L valuation studies using the EQ-5D-5L valuation protocol 1.1. Interviews were conducted between March and June 2014.

(ii) **Sample size; sample frame**

1098 interviews with the adult general population > 20 years of age were conducted in five cities in Japan: Tokyo, Okayama, Nagoya, Osaka, and Niigata. Respondents were recruited by a research company (ANTE-RIO Inc.) that sampled approximately 200 respondents at each location. The sample number was not determined on the basis of statistical considerations; respondents were stratified by sex and age group in each location to collect the same number in each cell.

Following the application of quality control, data from respondents interviewed by three interviewers were excluded from analysis. Of the 1026 respondents included in the analysis, 49.8% were female and 50.2% were male. The age distribution of the respondents was:

18–24 years	10.33%
25–29 years	9.65%
30–39 years	19.98%
40–49 years	19.88%
50–64 years	29.24%
65–74 years	9.75%
75+ years	1.17%

(iii) **Representativeness of achieved sample**

The study sample was indicated to be broadly representative of the adult general public of Japan – however the paper does not report descriptive statistics for the general population to enable direct comparison with the characteristics of the analysis sample. The sample characteristics are provided in Table 4.22.

Table 4.22 Characteristics of the sample in the Japanese valuation study

		Study sample (N=1026)	General population[a]
Sampling characteristics			
Age, n (%)	20-29	203 (19.8%)	15.6%
	30-39	204 (19.9%)	18.2%
	40-49	206 (20.1%)	23.9%
	50-59	206 (20.1%)	21.1%
	≥ 60	207 (20.2%)	21.2%
Gender, n (%)	Female	511 (49.8%)	51.3%
	Male	515 (50.2%)	48.7%
Education, n (%)	Junior High School	33 (3.2%)	14.8%
	High School	415 (40.4%)	39.7%
	Vocational School or Junior College	247 (24.1%)	20.5%
	University or graduate school	331 (32.3%)	24.3%

Reproduced from Shiroiwa et al. (2016)

[a]% age and gender are based on 'Vital Statistics', Ministry of Health, Labour and Welfare; education statistics are from the Japan 2010 National Census

(iv)   **Mean observed cTTO values by EQ-5D-5L state** (Table 4.23)

Table 4.23 Mean observed cTTO values by health state

State	Mean	SE	State	Mean	SE	State	Mean	SE
11112	0.907	0.014	21345	0.417	0.043	43315	0.391	0.043
11121	0.900	0.015	21444	0.397	0.037	43514	0.308	0.050
11122	0.859	0.018	22434	0.445	0.045	43542	0.329	0.045
11211	0.908	0.012	23152	0.489	0.045	43555	0.133	0.041
11212	0.810	0.031	23242	0.524	0.041	44125	0.375	0.044
11221	0.849	0.030	23514	0.543	0.038	44345	0.227	0.049
11235	0.598	0.039	24342	0.457	0.041	44553	0.173	0.048
11414	0.601	0.032	24443	0.383	0.039	45133	0.485	0.039
11421	0.721	0.032	24445	0.301	0.037	45144	0.323	0.044
11425	0.536	0.042	24553	0.221	0.051	45233	0.359	0.046
12111	0.892	0.014	25122	0.550	0.045	45413	0.321	0.045
12112	0.817	0.028	25222	0.566	0.038	51152	0.359	0.043
12121	0.870	0.016	25331	0.559	0.037	51451	0.326	0.044
12244	0.503	0.045	31514	0.448	0.038	52215	0.403	0.045
12334	0.606	0.041	31524	0.459	0.043	52335	0.323	0.031
12344	0.508	0.041	31525	0.394	0.043	52431	0.435	0.040
12513	0.611	0.040	32314	0.521	0.042	52455	0.155	0.051
12514	0.534	0.035	32443	0.453	0.039	53221	0.580	0.032
12543	0.474	0.040	33253	0.406	0.042	53243	0.364	0.040
13122	0.755	0.034	34155	0.361	0.042	53244	0.261	0.045
13224	0.608	0.026	34232	0.532	0.024	53412	0.357	0.047
13313	0.633	0.039	34244	0.342	0.047	54153	0.285	0.043
14113	0.703	0.034	34515	0.300	0.044	54231	0.400	0.046
14554	0.307	0.045	35143	0.396	0.038	54342	0.342	0.045
15151	0.545	0.038	35245	0.303	0.045	55225	0.209	0.048
21111	0.897	0.014	35311	0.601	0.028	55233	0.273	0.048
21112	0.813	0.026	35332	0.385	0.048	55424	0.169	0.050
21315	0.599	0.034	42115	0.483	0.036	55555	−0.019	0.015
21334	0.535	0.043	42321	0.590	0.028			

SE standard error

(v)   **Proportions choosing A in the DCE based on relative severities of A and B** (Fig. 4.12)

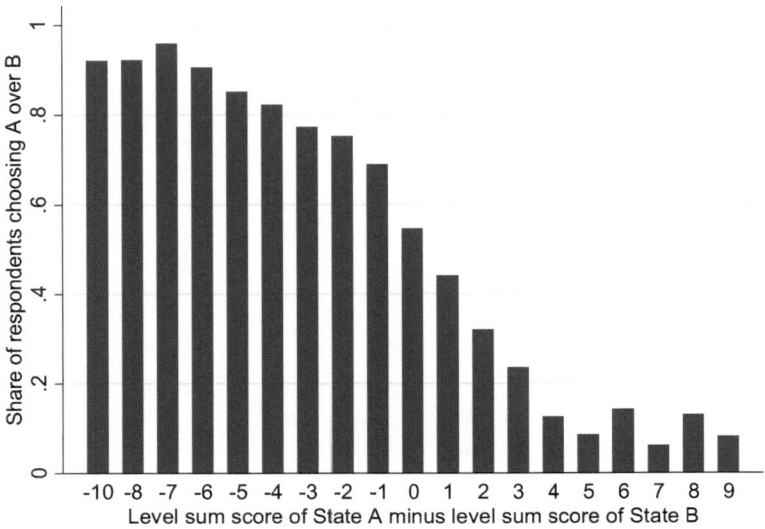

Fig. 4.12   Proportions choosing A based on relative severities of A and B

(vi) **Exclusion criteria**
      Quality control flagged three interviewers as failing to comply with the protocol; some or all of the data from the 72 respondents who were interviewed were excluded from the analysis data set.

(vii) **Number of interviewers; Interviewer effects**
      In total, 1098 interviews were conducted by 31 interviewers. The variance of the responses can be partitioned into variance related to differences between interviewers (0.95%), respondents (38.77%), and responses (60.28%).

(viii) **Description of modelling choices**
      The preferred value set is modelled using only cTTO data. The data were analysed by a linear mixed model with "1 - QOL score" as the dependent variable. To account for the intra-respondent correlation, a constant term and dummy variables representing the levels of the five dimensions were treated as fixed effects and the respondents were treated as random effects.

(ix) **Value Set** (Table 4.24 and Fig. 4.13)

Table 4.24 Key characteristics of the Japanese value set

Characteristics	Japan EQ-5D-5L value set
% states with negative values	0.0003% (1 out of 3125)
Rank order of dimensions (from most to least relative importance)	Mobility Anxiety/depression Usual activities Pain/discomfort Self-care
Coefficient with highest weight	0.2429 (level 5 of mobility)
Range of values	Maximum value: 1 Minimum value: −0.025
Max value < 1:	0.895 (value of health state 12111)
Linearity/non-linearity of value decrements by level	There is a large fall in value for any move away from no problems on every dimension, with smaller decrements for other 1-level changes. Values continue to fall sharply in increased problems in mobility, such that it has the highest value decrement at level 5 across all dimensions.

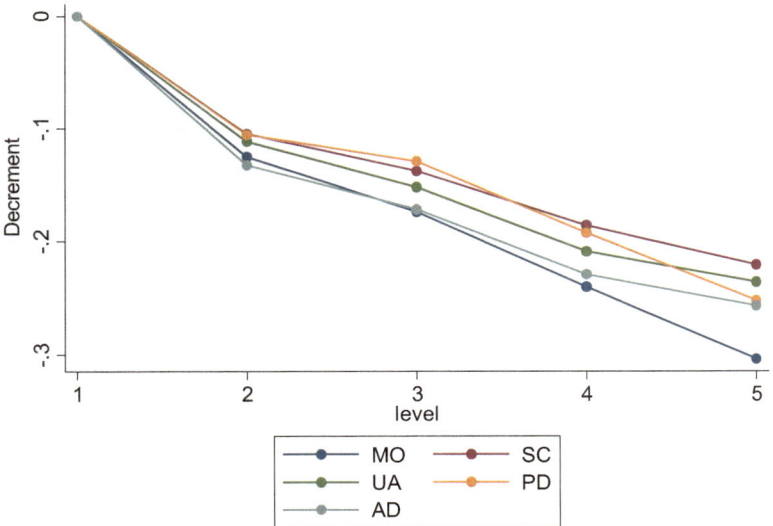

Fig. 4.13 Value decrements across dimensions (*AD* anxiety/depression, *MO* mobility, *PD* pain/discomfort, *SC* self-care, *UA* usual activities)

(x)   **Uptake by local HTA/health care decision makers**

According to Sect. 8.2.1 of the Japanese HTA Guidelines, "If Japanese quality of life scores are newly collected for a cost-effectiveness analysis, the use
of preference-based measures with a value set developed in Japan using TTO
(or mapped onto a TTO score) is recommended as the first choice."
(C2H. 2019) The characteristics of the Japanese EQ-5D-5L reported here
therefore meets the stated requirements of Japan's HTA body, although it is
unclear how often it has been used in evidence submitted to it.

(xi) **Reference(s) for this value set**

Shiroiwa T, Ikeda S, Noto S, Igarashi A, Fukuda T, Saito S, Shimozuma K
(2016) Comparison of value set based on DCE and/or TTO data: scoring
for EQ-5D-5L health states in Japan. Value Health 19(5): 648–655

Further Literature

Center for Outcomes Research and Economic Evaluation for Health, National
Institute of Public Health (C2H) (2019) Guideline for Preparing Cost-
Effectiveness Evaluation to the Central Social Insurance Medical Council.
https://c2h.niph.go.jp/tools/guideline/guideline_en.pdf. Accessed 16 June 2021
Ministry of Health, Labour and Welfare (2018) Vital Statistics. https://www.mhlw.
go.jp. Accessed 29 July 2021
Statistics of Japan (2010) 2010 Population Census. https://e-stat.go.jp. Accessed 29
July 2021

4.3.2.2   Country/Region: Korea (Table 4.25)

Table 4.25 Overview of EQ-5D-5L value set for Korea

Korean EQ-5D-5L value set		Example: the value for health state 21232	
Full health (11111)	1	Full health	=1
constant	0.096	Minus constant	−0.096
Mobility = 2	0.046	Minus MO level 2	−0.046
Mobility = 3	0.058		
Mobility = 4	0.133		
Mobility = 5	0.251		
Self-care = 2	0.032	Minus SC level 1	−0.000
Self-care = 3	0.050		
Self-care = 4	0.078		
Self-care = 5	0.122		
Usual activities = 2	0.021	Minus UA level 2	−0.021
Usual activities = 3	0.051		
Usual activities = 4	0.100		
Usual activities = 5	0.175		
Pain/discomfort = 2	0.042		
Pain/discomfort = 3	0.053	Minus PD level 3	−0.053
Pain/discomfort = 4	0.166		
Pain/discomfort = 5	0.207		
Anxiety/depression = 2	0.033	Minus AD level 2	−0.033
Anxiety/depression = 3	0.046		
Anxiety/depression = 4	0.102		
Anxiety/depression = 5	0.137		
N4	0.078		
		State 21232	= 0.751

N4 is a dummy variable set to 1 where *any* dimension has *at least* a level 4; and 0 otherwise
AD anxiety/depression, *MO* mobility, *PD* pain/discomfort, *SC* self-care, *UA* usual activities

The mathematical representation of the model for health state X is:

$$
\begin{aligned}
V(X) = 1 & - 0.096 - 0.046\,MO_2 - 0.058\,MO_3 - 0.133\,MO_4 - 0.251\,MO_5 \\
& - 0.032\,SC_2 - 0.050\,SC_3 - 0.078\,SC_4 - 0.122\,SC_5 - 0.021\,UA_2 \\
& - 0.051\,UA_3 - 0.100\,UA_4 - 0.175\,UA_5 - 0.042\,PD_2 - 0.053\,PD_3 \\
& - 0.166\,PD_4 - 0.207\,PD_5 - 0.033\,AD_2 - 0.046\,AD_3 - 0.102\,AD_4 \\
& - 0.137\,AD_5 - 0.078\,N4
\end{aligned}
$$

(i)   **Date/wave of study**

Data were collected in the second wave of EQ-5D-5L valuation studies using the EQ-5D-5L valuation protocol 1.1. Interviews were performed between August 9 and November 13, 2013.

(ii) **Sample size; sample frame**

Sampling was performed using a multistage stratified quota method. A sample quota was assigned to each of the 15 regions according to population structure (population in region, sex, age, and education level), as defined in the June 2013 resident registration data available through the Ministry of Administration and Security, South Korea.

Of the 1080 respondents included in the analysis, 50.6% were female and 49.4% were male.

The age distribution of the respondents was:

18–24 years	8.98%
25–34 years	9.35%
35–44 years	19.35%
45–54 years	21.30%
55–64 years	33.33%
65–74 years	6.94%
75+ years	0.74%

(iii) **Representativeness of achieved sample**

The study sample was representative for the Korean population in terms of age (over 18 years), sex, education and employment status (Table 4.26).

Table 4.26 Representativeness of the sample in the Korean valuation study

		Study sample (N=1080)	Korean general population[a]
Sampling characteristics			
Age, n (%)	19 –29	197 (18.2%)	17.9%
	30–39	212 (19.6%)	19.9%
	40–49	229 (21.2%)	21.7%
	50–59	213 (19.7%)	19.5%
	≥ 60	229 (21.2%)	21.0%
Gender, n (%)	Female	546 (50.6%)	50.5%
	Male	534(49.4%)	49.5%
Education, n (%)	8 years or below	50 (4.6%)	13.2%
	9–11 years	101 (9.4%)	9.4%
	12–15 years	651(60.3%)	53.6%
	16 or more years	278 (25.7%)	23.8%

Reproduced from Kim et al. (2016)

[a]2010 Census

(iv)   **Mean observed cTTO values of EQ-5D-5L states** (Table 4.27)

Table 4.27   Mean observed cTTO values by health state

State	Mean	SE	State	Mean	SE	State	Mean	SE
11112	0.880	0.011	21345	0.445	0.033	43315	0.421	0.023
11121	0.891	0.008	21444	0.384	0.033	43514	0.416	0.030
11122	0.840	0.017	22434	0.476	0.027	43542	0.266	0.039
11211	0.872	0.011	23152	0.510	0.031	43555	0.156	0.038
11212	0.842	0.016	23242	0.448	0.040	44125	0.423	0.025
11221	0.836	0.015	23514	0.479	0.022	44345	0.303	0.031
11235	0.628	0.022	24342	0.372	0.045	44553	0.207	0.040
11414	0.624	0.026	24443	0.349	0.034	45133	0.457	0.025
11421	0.729	0.018	24445	0.321	0.035	45144	0.339	0.029
11425	0.528	0.024	24553	0.291	0.031	45233	0.458	0.031
12111	0.885	0.011	25122	0.629	0.029	45413	0.391	0.028
12112	0.850	0.014	25222	0.600	0.028	51152	0.274	0.033
12121	0.803	0.016	25331	0.550	0.028	51451	0.325	0.023
12244	0.541	0.032	31514	0.509	0.028	52215	0.408	0.026
12334	0.567	0.035	31524	0.398	0.029	52335	0.321	0.031
12344	0.489	0.027	31525	0.461	0.028	52431	0.364	0.028
12513	0.580	0.020	32314	0.557	0.035	52455	0.180	0.040
12514	0.505	0.027	32443	0.434	0.025	53221	0.489	0.025
12543	0.399	0.030	33253	0.389	0.038	53243	0.277	0.035
13122	0.747	0.020	34155	0.335	0.030	53244	0.207	0.035
13224	0.663	0.019	34232	0.558	0.026	53412	0.336	0.043
13313	0.763	0.017	34244	0.422	0.033	54153	0.215	0.033
14113	0.666	0.020	34515	0.382	0.028	54231	0.455	0.030
14554	0.272	0.032	35143	0.460	0.028	54342	0.295	0.031
15151	0.463	0.030	35245	0.367	0.025	55225	0.230	0.041
21111	0.878	0.011	35311	0.585	0.025	55233	0.429	0.025
21112	0.837	0.013	35332	0.511	0.025	55424	0.187	0.042
21315	0.545	0.026	42115	0.485	0.029	55555	−0.073	0.014
21334	0.512	0.034	42321	0.573	0.025			

SE standard error

(v) **Proportions choosing A in the DCE based on relative severities of A and B** (Fig. 4.14)

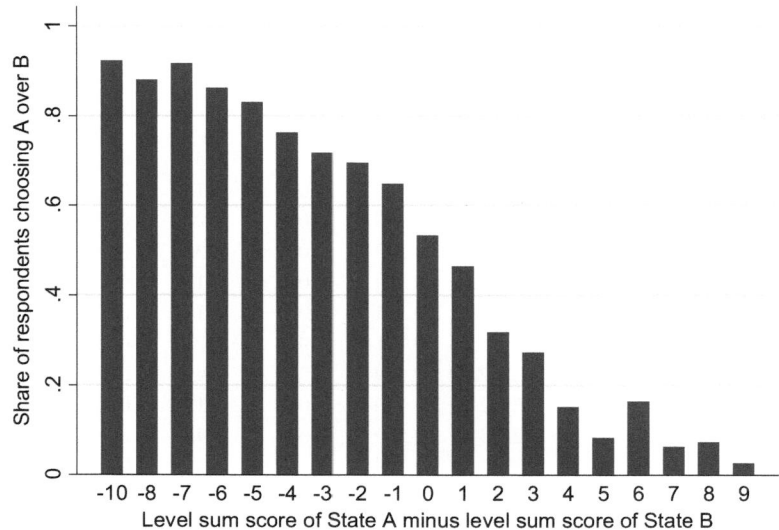

Fig. 4.14 Proportions choosing A based on relative severities of A and B

(vi) **Exclusion criteria**
Five respondents who responded with the same answer for all 10 health states of cTTO were excluded from the modelling dataset.

(vii) **Number of interviewers; Interviewer effects**
In total, 1080 interviews were conducted by 27 interviewers. The variance of the responses can be partitioned into variance related to differences between interviewers (12.54%), respondents (20.69%), and responses (66.77%).

(viii) **Description of modelling choice**
The value set was based on cTTO data only, using 20 dummy variables (4 levels for each of 5 dimensions). Three criteria were used to select the final model (1) the model must demonstrate logically consistent predictions; (2) goodness of fit of the model, judged using mean absolute error (MAE), generalized R^2 and the number of health states with absolute error <0.05 or 0.1; and (3) where models with similar MAEs were consistent, the simplest model was selected to maintain parsimony. The final model includes a constant, and a term that picked up whether any dimension in the state was at a level 4 or 5.

(ix) **Value Set** (Table 4.28 and Fig. 4.15)

Table 4.28 Key characteristics of the Korean value set

Characteristics	Korea EQ-5D-5L value set
% states with negative values	0.1% (4 out of 3125)
Rank order of dimensions (from most to least relative importance)	Mobility Pain/discomfort Usual activities Anxiety/depression Self-care
Coefficient with highest weight	0.251 (level 5 of mobility)
Range of values	Maximum value: 1 Minimum value: −0.066
Max value < 1:	0.883 (value of health state11211)
Linearity/non-linearity of value decrements by level	All dimensions follow a broadly similar pattern: a sharp drop in value for any movement away from 'no problem', small differences between levels 2 and 3, then a sharp drop between levels 3 and 4. In the case of mobility, there is a further large change in value between levels 4 and 5; to the extent that at level 5 mobility has the largest value decrement of all dimensions.

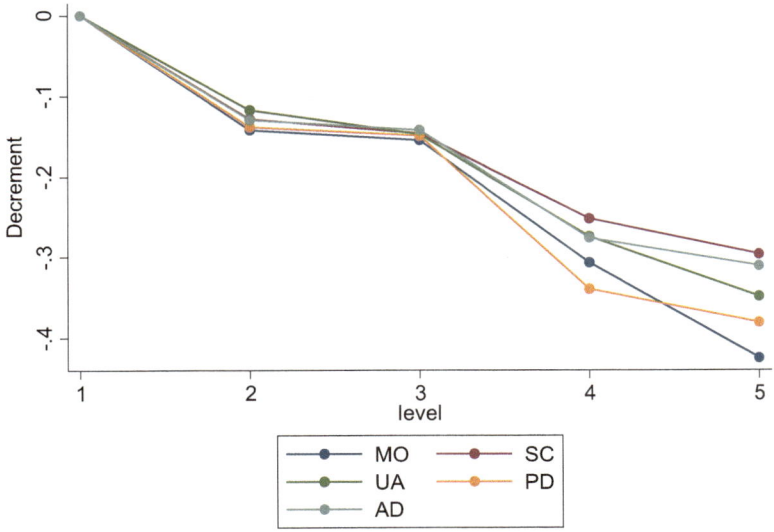

Fig. 4.15 Value decrements across dimensions (*AD* anxiety/depression, *MO* mobility, *PD* pain/discomfort, *SC* self-care, *UA* usual activities)

(x)   **Uptake by local HTA/health care decision makers**
CUA is currently the preferred form of economic evaluation in the 3ʳᵈ version
of Pharmacoeconomic Guideline revised by HIRA (Health Insurance Review
Agency), the institute that assesses the cost-effectiveness of healthcare services to determine whether to include the service into the benefit package and
decides the reimbursement price of the service (HIRA 2021), in 2021. There
is no preference for a specific multi-attribute utility instrument but the recommended source of values is a representative sample of the general population,
preferably Korean (Bae et al. 2013). For EQ-5D, value sets for both 3-level
version and 5-level version were developed from the general population in
Korea (Jo et al. 2008; Lee et al. 2009; Kim et al., 2016) and those instruments
have been applied for economic evaluations informing the reimbursement
decision making regarding new drugs.

(xi) **Reference(s) for this value set**
Kim SH, Ahn J, Ock M, Shin S, Park J, Luo N, Jo MW (2016) The EQ-5D-5L
valuation study in Korea. Qual Life Res 25(7):1845–1852

Further Literature

Health Insurance review agency (2021) http://www.hira.or.kr/dummy.
do?pgmid=HIRAJ010000009001 (Korean) Accessed 28 July 2021
Bae S, Lee S, Bae EY, Jang S (2013) Korean guidelines for pharmacoeconomic
evaluation (second and updated version): consensus and compromise.
Pharmacoeconomics 31(4):257–267
Jo MW, Yun SC, Lee SI (2008) Estimating quality weights for EQ-5D health states
with the time trade-off method in South Korea. Value Health 11(7):1186–1189
Lee YK, Nam HS, Chuang LH, Kim KY, Yang HK, Kwon IS, Kind P, Kweon SS,
Kim YT (2009) South Korean time trade-off values for EQ-5D health states:
modeling with observed values for 101 health states. Value Health
12(8):1187–1893

4.3.2.3   Country/Region: Thailand (Table 4.29)

Table 4.29   Overview of EQ-5D-5L value set for Thailand

Thai EQ-5D-5L value set		Example: the value for health state 21232	
Full health (11111)	1	Full health	=1
Mobility = 2	0.066	Minus MO level 2	−0.066
Mobility = 3	0.087		
Mobility = 4	0.211		
Mobility = 5	0.371		
Self-care = 2	0.058	Minus SC level 1	−0.000
Self-care = 3	0.071		
Self-care = 4	0.193		
Self-care = 5	0.250		
Usual activities = 2	0.058	Minus UA level 2	−0.058
Usual activities = 3	0.071		
Usual activities = 4	0.154		
Usual activities = 5	0.248		
Pain/discomfort = 2	0.056		
Pain/discomfort = 3	0.067	Minus PD level 3	−0.067
Pain/discomfort = 4	0.207		
Pain/discomfort = 5	0.256		
Anxiety/depression = 2	0.058	Minus AD level 2	−0.058
Anxiety/depression = 3	0.096		
Anxiety/depression = 4	0.233		
Anxiety/depression = 5	0.295		
Constant	-		
		State 21232	=0.751

AD anxiety/depression, *MO* mobility, *PD* pain/discomfort, *SC* self-care, *UA* usual activities

The mathematical representation of the model for health state X is:

$$V(X) = 1 - 0.066\,MO_2 - 0.087\,MO_3 - 0.211\,MO_4 - 0.371\,MO_5 - 0.058\,SC_2$$
$$- 0.071\,SC_3 - 0.193\,SC_4 - 0.250\,SC_5 - 0.058\,UA_2 - 0.071\,UA_3$$
$$- 0.154\,UA_4 - 0.248\,UA_5 - 0.056\,PD_2 - 0.067\,PD_3 - 0.207\,PD_4$$
$$- 0.256\,PD_5 - 0.058\,AD_2 - 0.096\,AD_3 - 0.233\,AD_4 - 0.295\,AD_5$$

(i)   **Date/wave of study**

Data were collected in the second wave of EQ-5D-5L valuation studies using the EQ-5D-5L valuation protocol 1.1. Interviews were conducted between August 2013 and January 2014.

(ii)   **Sample size; sample frame**
       1207 interviews with the general population were conducted in the capital
       Bangkok and the following 11 provinces: Sing Buri, Trat, Suphan Buri,
       Chiang Mai, Chiang Rai, Sukhothai, Surin, Nong Bua Lam Phu, Roi Et,
       Krabi, and Nakhon Si Thammarat. Within these provinces, probability-based
       sampling was used to select geographical subunits, from each of which 10
       respondents were selected using quota sampling with respect to age and gen-
       der. Of the 1207 respondents included in the final value set, 51.6% were
       female and 48.4% were male. The age distribution of the respondents was:

18–24 years	12.8%
25–29 years	8.0%
30–39 years	21.7%
40–49 years	22.6%
50–64 years	25.4%
65–74 years	8.0%
75+ years	1.4%

(iii) **Representativeness of achieved sample**
       The study sample was representative for the Thai population in terms of age
       (over 18 years), gender, residential area, and number of children (Table 4.30).

Table 4.30 Representativeness of the sample in the Thai valuation study

		Study sample (N=1207)	Thai general population[a]
Sampling characteristics			
Age, n (%)	18–29	251 (20.8%)	20.2%
	30–39	262 (21.7%)	22.7%
	40–49	273 (22.6%)	22.6%
	50–59	208 (17.2%)	16.9%
	≥60	213 (17.7%)	17.6%
Gender, n (%)	Female	623 (51.6%)	50.9%
	Male	584 (48.4%)	49.1%
Residential area, n (%)	Urban	523 (43.3%)	44.2%
	Rural	684 (56.7%)	55.8%
Education, n (%)	Primary school or lower	543 (45.0%)	52.8%
	High school	533 (44.2%)	30.1%
	Bachelor or higher	131 (10.9%)	17.1%
Number of children (mean (SD))		1.7 (1.6)	1.5

Reproduced from Pattanaphesaj et al. (2018)
[a]National Statistics Office 2012 and 2013

(iv)   **Mean observed cTTO values of EQ-5D-5L states** (Table 4.31)

Table 4.31   Mean observed cTTO values by health state

State	Mean	SE	State	Mean	SE	State	Mean	SE
11112	0.932	0.006	21345	0.383	0.037	43315	0.287	0.038
11121	0.931	0.006	21444	0.325	0.040	43514	0.250	0.042
11122	0.899	0.012	22434	0.392	0.036	43542	0.106	0.040
11211	0.923	0.006	23152	0.585	0.026	43555	−0.100	0.048
11212	0.879	0.011	23242	0.566	0.030	44125	0.287	0.036
11221	0.870	0.012	23514	0.405	0.030	44345	−0.071	0.043
11235	0.590	0.029	24342	0.390	0.035	44553	−0.031	0.045
11414	0.590	0.038	24443	0.175	0.042	45133	0.324	0.034
11421	0.770	0.016	24445	0.007	0.045	45144	0.022	0.045
11425	0.600	0.023	24553	0.027	0.045	45233	0.285	0.040
12111	0.936	0.006	25122	0.617	0.028	45413	0.184	0.042
12112	0.876	0.010	25222	0.604	0.035	51152	0.338	0.036
12121	0.854	0.013	25331	0.530	0.035	51451	0.222	0.039
12244	0.491	0.029	31514	0.432	0.038	52215	0.331	0.037
12334	0.548	0.029	31524	0.382	0.035	52335	0.235	0.040
12344	0.442	0.032	31525	0.369	0.038	52431	0.397	0.034
12513	0.580	0.031	32314	0.580	0.032	52455	−0.036	0.047
12514	0.462	0.035	32443	0.364	0.031	53221	0.460	0.035
12543	0.472	0.032	33253	0.299	0.038	53243	0.168	0.042
13122	0.783	0.017	34155	0.043	0.042	53244	0.027	0.045
13224	0.684	0.021	34232	0.560	0.022	53412	0.330	0.037
13313	0.736	0.015	34244	0.168	0.043	54153	0.046	0.044
14113	0.752	0.013	34515	0.130	0.042	54231	0.354	0.040
14554	0.064	0.042	35143	0.319	0.041	54342	0.108	0.041
15151	0.457	0.035	35245	0.000	0.044	55225	−0.035	0.048
21111	0.940	0.005	35311	0.589	0.021	55233	0.201	0.041
21112	0.873	0.012	35332	0.371	0.034	55424	−0.013	0.044
21315	0.593	0.027	42115	0.507	0.031	55555	−0.316	0.014
21334	0.535	0.028	42321	0.612	0.025			

SE standard error

(v)   **Proportions choosing A in the DCE based on relative severities of A and B** (Fig. 4.16)

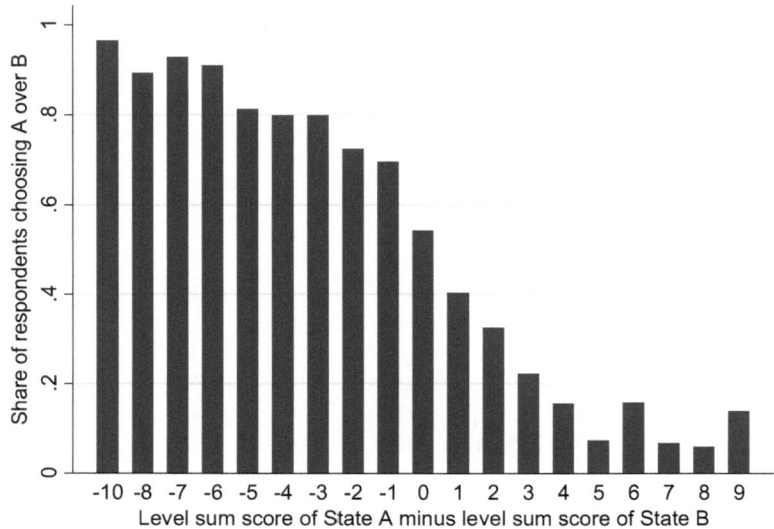

Fig. 4.16 Proportions choosing A based on relative severities of A and B

(vi)   **Exclusion criteria**
       cTTO responses were excluded if (1) a respondent assigned the same value to
       all 10 states valued, (2) a respondent had a positive slope on the regression
       between respondent's cTTO values and level sum score and (3) there were
       severe irrational responses, defined as major inconsistent responses (e.g.
       severe dominance violations). Two respondents were excluded from analysis.
       No DCE data were excluded from the analysis.

(vii) **Number of interviewers; Interviewer effects**
       In total, 1207 interviews were conducted by 6 interviewers. The variance of
       the responses included in the final analysis can be partitioned into variance
       related to differences between interviewers (1.8%), respondents (17.1%) and
       responses (81.1%).

(viii) **Description of modelling choices**
       The Thai EQ-5D-5L value set was based on a hybrid model combining a
       conditional logit model for the DCE data and a censored at −1 Tobit model
       for the cTTO data, correcting for heteroskedasticity. The intercept was con-
       strained in the final model.

(ix)   **Value Set** (Table 4.32 and Fig. 4.17)

Table 4.32 Key characteristics of the Thai value set

Characteristics	Thai EQ-5D-5L value set
% states with negative values	6.0% (188 out of 3125)
Rank order of dimensions (from most to least relative importance)	Mobility Anxiety/depression Pain/discomfort Self-care Usual activities
Coefficient with highest weight	0.371 (level 5 of mobility)
Range of values	Maximum value: 1 Minimum value: −0.421
Max value < 1:	0.944 (value of health state 11121)
Linearity/non-linearity of value decrements by level	Kink at level 3 for all dimensions (see Fig. 4.17). Anxiety/depression receives the largest weight for levels 3 and 4. There is a reverse kink between level 4 and 5 for all dimensions except mobility, causing mobility to receive the largest weight at level 5.

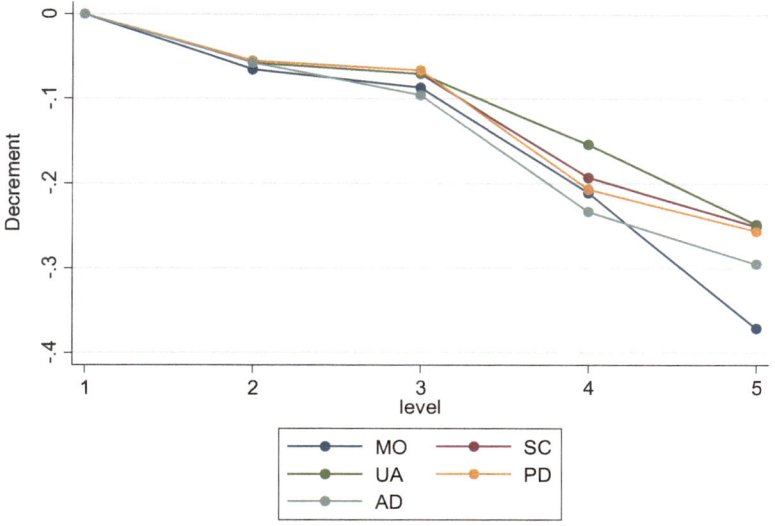

Fig. 4.17 Value decrements across dimensions (*AD* anxiety/depression, *MO* mobility, *PD* pain/discomfort, *SC* self-care, *UA* usual activities)

(x)   **Uptake by local HTA/health care decision makers**

Economic evidence is one type of evidence to be considered during the decision-making process for both pharmaceutical and non-pharmaceutical interventions in Thailand (Leelahavarong et al. 2019). Cost-utility analysis (CUA) using QALYs is required for economic evidence (such as when considering high-cost medicines for public funding). EQ-5D-5L and its value set are recommended in the National Health Technology Assessment (HTA) guideline as a method to estimate health utility and subsequently QALYs. Health Intervention and Technology Assessment Program (HITAP) has been offering an annual economic evaluation training to policymakers and researchers which includes how to interpret and use EQ-5D-5L values in health technology assessment (HTA). Currently, EQ-5D-5L is being widely adopted in health economic evaluations in Thailand.

(xi)   **Reference(s) of value set**

Pattanaphesaj J, Thavorncharoensap M, Ramos-Goñi JM, Tongsiri S, Ingsrisawang L, Teerawattananon Y (2018) The EQ-5D-5L valuation study in Thailand. Expert Rev Pharmacoecon Outcomes Res 18(5): 551–558

Further Literature

Chaikledkaew U, Kittrongsiri K (2014) Guidelines for Health Technology Assessment in Thailand (Second Edition)-The Development Process. J Med Assoc Thai 97: 4–9

Leelahavarong P, Doungthipsirikul S, Kumluang S, Poonchai A, Kittiratchakool N, Chinnacom D, Suchonwanich N, Tantivess S (2019) Health technology assessment in Thailand: institutionalization and contribution to healthcare decision making: review of literature. Int J Tech Assess Health Care 35(6): 467–473

Teerawattananon Y, Luz AC, Culyer A, Chalkidou K (2020) Charging for the use of survey instruments on population health: the case of quality-adjusted life years. Bull World Health Organ 98(1):59–65

National Statistics Office (2012) The 2010 Population and Housing Census. National Statistics Office, Bangkok

National Statistics Office (2013). The Labor Force Survey 2012. National Statistics Office, Bangkok

4.3.2.4   Country/Region: Uruguay (Table 4.33)

Table 4.33 Overview of EQ-5D-5L value set for Uruguay

Uruguayan EQ-5D-5L value set		Example: the value for health state 21232	
Full health (11111)	1	Full health	=1
At least one 2, 3, 4 or 5 (constant)	0.013	Minus constant	−0.013
Mobility = 2	0.014	Minus MO level 2	−0.014
Mobility = 3	0.032		
Mobility = 4	0.108		
Mobility = 5	0.299		
Self-care = 2	0.026	Minus SC level 1	−0.000
Self-care = 3	0.061		
Self-care = 4	0.117		
Self-care = 5	0.273		
Usual activities = 2	0.042	Minus UA level 2	−0.042
Usual activities = 3	0.046		
Usual activities = 4	0.118		
Usual activities = 5	0.232		
Pain/discomfort = 2	0.017		
Pain/discomfort = 3	0.061	Minus PD level 3	−0.061
Pain/discomfort = 4	0.187		
Pain/discomfort = 5	0.271		
Anxiety/depression = 2	0.010	Minus AD level 2	−0.010
Anxiety/depression = 3	0.044		
Anxiety/depression = 4	0.104		
Anxiety/depression = 5	0.177		
		State 21232	=0.860

AD anxiety/depression, *MO* mobility, *PD* pain/discomfort, *SC* self-care, *UA* usual activities

The mathematical representation of the model for health state X is:

$$\begin{aligned} V(X) = 1 &- 0.013 - 0.014\,MO_2 - 0.032\,MO_3 - 0.108\,MO_4 - 0.299\,MO_5 \\ &- 0.026\,SC_2 - 0.061\,SC_3 - 0.117\,SC_4 - 0.273\,SC_5 - 0.042\,UA_2 \\ &- 0.046\,UA_3 - 0.118\,UA_4 - 0.232\,UA_5 - 0.017\,PD_2 - 0.061\,PD_3 \\ &- 0.187\,PD_4 - 0.271\,PD_5 - 0.010\,AD_2 - 0.044\,AD_3 - 0.104\,AD_4 \\ &- 0.177\,AD_5 \end{aligned}$$

(i)   **Date/wave of study**
    Data were collected in the second wave of EQ-5D-5L valuation studies using the EQ-5D-5L valuation protocol 1.1. Interviews were conducted between October 2013 and June 2014.

(ii) **Sample size; sample frame**

805 interviews with the general population were conducted. Respondents were recruited from 3 Uruguayan regions: Montevideo and the departments of Maldonado and Paysandú, using a stratified approach. Respondents were recruited using quotas for location, age, gender and socio-economic status. Of the 794 respondents included in the final value set, 55.3% were female and 44.7% were male. The age distribution of the respondents was:

18–24 years	12.1%
25–29 years	11.7%
30–39 years	24.8%
40–49 years	16.3%
50–64 years	23.6%
65–74 years	9.8%
75+ years	1.8%

(iii) **Representativeness of achieved sample**

The study sample was broadly representative for the Uruguayan population. However, younger and higher educated respondents were slightly over-represented (Table 4.34).

Table 4.34 Representativeness of the sample in the Uruguayan valuation study

		Study sample (N=794)	Uruguayan general population[a]
Sampling characteristics			
Age, n (%)	20–39	386 (48.6%)	42.4%
	40–59	271 (34.1%)	35.2%
	≥60	137 (17.3%)	22.4%
Gender, n (%)	Female	439 (55.3%)	52.0%
	Male	355 (44.7%)	48.0%
Education[b], n (%)	Primary school	137 (17.3%)	36.2%
	Secondary school	406 (51.3%)	44.5%
	Tertiary school	249 (31.4%)	18.5%

Reproduced from Augustovski et al. (2016)
[a]National Institute of Statistics Uruguay 2011
[b]Missing values (N=2)

(iv) **Mean observed cTTO values of EQ-5D-5L states** (Table 4.35)

Table 4.35 Mean observed cTTO values by health state

State	Mean	SE	State	Mean	SE	State	Mean	SE
11112	0.950	0.012	21345	0.416	0.061	43315	0.495	0.059
11121	0.969	0.007	21444	0.274	0.073	43514	0.315	0.070
11122	0.939	0.014	22434	0.592	0.046	43542	0.254	0.069
11211	0.940	0.008	23152	0.450	0.064	43555	0.046	0.069
11212	0.864	0.041	23242	0.555	0.057	44125	0.444	0.062
11221	0.927	0.013	23514	0.489	0.056	44345	0.213	0.069
11235	0.655	0.042	24342	0.514	0.055	44553	−0.055	0.069
11414	0.644	0.045	24443	0.359	0.058	45133	0.346	0.067
11421	0.826	0.023	24445	0.278	0.061	45144	0.346	0.054
11425	0.661	0.041	24553	0.310	0.059	45233	0.252	0.076
12111	0.933	0.011	25122	0.578	0.063	45413	0.375	0.058
12112	0.856	0.032	25222	0.430	0.073	51152	0.363	0.063
12121	0.909	0.019	25331	0.401	0.069	51451	0.255	0.063
12244	0.536	0.062	31514	0.421	0.073	52215	0.321	0.068
12334	0.682	0.042	31524	0.520	0.051	52335	0.255	0.063
12344	0.594	0.053	31525	0.514	0.058	52431	0.435	0.056
12513	0.788	0.030	32314	0.706	0.045	52455	−0.024	0.075
12514	0.596	0.038	32443	0.483	0.052	53221	0.555	0.064
12543	0.415	0.062	33253	0.381	0.065	53243	0.097	0.076
13122	0.843	0.030	34155	0.269	0.065	53244	0.066	0.075
13224	0.709	0.041	34232	0.589	0.046	53412	0.437	0.063
13313	0.791	0.032	34244	0.233	0.070	54153	0.192	0.070
14113	0.755	0.035	34515	0.315	0.055	54231	0.378	0.058
14554	0.316	0.067	35143	0.243	0.075	54342	0.277	0.074
15151	0.402	0.059	35245	0.256	0.060	55225	0.138	0.067
21111	0.952	0.008	35311	0.576	0.047	55233	0.147	0.074
21112	0.943	0.014	35332	0.510	0.056	55424	0.012	0.067
21315	0.673	0.051	42115	0.665	0.039	55555	−0.287	0.022
21334	0.672	0.047	42321	0.653	0.038			

SE standard error

(v)   **Proportions choosing A in the DCE based on relative severities of A and B** (Fig. 4.18)

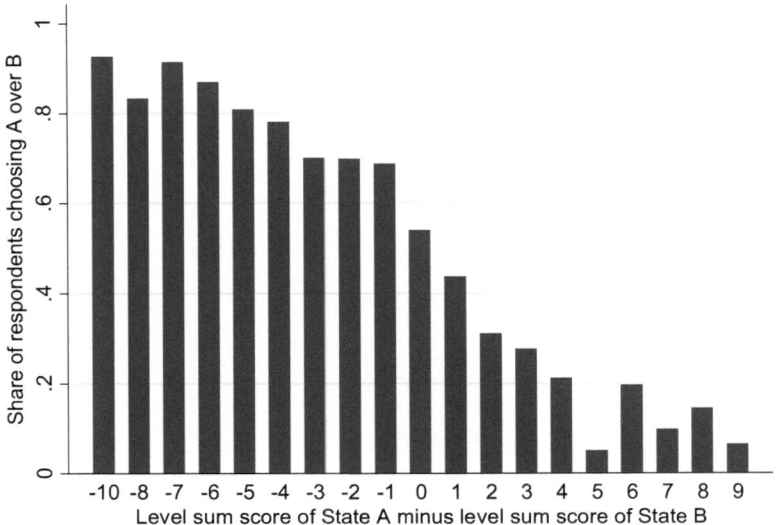

Fig. 4.18 Proportions choosing A based on relative severities of A and B

(vi)   **Exclusion criteria**
       Respondents were excluded (1) if they had a positive slope on the regression
       between respondent's cTTO values and level sum score, or (2) if they assigned
       the same value to all health states (except if all states were assigned the value
       1, i.e., non-traders). 11 respondents were excluded from analysis.

(vii) **Number of interviewers; Interviewer effects**
       In total, 805 interviews were conducted by 11 interviewers. The variance of
       the responses included in the final value set can be partitioned into variance
       related to differences between interviewers (5.5%), respondents (26.9%) and
       responses (67.6%).

(viii) **Description of modelling choices**
       The Uruguayan EQ-5D-5L value set was based on cTTO data only. The
       selected model was based on a robust regression. A tuning variable was used,
       which was set to equal 8.5.

(ix)   **Value Set** (Table 4.36 Fig. 4.19)

Table 4.36   Key characteristics of the Uruguayan value set

Characteristics	Uruguayan EQ-5D-5L value set
% states with negative values	0.90% (28 out of 3125)
Rank order of dimensions (from most to least relative importance)	Pain/discomfort Self-care Mobility Usual activities Anxiety/depression
Coefficient with highest weight	0.299 (level 5 of mobility)
Range of values	Maximum value: 1 Minimum value: −0.265
Max value < 1:	0.977 (value of health state 11112)
Linearity/non-linearity of value decrements by level	Kink at level 3 for all dimensions (see Fig. 4.19). The value decrement is largest for PD. Kink at level 4 for all dimensions except anxiety/depression and pain/discomfort.

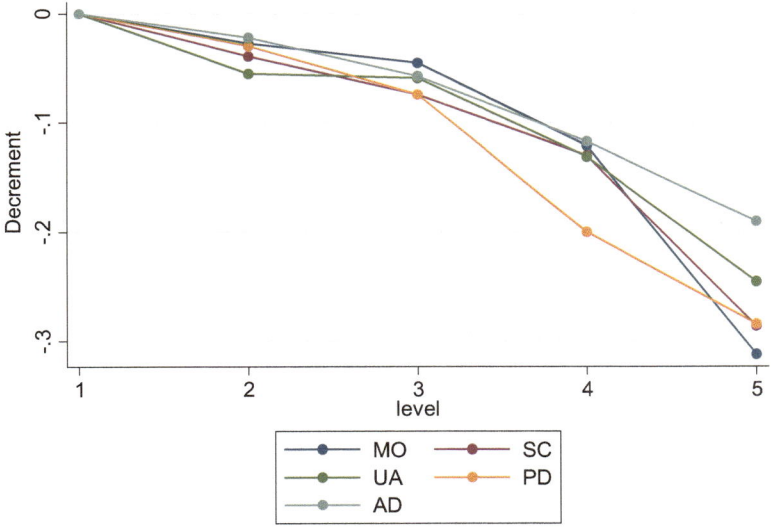

Fig. 4.19 Value decrements across dimensions (*AD* anxiety/depression, *MO* mobility, *PD* pain/discomfort, *SC* self-care, *UA* usual activities)

(x)   **Uptake by local HTA/health care decision makers**
      The Uruguayan EQ-5D-5L value set has been disseminated in scientific
      meetings in Uruguay and Latin America and used in several scientific proj-
      ects. Research is currently ongoing to collect population health data using
      EQ-5D-5L in relevant health conditions, in order to use the Uruguayan
      weights. There are two HTA bodies in Uruguay; División de Evaluación
      Sanitaria/Ministerio de Salud Publica and Fondo Nacional de Recursos
      (FNR). Neither of these HTA bodies currently makes a specific recommenda-
      tion to use the Uruguayan EQ-5D-5L value set in economic evaluations.

(xi) **Reference(s) of value set**
      Augustovski F, Rey-Ares L, Irazola V, Garay OU, Gianneo O, Fernández G,
         Morales M, Gibbons L, Ramos-Goñi JM (2016) An EQ-5D-5L value set
         based on Uruguayan population preferences. Qual Life Res 25(2):323–333

Further Literature

National Institute of Statistics Uruguay (Instituto Nacional de Estadística) (2011)
   Census http://www.ine.gub.uy/censos2011/index.html. Accessed 18 July 2021

4.3.2.5 Country/Region: Hong Kong (Table 4.37)

Table 4.37 Overview of EQ-5D-5L value set for Hong Kong

Hong Kong EQ-5D-5L value set		Example: the value for health state 21232	
Full health (11111)	1	Full health	=1
Mobility = 2	0.109	Minus MO level 2	−0.109
Mobility = 3	0.182		
Mobility = 4	0.371		
Mobility = 5	0.529		
Self-care = 2	0.087	Minus SC level 1	−0.000
Self-care = 3	0.113		
Self-care = 4	0.271		
Self-care = 5	0.352		
Usual activities = 2	0.067	Minus UA level 2	−0.067
Usual activities = 3	0.094		
Usual activities = 4	0.234		
Usual activities = 5	0.282		
Pain/discomfort = 2	0.076		
Pain/discomfort = 3	0.147	Minus PD level 3	−0.147
Pain/discomfort = 4	0.307		
Pain/discomfort = 5	0.354		
Anxiety/depression = 2	0.080	Minus AD level 2	−0.080
Anxiety/depression = 3	0.140		
Anxiety/depression = 4	0.293		
Anxiety/depression = 5	0.348		
		State 21232	=0.597

AD anxiety/depression, *MO* mobility, *PD* pain/discomfort, *SC* self-care, *UA* usual activities

The mathematical representation of the model for health state X is:

$$V(X) = 1 - 0.109\,MO_2 - 0.182\,MO_3 - 0.371\,MO_4 - 0.529\,MO_5 - 0.087\,SC_2$$
$$- 0.113\,SC_3 - 0.271\,SC_4 - 0.352\,SC_5 - 0.067\,UA_2 - 0.094\,UA_3$$
$$- 0.234\,UA_4 - 0.282\,UA_5 - 0.076\,PD_2 - 0.147\,PD_3 - 0.307\,PD_4$$
$$- 0.354\,PD_5 - 0.080\,AD_2 - 0.140\,AD_3 - 0.293\,AD_4 - 0.348\,AD_5$$

(i)   **Date/wave of study**
Data were collected in the second wave of EQ-5D-5L valuation studies using the EQ-5D-5L valuation protocol 1.1. Interviews were conducted between June 2014 and October 2015.

(ii)   **Sample size; sample frame**
A total of 1014 Hong Kong residents aged 18 and above participated in this study. Stratified quota sampling was applied based on age, sex and educa-

tional attainment over three geographical areas of Hong Kong: Hong Kong Island, Kowloon, and New Territories. Of the 999 respondents included in the final value set, 59.2% were female, and 40.8% were male. Furthermore, 29.8% of the respondents had at least 1 chronic health condition. The age distribution of the respondents was:

18–24 years	16.52%
25–29 years	8.71%
30–39 years	17.62%
40–49 years	12.61%
50–64 years	29.43%
65–74 years	10.01%
75+ years	5.11%

(iii) **Representativeness of achieved sample**

The study sample was representative for the Hong Kong general population in terms of age, sex and highest education attainment. The distribution of the study sample in terms of marital status, employment status, and area of residence approximated that of the general population (Table 4.38).

Table 4.38 Representativeness of the sample in the Hong Kong valuation study

		Study sample (N=1014)	Hong Kong general population[a]
Sampling characteristics			
Age, n (%)	18–24	166 (16.4%)	12.1%
	25–34	173 (17.1%)	16.7%
	35–44	173 (17.1%)	17.5%
	45–54	119 (11.7%)	18.6%
	55–64	223 (22.0%)	17.2%
	≥ 65	160 (15.8%)	17.9%
Gender, n (%)	Female	600 (59.2%)	55.0%
	Male	414 (40.8%)	45.0%
Highest level of education, n (%)	Primary and below	201 (19.8%)	20.0%
	Secondary/sub degree	615 (60.7%)	57.8%
	Post-secondary/degree	198 (19.5%)	22.2%
Marital status, n (%)	Single	322 (31.8%)	30.1%
	Married	583 (57.5%)	58.4%
	Divorced/separated	52 (5.1%)	5.1%
	Widow	57 (5.6%)	6.4%
Employment status, n (%)	Full time student	109 (10.7%)	16.9%
	Retired/homemaker/unemployed	470 (46.3%)	31.8%
	Employed	435 (42.9%)	51.3%

Reproduced from Wong et al. (2018)
[a]Census and Statistics Department. (2012)

(iv)   **Mean observed cTTO values of EQ-5D-5L states** (Table 4.39)

Table 4.39   Mean observed cTTO values by health state

State	Mean	SE	State	Mean	SE	State	Mean	SE
11112	0.908	0.014	21345	0.194	0.072	43315	0.159	0.062
11121	0.934	0.009	21444	0.090	0.068	43514	0.036	0.079
11122	0.870	0.024	22434	0.074	0.074	43542	−0.078	0.071
11211	0.909	0.012	23152	0.343	0.070	43555	−0.098	0.066
11212	0.885	0.020	23242	0.263	0.062	44125	0.111	0.065
11221	0.880	0.018	23514	0.220	0.065	44345	−0.106	0.066
11235	0.388	0.059	24342	0.161	0.065	44553	−0.221	0.076
11414	0.531	0.045	24443	0.010	0.064	45133	0.040	0.074
11421	0.670	0.037	24445	−0.011	0.068	45144	−0.207	0.070
11425	0.245	0.068	24553	−0.098	0.069	45233	−0.001	0.067
12111	0.900	0.014	25122	0.398	0.061	45413	−0.080	0.070
12112	0.861	0.024	25222	0.469	0.064	51152	0.034	0.076
12121	0.843	0.026	25331	0.325	0.063	51451	−0.089	0.072
12244	0.175	0.062	31514	0.348	0.059	52215	0.140	0.069
12334	0.410	0.049	31524	0.206	0.062	52335	−0.063	0.073
12344	0.232	0.062	31525	0.183	0.063	52431	0.131	0.063
12513	0.499	0.054	32314	0.403	0.051	52455	−0.262	0.064
12514	0.259	0.066	32443	0.135	0.068	53221	0.268	0.067
12543	0.183	0.068	33253	0.107	0.065	53243	0.012	0.063
13122	0.690	0.044	34155	−0.099	0.070	53244	−0.122	0.063
13224	0.451	0.063	34232	0.388	0.058	53412	0.037	0.071
13313	0.620	0.038	34244	−0.002	0.081	54153	−0.103	0.066
14113	0.548	0.046	34515	−0.075	0.074	54231	0.126	0.067
14554	−0.024	0.064	35143	0.101	0.062	54342	−0.098	0.064
15151	0.235	0.067	35245	−0.143	0.068	55225	−0.265	0.067
21111	0.908	0.014	35311	0.363	0.065	55233	−0.073	0.065
21112	0.841	0.030	35332	0.121	0.072	55424	−0.226	0.076
21315	0.428	0.057	42115	0.160	0.073	55555	−0.448	0.019
21334	0.413	0.054	42321	0.434	0.052			

SE standard error

(v)   **Proportions choosing A in the DCE based on relative severities of A and
        B** (Fig. 4.20)

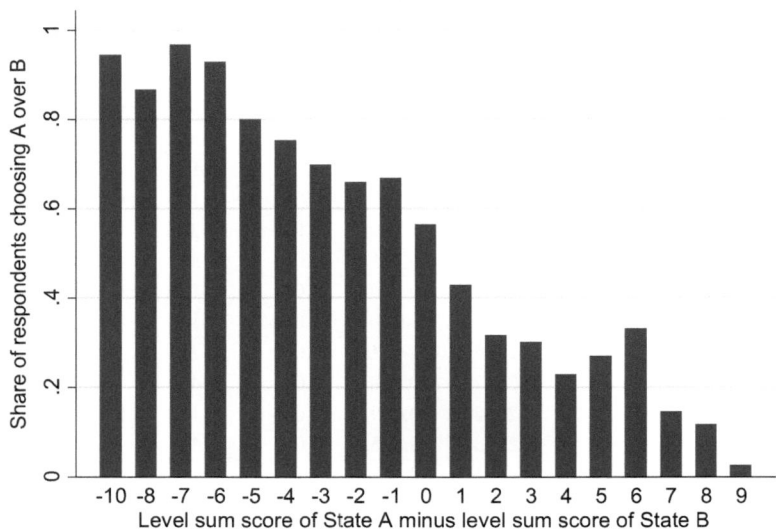

Fig. 4.20 Proportions choosing A based on relative severities of A and B

(vi)   **Exclusion criteria**
        Three respondents with a positive slope on a regression between their cTTO
        values and the severity of the states were excluded from analysis. In addition,
        one respondent who valued all states at zero and 11 respondents who valued
        all states as −1 were removed from analysis. All DCE data were included in
        the analysis. A further 515 out of 9990 (5.16%) cTTO responses were
        removed following issues flagged in the feedback module.

(vii) **Number of interviewers; Interviewer effects**
        In total, 1014 interviews were conducted by 6 interviewers. The variance of
        the responses included in the final value set can be partitioned into variance
        related to differences between interviewers (2.2%), respondents (33.1%), and
        responses (64.7%).

(viii) **Description of modelling choices**
        The Hong Kong EQ-5D-5L value set was based on a hybrid model combin-
        ing a conditional logit model for the DCE data and a censored at −1 Tobit
        model for the cTTO data. The intercept was constrained in the final model as
        it was not statistically significant.

(ix)   **Value Set** (Table 4.40 and Fig. 4.21)

Table 4.40   Key characteristics of the Hong Kong value set

Characteristics	Hong Kong EQ-5D-5L value set
% states with negative values	35.65% (1114 out of 3125)
Rank order of dimensions (from most to least relative importance)	Mobility Pain/discomfort Anxiety/depression Self care Usual activities
Coefficient with highest weight	0.529 (level 5 of mobility)
Range of values	Maximum value: 1 Minimum value: −0.864
Max value < 1:	0.933 (value of health state 11211)
Linearity/non-linearity of value decrements by level	Kink at level 3 for all dimensions. The largest change in value occurs between levels 3 and 4 on all dimensions. Reverse kink at level 4 for all dimensions except mobility. At all levels of problems, mobility has the largest value decrement of all five dimensions.

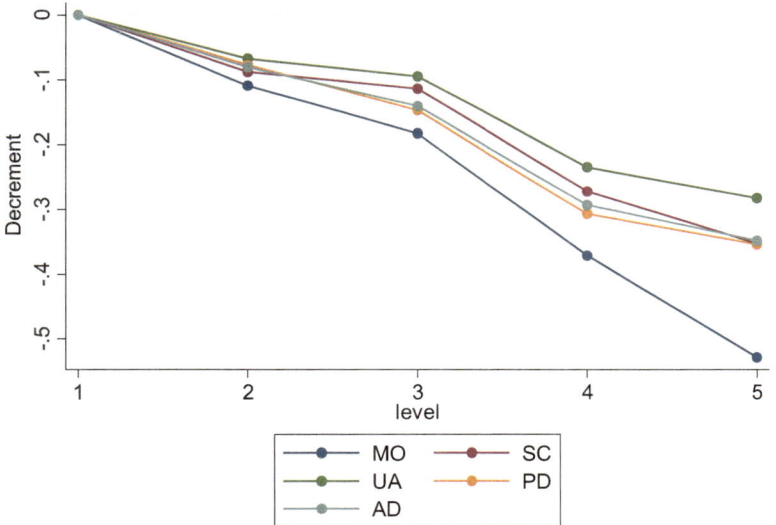

Fig. 4.21 Value decrements across dimensions (*MO* mobility, *SC* self-care, *UA* usual activities, *PD* pain/discomfort, *AD* anxiety/depression)

(x)   **Uptake by local HTA/health care decision makers**

The EQ-5D-5L has been adopted in healthcare management for individual patients, education in healthcare delivery and health policy to promote patient-centred care in hospital settings in Hong Kong. The association between health-related quality of life and shared decision-making among patients was explored using the EQ-5D-5L in enhancing health professional-patient communications. The tool was incorporated into the local validated patient-reported experience measures (PREMs) among patients as a measure of health outcomes together with patient experience in different healthcare settings including inpatient, specialist outpatient, and accident and emergency department under the Hospital Authority (HA) in Hong Kong. It was also applied in health-related population surveys and routine measurement among patients with chronic conditions such as musculoskeletal problems, diabetes mellitus and elderly with hypertension in both clinical and non-clinical settings.

(xi) **Reference(s) for this value set**

Wong EL, Ramos-Goni JM, Cheung AW, Wong AY, Rivero-Arias O (2018) Assessing the **use of a feedback module to model EQ-5D-5L health states values in Hong Kong.** Patient 11(2):235–247

Further Literature

Coulter A, Cheung AWL, Yam CHK, Yeoh EK, Griffiths S (2013) Validation of inpatient experience questionnaire. Int J Qual Health Care 25(4):443–451.

Lam CLK, Chao DVK, Cheung JPY, Fong D, Kind P, Ko WWK, Or CKL, Wong CKH, Wong ELY (2020) Effectiveness of routine measurement of health-related quality of life in improving the outcomes of patients with Musculoskeletal problems – A randomized controlled trial. 2019/2020 Research Grants Council Funded Study

Wong ELY, Xu RH, Cheung AWL (2020) Health-related quality of life in elderly people with hypertension and the estimation of minimally important difference using EQ-5D-5L in Hong Kong SAR, China. Eur J Health Econ 21(6):869–879

Wong ELY, Xu RH, Cheung AWL (2020) Measurement of health-related quality of life in patients with diabetes mellitus using EQ-5D-5L in Hong Kong, China. Qual Life Res 29(7):1913–921.

Wong ELY, Ho KF, Wong SYS, Cheung AWL, Yau PSY, Dong D, Yeoh EK (2020) Views on workplace policies and its impact on health-related quality of life during Coronavirus Disease (COVID-19) pandemic: Cross-sectional survey of employees. Int J Health Policy Manag. https://doi.org/10.34172/ijhpm.2020.127

Wong ELY, Xu RH, Cheung AWL. (2019) Health-related quality of life among patients with hypertension: population-based survey using EQ-5D-5L in Hong Kong SAR, China. BMJ Open 9(9):e032544. https://doi.org/10.1136/bmjopen-2019-032544

Wong ELY, Cheung AWL, Xu RH, Yam CHK, Lui SF, Yeoh EK (2019) Development and validation of a generic patient experience instrument for measuring specialist outpatient service in Hong Kong. Int J Qual Health Care 31(10):G158-G164

Wong ELY, Cheung AWL, Wong AYK, Xu RH, Ramos-Goni JM, Rivero-Arias O (2019) Normative profile of health-related quality of life for Hong Kong general population using preference-based instrument EQ-5D-5L. Value Health 22(8):916–924

Wong ELY, Shah K, Cheung AWL, Wong AYK, Visser M, Stolk E (2018) Evaluation of split version and feedback module on the improvement of Time Trade-Off Data. Value Health 21(6):732–741

Wong ELY, Coulter A, Hewitson P, Cheung AWL, Yam CHK, Lui SF, Tam WWS, Yeoh EK (2015) Patient experience and satisfaction with inpatient service: Development of short form survey instrument measuring the core aspect of inpatient experience. PLoS One 10(4):e0122299.https://doi.org/10.1371/journal.pone.0122299

Wong ELY, Xu RH, Cheung AWL, Wong ELY (2017) The relationship between shared decision-making and health-related quality of life among patients in Hong Kong SAR, China. Int J Qual Health Care. 29(4), 534–540. 11.

Census and Statistics Department (2012) 2011 Population census main report: Volume I. Census and Statistics Department, Hong Kong. http://www.statistics.gov.hk/pub/B11200592012XXXXB0100.pdf. Accessed 28 July 2021

4.3.3   Wave 3

4.3.3.1   Country/Region: France (Table 4.41)

Table 4.41 Overview of EQ-5D-5L value set for France

French EQ-5D-5L value set[a]		Example: the value for health state 21232	
Full health (11111)	1	Full health	=1
Mobility = 2	0.038	Minus MO level 2	−0.038
Mobility = 3	0.048		
Mobility = 4	0.179		
Mobility = 5	0.325		
Self-care = 2	0.037	Minus SC level 1	−0.000
Self-care = 3	0.051		
Self-care = 4	0.172		
Self-care = 5	0.258		
Usual activities = 2	0.033	Minus UA level 2	−0.033
Usual activities = 3	0.040		
Usual activities = 4	0.157		
Usual activities = 5	0.240		
Pain/discomfort = 2	0.022		
Pain/discomfort = 3	0.047	Minus PD level 3	−0.047
Pain/discomfort = 4	0.264		
Pain/discomfort = 5	0.444		
Anxiety/depression = 2	0.020	Minus AD level 2	−0.020
Anxiety/depression = 3	0.047		
Anxiety/depression = 4	0.200		
Anxiety/depression = 5	0.258		
		State 21232	=0.862

AD anxiety/depression, *MO* mobility, *PD* pain/discomfort, *SC* self-care, *UA* usual activities
[a]The preferred model is the adjusted hybrid model – these values are taken from Andrade et al. 2020, Table 3 ('weighted model') and rounded to 3 decimal places

The mathematical representation of the model for health state X is:

$$V(X) = 1 - 0.038\,MO_2 - 0.048\,MO_3 - 0.179\,MO_4 - 0.325\,MO_5 - 0.037$$
$$SC_2 - 0.051\,SC_3 - 0.172\,SC_4 - 0.258\,SC_5 - 0.033\,UA_2 - 0.040\,UA_3 - 0.157$$
$$UA_4 - 0.240\,UA_5 - 0.022\,PD_2 - 0.047\,PD_3 - 0.264\,PD_4 - 0.444\,PD_5 - 0.020$$
$$AD_2 - 0.047\,AD_3 - 0.200\,AD_4 - 0.258\,AD_5$$

(i)   **Date/wave of study**
Data were collected in the third wave of EQ-5D-5L valuation studies using the EQ-5D-5L valuation protocol 2.0. Interviews were conducted from March until November 2018.

(ii) **Sample size; sample frame**
1143 interviews with the general population were conducted. Quota-based sampling with respect to age, sex, and socioeconomic status was applied (National Institute for Statistics and Economic Studies [INSEE] 2018). Interviewers were selected to provide reasonable coverage of the territory and population size of the respondents' residence. Of the 1048 respondents included in the final value set, 55.4% were female and 44.6% were male. The age distribution of the respondents was:

18–24 years	9.6%
25–29 years	9.6%
30–39 years	15.4%
40–49 years	15.6%
50–64 years	26.0%
65–74 years	14.5%
75+ years	9.4%

(iii) **Representativeness of achieved sample**
The study sample was broadly representative for the French population aged over 18. However, the composition of the final sample used in modelling (following exclusions – see (vi) below) differed from the French general population in terms of age and gender. An overrepresentation of female respondents was observed. Respondents aged 25–34 years were overrepresented for both sexes. Moreover, women aged 75 and older were underrepresented in the sample, whereas woman in the age group 55–64 years were overrepresented (Table 4.42).

Table 4.42 Representativeness of the sample in the French valuation study

		Study sample (N=1048)		French general population[a]	
Sampling characteristics		Male	Female	Male	Female
Age, n (%)	18–24	9.6%	9.6%	10.9%	9.6%
	25–34	18.6%	15.9%	15.6%	14.7%
	35–44	14.5%	14.4%	16.7%	15.6%
	45–54	16.7%	16.1%	17.9%	16.7%
	55–64	17.7%	19.1%	16.1%	15.8%
	65–74	13.4%	15.9%	13.2%	13.7%
	≥ 75	9.5%	9.2%	9.6%	13.9%
Gender, n (%)	Female	55.4%		52.3%	
	Male	44.6%		47.7%	

[a]National Institute for Statistics and Economic Studies (INSEE) 2018

(iv)   **Mean observed cTTO values of EQ-5D-5L states** (Table 4.43)

Table 4.43   Mean observed cTTO values by health state

State	Mean	SE	State	Mean	SE	State	Mean	SE
11112	0.973	0.007	21345	0.402	0.043	43315	0.476	0.049
11121	0.985	0.002	21444	0.398	0.051	43514	0.358	0.047
11122	0.953	0.011	22434	0.620	0.028	43542	0.280	0.050
11211	0.980	0.003	23152	0.360	0.051	43555	−0.162	0.051
11212	0.954	0.008	23242	0.542	0.043	44125	0.355	0.049
11221	0.942	0.013	23514	0.522	0.041	44345	0.053	0.053
11235	0.665	0.041	24342	0.422	0.045	44553	−0.104	0.051
11414	0.651	0.033	24443	0.299	0.047	45133	0.452	0.051
11421	0.807	0.020	24445	0.076	0.054	45144	0.172	0.050
11425	0.595	0.043	24553	0.067	0.055	45233	0.482	0.039
12111	0.959	0.010	25122	0.739	0.024	45413	0.385	0.046
12112	0.945	0.009	25222	0.726	0.035	51152	0.150	0.058
12121	0.959	0.009	25331	0.684	0.040	51451	0.155	0.057
12244	0.420	0.046	31514	0.592	0.041	52215	0.332	0.055
12334	0.616	0.041	31524	0.517	0.043	52335	0.308	0.050
12344	0.413	0.046	31525	0.438	0.046	52431	0.498	0.051
12513	0.665	0.037	32314	0.636	0.040	52455	−0.121	0.054
12514	0.554	0.043	32443	0.482	0.044	53221	0.610	0.044
12543	0.449	0.044	33253	0.281	0.054	53243	0.415	0.046
13122	0.912	0.012	34155	0.131	0.054	53244	0.243	0.055
13224	0.690	0.033	34232	0.682	0.033	53412	0.375	0.059
13313	0.888	0.014	34244	0.283	0.046	54153	0.039	0.058
14113	0.795	0.026	34515	0.269	0.055	54231	0.446	0.055
14554	−0.011	0.056	35143	0.496	0.043	54342	0.227	0.051
15151	0.225	0.058	35245	0.216	0.049	55225	−0.006	0.057
21111	0.973	0.006	35311	0.650	0.045	55233	0.302	0.051
21112	0.943	0.012	35332	0.650	0.034	55424	−0.116	0.049
21315	0.682	0.038	42115	0.554	0.045	55555	−0.510	0.013
21334	0.626	0.039	42321	0.725	0.027			

SE standard error

(v)   **Proportions choosing A in the DCE based on relative severities of A and B** (Fig. 4.22)

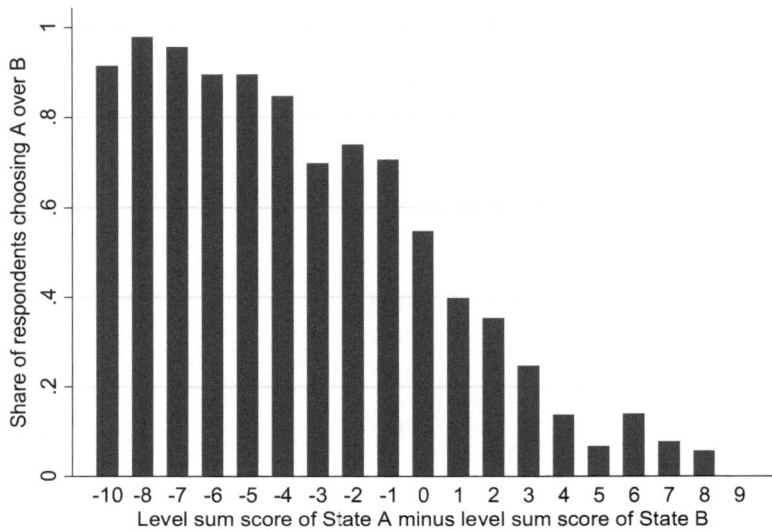

Fig. 4.22 Proportions choosing A based on relative severities of A and B

(vi)   **Exclusion criteria**
95 interviews were excluded from data analysis due to poor data quality. Interviews were excluded if the interviewer did not show the WTD task in the wheelchair example or if the respondent gave state 55555 a value that was higher than the value given to the mildest health state presented in the cTTO tasks. Moreover, a total of 6.5% of cTTO responses (n = 677) were removed following the feedback module. No DCE data were excluded from the analysis.

(vii) **Number of interviewers; Interviewer effects**
In total, 1143 interviews were conducted by 11 interviewers. The variance of the responses included in the final value set can be partitioned into variance related to differences between interviewers (3.3%), respondents (11.1%), and responses (85.6%).

(viii) **Description of modelling choices**
The French EQ-5D-5L value set was based on a hybrid model combining a conditional logit model for the DCE data and a censored at -1 tobit model for the cTTO data, correcting for heteroskedasticity. The model was additionally adjusted to correct for imbalance in the sample in terms of age and gender distribution compared to the general population in France. The intercept was constrained in the final model because it was marginal and non-significant.

(ix)   **Value Set** (Table 4.44 and Fig. 4.23)

Table 4.44   Key characteristics of the French value set

Characteristics	French EQ-5D-5L value set
% states with negative values	20.2% (631 out of 3125)
Rank order of dimensions (from most to least relative importance)	Pain/discomfort Mobility Anxiety/depression Self-care Usual activities
Coefficient with highest weight	0.444 (level 5 of pain/discomfort)
Range of values	Maximum value: 1 Minimum value: −0.525
Max value < 1:	0.980 (value of health state 11112)
Linearity/non-linearity of value decrements by level	Kink at level 3 for all dimensions (see Fig. 4.23). Value decrements for all dimensions were very similar to each other for levels 2 and 3. The decrements in value for problems with self-care, usual activities and anxiety/depression were similar to each other for all levels, whereas the value of mobility level 5 was higher. The value decrements of pain/discomfort were much higher in levels 4 and 5 than all other dimensions.

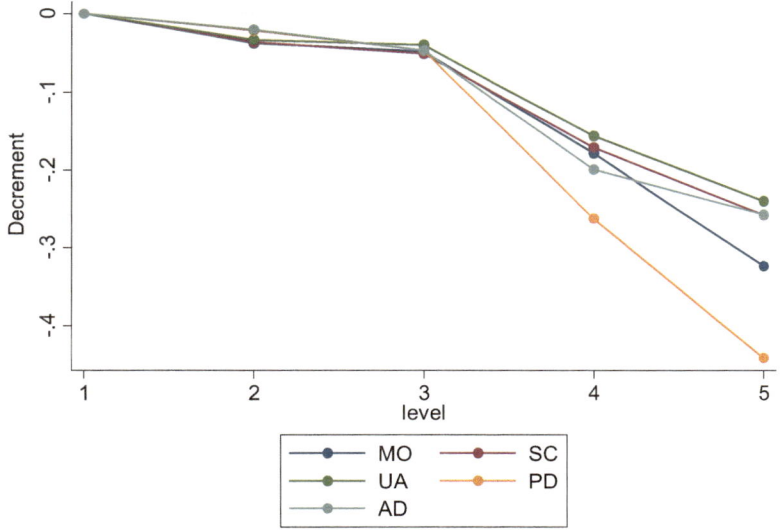

Fig. 4.23   Value decrements across dimensions (*AD* anxiety/depression, *MO* mobility, *PD* pain/discomfort, *SC* self-care, *UA* usual activities)

(x)   **Uptake by local HTA/health care decision makers**
       The French National Authority for Health (Haute Autorité de Santé [HAS]) rec-
       ommends in its updated official methodological guide for economic evaluation
       that the EQ-5D-5L questionnaire and the French EQ-5D-5L value set should be
       the preferred measure used to derive utility values for use in HTA (HAS 2020).

(xi)   **Reference(s) for this value set**
       Andrade LF, Ludwig K, Ramos-Goñi JM, Oppe M, de Pouvourville G (2020)
           A French Value Set for the EQ-5D-5L. Pharmacoeconomics 38(4):413–425

Further Literature

National Institute for Statistics and Economic Studies (INSSE) (2018) Total popula-
    tion age and sex, January 1st, 2018. https://www.insee.fr/fr/statistiques/1892086
    ?sommaire=1912926. Accessed 1 Jan 2018
Haute Autorité de Santé (HAS) (2020) The Choix méthodologiques pour l'évaluation
    économique à la HAS guideline. https://www.has-sante.fr/upload/docs/applica-
    tion/pdf/2020-07/guide_methodologique_evaluation_economique_has_2020_
    vf.pdf. Accessed 25 June 2021

4.3.3.2 Country/Region: Germany (Table 4.45)

Table 4.45 Overview of EQ-5D-5L value set for Germany

German EQ-5D-5L value set		Example: the value for health state 21232	
Full health (11111)	1	Full health	=1
Mobility = 2	0.026	Minus MO level 2	−0.026
Mobility = 3	0.042		
Mobility = 4	0.139		
Mobility = 5	0.224		
Self-care = 2	0.050	Minus SC level 1	−0.000
Self-care = 3	0.056		
Self-care = 4	0.169		
Self-care = 5	0.260		
Usual activities = 2	0.036	Minus UA level 2	−0.036
Usual activities = 3	0.049		
Usual activities = 4	0.129		
Usual activities = 5	0.209		
Pain/discomfort = 2	0.057		
Pain/discomfort = 3	0.109	Minus PD level 3	−0.109
Pain/discomfort = 4	0.404		
Pain/discomfort = 5	0.612		
Anxiety/depression = 2	0.030	Minus AD level 2	−0.030
Anxiety/depression = 3	0.082		
Anxiety/depression = 4	0.244		
Anxiety/depression = 5	0.356		
		State 21232	=0.799

AD anxiety/depression, *MO* mobility, *PD* pain/discomfort, *SC* self-care, *UA* usual activities

The mathematical representation of the model for health state X is:

$$V(X) = 1 - 0.026\,MO_2 - 0.042\,MO_3 - 0.139\,MO_4 - 0.224\,MO_5 - 0.050$$
$$SC_2 - 0.056\,SC_3 - 0.169\,SC_4 - 0.260\,SC_5 - 0.036\,UA_2 - 0.049\,UA_3 - 0.129$$
$$UA_4 - 0.209\,UA_5 - 0.057\,PD_2 - 0.109\,PD_3 - 0.404\,PD_4 - 0.612\,PD_5 - 0.030$$
$$AD_2 - 0.082\,AD_3 - 0.244\,AD_4 - 0.356\,AD_5$$

(i) **Date/wave of study**
   Data were collected in the third wave of EQ-5D-5L valuation studies using the EQ-5D-5L valuation protocol 2.0. Interviews were conducted between December 2014 and March 2015.

(ii) **Sample size; sample frame**

1158 interviews with the general population were conducted in six cities and surrounds located in different parts of Germany: Berlin, Leipzig, Hamburg, Bielefeld, Munich, and Frankfurt. Quota-based sampling with respect to age, sex, educational level, and employment status was applied (Federal Statistical Office 2015). Of the 1158 respondents included in the final value set, 53.4% were female and 46.6% were male. The age distribution of the respondents was:

18–24 years	8.1%
25–29 years	6.3%
30–39 years	13.4%
40–49 years	19.5%
50–64 years	27.6%
65–74 years	14.2%
75+ years	10.9%

(iii) **Representativeness of achieved sample**

The study sample was representative for the German population in terms of age, sex, education, and employment status (Table 4.46).

Table 4.46 Representativeness of the sample in the German valuation study

		Study sample (N=1158)	German general population[a]
Sampling characteristics			
Age, n (%)	18–24	94 (8.1%)	9.3%
	25–29	73 (6.3%)	7.3%
	30–39	155 (13.4%)	14.2%
	40–49	226 (19.5%)	19.2%
	50–64	320 (27.6%)	24.9%
	65–74	164 (14.2%)	13.4%
	≥ 75	126 (10.9%)	11.7%
Gender, n (%)	Female	618 (53.4%)	51.6%
	Male	540 (46.6%)	48.4%
Education, n (%)	Still in education	5 (0.4%)	1.2%
	Lower education	410 (35.4%)	40.7%
	Middle education	396 (34.2%)	29.8%
	Higher education	347 (30%)	28.3%
Employment status, n (%)	Employed	608 (52.5%)	49.9%
	Non-employed	550 (47.5%)	50.1%

Reproduced from Ludwig et al. (2018)

[a]Federal Statistical Office 2015

(iv)   **Mean observed cTTO values of EQ-5D-5L states** (Table 4.47)

Table 4.47 Mean observed cTTO values by health state

State	Mean	SE	State	Mean	SE	State	Mean	SE
11112	0.957	0.008	21345	0.206	0.048	43315	0.379	0.055
11121	0.951	0.008	21444	0.180	0.049	43514	0.392	0.047
11122	0.939	0.011	22434	0.520	0.034	43542	0.204	0.053
11211	0.949	0.008	23152	0.245	0.048	43555	−0.133	0.053
11212	0.929	0.018	23242	0.435	0.040	44125	0.217	0.051
11221	0.913	0.013	23514	0.463	0.050	44345	−0.184	0.056
11235	0.519	0.035	24342	0.345	0.045	44553	−0.130	0.052
11414	0.596	0.037	24443	0.109	0.058	45133	0.444	0.041
11421	0.758	0.029	24445	−0.038	0.052	45144	0.064	0.053
11425	0.511	0.038	24553	0.055	0.052	45233	0.335	0.052
12111	0.952	0.005	25122	0.595	0.046	45413	0.437	0.046
12112	0.934	0.008	25222	0.627	0.038	51152	0.213	0.049
12121	0.880	0.019	25331	0.548	0.040	51451	0.127	0.052
12244	0.201	0.048	31514	0.531	0.040	52215	0.406	0.056
12334	0.593	0.032	31524	0.452	0.047	52335	0.307	0.047
12344	0.185	0.053	31525	0.309	0.049	52431	0.523	0.045
12513	0.674	0.028	32314	0.647	0.029	52455	−0.176	0.052
12514	0.458	0.046	32443	0.292	0.052	53221	0.589	0.042
12543	0.288	0.049	33253	0.240	0.046	53243	0.192	0.050
13122	0.876	0.014	34155	−0.007	0.062	53244	0.043	0.052
13224	0.643	0.033	34232	0.677	0.026	53412	0.604	0.032
13313	0.797	0.022	34244	0.196	0.049	54153	−0.033	0.057
14113	0.762	0.030	34515	0.235	0.055	54231	0.501	0.041
14554	−0.197	0.055	35143	0.211	0.049	54342	0.080	0.054
15151	0.128	0.057	35245	0.008	0.055	55225	0.246	0.053
21111	0.973	0.005	35311	0.708	0.026	55233	0.256	0.053
21112	0.929	0.013	35332	0.512	0.044	55424	0.162	0.049
21315	0.477	0.051	42115	0.442	0.044	55555	−0.462	0.016
21334	0.577	0.035	42321	0.764	0.028			

SE standard error

(v) **Proportions choosing A in the DCE based on relative severities of A and B** (Fig. 4.24)

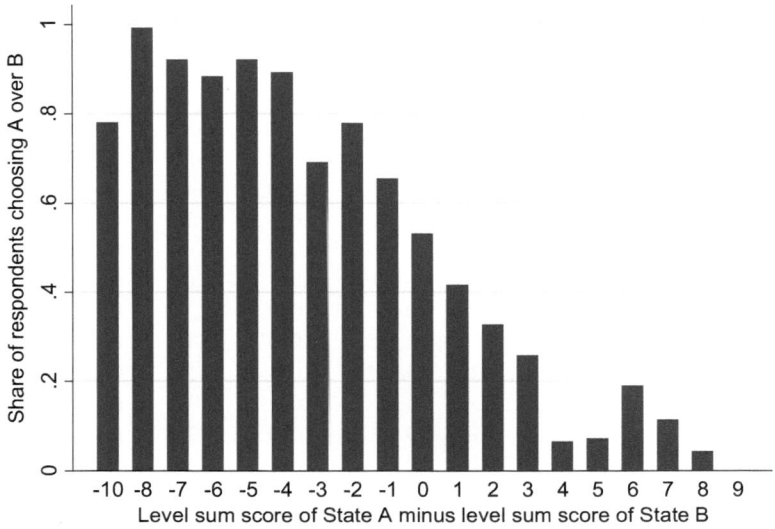

Fig. 4.24 Proportions choosing A based on relative severities of A and B

(vi) **Exclusion criteria**
A total of 6.2% of cTTO responses (n = 713) were removed following the feedback module; but no respondent's entire cTTO responses were excluded. No DCE data were excluded from the analysis.

(vii) **Number of interviewers; Interviewer effects**
In total, 1158 interviews were conducted by 19 interviewers. The variance of the responses can be partitioned into variance related to differences between interviewers (2.7%), respondents (16.0%), and responses (81.3%).

(viii) **Description of modelling choices**
The German EQ-5D-5L value set was based on a hybrid model combining a conditional logit model for the DCE data and a censored at −1 tobit model for the cTTO data, correcting for heteroskedasticity. The intercept was constrained in the final model because it was marginal and non-significant.

(ix)   **Value Set** (Table 4.48 and Fig. 4.25)

Table 4.48   Key characteristics of the German value set

Characteristics	German EQ-5D-5L value set
% states with negative values	15.1% (471 out of 3125)
Rank order of dimensions (from most to least relative importance)	Pain/discomfort Anxiety/depression Self-care Mobility Usual activities
Coefficient with highest weight	0.612 (level 5 of pain/discomfort)
Range of values	Maximum value: 1 Minimum value: −0.661
Max value < 1:	0.974 (value of health state 21111)
Linearity/non-linearity of value decrements by level	Kink at level 3 for all dimensions (see Fig. 4.25). Value decrements of the functional dimensions (mobility, self-care, and usual activities) were similar to each other over all levels. The value decrements for pain/discomfort and anxiety/depression were higher, especially for levels 4 and 5.

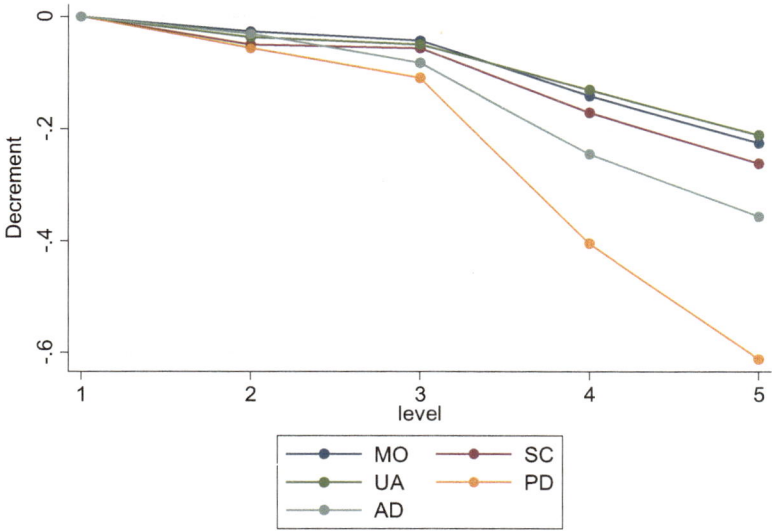

Fig. 4.25   Value decrements across dimensions (*AD* anxiety/depression, *MO* mobility, *PD* pain/discomfort, *SC* self-care, *UA* usual activities)

(x)   **Uptake by local HTA/health care decision makers**
      Cost-utility analysis (CUA) is currently not required and is not the preferred
      form of economic evaluation in pharmacoeconomics and health technology
      assessment guidelines provided by the Institute for Quality and Efficiency in
      Health Care (IQWiG), the official agency for providing evidence for reim-
      bursement decisions of drugs in Germany (IQWiG 2020; Kennedy-Martin
      et al. 2020; Rowen et al. 2017). Use of CUA is common in the assessment
      process for the development of vaccination recommendations by the Standing
      Committee on Vaccination (STIKO) but no preference for a specific multi-
      attribute utility instrument is recorded (STIKO 2016).

(xi) **Reference(s) for this value set**
      Ludwig K, Graf von der Schulenburg JM, Greiner W (2018) German Value
      Set for the EQ-5D-5L. Pharmacoeconomics 36(6):663–674

Further Literature

Federal Statistical Office (2015) Mikrozensus. Bevölkerung und Erwerbstätigkeit.
    Stand und Entwicklung der Erwerbstätigkeit in Deutschland 2014. Federal
    Statistical Office, Wiesbaden
    Thematisch/Arbeitsmarkt/Erwerbstaetige/StandEntwicklungErwerbstaetigkeit.
    html. Accessed 10 Aug 2017
Institute for Quality and Efficiency in Health Care (IQWiG) (2020) Allgemeine
    Methoden 6.0. IQWiG, Cologne. https://www.iqwig.de/ueber-uns/methoden/
    methodenpapier/. Accessed 25 June 2021
Standing Committee on Vaccination (STIKO) (2016) Methoden zur Durchführung
    und Berücksichtigung von Modellierungen zur Vorhersage epidemiologischer
    und gesundheitsökonomischer Effekte von Impfungen für die Ständige
    Impfkommission.   STIKO,   Berlin.   https://www.rki.de/DE/Content/
    Kommissionen/STIKO/Aufgaben_Methoden/methoden_node.html;jsessioni
    d=54B83BAC57F91FF652D8A285C014CD53.internet112.   Accessed   25
    June 2021
Kennedy-Martin M, Slaap B, Herdman M, van Reenen M, Kennedy-Martin T,
    Greiner W, Busschbach J, Boye K (2020) Which multi-attribute utility instru-
    ments are recommended for use in cost-utility analysis? A review of national
    health technology assessment (HTA) guidelines. Eur J Health Econ
    21(8):1245–1257
Rowen D, Azzabi ZI, Chevrou-Severac H, van Hout B (2017) International
    Regulations and Recommendations for Utility Data for Health Technology
    Assessment. Pharmacoeconomics 35(Suppl 1):11–19

4.3.3.3   Country/Region: Indonesia (Table 4.49)

Table 4.49 Overview of EQ-5D-5L value set for Indonesia[a]

Indonesian EQ-5D-5L value set		Example: the value for health state 21232	
Full health (11111)	1	Full health	=1
Mobility = 2	0.119	Minus MO level 2	−0.119
Mobility = 3	0.192		
Mobility = 4	0.410		
Mobility = 5	0.613		
Self-care = 2	0.101	Minus SC level 1	−0.000
Self-care = 3	0.140		
Self-care = 4	0.248		
Self-care = 5	0.316		
Usual activities = 2	0.090	Minus UA level 2	−0.090
Usual activities = 3	0.156		
Usual activities = 4	0.301		
Usual activities = 5	0.385		
Pain/discomfort = 2	0.086		
Pain/discomfort = 3	0.095	Minus PD level 3	−0.095
Pain/discomfort = 4	0.198		
Pain/discomfort = 5	0.246		
Anxiety/depression = 2	0.079	Minus AD level 2	−0.079
Anxiety/depression = 3	0.134		
Anxiety/depression = 4	0.227		
Anxiety/depression = 5	0.305		
		State 21232	=0.617

AD anxiety/depression, *MO* mobility, *PD* pain/discomfort, *SC* self-care, *UA* usual activities
[a]These coefficients present the decrement from level 1 to the respective level (regular dummies), whereas Purba et al. (2017a) report coefficients representing the additional decrement of moving from one level to another (incremental dummies)

The mathematical representation of the model for health state X is:

$$V(X) = 1 - 0.119\, MO_2 - 0.192\, MO_3 - 0.410\, MO_4 - 0.613\, MO_5 - 0.101$$
$$SC_2 - 0.140\, SC_3 - 0.248\, SC_4 - 0.316\, SC_5 - 0.090\, UA_2 - 0.156\, UA_3 - 0.301$$
$$UA_4 - 0.385\, UA_5 - 0.086\, PD_2 - 0.095\, PD_3 - 0.198\, PD_4 - 0.246\, PD_5 - 0.079$$
$$AD_2 - 0.134\, AD_3 - 0.227\, AD_4 - 0.305\, AD_5$$

(i)   **Date/wave of study**
Data were collected in the third wave of EQ-5D-5L valuation studies using the EQ-5D-5L valuation protocol 2.0. Interviews were conducted between March 2015 and January 2016.

(ii)   **Sample size; sample frame**

1056 interviews with the general population were conducted in six cities and surrounds located in different parts of Indonesia: Jakarta, Bandung, Jogjakarta, Surabaya, Medan, and Makassar. A multi-stage stratified quota sampling with respect to residence, gender, age, and level of education (stage 1) and with respect to religion and ethnicity (stage 2) was applied (Indonesian Bureau of Statistics (BPS) 2015). Of the 1054 respondents included in the final value set, 49.9% were female and 50.1% were male. The age distribution of the respondents was:

17–24 years	26.28%
25–29 years	11.20%
30–39 years	25.05%
40–49 years	17.08%
50–64 years	18.22%
65–74 years	2.09%
75+ years	0.09%

(iii)   **Representativeness of achieved sample**

The study sample was representative for the Indonesian general population (over 17 years). The distribution of the study sample in terms of residence, gender, and religion was similar to that of the general population. There were some small differences between the Indonesian general population and some of the age groups, education levels, and ethnicities in the study sample (Table 4.50).

Table 4.50 Representativeness of the sample in the Indonesian valuation study

		Study sample (N=1054)	Indonesian general population[a]
Sampling characteristics			
Age, n (%)	17–19	159 (15.1%)	12.3%
	20–29	236 (22.4%)	24.4%
	30–39	264 (25.1%)	22.7%
	40–49	180 (17.1%)	18.1%
	50–59	164 (15.6%)	11.8%
	60–69	43 (4.1%)	6.4%
	≥ 70	8 (0.8%)	4.3%
Gender, n (%)	Female	526 (49.9%)	49.7%
	Male	528 (50.1%)	50.3%
Ethnicity, n (%)	Jawa	441 (41.8%)	40.2%
	Sunda	199 (18.9%)	15.5%
	Sumatera	128 (12.1%)	15.0%
	Sulawesi	63 (6.0%)	8.1%
	Madura—Bali	52 (4.9%)	4.7%
	Others	171 (16.2%)	16.5%
Residence, n (%)	Urban	549 (52.1%)	53.3%
	Rural	505 (47.9%)	46.7%

(continued)

Table 4.50 (continued)

		Study sample (N=1054)	Indonesian general population[a]
Education, n (%)	Low	339 (32.2%)	35.2%
	Middle	550 (52.2%)	51.7%
	High	165 (15.7%)	13.1%
Religion, n (%)	Islam	920 (87.3%)	87.2%
	Christian	103 (9.8%)	9.9%
	Others	31 (2.9)%)	2.9%

Reproduced from Purba et al. (2017a)
[a]BPS 2015

(iv)   **Mean observed cTTO values of EQ-5D-5L states** (Table 4.51)

Table 4.51 Mean observed cTTO values by health state

State	Mean	SE	State	Mean	SE	State	Mean	SE
11112	0.906	0.009	21345	0.237	0.055	43315	−0.136	0.051
11121	0.908	0.008	21444	0.077	0.052	43514	−0.132	0.052
11122	0.869	0.011	22434	0.223	0.052	43542	−0.214	0.049
11211	0.902	0.008	23152	0.389	0.048	43555	−0.381	0.048
11212	0.787	0.027	23242	0.426	0.043	44125	−0.093	0.054
11221	0.775	0.023	23514	0.217	0.045	44345	−0.354	0.047
11235	0.537	0.037	24342	0.200	0.047	44553	−0.452	0.046
11414	0.499	0.038	24443	−0.088	0.052	45133	0.017	0.052
11421	0.608	0.030	24445	−0.190	0.057	45144	−0.146	0.051
11425	0.333	0.055	24553	−0.035	0.061	45233	0.000	0.051
12111	0.909	0.007	25122	0.473	0.039	45413	−0.190	0.054
12112	0.764	0.028	25222	0.497	0.042	51152	0.091	0.060
12121	0.779	0.018	25331	0.360	0.048	51451	−0.112	0.055
12244	0.405	0.041	31514	0.164	0.047	52215	0.041	0.053
12334	0.438	0.044	31524	0.051	0.051	52335	−0.169	0.051
12344	0.157	0.055	31525	0.176	0.045	52431	−0.197	0.048
12513	0.351	0.051	32314	0.394	0.042	52455	−0.370	0.049
12514	0.359	0.039	32443	0.028	0.050	53221	0.052	0.058
12543	0.220	0.051	33253	0.233	0.048	53243	−0.140	0.051
13122	0.646	0.032	34155	0.028	0.054	53244	−0.253	0.048
13224	0.468	0.038	34232	0.269	0.042	53412	−0.113	0.052
13313	0.560	0.037	34244	−0.055	0.057	54153	−0.244	0.051
14113	0.553	0.037	34515	−0.054	0.049	54231	−0.036	0.051
14554	−0.010	0.058	35143	0.213	0.053	54342	−0.277	0.052
15151	0.409	0.049	35245	0.007	0.052	55225	−0.326	0.046
21111	0.876	0.015	35311	0.379	0.043	55233	−0.149	0.047
21112	0.763	0.023	35332	0.145	0.053	55424	−0.449	0.044
21315	0.364	0.045	42115	0.228	0.056	55555	−0.719	0.013
21334	0.469	0.039	42321	0.219	0.046			

SE standard error

(v)   **Proportions choosing A in the DCE based on relative severities of A and B** (Fig. 4.26)

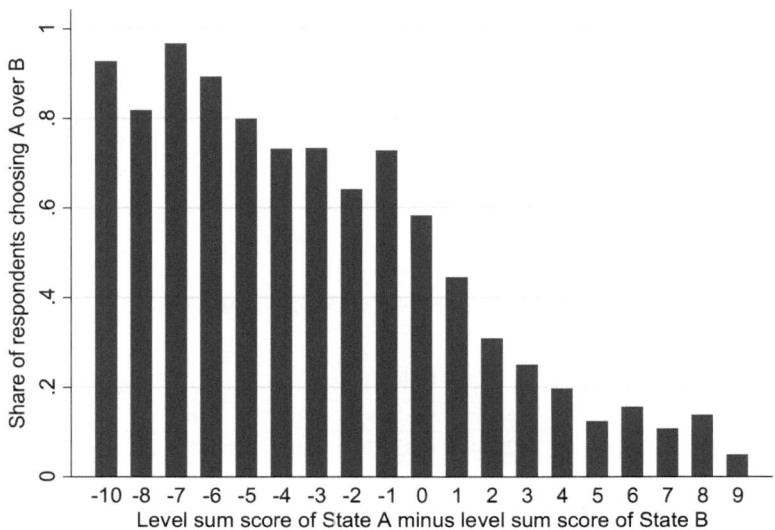

Fig. 4.26   Proportions choosing A based on relative severities of A and B

(vi)   **Exclusion criteria**
Due to data quality issues, after the first 102 interviews all interviewers were retrained and the interviews collected to that point were excluded from data analysis and regarded as pilot interviews (not included in the above-mentioned study sample, details are reported in Purba et al. 2017b).

A total of 9.8% of cTTO responses (n = 1033) were removed following the feedback module. Moreover, further 45 cTTO responses were excluded where the respondent preferred living in an impaired health state over full health. In addition, two respondents with a positive slope on the regression between his cTTO values and the level sum score were also excluded. No DCE data were excluded from the analysis.

(vii)   **Number of interviewers; Interviewer effects**
In total, 1056 interviews were conducted by 15 interviewers. The variance of the responses included in the final value set can be partitioned into variance related to differences between interviewers (2.7%), respondents (12.1%), and responses (85.2%).

(viii)   **Description of modelling choices**
The Indonesian EQ-5D-5L value set was based on a hybrid model combining a conditional logit model for the DCE data and a censored at −1 tobit model for the cTTO data, correcting for heteroskedasticity. The intercept was constrained in the final model.

(ix)   **Value Set** (Table 4.52 and Fig. 4.27)

Table 4.52 Key characteristics of the Indonesian value set

Characteristics	Indonesian EQ-5D-5L value set
% states with negative values	35.5% (1108 out of 3125)
Rank order of dimensions (from most to least relative importance)	Mobility Usual activities Self-care Anxiety/depression Pain/discomfort
Coefficient with highest weight	0.613 (level 5 of mobility)
Range of values	Maximum value: 1 Minimum value: −0.865
Max value < 1:	0.921 (value of health state 11112)
Linearity/non-linearity of value decrements by level	Value decrements for level 2 were similar to each other across all dimensions (see Fig. 4.27). Kink at level 3 for all dimensions. In level 3 and especially in levels 4 and 5, the value decrements were more differentiated, with decrements for usual activities and mobility higher than that for the other three dimensions. Mobility had by far the largest impact on value estimates.

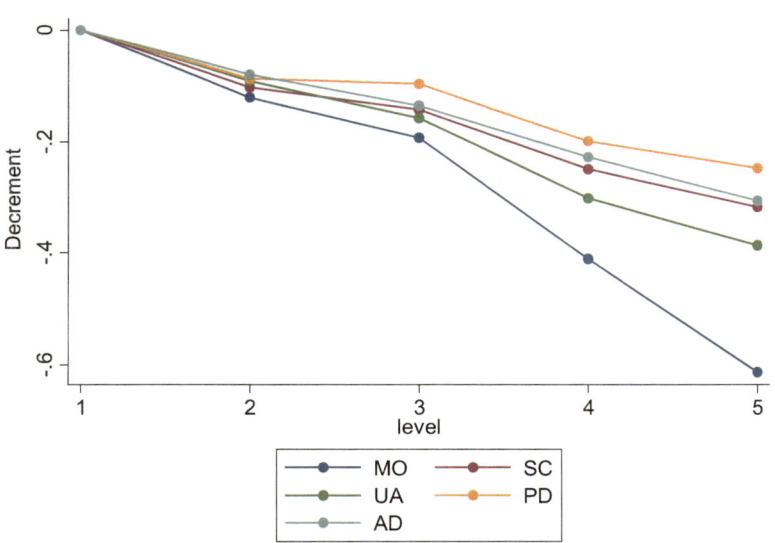

Fig. 4.27 Value decrements across dimensions (*AD* anxiety/depression, *MO* mobility, *PD* pain/discomfort, *SC* self-care, *UA* usual activities)

(x)   **Uptake by local HTA/health care decision makers**

The Indonesian Health Technology Assessment Committee (InaHTAC) produced an HTA guideline in 2017 that suggests use of cost-utility analysis (CUA) and cost-effectiveness analysis (CEA) for economic evaluations in Indonesia. The guideline also recommends EQ-5D as the preferred instrument for use in estimating QALYs (InaHTAC 2017). The availability of EQ-5D-5L value set from a societal, Indonesian perspective supported various HTA and non-HTA studies in Indonesia.

(xi)   **Reference(s) for this value set**

Purba FD, Hunfeld JAM, Iskandarsyah A, Fitriana TS, Sadarjoen SS, Ramos-Goñi JM, Passchier J, Busschbach JJV (2017a) The Indonesian EQ-5D-5L Value Set. Pharmacoeconomics 35(11):1153–1165

Further Literature

Badan Pusat Statistik (BPS) (2015) Statistik 70 Tahun Indonesia Merdeka. Badan Pusat Statistik, Jakarta

Indonesian Health Technology Assessment Committee (InaHTAC) (2017) Health Technology Assessment (HTA) Guideline. Pusat Pembiayaan dan Jaminan Kesehatan Kementerian Kesehatan RI, Jakarta

Purba FD, Hunfeld JAM, Iskandarsyah A, Fitriana TS, Sadarjoen SS, Passchier J, Busschbach JJV (2017b) Employing quality control and feedback to the EQ-5D-5L valuation protocol to improve the quality of data collection. Qual Life Res 26(5):1197–1208

4.3.3.4   Country/Region: Ireland (Table 4.53)

Table 4.53 Overview of EQ-5D-5L value set for Ireland

Irish EQ-5D-5L value set		Example: the value for health state 21232	
Full health (11111)	1	Full health	=1
Mobility = 2	0.063	Minus MO level 2	−0.063
Mobility = 3	0.097		
Mobility = 4	0.215		
Mobility = 5	0.344		
Self-care = 2	0.055	Minus SC level 1	−0.000
Self-care = 3	0.088		
Self-care = 4	0.229		
Self-care = 5	0.287		
Usual activities = 2	0.049	Minus UA level 2	−0.049
Usual activities = 3	0.072		
Usual activities = 4	0.154		
Usual activities = 5	0.187		
Pain/discomfort = 2	0.068		
Pain/discomfort = 3	0.093	Minus PD level 3	−0.093
Pain/discomfort = 4	0.373		
Pain/discomfort = 5	0.510		
Anxiety/depression = 2	0.080	Minus AD level 2	−0.080
Anxiety/depression = 3	0.202		
Anxiety/depression = 4	0.535		
Anxiety/depression = 5	0.646		
		State 21232	=0.715

AD anxiety/depression, *MO* mobility, *PD* pain/discomfort, *SC* self-care, *UA* usual activities

The mathematical representation of the model for health state X is:

$$V(X) = 1 - 0.063\,MO_2 - 0.097\,MO_3 - 0.215\,MO_4 - 0.344\,MO_5 - 0.055$$
$$SC_2 - 0.088\,SC_3 - 0.229\,SC_4 - 0.287\,SC_5 - 0.049\,UA_2 - 0.072\,UA_3 - 0.154$$
$$UA_4 - 0.187\,UA_5 - 0.068\,PD_2 - 0.093\,PD_3 - 0.373\,PD_4 - 0.510\,PD_5 - 0.080$$
$$AD_2 - 0.202\,AD_3 - 0.535\,AD_4 - 0.646\,AD_5$$

(i)   **Date/wave of study**
  Data were collected in the third wave of EQ-5D-5L valuation studies using the EQ-5D-5L valuation protocol 2.0. Interviews were conducted between March 2015 and September 2016.

(ii) **Sample size; sample frame**
  1160 interviews with the general population were conducted. A representative sample of Irish residents was obtained using a two-stage stratified clustering process. In the first stage, a sample of 54 small areas stratified by income and urban/rural classifications were drawn at random from across the

country. In the second stage, within each small area, a sample of approximately 20 households were selected at random. Random selection was achieved by using a random starting point and inviting a resident from every third household to participate in the survey. The recruited sample was then compared with Central Statistics Office for Ireland (CSO) national population estimates for age and sex. Purposive sampling was used to augment the number of younger individuals and males in the sample. Of the 1160 completed surveys, 102 were purposive; 37% were male and 63% female.

The age distribution of the respondents was:

18–24 years	7.84%
25–29 years	5.60%
30–39 years	18.02%
40–49 years	20.69%
50–64 years	25.95%
65–74 years	14.05%
75+ years	7.84%

(iii) **Representativeness of achieved sample**
Including the purposive sample, the sample broadly reflects the Irish population, with some over-representation of those aged > 45 years and of females. Those with tertiary-level education were over-represented and those with only primary- level education were under-represented compared with the population at large (Table 4.54).

Table 4.54 Representativeness of the sample in the Ireland valuation study

		Study sample (N=1160)[a]	Irish general population[b]
Sampling characteristics			
Age. n (%)	18–24	91 (8.0%)	12.0%
	25–34	166 (14.0%)	22.0%
	35–44	226 (19.0%)	20.0%
	45–54	233 (20.0%)	17.0%
	55–64	190 (16.0%)	13.0%
	65–74	163 (14.0%)	9.0%
	≥ 75	91 (8.0%)	7.0%
Gender. n (%)	Female	729 (63.0%)	51.0%
	Male	431 (37.0%)	49.0%
Education. n (%)	Primary	88 8.0%)	14.0%
	Second level or less	429 (37.0%)	37.0%
	Third level	643 (55.0%)	43.0%
	Not stated/no formal education	0 (0%)	6.0%
Employment status. n (%)	Employed (full- or part-time)	559 (48.0%)	50.0%
	Unemployed	72 (6.0%)	12.0%

(continued)

Table 4.54 (continued)

		Study sample (N=1160)[a]	Irish general population[b]
	Student	71 (6.0%)	11.0%
	Long-term sickness	48 (4.0%)	4.0%
	Home duties	129 (11.0%)	9.0%
	Retired	263 (23.0%)	13.0%
	Other	18 (2.0%)	0%

Reproduced from Hobbins et al. (2018)
[a]Decimal places are shown only for consistency in reporting. The percentages shown here are from Hobbins et al. (2018) and are rounded to the closest whole number.
[b]Central Statistics Office for Ireland (2011)

(iv)   **Mean values of cTTO states** (Table 4.55)

Table 4.55   Mean cTTO values by health state

State	Mean	SE	State	Mean	SE	State	Mean	SE
11112	0.918	0.017	21345	−0.055	0.068	43315	0.050	0.068
11121	0.928	0.016	21444	−0.018	0.060	43514	0.010	0.071
11122	0.905	0.014	22434	0.116	0.062	43542	0.130	0.058
11211	0.949	0.008	23152	0.188	0.066	43555	−0.389	0.059
11212	0.908	0.017	23242	0.236	0.059	44125	−0.080	0.064
11221	0.926	0.014	23514	0.251	0.059	44345	−0.339	0.060
11235	0.216	0.071	24342	0.113	0.063	44553	−0.284	0.062
11414	0.270	0.060	24443	−0.005	0.064	45133	0.295	0.059
11421	0.775	0.028	24445	−0.378	0.058	45144	−0.158	0.067
11425	0.146	0.060	24553	0.036	0.061	45233	0.284	0.057
12111	0.938	0.011	25122	0.565	0.049	45413	0.187	0.066
12112	0.890	0.018	25222	0.433	0.061	51152	0.188	0.060
12121	0.911	0.017	25331	0.443	0.056	51451	−0.031	0.070
12244	0.008	0.060	31514	0.262	0.058	52215	0.066	0.066
12334	0.238	0.060	31524	0.152	0.067	52335	−0.130	0.067
12344	0.034	0.066	31525	0.117	0.060	52431	0.349	0.061
12513	0.466	0.053	32314	0.213	0.062	52455	−0.332	0.059
12514	0.267	0.064	32443	0.176	0.059	53221	0.369	0.066
12543	0.233	0.059	33253	0.069	0.061	53243	0.088	0.062
13122	0.789	0.030	34155	−0.103	0.062	53244	−0.039	0.062
13224	0.122	0.065	34232	0.424	0.053	53412	0.319	0.059
13313	0.703	0.030	34244	−0.168	0.065	54153	−0.043	0.068
14113	0.557	0.050	34515	0.047	0.067	54231	0.240	0.069
14554	−0.175	0.062	35143	0.088	0.063	54342	−0.068	0.067
15151	0.159	0.068	35245	−0.139	0.067	55225	−0.268	0.062
21111	0.960	0.006	35311	0.453	0.053	55233	0.158	0.059
21112	0.862	0.027	35332	0.393	0.056	55424	−0.207	0.067
21315	0.182	0.069	42115	0.115	0.059	55555	−0.506	0.018
21334	0.253	0.060	42321	0.622	0.041			

SE standard error

(v)   **Proportions choosing A and B in DCE based on relative severities of A and B** (Fig. 4.28)

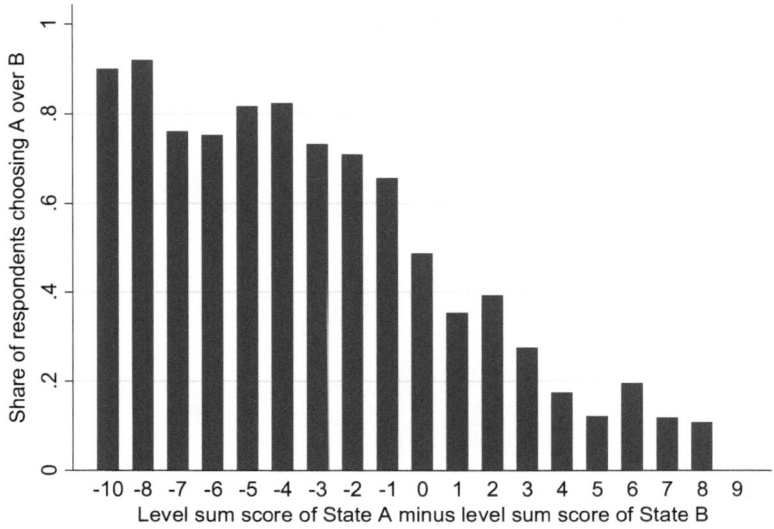

Fig. 4.28 Proportions choosing A and B based on relative severities of A and B

(vi)   **Exclusion criteria**
       No data were excluded from analysis.

(vii) **Number of interviewers; Interviewer effects**
       In total 1160 interviews were conducted by 7 interviewers. The variance of the responses can be partitioned into variance related to differences between interviewers (1.39%) respondents (30.98%) and responses (67.63%).

(viii) **Description of modelling choices**
       The observed cTTO values for the non-flagged health states after the feedback module were used i.e., the respondent's flagged cTTO observations – which accounted for 2% values) were excluded (details on the feedback module and its use are provided in Chap. 2). For the DCE data, the dependent variable was the binary stated choice (i.e., 0/1 indicated the choice for each health state pair). No DCE data were excluded.
       The Irish EQ-5D-5L value set was based on a main effects hybrid model combining DCE data and cTTO data, addressing the censoring of cTTO data at −1 and correcting for heteroskedasticity.

(ix)   **Value Set** (Table 4.56 and Fig. 4.29)

Table 4.56 Key characteristics of the Ireland value set

Characteristics	Irish EQ-5D-5L value set
% states with negative values	36.0% (1125 out of 3125)
Rank order of dimensions (from most to least relative importance)	Anxiety/depression Pain/discomfort Mobility Self-care Usual activities
Coefficient with highest weight	0.646 (level 5 of anxiety/depression)
Range of values	Maximum value: 1 Minimum value: −0.974
Max value < 1:	0.951 (value of health state 11211)
Linearity/non-linearity of value decrements by level	Values are non-linear with respect to severity in dimensions. For example, the decrement in value associated with a change in mobility, self-care and usual activities from level 3 to 4 is much greater than that from level 1 to 2 or from 2 to 3. The value decrements for anxiety/depression are higher at every level of problem than other dimensions.

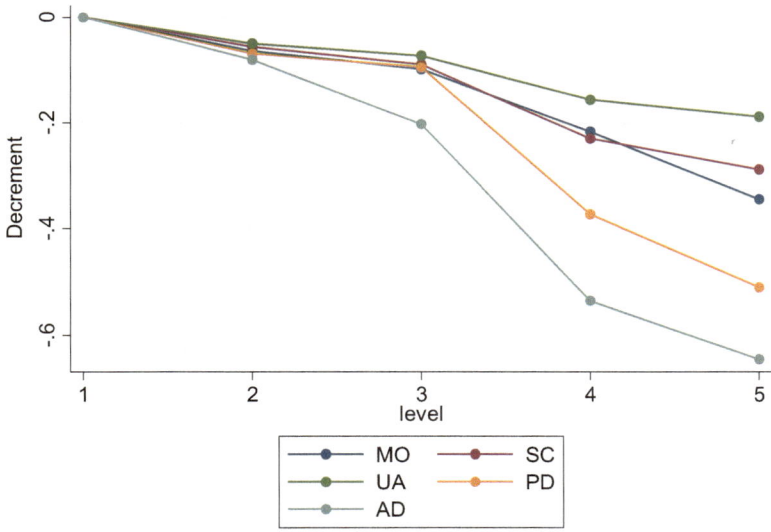

Fig. 4.29 Value decrements across dimensions (*AD* anxiety/depression, *MO* mobility, *PD* pain/discomfort, *SC* self-care, *UA* usual activities)

(x)   **Uptake by local HTA/health care decision makers**
        There are two principal public entities involved in cost-utility analysis (CUA)
        in Ireland: the Health Information and Quality Authority (HIQA) for non-
        pharmaceutical technologies and the National Centre for Pharmacoeconomics
        (NCPE) for pharmaceutical technologies. The former can undertake CUAs;
        the latter can request evidence from CUAs by pharmaceutical companies.
        While HIQA has used the Irish EQ-5D-5L value set (HIQA 2018) as have a
        number of academic studies (for example, see Murphy et al. 2019; Cardwell
        et al. 2020), NCPE have not yet adopted it for use.

(xi)   **Reference for this value set**
        Hobbins A, Barry L, Kelleher D, Shah K, Devlin N, Ramos Goni JM, O'Neill
        C (2018) Utility Values for Health States in Ireland: A Value Set for the
        EQ-5D-5L. Pharmacoeconomics 36(11):1345–1353

Further Literature

Central Statistics Office for Ireland (2011) Census 2011 reports. https://www.cso.ie/
    en/census/census2011reports/. Accessed 29 July 2021
HIQA (2018) HTA of extending the HPV vaccination to boys. https://www.hiqa.ie/
    reports-and-publications/health-technology-assessment/hta-extending-hpv-
    vaccination-boys. Accessed 21 July 2021
Cardwell K, Smith S M, Clyne B, McCullagh L, Wallace E, Kirke C, Fahey T,
    Moriarty F (2020) Evaluation of the General Practice Pharmacist (GPP) interven-
    tion to optimise prescribing in Irish primary care: a non-randomised pilot study.
    BMJ Open 10(6):e035087. https://doi.org/10.1136/bmjopen-2019-035087
Murphy A, Bourke J, Flynn D, Kells M, Joyce M (2019) A cost-effectiveness analy-
    sis of dialectical behaviour therapy for treating individuals with borderline per-
    sonality disorder in the community. Ir J Med Sci 189(2):415–423

4.3.3.5   Country/Region: Malaysia (Table 4.57)

Table 4.57 Overview of EQ-5D-5L value set for Malaysia

Malaysian EQ-5D-5L value set		Example: the value for health state 21232	
Full health (11111)	1	Full health	=1
Mobility = 2	0.081	Minus MO level 2	−0.081
Mobility = 3	0.108		
Mobility = 4	0.261		
Mobility = 5	0.340		
Self-care = 2	0.062	Minus SC level 1	−0.000
Self-care = 3	0.083		
Self-care = 4	0.200		
Self-care = 5	0.261		
Usual activities = 2	0.048	Minus UA level 2	−0.048
Usual activities = 3	0.064		
Usual activities = 4	0.155		
Usual activities = 5	0.202		
Pain/discomfort = 2	0.081		
Pain/discomfort = 3	0.107	Minus PD level 3	−0.107
Pain/discomfort = 4	0.259		
Pain/discomfort = 5	0.338		
Anxiety/depression = 2	0.072	Minus AD level 2	−0.072
Anxiety/depression = 3	0.095		
Anxiety/depression = 4	0.230		
Anxiety/depression = 5	0.300		
		State 21232	=0.692

AD anxiety/depression, *MO* mobility, *PD* pain/discomfort, *SC* self-care, *UA* usual activities

The mathematical representation of the model for health state X is:

$$V(X) = 1 - 0.081\,MO_2 - 0.108\,MO_3 - 0.261\,MO_4 - 0.340\,MO_5 - 0.062$$
$$SC_2 - 0.083\,SC_3 - 0.200\,SC_4 - 0.261\,SC_5 - 0.048\,UA_2 - 0.064\,UA_3 - 0.155$$
$$UA_4 - 0.202\,UA_5 - 0.081\,PD_2 - 0.107\,PD_3 - 0.259\,PD_4 - 0.338\,PD_5 - 0.072$$
$$AD_2 - 0.095\,AD_3 - 0.230\,AD_4 - 0.300\,AD_5$$

(i)   **Date/wave of study**
Data were collected in the third wave of EQ-5D-5L valuation studies using the EQ-5D-5L valuation protocol 2.0. Interviews were conducted between August and September 2016.

(ii)   **Sample size; sample frame**
1137 interviews with the general population were conducted in four Malaysian states: Penang (Northern), Selangor (Central), Kelantan (Eastern), and

Malacca (Southern). A quota-based sampling with respect to urbanicity, gender, age (over 18 years) and ethnicity based on the Malaysian National Census (Department of Statistics Malaysia 2010). Of the 1125 respondents included in the final value set, 48.8% were female and 51.2% were male. The age distribution of the respondents was:

18–24 years	26.8%
25–29 years	13.7%
30–39 years	15.6%
40–49 years	14.6%
50–64 years	21.4%
65–74 years	6.3%
75+ years	1.5%

(iii) **Representativeness of achieved sample**
The study sample was largely representative for the Malaysian general population in terms of gender, age, ethnicity, and residential area. Employed (full time)/self-employed respondents were slightly underrepresented in the study sample (Table 4.58).

Table 4.58 Representativeness of the sample in the Malaysian valuation study

		Study sample (N=1125)	Malaysian general population[a]
Sampling characteristics			
Age, n (%)	18–39	632 (56.2%)	53.9%
	40–64	405 (36.0%)	37.5%
	≥ 65	88 (7.8%)	8.6%
Gender, n (%)	Female	549 (48.8%)	48.5%
	Male	576 (51.2%)	51.5%
Ethnicity, n (%)	Indigenous	770 (68.4%)	67.4%
	Non-indigenous	355 (31.6%)	32.6%
Residential area, n (%)	Urban	790 (70.2%)	71.0%
	Rural	355 (29.8%)	29.0%
Employment status, n (%)	Employed full time/ self-employed	629 (55.9%)	64.3%
	Unemployed (able to work)	48 (4.3%)	3.4%
	Outside labor force[b]	313 (37.8%)	32.0%
	Others	14 (1.2%)	/
	Missing	9 (0.8%)	/

Reproduced from Shafie et al. (2019)
[a]Department of Statistics Malaysia 2010 and 2016
[b]Outside labour force: respondents with sickness or disability, caretakers of households, students, and the retired

(iv)   **Mean observed cTTO values of EQ-5D-5L states** (Table 4.59)

Table 4.59 Mean observed cTTO values by health state

State	Mean	SE	State	Mean	SE	State	Mean	SE
11112	0.928	0.009	21345	0.290	0.050	43315	0.340	0.045
11121	0.945	0.006	21444	0.188	0.056	43514	0.195	0.053
11122	0.919	0.011	22434	0.350	0.045	43542	0.129	0.047
11211	0.937	0.007	23152	0.368	0.048	43555	−0.139	0.052
11212	0.870	0.022	23242	0.462	0.043	44125	0.110	0.054
11221	0.884	0.019	23514	0.417	0.043	44345	−0.087	0.053
11235	0.588	0.035	24342	0.216	0.050	44553	−0.044	0.052
11414	0.547	0.046	24443	0.165	0.047	45133	0.307	0.047
11421	0.760	0.026	24445	−0.053	0.049	45144	0.052	0.050
11425	0.435	0.040	24553	0.103	0.053	45233	0.342	0.052
12111	0.922	0.010	25122	0.608	0.039	45413	0.177	0.049
12112	0.859	0.022	25222	0.494	0.051	51152	0.150	0.054
12121	0.861	0.023	25331	0.456	0.051	51451	0.226	0.049
12244	0.431	0.042	31514	0.434	0.048	52215	0.191	0.051
12334	0.444	0.046	31524	0.456	0.038	52335	0.191	0.046
12344	0.394	0.042	31525	0.398	0.043	52431	0.367	0.042
12513	0.662	0.025	32314	0.496	0.044	52455	−0.026	0.052
12514	0.463	0.042	32443	0.306	0.044	53221	0.412	0.048
12543	0.319	0.050	33253	0.190	0.052	53243	0.111	0.057
13122	0.788	0.025	34155	0.070	0.050	53244	0.002	0.056
13224	0.589	0.030	34232	0.470	0.040	53412	0.247	0.051
13313	0.762	0.025	34244	0.165	0.055	54153	0.100	0.048
14113	0.644	0.036	34515	0.233	0.045	54231	0.296	0.047
14554	0.025	0.054	35143	0.210	0.060	54342	0.074	0.052
15151	0.360	0.048	35245	0.119	0.050	55225	−0.044	0.052
21111	0.934	0.008	35311	0.554	0.037	55233	0.283	0.052
21112	0.897	0.011	35332	0.432	0.042	55424	−0.007	0.054
21315	0.576	0.038	42115	0.339	0.046	55555	−0.455	0.015
21334	0.453	0.048	42321	0.503	0.042			

SE standard error

(v)   **Proportions choosing A in the DCE based on relative severities of A and B** (Fig. 4.30)

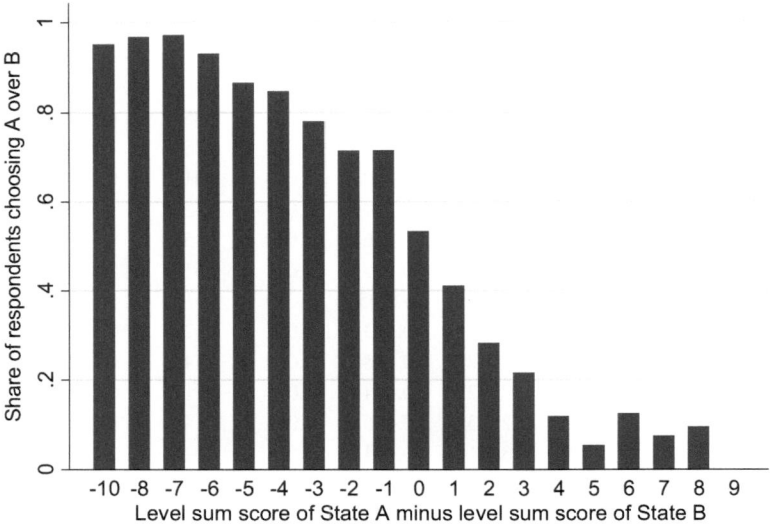

Fig. 4.30 Proportions choosing A based on relative severities of A and B

(vi)   **Exclusion criteria**
       Respondents whose cTTO value increased with health state severity and those who valued all health states at −1 were excluded from data analysis (n=12). No DCE data were excluded from the analysis.

(vii) **Number of interviewers; Interviewer effects**
       In total, 1137 interviews were conducted by 18 interviewers. The variance of the responses included in the final value set can be partitioned into variance related to differences between interviewers (1.1%), respondents (21.8%), and responses (77.1%).

(viii) **Description of modelling choices**
       The Malaysian EQ-5D-5L value set was based on a non-linear constrained hybrid model combining a conditional logit model for the DCE data and an additive model assuming a normal distribution for the cTTO data. A constrained eight-parameter model was selected that fits a single parameter per dimension, taking a value representing level 5; and one parameter for each of levels 2, 3, and 4 that are multiplied by the respective dimension parameters. The eight-parameter model can be converted to 20 parameters, as presented in Table 4.57 for consistency purposes in this chapter. The intercept was constrained in the final model because it was non-significant.

(ix)   **Value Set** (Table 4.60 and Fig. 4.31)

Table 4.60 Key characteristics of the Malaysian value set

Characteristics	Malaysian EQ-5D-5L value set
% states with negative values	8.9% (281 out of 3125)
Rank order of dimensions (from most to least relative importance)	Mobility Pain/discomfort Anxiety/depression Self-care Usual activities
Coefficient with highest weight	0.340 (level 5 of mobility)
Range of values	Maximum value: 1 Minimum value: −0.442[a]
Max value < 1:	0.952 (value of health state 11211)
Linearity/non-linearity of value decrements by level	Kink at level 3 for all dimensions (see Fig. 4.31). Value decrements for the dimensions were similar at levels 2 and 3. In levels 4 and 5, the value decrements were more differentiated across dimensions. At level 5, the decrements of pain/discomfort and mobility were the highest and are nearly identical.

[a]Minimum value was calculated using the non-rounded values as reported in Shafie et al. (2019)

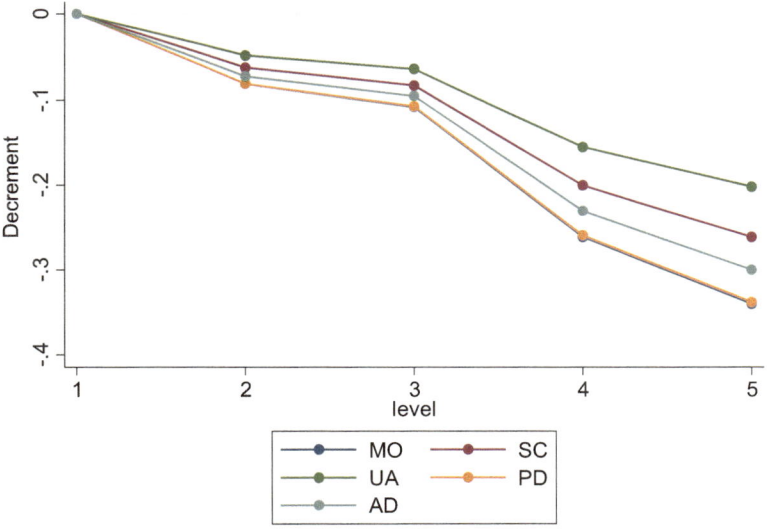

Fig. 4.31 Value decrements across dimensions. (Please note that the lines of MO and PD are virtually identical. The line for MO is obscured by the yellow line for PD; AD anxiety/depression, MO mobility, PD pain/discomfort, SC self-care, UA usual activities)

(x)   **Uptake by local HTA/health care decision makers**
       According to the current Malaysia Pharmacoeconomic Guidelines, the pre-
       ferred economic evaluation techniques to inform health technology assess-
       ment decisions are cost-effectiveness analysis (CEA) and cost-utility analysis
       (CUA) (Ministry of Health Malaysia 2019). CUA is the recommended tech-
       nique when HRQOL is an important outcome and when the intervention
       affects both morbidity and mortality. The guideline also states that EQ-5D is
       the preferred patient-reported outcomes measure and that a locally derived
       value set is strongly recommended for use, with the Malaysian EQ-5D-5L
       value set study being cited in the document.

(xi)   **Reference(s) for this value set**
       Shafie AA, Vasan Thakumar A, Lim CJ, Luo N, Rand-Hendriksen K, Yusof
            FAM (2019) EQ-5D-5L Valuation for the Malaysian Population.
            Pharmacoeconomics 37(5):715–725

Further Literature

Department of Statistics Malaysia (2010) Population distribution and basic demo-
     graphic characteristic report 2010. Department of Statistics Malaysia, Putrajaya
Department of Statistics Malaysia (2016) Labour Force Survey Report Malaysia
     2016. Department of Statistics Malaysia, Putrajaya. https://www.dosm.gov.my/
     v1/index.php?r=column/cthemeByCat&cat=126&bul_id=SGZCNnMrWW9ZT
     EdpYys4YW0yRlhoQT09&menu_id=U3VPMldoYUxzVzFaYmNkWXZteGd
     uZz09. Accessed 14 July 2021
Ministry of Health Malaysia (2019) Pharmacoeconomic guidelines for Malaysia.
     Ministry of Health Malaysia, Petaling Jaya. https://www.pharmacy.gov.my/v2/
     sites/default/files/document-upload/pharmacoeconomic-guidelines-malaysia-
     malaysia-second-edition-2019-final-page-adjustment.pdf.   Accessed   25
     June 2021

4.3.3.6   Country/Region: Poland (Table 4.61)

Table 4.61 Overview of EQ-5D-5L value set for Poland

Polish EQ-5D-5L value set		Example: the value for health state 21232	
Full health (11111)	1	Full health	=1
Mobility = 2	0.025	Minus MO level 2	−0.025
Mobility = 3	0.034		
Mobility = 4	0.126		
Mobility = 5	0.314		
Self-care = 2	0.031	Minus SC level 1	−0.000
Self-care = 3	0.047		
Self-care = 4	0.111		
Self-care = 5	0.264		
Usual activities = 2	0.023	Minus UA level 2	−0.023
Usual activities = 3	0.040		
Usual activities = 4	0.097		
Usual activities = 5	0.205		
Pain/discomfort = 2	0.030		
Pain/discomfort = 3	0.050	Minus PD level 3	−0.050
Pain/discomfort = 4	0.261		
Pain/discomfort = 5	0.575		
Anxiety/depression = 2	0.018	Minus AD level 2	−0.018
Anxiety/depression = 3	0.029		
Anxiety/depression = 4	0.108		
Anxiety/depression = 5	0.232		
		State 21232	=0.884

AD anxiety/depression, *MO* mobility, *PD* pain/discomfort, *SC* self-care, *UA* usual activities

The mathematical representation of the model for health state X is:

$$V(X) = 1 - 0.025\,MO_2 - 0.034\,MO_3 - 0.126\,MO_4 - 0.314\,MO_5 - 0.031$$
$$SC_2 - 0.047\,SC_3 - 0.111\,SC_4 - 0.264\,SC_5 - 0.023\,UA_2 - 0.040\,UA_3 - 0.097$$
$$UA_4 - 0.205\,UA_5 - 0.030\,PD_2 - 0.050\,PD_3 - 0.261\,PD_4 - 0.575\,PD_5 - 0.018$$
$$AD_2 - 0.029\,AD_3 - 0.108\,AD_4 - 0.232\,AD_5$$

(i)   **Date/wave of study**
Data were collected in the third wave of EQ-5D-5L valuation studies using the EQ-5D-5L valuation protocol 2.0. Interviews were conducted from June until October 2016.

(ii)   **Sample size; sample frame**
1281 interviews with the general population were conducted. Quota-based sampling was applied using Polish census data from November 2014, based on personal identification number registry and Central Statistical Office data on education (Central Statistical Office 2015). Of the 1252 respondents included in the final value set, 52.5% were female and 47.5% were male. The age distribution of the respondents was:

18–24 years	14.8%
25–29 years	7.0%
30–39 years	17.5%
40–49 years	15.9%
50–64 years	26.5%
65–74 years	13.9%
75+ years	4.5%

(iii) **Representativeness of achieved sample**

The study sample was representative for the Polish general population in terms of age, sex, education, employment status, as well as size and geographical location of the place of residence (Table 4.62).

Table 4.62 Representativeness of the sample in the Polish valuation study

		Study sample (N=1252)	Polish general population[a]
Sampling characteristics			
Age, n (%)	18–34	378 (30.2%)	30.2%
	35–49	313 (25.0%)	25.1%
	50–64	332 (26.5%)	25.6%
	≥ 65	229 (18.3%)	19.2%
Gender, n (%)	Female	657 (52.5%)	52.6%
	Male	595 (47.5%)	47.4%
Geographical location of residence, n (%)	Central	242 (19.4%)	20.3%
	Southwest	136 (10.9%)	10.3%
	South	245 (19.6%)	20.6%
	Northwest	199 (15.9%)	16.0%
	North	187 (15.0%)	15.0%
	East	241 (19.3%)	17.9%
Size of place of residence, n (%)	Rural area	501 (40.1%)	39.5%
	Town of less than 100,000 inhabitants	404 (32.3%)	32.9%
	City of 100,000 and more inhabitants	345 (27.6%)	27.6%
Education, n (%)	Primary or middle school	221 (17.7%)	17.9%
	Vocational school	328 (26.2%)	24.9%
	Secondary school	428 (34.2%)	35.9%
	Higher	273 (21.8%)	21.3%
Employment status, n (%)	Employed/self-employed	637 (51.2%)	49.7%
	Unemployed (able to work)	90 (7.2%)	8.4%
	Unemployed (unable to work, annuitant)	77 (6.2%)	6.7%
	Student (full time)	114 (9.2%)	7.2%
	Homemaker, housewife	32 (2.6%)	3.4%
	Retired person	295 (23.7%)	24.7%

Reproduced from Golicki et al. (2019)
[a]Central Statistical Office 2015

(iv) **Mean observed cTTO values of EQ-5D-5L states** (Table 4.63)

Table 4.63 Mean observed cTTO values by health state

State	Mean	SE	State	Mean	SE	State	Mean	SE
11112	0.981	0.002	21345	0.519	0.032	43315	0.670	0.029
11121	0.966	0.004	21444	0.548	0.035	43514	0.602	0.029
11122	0.948	0.006	22434	0.706	0.026	43542	0.408	0.044
11211	0.973	0.002	23152	0.443	0.040	43555	0.024	0.048
11212	0.957	0.004	23242	0.577	0.034	44125	0.466	0.038
11221	0.940	0.009	23514	0.640	0.033	44345	0.270	0.046
11235	0.720	0.019	24342	0.537	0.035	44553	0.106	0.047
11414	0.786	0.022	24443	0.518	0.036	45133	0.533	0.036
11421	0.821	0.024	24445	0.272	0.043	45144	0.317	0.045
11425	0.651	0.033	24553	0.205	0.051	45233	0.503	0.042
12111	0.965	0.003	25122	0.656	0.037	45413	0.552	0.037
12112	0.943	0.009	25222	0.694	0.031	51152	0.252	0.049
12121	0.950	0.005	25331	0.663	0.034	51451	0.212	0.048
12244	0.582	0.033	31514	0.685	0.028	52215	0.424	0.047
12334	0.773	0.016	31524	0.682	0.029	52335	0.439	0.044
12344	0.535	0.039	31525	0.568	0.033	52431	0.649	0.031
12513	0.728	0.027	32314	0.791	0.023	52455	0.018	0.050
12514	0.674	0.028	32443	0.594	0.026	53221	0.666	0.035
12543	0.518	0.036	33253	0.317	0.047	53243	0.439	0.044
13122	0.919	0.007	34155	0.126	0.050	53244	0.384	0.048
13224	0.754	0.024	34232	0.739	0.022	53412	0.530	0.046
13313	0.873	0.015	34244	0.507	0.036	54153	0.237	0.048
14113	0.875	0.010	34515	0.517	0.033	54231	0.593	0.041
14554	0.158	0.048	35143	0.490	0.040	54342	0.324	0.046
15151	0.321	0.046	35245	0.343	0.041	55225	0.179	0.050
21111	0.961	0.006	35311	0.651	0.039	55233	0.335	0.049
21112	0.939	0.012	35332	0.637	0.038	55424	0.246	0.049
21315	0.750	0.027	42115	0.617	0.033	55555	−0.408	0.016
21334	0.793	0.014	42321	0.767	0.028			

SE standard error

(v)   **Proportions choosing A in the DCE based on relative severities of A and B** (Fig. 4.32)

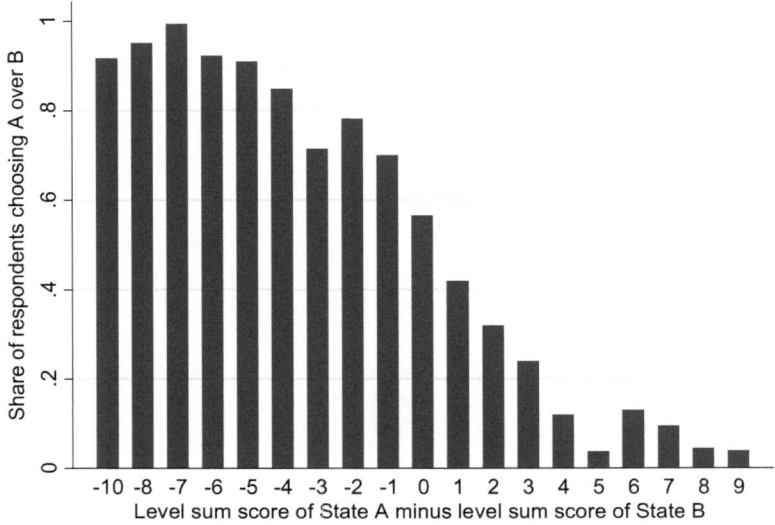

Fig. 4.32 Proportions choosing A based on relative severities of A and B

(vi) **Exclusion criteria**
      29 interviews with data quality issues in the cTTO part were excluded from the data analysis (i.e. flagged interviews in QC tool; see Chap. 2 for more details). A total of 8.3% of cTTO responses (n = 1040) were removed following the feedback module. No DCE data were excluded from the analysis.

(vii) **Number of interviewers; Interviewer effects**
      In total, 1281 interviews were conducted by 15 interviewers. The variance of the responses included in the final value set can be partitioned into variance related to differences between interviewers (3.5%), respondents (13.7%), and responses (82.8%).

(viii) **Description of modelling choices**
      The Polish EQ-5D-5L value set was based on a hybrid model that accounted for random parameters, error scaling with fat tails, censoring at −1, unwillingness to trade life years in cTTO by the religious people and Cauchy distribution in DCE. The intercept was constrained in the final model.

(ix)   **Value Set** (Table 4.64 and Fig. 4.33)

Table 4.64   Key characteristics of the Polish value set

Characteristics	Polish EQ-5D-5L value set
% states with negative values	6.7% (208 out of 3125)
Rank order of dimensions (from most to least relative importance)	Pain/discomfort Mobility Self-care Anxiety/depression Usual activities
Coefficient with highest weight	0.575 (level 5 of pain/discomfort)
Range of values	Maximum value: 1 Minimum value: −0.590
Max value < 1:	0.982 (value of health state 11112)
Linearity/non-linearity of value decrements by level	For all five dimensions, changes from level 3 to 2, and from level 2 to 1, confer relatively modest, and very similar, changes in value (see Fig. 4.33). A change in health between levels 5 and 4, and between levels 4 and 3, results in larger changes in value – and this is especially marked in the case of pain/discomfort.

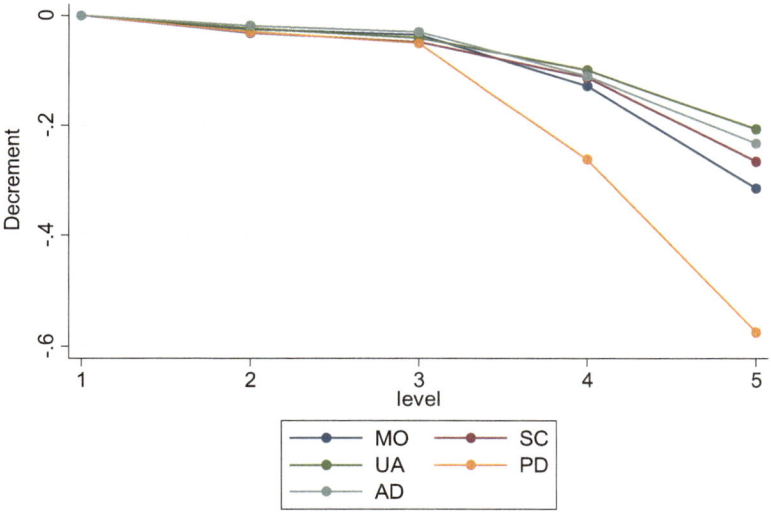

Fig. 4.33 Value decrements across dimensions (*AD* anxiety/depression, *MO* mobility, *PD* pain/discomfort, *SC* self-care, *UA* usual activities)

(x)   **Uptake by local HTA/health care decision makers**
        A pharmacoeconomic analysis is required in Polish HTA submissions, and
        cost-utility analysis is the preferred form of economic evaluation in HTA
        reports and reimbursement dossiers of drugs, according to Reimbursement
        Act (2011) and Polish HTA agency (Agencja Oceny Technologii Medycznych
        i Taryfikacji, AOTMiT) guidelines (AOTMiT 2016). The preferred way of
        obtaining health state values is based on secondary sources – published data
        collected using questionnaires accompanied by values. The first choice is
        EQ-5D (EQ-5D-5L or EQ-5D-3L). If EQ-5D-based data are not available,
        the second choice is SF-6D- or HUI-based utilities. The third choice covers
        health state values based on other instruments. In the case of primary collec-
        tion of health states valuation data, the use of EQ-5D (EQ-5D-3L or
        EQ-5D-5L) and Polish values sets are recommended.

(xi)   **Reference(s) for this value set**
        Golicki D, Jakubczyk M, Graczyk K, Niewada M (2019) Valuation of
        EQ-5D-5L Health States in Poland: the First EQ-VT-Based Study in
        Central and Eastern Europe. Pharmacoeconomics 37(9):1165–1176

Further Literature

Agencja Oceny Technologii Medycznych i Taryfikacji (AOTMiT) (2016) Health
    Technology Assessment Guidelines (Version 3.0). AOTMiT, Warsaw.
    https://www.aotm.gov.pl/media/2020/07/20160913_Wytyczne_AOTMiT.pdf
    [Polish version];
https://www2.aotm.gov.pl/wp-content/uploads/wytyczne_hta/2016/20161104_
    HTA_Guidelines_AOTMiT.pdf [English version]. Accessed 13 July 2021
Central Statistical Office (2015) Demographic yearbook of Poland. Zakład
    Wydawnictw Statystycznych, Warsaw

4.3.3.7   Country/Region: Portugal (Table 4.65)

Table 4.65 Overview of EQ-5D-5L value set for Portugal

Portuguese EQ-5D-5L value set		Example: the value for health state 21232	
Full health (11111)	1	Full health	=1
Mobility = 2	0.048	Minus MO level 2	−0.048
Mobility = 3	0.092		
Mobility = 4	0.182		
Mobility = 5	0.356		
Self-care = 2	0.048	Minus SC level 1	−0.000
Self-care = 3	0.070		
Self-care = 4	0.156		
Self-care = 5	0.294		
Usual activities = 2	0.044	Minus UA level 2	−0.044
Usual activities = 3	0.063		
Usual activities = 4	0.135		
Usual activities = 5	0.263		
Pain/discomfort = 2	0.041		
Pain/discomfort = 3	0.101	Minus PD level 3	−0.101
Pain/discomfort = 4	0.254		
Pain/discomfort = 5	0.406		
Anxiety/depression = 2	0.036	Minus AD level 2	−0.036
Anxiety/depression = 3	0.085		
Anxiety/depression = 4	0.212		
Anxiety/depression = 5	0.284		
		State 21232	=0.771

AD anxiety/depression, *MO* mobility, *PD* pain/discomfort, *SC* self-care, *UA* usual activities

The mathematical representation of the model for health state X is:

$$V(X) = 1 - 0.048\,MO_2 - 0.092\,MO_3 - 0.182\,MO_4 - 0.356\,MO_5 - 0.048$$
$$SC_2 - 0.070\,SC_3 - 0.156\,SC_4 - 0.294\,SC_5 - 0.044\,UA_2 - 0.063\,UA_3 - 0.135$$
$$UA_4 - 0.263\,UA_5 - 0.041\,PD_2 - 0.101\,PD_3 - 0.254\,PD_4 - 0.406\,PD_5 - 0.036$$
$$AD_2 - 0.085\,AD_3 - 0.212\,AD_4 - 0.284\,AD_5$$

(i)   **Date/wave of study**

Data were collected in the third wave of EQ-5D-5L valuation studies using the EQ-5D-5L valuation protocol 2.0. Interviews were conducted between October 2015 and July 2016.

(ii)   **Sample size; sample frame**

1451 interviews with the general population were conducted over the country. Random sampling stratified by gender and age group, based on the Portuguese census (Portuguese Statistical Office 2012), was applied that was originally designed based on the random route sampling method. Of the 1450 respondents included in the final value set, 56.9% were female and 43.1% were male. The age distribution of the respondents was:

18–24 years	10.6%
25–29 years	5.9%
30–39 years	16.3%
40–49 years	13.8%
50–64 years	21.2%
65–74 years	19.0%
75+ years	13.2%

(iii) **Representativeness of achieved sample**

The study sample was representative for the Portuguese population in terms of age (over 18 years), and gender of the general population of mainland Portugal and the islands (Table 4.66).

Table 4.66 Representativeness of the sample in the Portuguese valuation study

		Study sample (N=1450)[a]	Portuguese general population[b]
Sampling characteristics			
Age, n (%)	18–29	239 (16.5%)	17.0%
	30–39	236 (16.3%)	18.5%
	40–49	200 (13.8%)	17.8%
	50–59	232 (16.0%)	16.2%
	60–69	155 (10.7%)	13.7%
	≥ 70	388 (26.7%)	16.8%
Gender, n (%)	Female	825 (56.9%)	53.0%
	Male	625 (43.1%)	47.0%
Education, n (%)	No formal education	47 (3.2%)	6.2%
	4 years	239 (16.5%)	31.2%
	6 years	86 (5.9%)	9.7%
	9 years	176 (12.2%)	14.9%
	12 years	322 (22.2%)	19.2%
	Higher education	580 (40.0%)	18.8%
Employment status, n (%)	Employed/self-employed	725 (50.0%)	49.4%
	Unemployed but able to work	70 (4.8%)	7.4%
	Unemployed but unable to work for health reasons	3 (0.2%)	1.6%
	Student	146 (10.1%)	5.8%
	Housekeeper	43 (3.0%)	4.7%
	Retired	463 (31.9%)	31.1%
Family status, n (%)	Married or living in common law	731 (50.4%)	56.9%
	Single	409 (28.2%)	27.4%
	Widower	173 (11.9%)	8.9%
	Divorced or separated	137 (9.5%)	6.8%

Reproduced from Ferreira et al. (2019)
[a]All respondents included in the final value set are presented
[b]Portuguese Statistical Office 2012

(iv)　**Mean observed cTTO values of EQ-5D-5L states** (Table 4.67)

Table 4.67　Mean observed cTTO values by health state

State	Mean	SE	State	Mean	SE	State	Mean	SE
11112	0.951	0.008	21345	0.380	0.043	43315	0.387	0.045
11121	0.952	0.005	21444	0.349	0.044	43514	0.308	0.046
11122	0.921	0.009	22434	0.491	0.038	43542	0.176	0.047
11211	0.951	0.003	23152	0.420	0.041	43555	−0.146	0.049
11212	0.907	0.017	23242	0.580	0.037	44125	0.283	0.053
11221	0.940	0.006	23514	0.421	0.042	44345	−0.039	0.051
11235	0.581	0.041	24342	0.498	0.041	44553	−0.051	0.046
11414	0.635	0.033	24443	0.364	0.041	45133	0.271	0.050
11421	0.820	0.014	24445	0.062	0.049	45144	0.126	0.052
11425	0.487	0.044	24553	0.142	0.046	45233	0.363	0.043
12111	0.951	0.004	25122	0.664	0.031	45413	0.364	0.040
12112	0.896	0.018	25222	0.617	0.036	51152	0.274	0.040
12121	0.936	0.006	25331	0.574	0.036	51451	0.111	0.053
12244	0.436	0.039	31514	0.456	0.038	52215	0.228	0.054
12334	0.601	0.037	31524	0.416	0.043	52335	0.205	0.047
12344	0.335	0.047	31525	0.388	0.040	52431	0.383	0.046
12513	0.631	0.034	32314	0.584	0.043	52455	−0.027	0.044
12514	0.457	0.041	32443	0.336	0.045	53221	0.524	0.046
12543	0.318	0.045	33253	0.317	0.044	53243	0.271	0.047
13122	0.842	0.013	34155	0.050	0.051	53244	0.137	0.049
13224	0.566	0.040	34232	0.557	0.037	53412	0.397	0.049
13313	0.777	0.019	34244	0.292	0.044	54153	0.055	0.048
14113	0.741	0.024	34515	0.226	0.051	54231	0.373	0.050
14554	−0.078	0.050	35143	0.363	0.040	54342	0.114	0.052
15151	0.268	0.047	35245	0.120	0.052	55225	0.097	0.050
21111	0.944	0.008	35311	0.499	0.045	55233	0.187	0.047
21112	0.919	0.010	35332	0.475	0.038	55424	−0.029	0.047
21315	0.564	0.041	42115	0.487	0.042	55555	−0.462	0.013
21334	0.612	0.040	42321	0.660	0.036			

SE standard error

(v) **Proportions choosing A in the DCE based on relative severities of A and B** (Fig. 4.34)

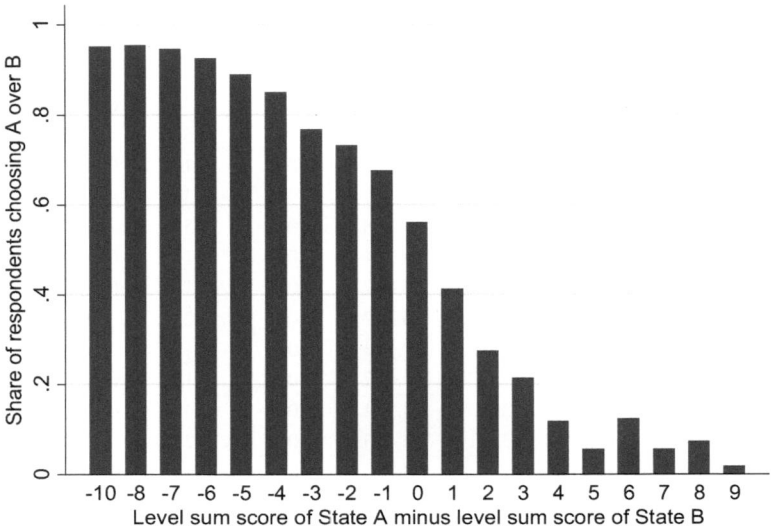

Fig. 4.34 Proportions choosing A based on relative severities of A and B

(vi) **Exclusion criteria**
A total of 7.7% of cTTO responses (n = 1119) were removed following the feedback module. In addition, one participant with a positive slope on the regression between his cTTO values and the level sum score was also excluded. No DCE data were excluded from the analysis.

(vii) **Number of interviewers; Interviewer effects**
In total, 1451 interviews were conducted by 28 interviewers. The variance of the responses included in the final value set can be partitioned into variance related to differences between interviewers (5.7%), respondents (20.0%), and responses (74.3%).

(viii) **Description of modelling choices**
The Portuguese EQ-5D-5L value set was based on a hybrid model combining a conditional logit model for the DCE data and a censored at -1 tobit model for the cTTO data, correcting for heteroskedasticity. The intercept was constrained in the final model.

(ix)   **Value Set** (Table 4.68 and Fig. 4.35)

Table 4.68 Key characteristics of the Portuguese value set

Characteristics	Portuguese EQ-5D-5L value set
% states with negative values	9.3% (292 out of 3125)
Rank order of dimensions (from most to least relative importance)	Pain/discomfort Mobility Anxiety/depression Self-care Usual activities
Coefficient with highest weight	0.406 (level 5 of pain/discomfort)
Range of values	Maximum value: 1 Minimum value: −0.603
Max value < 1:	0.964 (value of health state 11112)
Linearity/non-linearity of value decrements by level	Value decrements for levels 2 and 3 were similar across all dimensions (see Fig. 4.35). Kink at level 3 for all dimensions and in levels 4 and 5, the value decrements were more differentiated. Decrements for pain/discomfort and mobility were the highest.

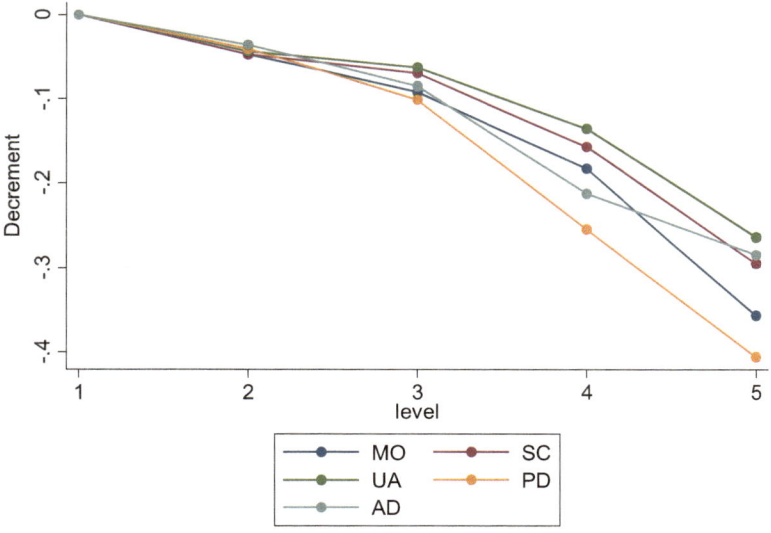

Fig. 4.35 Value decrements across dimensions (*AD* anxiety/depression, *MO* mobility, *PD* pain/discomfort, *SC* self-care, *UA* usual activities)

(x)   **Uptake by local HTA/health care decision makers**
The National Authority of Medicines and Health Products (Infarmed) recommends in its official methodological guidelines for economic evaluation studies of health technologies that the EQ-5D-5L questionnaire and the Portuguese EQ-5D-5L value set should be the preferred measure used to assess HRQoL in cost-utility analyses (CUA) (Perelman et al. 2019).

(xi) **Reference(s) for this value set**
Ferreira PL, Antunes P, Ferreira LN, Pereira LN, Ramos-Goñi JM (2019) A hybrid modelling approach for eliciting health states preferences: the Portuguese EQ-5D-5L value set. Qual Life Res 28(12):3163–3175

Further Literature

Perelman J, Soares M, Mateus C, Duarte A, Faria R, Ferreira L, Saramago P, Veiga P, Furtado C, Caldeira S, Teixeira MC, Sculpher M (2019) Methodological Guidelines for Economic Evaluation Studies of Health Technologies. INFARMED – National Authority of Medicines and Health Products, I.P., Lisbon. https://www.infarmed.pt/web/infarmed-en/human-medicines. Accessed 25 June 2021

Portuguese Statistical Office (2012) Census 2011. Portuguese Statistical Office, Lisbon

4.3.3.8   Country/Region: Taiwan (Table 4.69)

Table 4.69   Overview of EQ-5D-5L value set for Taiwan[a]

Taiwanese EQ-5D-5L value set		Example: the value for health state 21232	
Full health (11111)	1	Full health	=1
Mobility = 2	0.108	Minus MO level 2	−0.108
Mobility = 3	0.200		
Mobility = 4	0.365		
Mobility = 5	0.477		
Self-care = 2	0.076	Minus SC level 1	−0.000
Self-care = 3	0.132		
Self-care = 4	0.264		
Self-care = 5	0.324		
Usual activities = 2	0.073	Minus UA level 2	−0.073
Usual activities = 3	0.123		
Usual activities = 4	0.280		
Usual activities = 5	0.351		
Pain/discomfort = 2	0.087		
Pain/discomfort = 3	0.158	Minus PD level 3	−0.158
Pain/discomfort = 4	0.340		
Pain/discomfort = 5	0.453		
Anxiety/depression = 2	0.064	Minus AD level 2	−0.064
Anxiety/depression = 3	0.183		
Anxiety/depression = 4	0.340		
Anxiety/depression = 5	0.421		
		State 21232	=0.597

AD anxiety/depression, *MO* mobility, *PD* pain/discomfort, *SC* self-care, *UA* usual activities
[a]These coefficients present the decrement from level 1 to the respective level (regular dummies), whereas Lin et al. (2018) report coefficients representing the additional decrement of moving from one level to another (incremental dummies)

The mathematical representation of the model for health state X is:

$$V(X) = 1 - 0.108\,MO_2 - 0.200\,MO_3 - 0.365\,MO_4 - 0.477\,MO_5 - 0.076$$
$$SC_2 - 0.132\,SC_3 - 0.264\,SC_4 - 0.324\,SC_5 - 0.073\,UA_2 - 0.123\,UA_3 - 0.280$$
$$UA_4 - 0.351\,UA_5 - 0.087\,PD_2 - 0.158\,PD_3 - 0.340\,PD_4 - 0.453\,PD_5 - 0.064$$
$$AD_2 - 0.183\,AD_3 - 0.340\,AD_4 - 0.421\,AD_5$$

(i)   **Date/wave of study**
Data were collected in the third wave of EQ-5D-5L valuation studies using the EQ-5D-5L valuation protocol 2.0. Interviews were conducted between January and July 2017.

(ii) **Sample size; sample frame**

1000 interviews with the general population were conducted in nine randomly selected cities located in six geographic regions in Taiwan: Taipei, New Taipei, Tauyuan, Chinju, Hualien, Taichung, Chiayi, Tainan, and Kaohsiung. Multi-stage stratified quota sampling with respect to region (stage 1) and age (over 20), gender, and education (stage 2) was applied (Department of household registration, Ministry of the Interior, Taiwan 2016). Of the 1000 respondents included in the final value set, 50.5% were female and 49.5% were male. The age distribution of the respondents was:

20–24 years	7.9%
25–29 years	9.4%
30–39 years	20.8%
40–49 years	19.0%
50–64 years	28.8%
65–74 years	11.5%
75+ years	2.6%

(iii) **Representativeness of achieved sample**

The study sample was representative for the Taiwanese population in terms of age, gender, and living area. Respondents with higher education were overrepresented while respondents with primary school education were underrepresented in the study sample (Table 4.70).

Table 4.70 Representativeness of the sample in the Taiwanese valuation study

		Study sample (N=1000)	Taiwanese general population[a]
Sampling characteristics			
Age, n (%)	20–29	173 (17.3%)	17.8%
	30–39	208 (20.8%)	21.4%
	40–49	190 (19.0%)	19.1%
	50–59	193 (19.3%)	19.0%
	≥ 60	236 (23.6%)	22.7%
Gender, n (%)	Female	505 (50.5%)	50.8%
	Male	495 (49.5%)	49.2%
Living area, n (%)	North & East	500 (50.0%)	50.7%
	Central	225 (22.5%)	21.5%
	South	275 (27.5%)	27.8%
Education, n (%)	Primary school	130 (13.0%)	44.1%
	High school	277 (27.7%)	28.8%
	Higher education	593 (59.3%)	27.1%

Reproduced from Lin et al. (2018)

[a]Department of household registration, Ministry of the Interior, Taiwan 2016

(iv)   **Mean observed cTTO values of EQ-5D-5L states** (Table 4.71)

Table 4.71 Mean observed cTTO values by health state

State	Mean	SE	State	Mean	SE	State	Mean	SE
11112	0.957	0.005	21345	−0.007	0.059	43315	−0.078	0.052
11121	0.931	0.009	21444	−0.111	0.058	43514	−0.160	0.060
11122	0.895	0.015	22434	0.014	0.053	43542	−0.265	0.050
11211	0.950	0.005	23152	0.204	0.052	43555	−0.603	0.043
11212	0.886	0.016	23242	0.325	0.049	44125	−0.098	0.057
11221	0.908	0.012	23514	0.027	0.051	44345	−0.390	0.047
11235	0.315	0.044	24342	0.073	0.058	44553	−0.430	0.052
11414	0.339	0.053	24443	−0.173	0.054	45133	−0.069	0.052
11421	0.583	0.040	24445	−0.381	0.052	45144	−0.422	0.048
11425	0.139	0.052	24553	−0.252	0.054	45233	−0.025	0.058
12111	0.930	0.010	25122	0.469	0.051	45413	−0.170	0.056
12112	0.902	0.015	25222	0.387	0.055	51152	−0.030	0.053
12121	0.894	0.013	25331	0.212	0.059	51451	−0.219	0.052
12244	0.167	0.054	31514	0.076	0.056	52215	−0.090	0.050
12334	0.296	0.052	31524	−0.001	0.052	52335	−0.342	0.053
12344	0.056	0.052	31525	−0.048	0.056	52431	−0.013	0.054
12513	0.267	0.049	32314	0.331	0.049	52455	−0.486	0.050
12514	0.225	0.046	32443	−0.064	0.048	53221	0.202	0.049
12543	−0.027	0.050	33253	−0.124	0.057	53243	−0.220	0.055
13122	0.745	0.022	34155	−0.388	0.046	53244	−0.314	0.054
13224	0.291	0.056	34232	0.204	0.053	53412	0.002	0.057
13313	0.551	0.041	34244	−0.095	0.057	54153	−0.301	0.050
14113	0.474	0.041	34515	−0.245	0.052	54231	−0.025	0.052
14554	−.318	0.048	35143	−0.097	0.059	54342	−0.223	0.050
15151	0.105	0.058	35245	−0.323	0.048	55225	−0.344	0.054
21111	0.947	0.007	35311	0.244	0.054	55233	−0.099	0.061
21112	0.871	0.015	35332	0.096	0.055	55424	−0.370	0.053
21315	0.298	0.048	42115	0.096	0.052	55555	−0.739	0.012
21334	0.293	0.052	42321	0.253	0.053			

SE standard error

(v) **Proportions choosing A in the DCE based on relative severities of A and B** (Fig. 4.36)

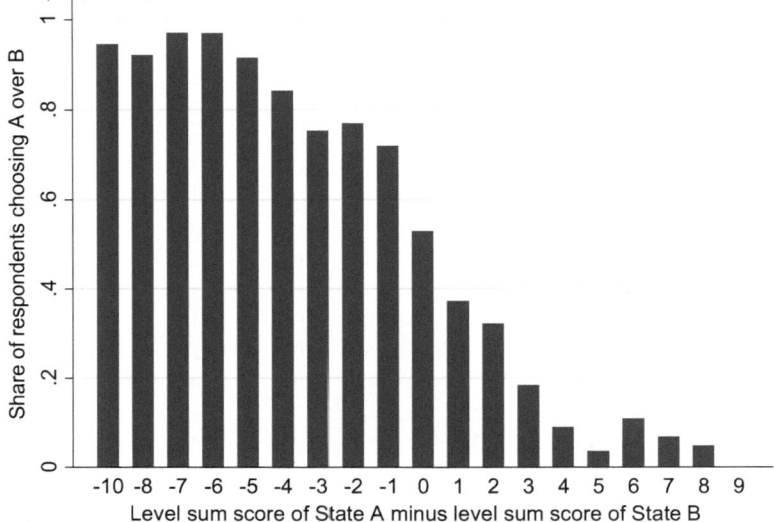

Fig. 4.36 Proportions choosing A based on relative severities of A and B

(vi) **Exclusion criteria**
No data were excluded from the analysis.

(vii) **Number of interviewers; Interviewer effects**
In total, 1000 interviews were conducted by 10 interviewers. The variance of the responses can be partitioned into variance related to differences between interviewers (1.3%), respondents (15.5%), and responses (83.2%).

(viii) **Description of modelling choices**
The Taiwanese EQ-5D-5L value set was based on a hybrid model combining a conditional logit model for the DCE data and a censored at -1 tobit GLS model for the cTTO data. The intercept was constrained in the final model because it was non-significant.

(ix)   **Value Set** (Table 4.72 and Fig. 4.37)

Table 4.72   Key characteristics of the Taiwanese value set

Characteristics	Taiwanese EQ-5D-5L value set
% states with negative values	45.1% (1410 out of 3125)
Rank order of dimensions (from most to least relative importance)	Mobility Pain/discomfort Anxiety/depression Usual activities Self-care
Coefficient with highest weight	0.477 (level 5 of mobility)
Range of values	Maximum value: 1 Minimum value: −1.026
Max value < 1:	0.936 (value of health state 11112)
Linearity/non-linearity of value decrements by level	Value decrements for mobility are higher than those for other dimensions across all levels (see Fig. 4.37). The biggest change in value occurs between levels 3 and 4 on all dimensions, with further large reductions in value between levels 4 and 5.

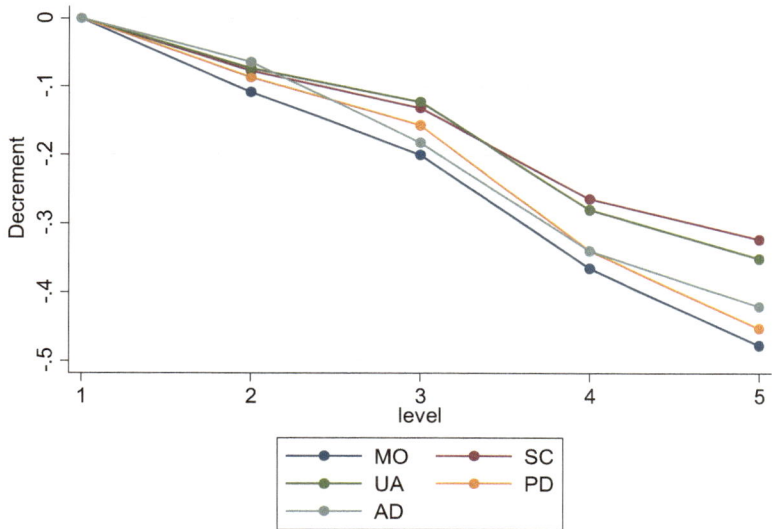

Fig. 4.37   Value decrements across dimensions (AD anxiety/depression, MO mobility, PD pain/discomfort, SC self-care, UA usual activities)

(x)   **Uptake by local HTA/health care decision makers**
        Conducting local cost-effectiveness analyses for new technologies is encour-
        aged in the official guideline of the Center for Drug Evaluation (CDE) in
        Taiwan (CDE 2021a, 2021b; Taiwan Society for Pharmacoeconomics and
        Outcomes Research [TaSPOR] 2014). The EQ-5D is listed as one of three
        recommended tools for multi-attribute utility system in this HTA guideline
        (TaSPOR 2014). A local value set was recommended, although no local value
        sets were available at the time of publishing this HTA guideline. Under the
        implementation of NHI in Taiwan, it was announced that "new drug applica-
        tions with local pharmacoeconomic studies are more likely to get reimburse-
        ment (…) [and the] additional markup of up to 10% of pricing decision (…)
        [can be added once the] applicants conduct a local pharmacoeconomic study"
        after quality review of the HTA/CDE (Chen et al. 2018). As a result, the
        EQ-5D-5L value set for Taiwan reported here was endorsed by CDE and
        TaSPOR in a joint conference ("Workshop of health utility applications -
        How to use Taiwan EQ-5D-5L value set to promote the impacts of pharma-
        coeconomics and outcomes research?" November 29, 2019). Given that the
        large value range of the Taiwanese value set might influence the future calcu-
        lation of quality-adjusted life years (QALYs) in cost-utility analyses, it was
        also agreed that there was a need for further research and discussions to facil-
        itate more reasonable decision-making about adopting a national set of
        EQ-5D-5L weights for QALYs calculations in that aforementioned confer-
        ence. This was also endorsed by HTA/CDE. In addition to its use in HTA, the
        EQ-5D-5L is also included in the National Health Interview Survey.

(xi)   **Reference(s) for this value set**
        Lin HW, Li CI, Lin FJ, Chang JY, Gau CS, Luo N, Pickard AS, Ramos Goñi
        JM, Tang CH, Hsu CN (2018) Valuation of the EQ-5D-5L in Taiwan.
        PLoS ONE 13(12). https://doi.org/10.1371/journal.pone.0209344

Further Literature

Center for Drug Evaluation (CDE) (2021a) Health Technology Assessment.
    Introduction. https://www.cde.org.tw/eng/HTA/. Accessed 21 June 2021
CDE (2021b) HTA Consultation Services. The Process of HTA Assessment for
    Applications of NHI New Drug Listing. http://www.cde.org.tw/eng/HTA/busi-
    ness. Accessed 21 June 2021
Chen GT, Chang SC, Chang CJ (2018) New Drug Reimbursement and Pricing
    Policy in Taiwan. Value Health Reg Issues 15:127–132
Department of household registration, Ministry of the Interior, Taiwan (2016)
    Household registration statistic data analysis 2016. http://www.ris.gov.tw/en/
    web/ris3-english/home. Accessed 12 Jan 2021
Taiwan Society for Pharmacoeconomics and Outcomes Research (TaSPOR) (2014)
    HTA guidelines in Taiwan 2014. Taiwan PE guideline, Pharmacoeconomic
    Guidelines Around the World. https://tools.ispor.org/PEguidelines/countrydet.
    asp?c=31&t=1. Accessed 15 June 2021

4.3.3.9   Country/Region: Denmark (Table 4.73)

Table 4.73 Overview of EQ-5D-5L value set for Denmark

Danish EQ-5D-5L value set		Example: the value for health state 21232	
Full health (11111)	1	Full health	=1
Mobility = 2	0.041	Minus MO level 2	−0.041
Mobility = 3	0.054		
Mobility = 4	0.157		
Mobility = 5	0.220		
Self-care = 2	0.035	Minus SC level 1	−0.000
Self-care = 3	0.050		
Self-care = 4	0.144		
Self-care = 5	0.209		
Usual activities = 2	0.033	Minus UA level 2	−0.033
Usual activities = 3	0.040		
Usual activities = 4	0.139		
Usual activities = 5	0.174		
Pain/discomfort = 2	0.048		
Pain/discomfort = 3	0.094	Minus PD level 3	−0.094
Pain/discomfort = 4	0.381		
Pain/discomfort = 5	0.537		
Anxiety/depression = 2	0.072	Minus AD level 2	−0.072
Anxiety/depression = 3	0.191		
Anxiety/depression = 4	0.430		
Anxiety/depression = 5	0.618		
		State 21232	=0.760

AD anxiety/depression, *MO* mobility, *PD* pain/discomfort, *SC* self-care, *UA* usual activities

The mathematical representation of the model for health state X is:

$$V(X) = 1 - 0.041\,MO_2 - 0.054\,MO_3 - 0.157\,MO_4 - 0.220\,MO_5 - 0.035$$
$$SC_2 - 0.050\,SC_3 - 0.144\,SC_4 - 0.209\,SC_5 - 0.033\,UA_2 - 0.040\,UA_3 - 0.139$$
$$UA_4 - 0.174\,UA_5 - 0.048\,PD_2 - 0.094\,PD_3 - 0.381\,PD_4 - 0.537\,PD_5 - 0.072$$
$$AD_2 - 0.191\,AD_3 - 0.430\,AD_4 - 0.618\,AD_5$$

(i)   **Date/wave of study**

Data were collected in the third wave of EQ-5D-5L valuation studies using the EQ-5D-5L valuation protocol 2.1. Interviews were conducted between October 2018 and November 2019.

(ii) **Sample size; sample frame**

1052 interviews with the general population were conducted. Randomly selected representative samples with respect to age, gender, education, and geographical region were provided by Statistics Denmark and a panel from a Danish market research company, to be invited to the study. Of the 1014 respondents included in the final value set, 51.6% were female and 48.4% were male. The age distribution of the respondents was:

18–24 years	3.9%
25–29 years	7.3%
30–39 years	12.0%
40–49 years	15.7%
50–64 years	29.7%
65–74 years	21.6%
75+ years	9.8%

(iii) **Representativeness of achieved sample**

The study sample was representative for the Danish population in terms of age (over 18 years), gender, education, and geographical region. However, higher educated respondents were slightly overrepresented compared to the general population (Table 4.74).

Table 4.74 Representativeness of the sample in the Danish valuation study

		Study sample (N=1014)	Danish general population[a]
Sampling characteristics			
Age, n (%)	18–24	40 (3.9%)	11.4%
	25–34	136 (13.4%)	15.8%
	35–44	135 (13.3%)	15.3%
	45–54	198 (19.5%)	17.6%
	55–64	187 (18.4%)	15.4%
	65–74	219 (21.6%)	14.1%
	≥75	99 (9.8%)	10.5%
Gender, n (%)	Female	523 (51.6%)	50.6%
	Male	491 (48.4%)	49.4%
Geographical region, n (%)	The North Denmark Region	152 (15.0%)	11.1%
	Central Denmark Region	251 (24.7%)	24.2%
	The Region of Southern Denmark	197 (19.4%)	20.4%
	The Capital Region of Denmark	282 (27.8%)	31.2%
	Region Zealand	132 (13.0%)	13.0%
Highest education (n=1010), n (%)	Secondary school	82 (8.1%)	25.9%
	High school/other	67 (6.6%)	12.0%
	Skilled worker	277 (27.4%)	29.9%
	Short-cycle higher education	126 (12.5%)	4.9%
	Medium-cycle higher education	279 (27.6%)	16.9%
	Long-cycle higher education	179 (17.7%)	10.3%

Reproduced from Jensen et al. (2021)
[a]Danmarks Statistik 2019

(iv)   **Mean observed cTTO values of EQ-5D-5L states** (Table 4.75)

Table 4.75 Mean observed cTTO values by health state

State	Mean	SE	State	Mean	SE	State	Mean	SE
11112	0.925	0.010	21345	0.009	0.063	43315	0.159	0.068
11121	0.956	0.008	21444	0.032	0.059	43514	0.257	0.052
11122	0.909	0.014	22434	0.205	0.064	43542	0.172	0.063
11211	0.943	0.012	23152	0.228	0.062	43555	−0.333	0.066
11212	0.910	0.013	23242	0.405	0.053	44125	0.154	0.058
11221	0.938	0.010	23514	0.294	0.062	44345	−0.085	0.062
11235	0.357	0.056	24342	0.322	0.057	44553	−0.159	0.061
11414	0.379	0.056	24443	0.192	0.060	45133	0.432	0.056
11421	0.855	0.016	24445	−0.233	0.067	45144	−0.027	0.065
11425	0.141	0.066	24553	−0.098	0.064	45233	0.354	0.059
12111	0.958	0.009	25122	0.683	0.042	45413	0.269	0.063
12112	0.903	0.018	25222	0.601	0.042	51152	0.130	0.063
12121	0.885	0.022	25331	0.573	0.047	51451	0.091	0.064
12244	0.236	0.057	31514	0.357	0.057	52215	0.157	0.064
12334	0.398	0.052	31524	0.304	0.061	52335	0.101	0.064
12344	0.130	0.063	31525	0.284	0.056	52431	0.593	0.045
12513	0.719	0.026	32314	0.423	0.052	52455	−0.234	0.061
12514	0.333	0.060	32443	0.156	0.064	53221	0.665	0.038
12543	0.205	0.062	33253	0.170	0.063	53243	0.176	0.059
13122	0.816	0.025	34155	−0.135	0.064	53244	−0.030	0.059
13224	0.409	0.054	34232	0.631	0.039	53412	0.563	0.047
13313	0.752	0.029	34244	0.018	0.061	54153	0.076	0.063
14113	0.682	0.039	34515	0.144	0.062	54231	0.550	0.051
14554	−0.093	0.061	35143	0.199	0.058	54342	0.167	0.059
15151	0.338	0.060	35245	−0.080	0.063	55225	0.050	0.060
21111	0.962	0.006	35311	0.683	0.040	55233	0.289	0.063
21112	0.860	0.030	35332	0.501	0.047	55424	0.092	0.057
21315	0.277	0.064	42115	0.153	0.062	55555	−0.480	0.017
21334	0.432	0.049	42321	0.717	0.040			

SE standard error

(v)   **Proportions choosing A in the DCE based on relative severities of A and B** (Fig. 4.38)

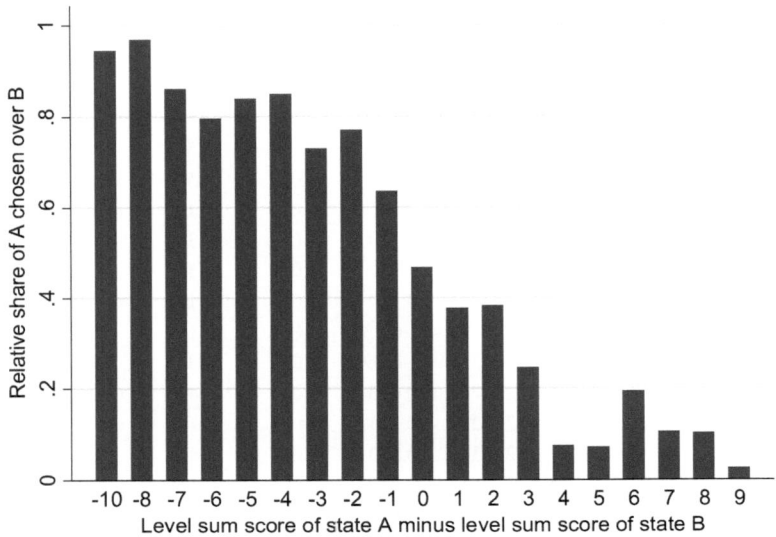

Fig. 4.38 Proportions choosing A based on relative severities of A and B

(vi)   **Exclusion criteria**
5 interviews were dropped because the two interviewers that conducted these interviews were not sufficiently available to do more interviews. Additionally, 12 interviews were dropped due to technical issues, respondents having cognitive or emotional issues, or withdrawing consent. Lastly, 21 respondents were excluded as they did not provide both cTTO and DCE data. A total of 7.0% of cTTO responses (n = 712) were removed following the feedback module.

(vii)   **Number of interviewers; Interviewer effects**
In total, 1014 interviews were conducted by 13 interviewers. 11 interviewers were included in the final interviewer team (see section vi). The variance of the responses included in the final value set can be partitioned into variance related to differences between interviewers (1.9%), respondents (23.8%), and responses (74.3%).

(viii)   **Description of modelling choices**
The Danish EQ−5D-5L value set was based on a hybrid model combining a conditional logit model for the DCE data and a censored at −1 Tobit model for the cTTO data, correcting for heteroskedasticity. The intercept was constrained in the final model.

(ix)   **Value Set** (Table 4.76 and Fig. 4.39)

Table 4.76 Key characteristics of the Danish value set

Characteristics	Danish EQ-5D-5L value set
% states with negative values	21.89% (684 out of 3125)
Rank order of dimensions (from most to least relative importance)	Anxiety/depression Pain/discomfort Mobility Self-care Usual activities
Coefficient with highest weight	0.618 (level 5 of anxiety/depression)
Range of values	Maximum value: 1 Minimum value: −0.757
Max value < 1:	0.967 (value of health state 11211)
Linearity/non-linearity of value decrements by level	Large kink at level 3 for anxiety/depression and pain/discomfort (see Fig. 4.39). Smaller kink at level 3 for the functioning dimensions, with a small reverse kink at level 4. The decrements for MO, SC and UA are very similar, while the decrements for PD and AD are much larger at each level.

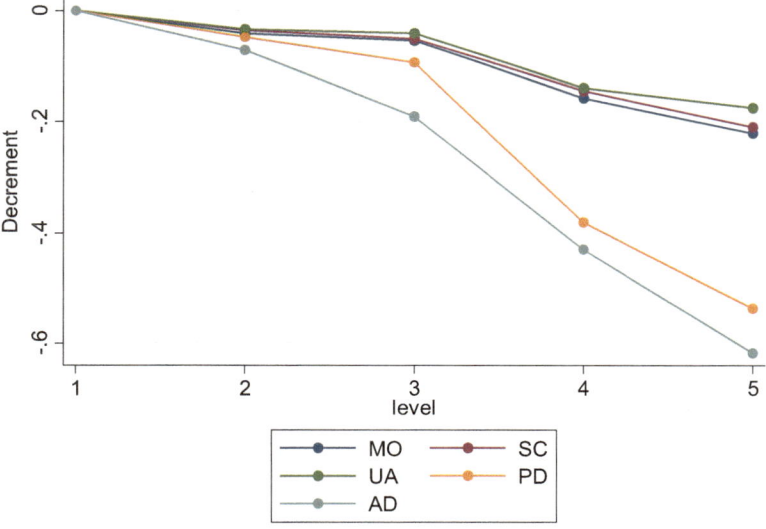

Fig. 4.39 Value decrements across dimensions (*AD* anxiety/depression, *MO* mobility, *PD* pain/discomfort, *SC* self-care, *UA* usual activities)

(x)   **Uptake by local HTA/health care decision makers**

As of 1st January 2021, the Danish Medicines Council started using quality-adjusted life years (QALYs) for the evaluation of new hospital-dispensed pharmaceuticals and change of indication. QALY estimates are expected to be based on EQ-5D-5L and the new Danish value set (Danish Medical Council 2021). Voluntary submissions of cost-utility analyses to the Reimbursement Committee (for prescription medicines prescribed by GPs) are also expected to make use of EQ-5D-5L with the Danish value set (Danish Medicines Agency). Furthermore, a new priority-setting council for new technology (excluding medicines) was established on 1st January 2021—the Danish Health Technology Council. Submissions to the council with cost-utility analysis are requested to use QALYs based on EQ-5D-5L and the Danish value set.

(xi)   **Reference(s) of value set**

Jensen CE, Sørensen SS, Gudex C, Jensen MB, Pedersen KM, Ehlers, LH (2021) The Danish EQ-5D-5L Value set A Hybrid Model Using cTTO and DCE Data. Appl Health Econ Health Policy 19(4):579–591

Further Literature

Danmarks Statistik (2019) Befolkningens udvikling 2019 (Vital Statistics 2019). https://www.dst.dk/Site/Dst/Udgivelser/GetPubFile.aspx?id=29444&sid=befudv2019 Accessed 28 July 2021

Danish Medicines Agency (2018) Health economic analyses in reimbursement applications https://laegemiddelstyrelsen.dk/en/reimbursement/general-reimbursement/application/health-economic-analyses-in-reimbursement-applications/. Accessed 15 July 2021

Danish HTA Agency (2021) Behandlingsrådet. https://behandlingsraadet.dk/proces-og-metode/. Accessed 15 July 2021

Danish Medicines Council (Medicinrådet) (2021) Medicinrådets metodevejledning for vurdering af nye lægemidler. Version 1.0. Published 3rd February 2021. https://medicinraadet.dk/media/5nvplk03/efter-1-januar-2021_medicinrådets-metodevejledning-for-vurdering-af-nye-lægemidler-vers-1-0_adlegacy.pdf. Accessed 15 July 2021

4.3.3.10   Country/Region: Ethiopia (Table 4.77)

Table 4.77 Overview of EQ-5D-5L value set for Ethiopia[a]

Ethiopian EQ-5D-5L value set		Example: the value for health state 21232	
Full health (11111)	1	Full health	=1
Mobility = 2	0.034	Minus MO level 2	−0.034
Mobility = 3	0.064		
Mobility = 4	0.228		
Mobility = 5	0.360		
Self-care = 2	0.024	Minus SC level 1	−0.000
Self-care = 3	0.040		
Self-care = 4	0.142		
Self-care = 5	0.222		
Usual activities = 2	0.032	Minus UA level 2	−0.032
Usual activities = 3	0.048		
Usual activities = 4	0.157		
Usual activities = 5	0.272		
Pain/discomfort = 2	0.036		
Pain/discomfort = 3	0.052	Minus PD level 3	−0.052
Pain/discomfort = 4	0.270		
Pain/discomfort = 5	0.406		
Anxiety/depression = 2	0.026	Minus AD level 2	−0.026
Anxiety/depression = 3	0.085		
Anxiety/depression = 4	0.299		
Anxiety/depression = 5	0.458		
Constant	−		
		State 21232	=0.856

AD anxiety/depression, *MO* mobility, *PD* pain/discomfort, *SC* self-care, *UA* usual activities
[a]In the valuation study manuscript, the value set is reported in incremental dummies. For consistency, we report regular dummies here

The mathematical representation of the model for health state X is:

$$V(X) = 1 - 0.034\,MO_2 - 0.064\,MO_3 - 0.228\,MO_4 - 0.360\,MO_5 - 0.024$$
$$SC_2 - 0.040\,SC_3 - 0.142\,SC_4 - 0.222\,SC_5 - 0.032\,UA_2 - 0.048\,UA_3 - 0.157$$
$$UA_4 - 0.272\,UA_5 - 0.036\,PD_2 - 0.052\,PD_3 - 0.270\,PD_4 - 0.406\,PD_5 - 0.026$$
$$AD_2 - 0.085\,AD_3 - 0.299\,AD_4 - 0.458\,AD_5$$

(i)   **Date/wave of study**
Data were collected in the third wave of EQ-5D-5L valuation studies using the EQ-VT protocol 2.1 and the EQ-PVT software. Interviews were conducted between March and May 2018.

(ii)   **Sample size; sample frame**

1050 interviews with the general population were conducted, recruited from the capital Addis Ababa city, and Butajira, which is a rural region. Multistage stratified quota sampling with respect to geographic area/residence, age, gender, and religion was applied. Of the 1048 respondents included in the final value set, 47.9% were female and 52.1% were male. The age distribution of the respondents was:

18–24 years	37.2%
25–29 years	23.7%
30–39 years	21.1%
40–49 years	7.1%
50–64 years	7.6%
65–74 years	3.2%
75+ years	0.1%

(iii) **Representativeness of achieved sample**

The study sample was representative for the Ethiopian population in terms of age (over 18 years), gender, residence and religion (Table 4.78).

Table 4.78 Representativeness of the sample in the Ethiopian valuation study

		Study sample (N=1050)	Ethiopian general population[a]
Sampling characteristics			
Age, n (%)	18–24	391 (37.2%)	36.0%
	25–54	575 (54.8%)	52.3%
	55–64	49 (4.7%)	6.9%
	≥65	35 (3.3%)	5.2%
Gender, n (%)	Female	503 (47.9%)	50.2%
	Male	547 (52.1%)	49.9%
Residence, n (%)	Urban	300 (28.6%)	19.9%
	Rural	750 (71.4%)	80.1%
Religion, n (%)	Christian	679 (64.7%)	63.0%
	Muslim	368 (35.1%)	34.0%
	Other	3 (0.3%)	3.0%

Reproduced from Welie et al. (2020)
[a]Central Statistical Agency 2017

(iv)   **Mean observed cTTO values of EQ-5D-5L states** (Table 4.79)

Table 4.79 Mean observed cTTO values by health state

State	Mean	SE	State	Mean	SE	State	Mean	SE
11112	0.971	0.004	21345	0.244	0.058	43315	0.257	0.042
11121	0.963	0.005	21444	0.202	0.046	43514	0.222	0.052
11122	0.941	0.006	22434	0.439	0.043	43542	0.158	0.050
11211	0.960	0.008	23152	0.526	0.038	43555	−0.372	0.052
11212	0.939	0.007	23242	0.607	0.036	44125	0.162	0.047
11221	0.923	0.010	23514	0.378	0.045	44345	−0.193	0.055
11235	0.503	0.039	24342	0.490	0.037	44553	−0.193	0.059
11414	0.519	0.036	24443	0.275	0.046	45133	0.457	0.036
11421	0.786	0.014	24445	−0.150	0.052	45144	−0.088	0.056
11425	0.335	0.054	24553	0.001	0.056	45233	0.447	0.034
12111	0.968	0.006	25122	0.730	0.023	45413	0.253	0.049
12112	0.940	0.008	25222	0.704	0.025	51152	0.225	0.052
12121	0.938	0.008	25331	0.603	0.027	51451	0.067	0.053
12244	0.418	0.040	31514	0.389	0.040	52215	0.210	0.054
12334	0.581	0.038	31524	0.398	0.042	52335	0.173	0.047
12344	0.370	0.042	31525	0.261	0.047	52431	0.463	0.033
12513	0.624	0.027	32314	0.590	0.032	52455	−0.309	0.058
12514	0.403	0.045	32443	0.416	0.040	53221	0.550	0.031
12543	0.376	0.044	33253	0.381	0.047	53243	0.242	0.043
13122	0.869	0.012	34155	−0.037	0.056	53244	0.004	0.052
13224	0.561	0.040	34232	0.664	0.025	53412	0.456	0.037
13313	0.796	0.015	34244	0.252	0.047	54153	0.076	0.048
14113	0.773	0.015	34515	0.064	0.053	54231	0.473	0.026
14554	−0.169	0.055	35143	0.374	0.037	54342	0.144	0.049
15151	0.369	0.044	35245	0.004	0.054	55225	−0.003	0.057
21111	0.969	0.004	35311	0.631	0.034	55233	0.406	0.034
21112	0.923	0.010	35332	0.562	0.036	55424	−0.096	0.054
21315	0.505	0.035	42115	0.307	0.049	55555	−0.737	0.011
21334	0.567	0.039	42321	0.707	0.017			

SE standard error

(v)   **Proportions choosing A in the DCE based on relative severities of A and B** (Fig. 4.40)

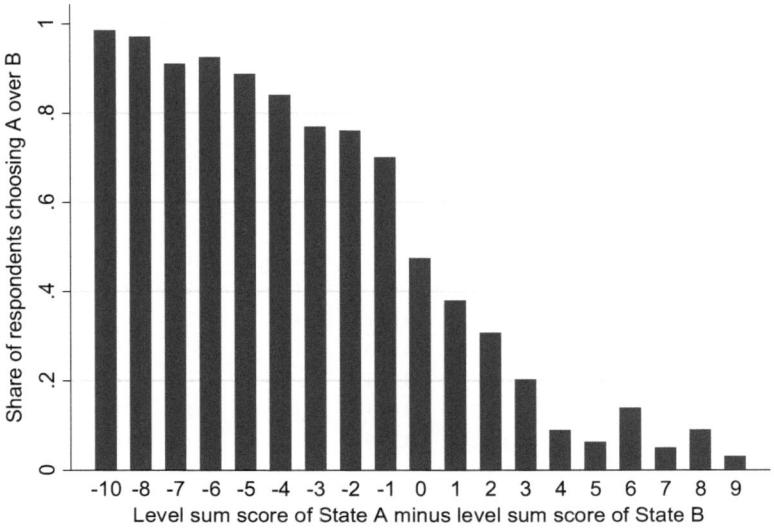

Fig. 4.40 Proportions choosing A based on relative severities of A and B

(vi)   **Exclusion criteria**
Respondents that valued all states as equal in the cTTO were excluded. Furthermore, respondents that valued the worst health state (55555) as higher than the mildest health state in their block were excluded. This amounts to 9 respondents excluded by the characteristics of their cTTO responses. Furthermore, 2 respondents' DCE data were excluded due to technical problems.

(vii)   **Number of interviewers; Interviewer effects**
In total, 1050 interviews were conducted by 10 interviewers. The variance of the responses included in the final value set can be partitioned into variance related to differences between interviewers (0.1%), respondents (10.5%) and responses (89.4%).

(viii) **Description of modelling choices**
The Ethiopian EQ-5D-5L value set was based on a hybrid model combining a conditional logit model for the DCE data and a censored at -1 Tobit model for the cTTO data, correcting for heteroskedasticity. The intercept was constrained in the final model.

(ix)   **Value Set** (Table 4.80 and Fig. 4.41)

Table 4.80 Key characteristics of the Ethiopian value set

Characteristics	Ethiopian EQ-5D-5L value set
% states with negative values	13.4% (419 out of 3125)
Rank order of dimensions (from most to least relative importance)	Anxiety/depression Pain/discomfort Mobility Usual activities Self-care
Coefficient with highest weight	0.458 (level 5 of anxiety/depression)
Range of values	Maximum value: 1 Minimum value: −0.718
Max value < 1:	0.976 (value of health state 12111)
Linearity/non-linearity of value decrements by level	Kink at level 3 for all dimensions (see Fig. 4.41). Linear value decrements for all other levels in all dimensions.

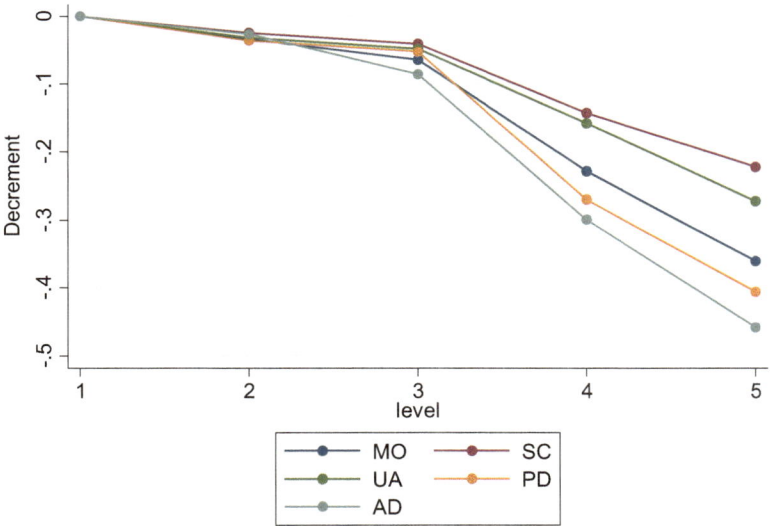

Fig. 4.41 Value decrements across dimensions (*AD* anxiety/depression, *MO* mobility, *PD* pain/discomfort, *SC* self-care, *UA* usual activities)

(x)   **Uptake by local HTA/health care decision makers**

The Ethiopian Federal Ministry of Health (FMOH) has set up an HTA agency in Ethiopia. However, HTA is not yet used for reimbursement decisions in Ethiopia.

(xi)   **Reference(s) of value set**

Welie AG, Gebretekle GB, Stolk E, Mukuria C, Krahn MD, Enquoselassie F, Fenta TG (2020) Valuing health state: an EQ-5D-5L value set for Ethiopians. Value Health Reg Issues 22:7–14

Further Literature

Central Statistical Agency (2017) Demographic and Health Survey 2016. https:// dhsprogram.com/pubs/pdf/FR328/FR328.pdf. Accessed 28 July 2021

4.3.3.11   Country/Region: Hungary (Table 4.81)

Table 4.81 Overview of EQ-5D-5L value set for Hungary

Hungarian EQ-5D-5L value set		Example: the value for health state 21232	
Full health (11111)	1	Full health	=1
Mobility = 2	0.035	Minus MO level 2	−0.035
Mobility = 3	0.089		
Mobility = 4	0.263		
Mobility = 5	0.455		
Self-care = 2	0.045	Minus SC level 1	−0.000
Self-care = 3	0.089		
Self-care = 4	0.241		
Self-care = 5	0.366		
Usual activities = 2	0.035	Minus UA level 2	−0.035
Usual activities = 3	0.085		
Usual activities = 4	0.217		
Usual activities = 5	0.276		
Pain/discomfort = 2	0.043		
Pain/discomfort = 3	0.073	Minus PD level 3	−0.073
Pain/discomfort = 4	0.288		
Pain/discomfort = 5	0.411		
Anxiety/depression = 2	0.040	Minus AD level 2	−0.040
Anxiety/depression = 3	0.093		
Anxiety/depression = 4	0.261		
Anxiety/depression = 5	0.340		
		State 21232	=0.817

AD anxiety/depression, MO mobility, PD pain/discomfort, SC self-care, UA usual activities

The mathematical representation of the model for health state X is:

$$V(X) = 1 - 0.035\,MO_2 - 0.089\,MO_3 - 0.263\,MO_4 - 0.455\,MO_5 - 0.045$$
$$SC_2 - 0.089\,SC_3 - 0.241\,SC_4 - 0.366\,SC_5 - 0.035\,UA_2 - 0.085\,UA_3 - 0.217$$
$$UA_4 - 0.276\,UA_5 - 0.043\,PD_2 - 0.073\,PD_3 - 0.288\,PD_4 - 0.411\,PD_5 - 0.040$$
$$AD_2 - 0.093\,AD_3 - 0.261\,AD_4 - 0.340\,AD_5$$

(i)   **Date/wave of study**
  Data were collected in the third wave of EQ-5D-5L valuation studies using the EQ-5D-5L valuation protocol 2.1. Interviews were conducted from May 2018 until March 2019.

(ii) **Sample size; sample frame**
  1000 interviews with the general population were conducted. A non-probability quota sampling was used, and quotas were set for age and sex accord-

ing to the latest data reported by the Hungarian Central Statistical Office (2016). Of the 1000 respondents included in the final value set, 53.3% were female and 46.7% were male. The age distribution of the respondents was:

18–24 years	10.0%
25–29 years	11.4%
30–39 years	14.4%
40–49 years	17.6%
50–64 years	24.0%
65–74 years	13.0%
75+ years	9.6%

(iii) **Representativeness of achieved sample**
The study sample was representative for the Hungarian general population in terms of age and sex. The distribution of the study sample in terms of marital status, employment status, and area of residence approximated that of the general population. Higher-educated respondents and inhabitants of Central Hungary were slightly overrepresented in the Hungarian valuation study (Table 4.82).

Table 4.82 Representativeness of the sample in the Hungarian valuation study

		Study sample (N=1000)	Hungarian general population[a]
Sampling characteristics			
Age, n (%)	18–24	100 (10.0%)	10.0%
	25–34	152 (15.2%)	15.2%
	35–44	194 (19.4%)	19.5%
	45–54	164 (16.4%)	16.0%
	55–64	164 (16.4%)	16.8%
	65–74	130 (13.0%)	13.0%
	≥ 75	96 (9.6%)	9.5%
Gender, n (%)	Female	533 (53.3%)	53.1%
	Male	467 (46.7%)	46.9%
Geographical region, n (%)	Central Hungary	533 (53.3%)	30.4%
	Transdanubia	177 (17.7%)	30.2%
	Great Plain and North	290 (29.0%)	39.5%
Place of residence, n (%)	Capital	348 (34.8%)	17.9%
	Other town	454 (45.4%)	52.6%
	Village	198 (19.8%)	29.5%
Highest level of education, n (%)	Primary school or less	157 (15.7%)	23.8%
	Secondary school	502 (50.2%)	55.0%
	College/university degree	341 (34.1%)	21.2%

(continued)

Table 4.82 (continued)

		Study sample (N=1000)	Hungarian general population[a]
Employment status, n (%)	Employed	620 (62.0%)	53.1%
	Unemployed	10 (1.0%)	3.1%
	Retired	250 (25.0%)	26.1%
	Disability pensioner	26 (2.6%)	3.1%
	Student	75 (7.5%)	4.7%
	Homemaker/ housewife	19 (1.9%)	1.0%
Marital status, n (%)	Single	239 (23.9%)	18.5%
	Married	419 (41.9%)	45.6%
	Domestic partnership	137 (13.7%)	13.4%
	Divorced	83 (8.3%)	11.1%
	Widowed	122 (12.2%)	11.4%

Reproduced from Rencz et al. (2020)
[a]Hungarian Central Statistical Office 2016

(iv)   **Mean observed cTTO values of EQ-5D-5L states** (Table 4.83)

Table 4.83 Mean observed cTTO values by health state

State	Mean	SE	State	Mean	SE	State	Mean	SE
11112	0.969	0.005	21345	0.313	0.038	43315	0.199	0.050
11121	0.957	0.008	21444	0.065	0.050	43514	0.092	0.050
11122	0.923	0.009	22434	0.395	0.038	43542	0.124	0.051
11211	0.964	0.005	23152	0.446	0.038	43555	−0.297	0.059
11212	0.920	0.012	23242	0.503	0.034	44125	0.113	0.047
11221	0.920	0.012	23514	0.374	0.046	44345	−0.228	0.052
11235	0.564	0.035	24342	0.347	0.042	44553	−0.339	0.051
11414	0.541	0.034	24443	0.122	0.051	45133	0.300	0.046
11421	0.711	0.022	24445	−0.134	0.052	45144	−0.177	0.057
11425	0.427	0.037	24553	−0.083	0.051	45233	0.153	0.050
12111	0.951	0.008	25122	0.490	0.045	45413	0.080	0.049
12112	0.909	0.014	25222	0.520	0.047	51152	0.030	0.053
12121	0.924	0.009	25331	0.422	0.040	51451	0.003	0.049
12244	0.398	0.037	31514	0.376	0.035	52215	0.143	0.058
12334	0.571	0.030	31524	0.361	0.041	52335	−0.062	0.058
12344	0.284	0.040	31525	0.243	0.044	52431	0.234	0.048
12513	0.596	0.026	32314	0.550	0.036	52455	−0.340	0.050
12514	0.430	0.041	32443	0.226	0.048	53221	0.391	0.048
12543	0.294	0.046	33253	0.335	0.043	53243	0.003	0.051
13122	0.806	0.015	34155	−0.112	0.055	53244	−0.124	0.054
13224	0.570	0.035	34232	0.490	0.037	53412	0.280	0.046
13313	0.708	0.023	34244	0.046	0.053	54153	−0.132	0.056
14113	0.681	0.027	34515	0.081	0.054	54231	0.201	0.049

(continued)

Table 4.83 (continued)

State	Mean	SE	State	Mean	SE	State	Mean	SE
14554	−0.194	0.052	35143	0.177	0.046	54342	−0.040	0.047
15151	0.258	0.047	35245	−0.038	0.051	55225	−0.179	0.057
21111	0.971	0.006	35311	0.461	0.042	55233	−0.067	0.056
21112	0.910	0.015	35332	0.304	0.045	55424	−0.372	0.050
21315	0.541	0.035	42115	0.312	0.042	55555	−0.642	0.015
21334	0.541	0.034	42321	0.578	0.025			

SE standard error

(v) **Proportions choosing A in the DCE based on relative severities of A and B** (Fig. 4.42)

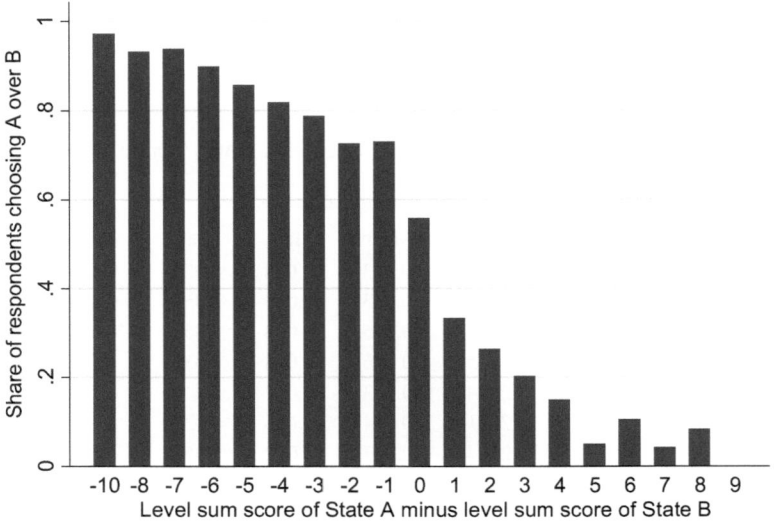

Fig. 4.42 Proportions choosing A based on relative severities of A and B

(vi) **Exclusion criteria**

A total of 6.3% of cTTO responses (n = 634) were removed following the feedback module, but no respondent's entire cTTO responses were excluded.

(vii) **Number of interviewers; Interviewer effects**

In total, 1000 interviews were conducted by 13 interviewers. The variance of the responses can be partitioned into variance related to differences between interviewers (1.7%), respondents (10.7%), and responses (87.6%).

(viii) **Description of modelling choices**

The Hungarian EQ-5D-5L value set was based on the cTTO data only. The selected model was a pooled heteroskedastic tobit model, left-censored at -1. The intercept was constrained in the final model because it was non-significant.

(ix)   **Value Set** (Table 4.84 and Fig. 4.43)

Table 4.84 Key characteristics of the Hungarian value set

Characteristics	Hungarian EQ-5D-5L value set
% states with negative values	21.7% (677 out of 3125)
Rank order of dimensions (from most to least relative importance)	Mobility Pain/discomfort Self-care Anxiety/depression Usual activities
Coefficient with highest weight	0.455 (level 5 of mobility)
Range of values	Maximum value: 1 Minimum value: −0.848
Max value < 1:	0.965 (value of health states 21111 and 11211)
Linearity/non-linearity of value decrements by level	Kink at level 3 for all dimensions (see Fig. 4.43). Value decrements of levels 2 and 3 were similar across all dimensions. In levels 4 and 5, the value decrements were more differentiated between dimensions, with the decrements for mobility and pain/discomfort being the highest.

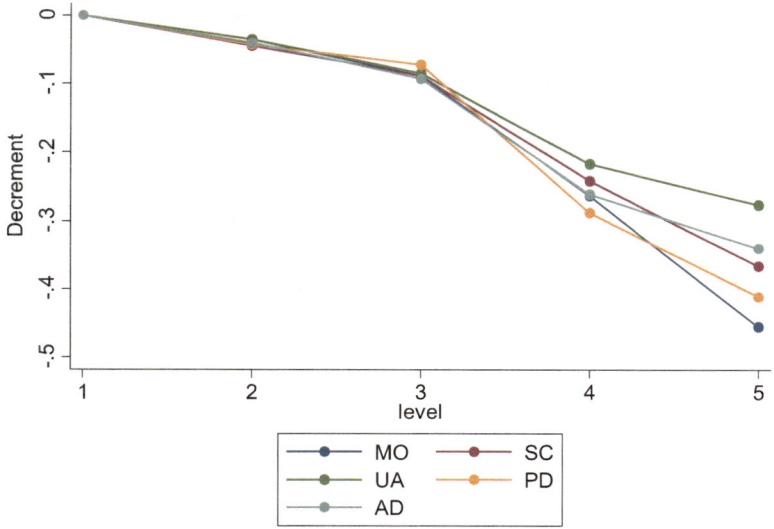

Fig. 4.43 Value decrements across dimensions (*AD* anxiety/depression, *MO* mobility, *PD* pain/discomfort, *SC* self-care, *UA* usual activities)

(x)   **Uptake by local HTA/health care decision makers**
In Hungary, guidelines on methods for economic evaluations in healthcare
are developed by the Ministry of Human Capacities (EMMI 2017), and submissions are critically appraised at the Division for HTA at the National
Institute for Pharmacy and Nutrition (OGYÉI 2019). Cost-utility analysis is
the preferred form of economic evaluation of new health technologies.
EQ-5D-5L is the preferred measure to calculate QALY's (EMMI 2017).
From 2020, the availability of the Hungarian value sets for both EQ-5D-5L
and EQ-5D-3L are expected to increase the use and diffusion of the EQ-5D
in Hungary.

(xi)   **Reference(s) for this value set**
Rencz F, Brodszky V, Gulácsi L, Golicki D, Ruzsa G, Pickard AS, Law EH,
Péntek M (2020) Parallel Valuation of the EQ-5D-3L and EQ-5D-5L by
Time Trade-Off in Hungary. Value Health 23(9):1235–1245

Further Literature

Hungarian Central Statistical Office (2016) Microcensus 2016. http://www.ksh.hu/
docs/eng/xftp/idoszaki/microcensus2016/microcensus_2016_3.pdf.   Accessed
24 Feb 2019
Ministry of Human Capacities of Hungary (Az Emberi Erőforrások Minisztériuma,
EMMI) (2017) Szakmai irányelve az egészségügyi technológia értékelés módsz-
ertanáról és ennek keretében költséghatékonysági elemzések készítéséről.
Egészségügyi Közlöny 3(10):821–842
Ministry of Human Capacities of Hungary (Az Emberi Erőforrások Minisztériuma,
EMMI) (2021) Egészségügyi szakmai irányelve az egészség-gazdaságtani
elemzések készítéséhez és értékeléséhez. Egészségügyi Közlöny 71(21):
2178-2200
National Institute of Pharmacy and Nutrition (Országos Gyógyszerészeti és
Élelmezés-egészségügyi Intézet, OGYÉI) (2019) A gyógyszer befogadási
kérelmek értékelésének OGYÉI Technológia-értékelő Főosztálya által figy-
elembe vett szempontjai. https://www.ogyei.gov.hu/ajanlasok. Accessed 8
Nov 2020
Rencz F, Gulacsi L, Drummond M, Golicki D, Prevolnik Rupel V, Simon J, Stolk
EA, Brodszky V, Baji P, Závada J, Petrova G, Rotar A, Péntek M (2016) EQ-5D
in Central and Eastern Europe: 2000–2015. Qual Life Res 25(11):2693–2710

4.3.3.12   Country/Region: Mexico (Table 4.85)

Table 4.85 Overview of EQ-5D-5L value set for Mexico

Mexican EQ-5D-5L value set		Example: the value for health state 21232	
Full health (11111)	1	Full health	=1
Mobility = 2	0.0160	Minus MO level 2	−0.0160
Mobility = 3	0.0473		
Mobility = 4	0.1786		
Mobility = 5	0.2697		
Self-care = 2	0.0476	Minus SC level 1	−0.000
Self-care = 3	0.0819		
Self-care = 4	0.1697		
Self-care = 5	0.2589		
Usual activities = 2	0.0553	Minus UA level 2	−0.0553
Usual activities = 3	0.0952		
Usual activities = 4	0.1798		
Usual activities = 5	0.2758		
Pain/discomfort = 2	0.0531		
Pain/discomfort = 3	0.0808	Minus PD level 3	−0.0808
Pain/discomfort = 4	0.2283		
Pain/discomfort = 5	0.4579		
Anxiety/depression = 2	0.0551	Minus AD level 2	−0.0551
Anxiety/depression = 3	0.0824		
Anxiety/depression = 4	0.1611		
Anxiety/depression = 5	0.3337		
		State 21232	=0.7928

AD anxiety/depression, *MO* mobility, *PD* pain/discomfort, *SC* self-care, *UA* usual activities

The mathematical representation of the model for health state X is:

$$V(X) = 1 - 0.0160\,MO_2 - 0.0473\,MO_3 - 0.1786\,MO_4 - 0.2697\,MO_5 - 0.0476$$
$$SC_2 - 0.0819\,SC_3 - 0.1697\,SC_4 - 0.2589\,SC_5 - 0.0553\,UA_2 - 0.0952\,UA_3 - 0.1798$$
$$UA_4 - 0.2758\,UA_5 - 0.0531\,PD_2 - 0.0808\,PD_3 - 0.2283\,PD_4 - 0.4579\,PD_5 - 0.0551$$
$$AD_2 - 0.0824\,AD_3 - 0.1611\,AD_4 - 0.3337\,AD_5$$

(i)   **Date/wave of study**
      Data were collected in the third wave of EQ-5D-5L valuation studies using
      the EQ-5D-5L valuation protocol 2.1. Interviews were conducted from June
      until August 2019.

(ii) **Sample size; sample frame**
      A nationally representative sample of Mexican adults > 18 years stratified by
      sex, age and socioeconomic level were obtained using sample frames devel-
      oped by CONAPO, the Mexican Office of Statistics and Geography and the

socioeconomic classification of households by the Mexican Association of Marketing Research and Public Opinion Agencies (AMAI). Of the 1000 respondents included in the analysis, 48.6% were female and 51.4% were male. The age distribution of the respondents was:

18–24 years	22.3%
25–34 years	15.4%
35–44 years	19.9%
45–54 years	16.5%
55–64 years	17.1%
65–74 years	5.9%
75+ years	2.9%

(iii) **Representativeness of achieved sample**

The study sample was representative for the adult Mexican population in terms of age, sex, geographical region and socioeconomic group (Table 4.86).

Table 4.86 Representativeness of the sample in the Mexican valuation study

		Study sample (N=1000)	Mexican general population[a]
Sampling characteristics			
Age, n (%)	18–24	223 (22.3%)	19.9%
	25–34	261 (26.1%)	24.0%
	35–44	198 (19.8%)	21.3%
	45–54	130 (13.0%)	15.3%
	55–64	100 (10.0%)	9.8%
	65–74	59 (5.9%)	5.8%
	75 and above	29 (2.9%)	3.8%
Gender, n (%)	Female	486 (48.6%)	48.1%
	Male	514 (51.4%)	51.9%
Regions, n (%)	Region 1	100 (10.0%)	10.1%
	Region 2	192 (19.2%)	19.2%
	Region 3	126 (12.6%)	12.3%
	Region 4	237 (23.7%)	23.8%
	Region 5	118 (11.8%)	11.6%
	Region 6	145 (14.5%)	14.3%
	Region 7	82 (8.2%	8.6%
Socioeconomic Status n (%)	A/B	107 (10.7%)	10.1%
	C+	297 (29.7%)	28.9%
	C	151 (15.1%)	15.7%
	C-	142 (14.2%)	14.4%
	D+	131 (13.1%)	13.5%
	D	111 (11.1%)	11.2%
	E	61 (6.1%)	6.2%

Reproduced from Gutierrez-Delgado et al. (2021)
[a]Instituto Nacional de Estadística y Geografía 2015

(iv) **Mean observed cTTO values of EQ-5D-5L states** (Table 4.87)

Table 4.87 Mean observed cTTO values by health state

State	Mean	SE	State	Mean	SE	State	Mean	SE
11112	0.935	0.007	21345	0.344	0.045	43315	0.287	0.049
11121	0.956	0.005	21444	0.391	0.045	43514	0.352	0.048
11122	0.878	0.017	22434	0.575	0.027	43542	0.197	0.053
11211	0.943	0.005	23152	0.362	0.046	43555	−0.134	0.058
11212	0.895	0.009	23242	0.578	0.035	44125	0.290	0.042
11221	0.902	0.010	23514	0.468	0.048	44345	0.008	0.051
11235	0.565	0.035	24342	0.511	0.033	44553	−0.102	0.056
11414	0.626	0.037	24443	0.291	0.048	45133	0.395	0.044
11421	0.706	0.028	24445	0.086	0.054	45144	0.140	0.050
11425	0.439	0.041	24553	0.176	0.045	45233	0.318	0.046
12111	0.942	0.007	25122	0.659	0.029	45413	0.293	0.050
12112	0.879	0.010	25222	0.698	0.027	51152	0.282	0.047
12121	0.889	0.010	25331	0.588	0.036	51451	0.099	0.058
12244	0.447	0.040	31514	0.542	0.036	52215	0.385	0.049
12334	0.647	0.027	31524	0.436	0.044	52335	0.193	0.052
12344	0.457	0.041	31525	0.389	0.039	52431	0.439	0.039
12513	0.603	0.038	32314	0.664	0.025	52455	−0.113	0.057
12514	0.522	0.040	32443	0.402	0.045	53221	0.519	0.047
12543	0.353	0.052	33253	0.276	0.052	53243	0.320	0.048
13122	0.777	0.016	34155	0.026	0.054	53244	0.257	0.050
13224	0.623	0.036	34232	0.497	0.043	53412	0.539	0.034
13313	0.718	0.018	34244	0.331	0.043	54153	0.161	0.053
14113	0.729	0.024	34515	0.197	0.054	54231	0.350	0.049
14554	0.033	0.051	35143	0.398	0.045	54342	0.179	0.050
15151	0.314	0.051	35245	0.146	0.052	55225	0.067	0.057
21111	0.952	0.005	35311	0.576	0.040	55233	0.242	0.046
21112	0.886	0.009	35332	0.503	0.037	55424	0.096	0.052
21315	0.509	0.042	42115	0.456	0.038	55555	−0.663	0.013
21334	0.631	0.032	42321	0.597	0.034			

SE standard error

(v)   **Proportions choosing A in the DCE based on relative severities of A and B** (Fig. 4.44)

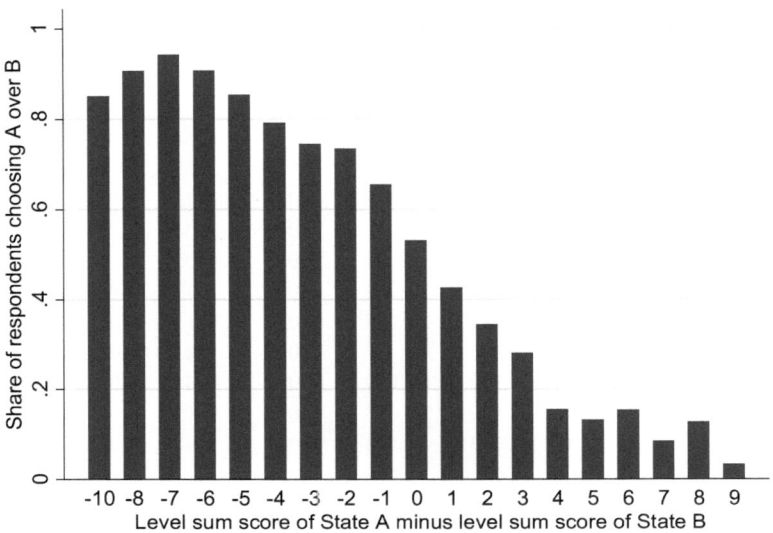

Fig. 4.44 Proportions choosing A based on relative severities of A and B

(vi)   **Exclusion criteria**
Using the feedback module, 2.1% of the cTTO responses were deemed problematic and were excluded from analysis. No DCE data were excluded from the analysis.

(vii)   **Number of interviewers; Interviewer effects**
In total, 1000 interviews were conducted by 15 interviewers. The variance of the responses can be partitioned into variance related to differences between interviewers (0.99%), respondents (7.61%), and responses (91.40%).

(viii)   **Description of modelling choices**
The observed cTTO values for the non-flagged health states after the feedback module were used (i.e. the respondent's flagged cTTO observations were excluded) (details on the feedback module and its use are provided in Chap. 2).
The Mexican EQ-5D-5L value set was based on a 20-parameter model estimated using only cTTO data. The value set is based on a heteroscedastic Bayesian model with censoring at −1.

(ix)   **Value Set** (Table 4.88 and Fig. 4.45)

Table 4.88 Key characteristics of the Mexican value set

Characteristics	Mexico EQ-5D-5L value set
% states with negative values	9.1% (284 out of 3125)
Rank order of dimensions (from most to least relative importance)	Pain/discomfort Anxiety/depression Usual activities Self-care Mobility
Coefficient with highest weight	0.4579 (level 5 of pain/discomfort)
Range of values	Maximum value: 1 Minimum value: −0.596
Max value < 1	0.984 (value of health state 21111)
Linearity/non-linearity of value decrements by level	With the exception of mobility, the dimensions have very similar value decrements at levels 2 and 3. There is a kink in the value decrements at level 3 for pain/discomfort and mobility. At level 5, the largest value decrement is for pain/discomfort, followed by anxiety/depression.

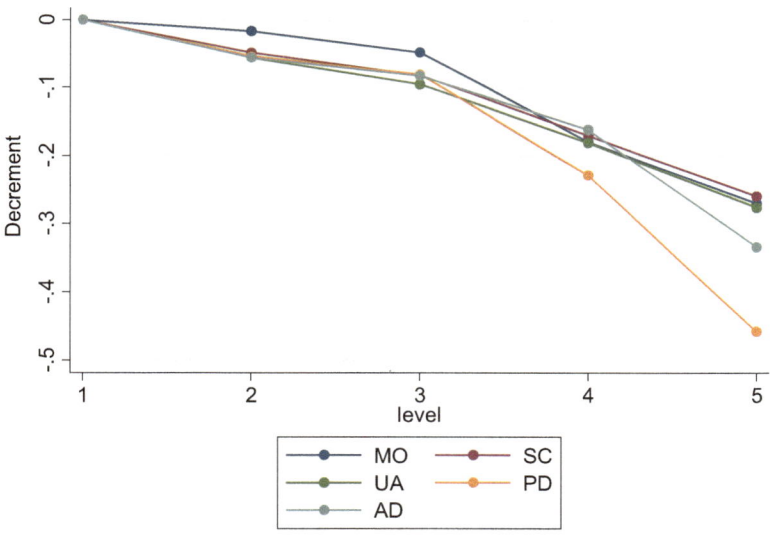

Fig. 4.45 Value decrements across dimensions (*AD* anxiety/depression, *MO* mobility, *PD* pain/discomfort, *SC* self-care, *UA* usual activities)

(x)   **Uptake by local HTA/health care decision makers**

Mexico's General Health Council (GHC) is the collegiate body responsible for updating the National Compendium of Healthcare Supplies of the public health care institutions. The Compendium aims to strengthen the evaluation of health care technologies, to optimize public resources directed at addressing health problems and to notify and update health professionals. The GHC periodically updates the health technology assessment (HTA) processes used to determine inclusion in the Compendium. The most recent update of the HTA process includes cost-utility analysis (CUA) as a complementary evaluation that can be presented to strengthen the cost-effectiveness and budget impact analyses of health technologies seeking inclusion in the Compendium. It can be foreseen that the Mexican value set will encourage the development of CUA in the near future.

(xi)   **Reference(s) for this value set**

Gutierrez-Delgado C, Galindo-Suárez RM, Cruz-Santiago C, Shah K, Papadimitropoulos M, Zamora B, Feng Y, Devlin N (2021) EQ-5D-5L Health-State Values for the Mexican Population. Appl Health Econ Health Policy. https://doi.org/10.1007/s40258-021-00658-0

Further Literature

Consejo de Salubridad General (2017) Guía para la Conducción de Estudios de Evaluación Económica para la Actualización del Cuadro Básico y Catálogo de Insumos del Sector Salud en México. Comisión Interinstitucional del Cuadro Básico y Catálogo de Insumos del Sector Salud. http://www.csg.gob.mx/descargas/pdf/priorizacion/cuadro-basico/guias/insumos_salud/GEI_2017_Diciembre.pdf. Accessed 28 July 2021

Consejo de Salubridad General (2017) Guía de Evaluación de Insumos para la Salud. Comisión Interinstitucional del Cuadro Básico y Catálogo de Insumos del Sector Salud. http://www.csg.gob.mx/descargas/pdf/priorizacion/cuadro-basico/guias/insumos_salud/GEI_2017_Diciembre.pdf. Accessed 28 July 2021

Consejo Nacional de Población (CONAPO) (2018) Proyecciones de la población de México y de las entidades federativas, 2016–2050 y conciliación demográfica de México 1950–2015. https://www.gob.mx/conapo/acciones-y-programas/conciliacion-demografica-de-mexico-1950-2015-y-proyecciones-de-la-poblacion-de-mexico-y-de-las-entidades-federativas-2016-2050. Accessed 28 July 2021

Instituto Nacional de Estadística y Geografía (INEGI) (2015) Regiones Socioeconómicas de México. http://sc.inegi.gob.mx/niveles/datosnbi/reg_soc_mexico.pdf. Accessed 28 July 2021

Asociación Mexicana de Agencias de Investigación de Mercado (AMAI) (2016) Niveles socioeconómicos. http://nse.amai.org/niveles-socio-economicos-amai/. Accessed 28 July 2021

4.3.3.13   Country/Region: Peru (Table 4.89)

Table 4.89 Overview of EQ-5D-5L value set for Peru[a]

Peruvian EQ-5D-5L value set		Example: the value for health state 21232	
Full health (11111)	1	Full health	=1
Mobility = 2	0.104	Minus MO level 2	−0.104
Mobility = 3	0.223		
Mobility = 4	0.312		
Mobility = 5	0.473		
Self-care = 2	0.117	Minus SC level 1	−0.000
Self-care = 3	0.214		
Self-care = 4	0.264		
Self-care = 5	0.355		
Usual activities = 2	0.143	Minus UA level 2	−0.143
Usual activities = 3	0.157		
Usual activities = 4	0.231		
Usual activities = 5	0.347		
Pain/discomfort = 2	0.072		
Pain/discomfort = 3	0.132	Minus PD level 3	−0.132
Pain/discomfort = 4	0.287		
Pain/discomfort = 5	0.476		
Anxiety/depression = 2	0.123	Minus AD level 2	−0.123
Anxiety/depression = 3	0.126		
Anxiety/depression = 4	0.188		
Anxiety/depression = 5	0.422		
		State 21232	=0.498

AD anxiety/depression, *MO* mobility, *PD* pain/discomfort, *SC* self-care, *UA* usual activities
[a]In the valuation study manuscript, the value set is reported in incremental dummies. For consistency, we report regular dummies here

The mathematical representation of the model for health state X is:

$$V(X) = 1 - 0.104\,MO_2 - 0.223\,MO_3 - 0.312\,MO_4 - 0.473\,MO_5 - 0.117$$
$$SC_2 - 0.214\,SC_3 - 0.264\,SC_4 - 0.355\,SC_5 - 0.143\,UA_2 - 0.157\,UA_3 - 0.231$$
$$UA_4 - 0.347\,UA_5 - 0.072\,PD_2 - 0.132\,PD_3 - 0.287\,PD_4 - 0.476\,PD_5 - 0.123$$
$$AD_2 - 0.126\,AD_3 - 0.188\,AD_4 - 0.422\,AD_5$$

(i)   **Date/wave of study**
      Data were collected in the third wave of EQ-5D-5L valuation studies using a "Lite" version of the EQ-5D-5L valuation protocol 2.1 (see also Chap. 3 for more details). Interviews were conducted between April 2018 and February 2019.

(ii)   **Sample size; sample frame**
       1000 interviews with the general population were conducted in three cities
       located in different parts of Peru: Lima, Arequipa and Iquitos. 300 of these
       respondents completed a full cTTO + DCE interview, while 700 completed
       DCE tasks only. Sampling was stratified by region, age and gender. Of the
       300 respondents included in the final value set, 49.7% were female and
       50.3% were male. The age distribution of the respondents was:

18–24 years	11.4%
25–29 years	16.2%
30–39 years	20.9%
40–49 years	19.1%
50–64 years	17.3%
65–74 years	14.1%
75+ years	1.0%

(iii) **Representativeness of achieved sample** (Table 4.90)

Table 4.90   Representativeness of the sample in the Peruvian valuation study

		cTTO sample (N=300)	Study sample (N=1000)	Peruvian general population
Sampling characteristics				
Age, n (%)[a]	18–24	38 (12.7%)	114 (11.4%)	18.1%
	25–34	26 (8.7%)	80 (8.0%)	24.1%
	35–44	46 (15.3%)	189 (18.9%)	21.2%
	45–54	46 (15.3%)	189 (18.9%)	16.7%
	55–64	88 (29.3%)	277 (27.7%)	12.0%
	65–74	50 (16.7%)	141 (14.1%)	7.4%
	≥75	6 (2.0%)	10 (1.0%)	0.6%
Gender, n (%)[a]	Female	149 (49.7%)	544 (54.4%)	50.8%
	Male	151 (50.3%)	456 (45.6%)	49.2%

Reproduced from Augustovski et al. (2020)
[a]Instituto Nacional de Estadística e Informática 2017

(iv)   **Mean observed cTTO values of EQ-5D-5L states** (Table 4.91)

Table 4.91 Mean observed cTTO values by health state

State	Mean	SE	State	Mean	SE	State	Mean	SE
11112	0.819	0.030	22445	−0.051	0.061	43241	0.064	0.067
11121	0.856	0.028	23554	−0.195	0.063	44355	−0.422	0.059
11211	0.809	0.035	24113	0.389	0.056	45414	−0.094	0.063
11215	0.332	0.063	25222	0.314	0.061	51144	−0.089	0.064
12111	0.836	0.035	31452	−0.057	0.066	52253	−0.198	0.063
12324	0.455	0.055	32511	0.181	0.061	53312	0.089	0.071
13433	0.288	0.065	33125	0.169	0.066	54421	−0.080	0.066
14542	−0.021	0.068	34234	0.139	0.063	55535	−0.498	0.058
15151	−0.075	0.068	35343	−0.039	0.063	55555	−0.686	0.027
21111	0.804	0.035	41523	0.134	0.061			
21331	0.596	0.047	42132	0.323	0.064			

SE standard error

(v)   **Proportions choosing A in the DCE based on relative severities of A and B** (Fig. 4.46)

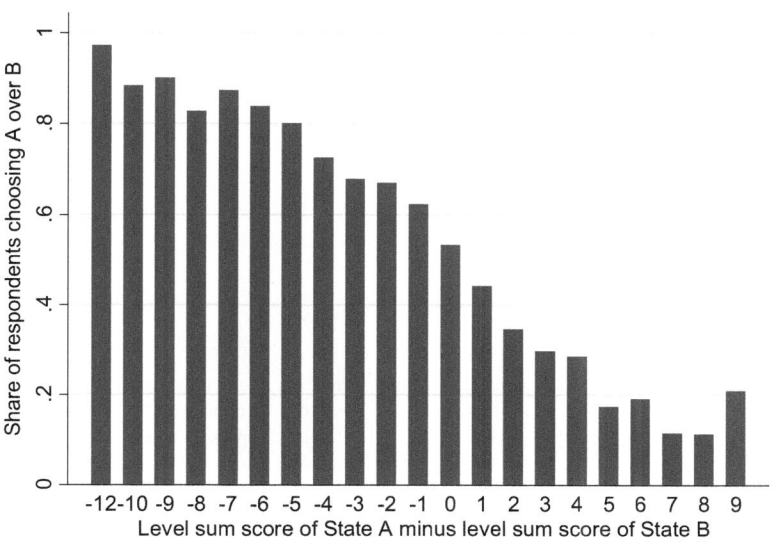

Fig. 4.46 Proportions choosing A based on relative severities of A and B

(vi) **Exclusion criteria**
Respondents were excluded if they did not belong to the age range that was intended to be sampled (18–75 years old). Furthermore, respondents were excluded if they did not live in a household selected through the sampling strategy. A total of 30 respondents were excluded for these reasons.

(vii) **Number of interviewers; Interviewer effects**
In total, 1000 interviews were conducted by 12 interviewers. 5 interviewers performed cTTO + DCE interviews, while the other 7 interviewers conducted DCE interviews only. The variance of the responses included in the final value set can be partitioned into variance related to differences between interviewers (0.7%), respondents (27.5%) and responses (71.8%).

(viii) **Description of modelling choices**
The Peruvian EQ-5D-5L value set was based on the cTTO data only. The selected model was a Tobit model, that accounts for censoring at −1, with a correction for heteroskedasticity. The model was additionally adjusted by differential weights to improve the representativeness of the sample compared to the general population in Peru. The intercept was constrained in the final model.

(ix) **Value Set** (Table 4.92 and Fig. 4.47)

Table 4.92 Key characteristics of the Peruvian value set

Characteristics	Peruvian EQ-5D-5L value set
% states with negative values	43.3% (1354 out of 3125)
Rank order of dimensions (from most to least relative importance)	Mobility Pain/discomfort Self-care Usual activities Anxiety/depression
Coefficient with highest weight	0.476 (level 5 of pain/discomfort)
Range of values	Maximum value: 1 Minimum value: −1.076
Max value < 1:	0.928 (value of health state 11121)
Linearity/non-linearity of value decrements by level	Reverse kink at level 2 for usual activities and anxiety/depression (see Fig. 4.47). Kink at level 3 for pain/discomfort. Kink at level 4 for anxiety/depression. Value decrements for mobility and self-care are relatively linear across levels.

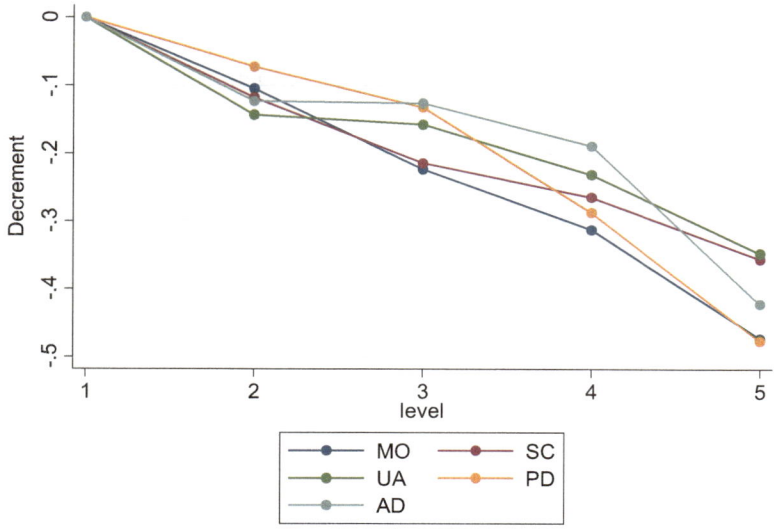

Fig. 4.47 Value decrements across dimensions (*AD* anxiety/depression, *MO* mobility, *PD* pain/discomfort, *SC* self-care, *UA* usual activities)

(x) **Uptake by local HTA/health care decision makers**

Cost-utility analysis (CUA) is currently not required by the Peruvian Ministry of Health, nor by national insurance agencies (Seguro Integral de Salud and Fondo Intangigle Solidario en Salud). However, previously CUAs have been used for decision making, especially on vaccination recommendations, using weights from other countries (Bolaños-Díaz et al. 2017; Bolaños-Días et al. 2016). Furthermore, researchers at CRONICAS institute for chronic diseases have been using the Peruvian EQ-5D-5L values in ongoing research. The National HTA Network, Red Nacional de Evaluación de Tecnologías Sanitarias (RENETSA), currently makes no specific recommendation on the use of EQ-5D-5L in economic evaluations in health care.

(xi) **Reference(s) of value set**

Augustovski F, Belizán M, Gibbons L, Reyes N, Stolk E, Craig BM, Tejada RA (2020) Peruvian Valuation of the EQ-5D-5L: A Direct Comparison of Time Trade-Off and Discrete Choice Experiments. Value Health 23(7):880–888

Further Literature

Bolaños-Díaz R, Tejada RA, Sanabria C, Escobedo-Palza S (2017) Cost-Effectiveness of two antiviral therapies for chronic Hepatitis B in Peru: Entecavir and Tenofovir. Rev Peru Med Exp Salud Publica 34(3):377–385

Bolaños-Díaz R, Tejada RA, Beltrán J, Escobedo-Palza S (2016) Evaluation of the cost-effectiveness of two alternative human papillomavirus vaccines as prophylaxis against uterine cervical cancer. Rev Peru Med Exp Salud Publica 33(3):411–418.

Instituto Nacional de Estadística e Informática (2017) Censos Nacionales. https://www.inei.gob.pe/. Accessed 29 July 2021

4.3.3.14   Country/Region: United States (Table 4.93)

Table 4.93 Overview of EQ-5D-5L value set for the United States

US EQ-5D-5L value set		Example: the value for health state 21232	
Full health (11111)	1	Full health	=1
Mobility = 2	0.096	Minus MO level 2	−0.096
Mobility = 3	0.122		
Mobility = 4	0.237		
Mobility = 5	0.322		
Self-care = 2	0.089	Minus SC level 1	−0.000
Self-care = 3	0.107		
Self-care = 4	0.220		
Self-care = 5	0.261		
Usual activities = 2	0.068	Minus UA level 2	−0.068
Usual activities = 3	0.101		
Usual activities = 4	0.255		
Usual activities = 5	0.255		
Pain/discomfort = 2	0.060		
Pain/discomfort = 3	0.098	Minus PD level 3	−0.098
Pain/discomfort = 4	0.318		
Pain/discomfort = 5	0.414		
Anxiety/depression = 2	0.057	Minus AD level 2	−0.057
Anxiety/depression = 3	0.123		
Anxiety/depression = 4	0.299		
Anxiety/depression = 5	0.321		
		State 21232	=0.681

AD anxiety/depression, *MO* mobility, *PD* pain/discomfort, *SC* self-care, *UA* usual activities

The mathematical representation of the model for health state X is:

$$V(X) = 1 - 0.096\,MO_2 - 0.122\,MO_3 - 0.237\,MO_4 - 0.322\,MO_5 - 0.089$$
$$SC_2 - 0.107\,SC_3 - 0.220\,SC_4 - 0.261\,SC_5 - 0.068\,UA_2 - 0.101\,UA_3 - 0.255$$
$$UA_4 - 0.255\,UA_5 - 0.060\,PD_2 - 0.098\,PD_3 - 0.318\,PD_4 - 0.414\,PD_5 - 0.057$$
$$AD_2 - 0.123\,AD_3 - 0.299\,AD_4 - 0.321\,AD_5$$

(i)   **Date/wave of study**

Data were collected in the third wave of EQ-5D-5L valuation studies using the EQ-5D-5L valuation protocol 2.1. Interviews were conducted between May and September 2017.

(ii)   **Sample size; sample frame**
       1134 interviews with the general population were conducted in 6 US metro-
       politan areas: Chicago, Philadelphia, Seattle, Birmingham, Phoenix, and
       Denver. Quota sampling with respect to age, gender, ethnicity, and race was
       applied based on the US census (US Census Bureau 2015). Of the 1062
       respondents included in the final value set, 51.0% were female and 48.5%
       were male. The age distribution of the respondents was:

18-24 years	9.6%
25–29 years	13.8%
30–39 years	17.4%
40–49 years	17.0%
50–64 years	23.1%
65–74 years	10.9%
75+ years	8.1%

(iii) **Representativeness of achieved sample**
       The study sample was representative for the US adult population in terms of
       age, gender, race, ethnicity, prevalence of chronic disease, and general health
       status (Table 4.94).

Table 4.94 Representativeness of the sample in the US valuation study

		Study sample[a] (N=1102)	cTTO sample (N=1062)	US general population[b]
Sampling characteristics				
Age, n (%)	18–34	354 (32.1%)	347 (32.7%)	30.5%
	35–54	381 (34.6%)	365 (34.4%)	34.5%
	>55	367 (33.3%)	350 (32.9%)	34.6%
Gender, n (%)	Female	553 (50.2%)	542 (51.0%)	51.4%
	Male	544 (49.3%)	515 (48.5%)	48.3%
	Other	5 (0.4%)	5 (0.5%)	0.3 %
Ethnicity, n (%)	White	679 (61.6%)	661 (62.2%)	65.5%
	Black	144 (13.1%)	128 (12.1%)	11.9%
	Asian or Pacific Islander	74 (6.7%)	70 (6.6%)	5.3%
	American Indian/ Alaskan Native	27 (2.5%)	27 (2.5%)	0.5%
Hispanic ethnicity, n (%)		197 (17.9%)	191 (18.0%)	15.0%
Education level greater than secondary, n (%)		718 (65.2%)	703 (66.3%)	58.9%

(continued)

Table 4.94 (continued)

		Study sample[a] (N=1102)	cTTO sample (N=1062)	US general population[b]
History of illness, n (%)	Hypertension	258 (23.4%)	245 (23.1%)	32.0%
	Arthritis	258 (23.4%)	244 (23.0%)	22.7%
	Diabetes	104 (9.4%)	95 (8.95%)	9.4%
	Heart failure	18 (1.6%)	18 (1.7%)	2.2%
	Stroke	22 (2.0%)	20 (1.9%)	1.8–2.4%
	Bronchitis	25 (2.3%)	23 (2.2%)	3.6%
	Asthma	130 (11.8%)	125 (11.8%)	7.5%
	Depression	285 (25.9%)	270 (25.5%)	25.7%
	Migraine	159 (14.4%)	154 (14.5%)	16.0%
	Cancer	64 (5.8%)	59 (5.6%)	5.9%
	None	364 (33.3%)	356 (33.6%)	-
Health status, n (%)	Excellent/very good/good	955 (86.7%)	923 (87.0%)	85.6%
	Fair/poor	146 (13.3%)	138 (13.0%)	14.4%

Reproduced from Pickard et al. (2019)
[a]All respondents of the 'analytic' sample are included, each of whom provided useable cTTO and DCE data (n=1102)
[b]Li et al. 2011; Centers for Disease Control and Prevention (CDC) 2018; US Census Bureau 2015

(iv) **Meactes** (Table 4.95)

Table 4.95 Mean observed cTTO values by health state

State	Mean	SE	State	Mean	SE	State	Mean	SE
11112	0.954	0.011	21345	0.059	0.078	43315	0.212	0.070
11121	0.965	0.006	21444	0.151	0.063	43514	0.132	0.077
11122	0.887	0.024	22434	0.320	0.072	43542	0.073	0.073
11211	0.949	0.009	23152	0.165	0.082	43555	−0.133	0.063
11212	0.907	0.025	23242	0.356	0.066	44125	0.177	0.068
11221	0.915	0.023	23514	0.230	0.069	44345	−0.046	0.071
11235	0.521	0.062	24342	0.147	0.071	44553	−0.225	0.071
11414	0.431	0.061	24443	0.013	0.071	45133	0.238	0.067
11421	0.672	0.051	24445	−0.109	0.061	45144	−0.040	0.072
11425	0.372	0.069	24553	0.069	0.077	45233	0.272	0.072
12111	0.939	0.012	25122	0.590	0.054	45413	0.142	0.076
12112	0.918	0.025	25222	0.481	0.063	51152	0.185	0.080
12121	0.884	0.024	25331	0.416	0.063	51451	0.144	0.071
12244	0.218	0.070	31514	0.327	0.062	52215	0.156	0.077
12334	0.442	0.064	31524	0.267	0.070	52335	0.126	0.066
12344	0.263	0.070	31525	0.215	0.067	52431	0.185	0.070
12513	0.583	0.052	32314	0.348	0.073	52455	−0.185	0.073
12514	0.428	0.059	32443	0.094	0.073	53221	0.492	0.067

(continued)

Table 4.95 (continued)

State	Mean	SE	State	Mean	SE	State	Mean	SE
12543	0.142	0.072	33253	0.202	0.068	53243	0.156	0.066
13122	0.820	0.040	34155	0.018	0.072	53244	−0.005	0.066
13224	0.431	0.063	34232	0.399	0.060	53412	0.265	0.074
13313	0.709	0.042	34244	−0.041	0.074	54153	−0.040	0.075
14113	0.590	0.054	34515	0.166	0.067	54231	0.315	0.076
14554	0.012	0.070	35143	0.247	0.063	54342	0.088	0.071
15151	0.167	0.077	35245	0.117	0.067	55225	−0.004	0.071
21111	0.945	0.013	35311	0.478	0.062	55233	0.179	0.071
21112	0.880	0.032	35332	0.481	0.063	55424	−0.176	0.071
21315	0.475	0.058	42115	0.367	0.069	55555	−0.366	0.021
21334	0.432	0.068	42321	0.530	0.058			

SE standard error

(v)   **Proportions choosing A in the DCE based on relative severities of A and B** (Fig. 4.48)

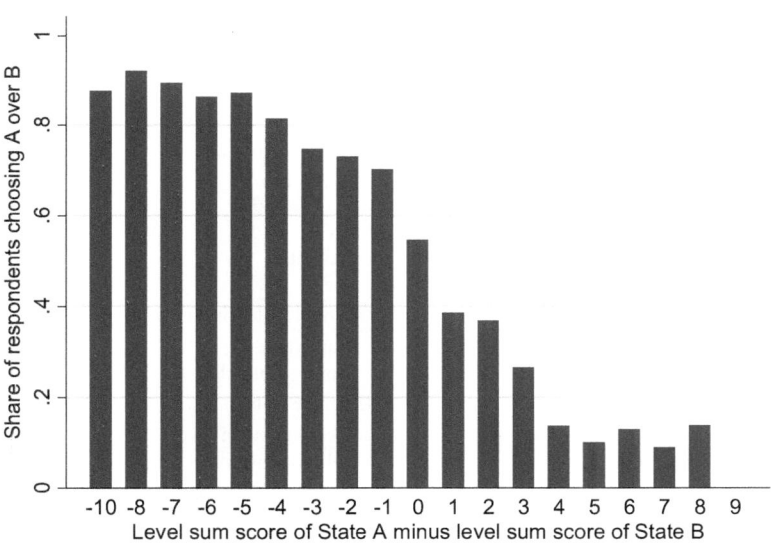

Fig. 4.48 Proportions choosing A based on relative severities of A and B

(vi)   **Exclusion criteria**

Respondents who did not understand the cTTO tasks (n = 72) were excluded from the analysis, based on interviewer assessment. Moreover, a total of 11.6% of cTTO responses (n = 1234) were removed following the feedback module from respondents who were deemed to have comprehended the task based on interviewer assessment.

(vii) **Number of interviewers; Interviewer effects**

In total, 1134 interviews were conducted by 11 interviewers. The variance of the responses included in the final value set can be partitioned into variance related to differences between interviewers (0.04%), respondents (35.25%), and responses (64.71%).

(viii) **Description of modelling choices**

The US EQ-5D-5L value set was based on the cTTO data only. The selected model was a tobit model, left-censored at -1, correcting for heteroskedasticity, and accounting for panel data (i.e., random intercept). Usual activities levels 4 and 5 were constrained to have the same value decrement. The intercept was constrained in the final model because it was non-significant.

(ix)   **Value Set** (Table 4.96 and Fig. 4.49)

Table 4.96 Key characteristics of the US value set

Characteristics	US EQ-5D-5L value set
% states with negative values	20% (624 out of 3125)
Rank order of dimensions (from most to least relative importance)	Pain/discomfort Anxiety/depression Mobility Usual activities Self-care
Coefficient with highest weight	0.414 (level 5 of pain/discomfort)
Range of values	Maximum value: 1 Minimum value: -0.573
Max value < 1:	0.943 (value of health state 11112)
Linearity/non-linearity of value decrements by level	Value decrements of levels 2 and 3 were similar across all dimensions (see Fig. 4.49). Kink at level 3 for all dimensions and for levels 4 and 5, the value decrements were more differentiated across dimensions. At level 5, the value decrement of pain/discomfort was the highest.

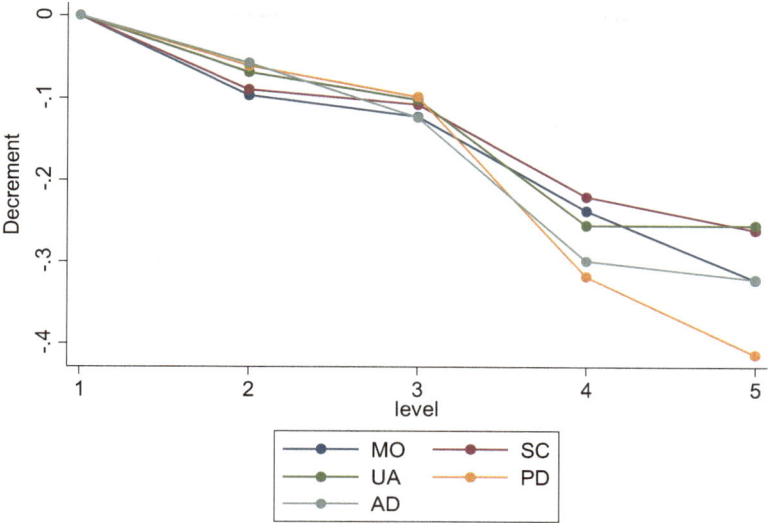

Fig. 4.49 Value decrements across dimensions (*AD* anxiety/depression, *MO* mobility, *PD* pain/discomfort, *SC* self-care, *UA* usual activities)

(x) **Uptake by local HTA/health care decision makers**

In the US, the Affordable Care Act prevents the denial of coverage of medical products or services in a manner that treats extending the life of an elderly, disabled, or terminally ill individual as of lower value than extending the life of healthy individuals. However, the absence of drug price regulation and instances of predatory business practices has led to the emergence of the non-profit Institute for Clinical Evaluation and Review as a highly influential organisation that assesses the fairness of drug prices using QALYs as one of the metrics. The EQ-5D-3L forms the basis for many utility inputs and this will likely extend to the EQ-5D-5L as greater use is seen in the literature. In the two years since the US value set was published, the EQ-5D-5L has been employed as an endpoint in clinical trials for pharmaceuticals as well as psychosocial interventions, with evidence that favorably supports its validity/responsiveness for a range of applications and health care interventions (Courtin et al. 2020; Hanmer et al. 2021; Reveille et al. 2021; Xiang et al. 2020).

(xi) **Reference(s) for this value set**

Pickard AS, Law EH, Jiang R, Pullenayegum E, Shaw JW, Xie F, Oppe M, Boye KS, Chapman RH, Gong CL, Balch A, Busschbach JJV (2019) United States Valuation of EQ-5D-5L Health States Using an International Protocol. Value Health 2(8):931–941

Further Literature

Centers for Disease Control and Prevention (CDC) (2018) Data and Statistics. 2018. https://www.cdc.gov/datastatistics/index.html. Accessed 30 Jan 2018

Courtin E, Aloisi K, Miller C, Allen HL, Katz LF, Muennig P (2020) The Health Effects Of Expanding The Earned Income Tax Credit: Results From New York City. Health Aff 39(7):1149–1156

Li C, Balluz LS, Okoro CA, Strine TW, Lin JMS, Town M, Garvin W, Murphy W, Bartoli W, Valluru B, CDC (2011) Surveillance of certain health behaviors and conditions among states and selected local areas. Behavioral Risk Factor Surveillance System, United States, 2009. MMWR Surveill Summ 60(9):1–250

Hanmer J, DeWalt DA, Berkowitz SA (2021) Association between Food Insecurity and Health-Related Quality of Life: a Nationally Representative Survey. J Gen Intern Med 36(6):1638–1647

Reveille JD, Hwang MC, Danve A, Kafka S, Peterson S, Lo KH, Kim L, Hsia EC, Chan EK, Deodhar A (2021) The effect of intravenous golimumab on health-related quality of life and work productivity in adult patients with active ankylosing spondylitis: results of the phase 3 GO-ALIVE trial. Clin Rheumatol 40(4):1331–1341

US Census Bureau (2015) 2015 American Community Survey 1-Year Estimates. US Census Bureau: Washington, DC

Xiang X, Sun Y, Smith S, Lai PHL, Himle J (2020) Internet-Based Cognitive Behavioral Therapy for Depression: A Feasibility Study for Home Care Older Adults. Res Soc Work Prac 30(7):791–801

4.3.3.15 Country/Region: Vietnam (Table 4.97)

Table 4.97 Overview of EQ-5D-5L value set for Vietnam

Vietnamese EQ-5D-5L value set		Example: the value for health state 21232	
Full health (11111)	1	Full health	=1
Mobility = 2	0.069	Minus MO level 2	−0.069
Mobility = 3	0.079		
Mobility = 4	0.206		
Mobility = 5	0.376		
Self-care = 2	0.043	Minus SC level 1	−0.000
Self-care = 3	0.046		
Self-care = 4	0.147		
Self-care = 5	0.231		
Usual activities = 2	0.046	Minus UA level 2	−0.046
Usual activities = 3	0.059		
Usual activities = 4	0.174		
Usual activities = 5	0.299		
Pain/discomfort = 2	0.084		
Pain/discomfort = 3	0.152	Minus PD level 3	−0.152
Pain/discomfort = 4	0.270		
Pain/discomfort = 5	0.367		
Anxiety/depression = 2	0.064	Minus AD level 2	−0.064
Anxiety/depression = 3	0.113		
Anxiety/depression = 4	0.171		
Anxiety/depression = 5	0.239		
		State 21232	=0.669

AD anxiety/depression, *MO* mobility, *PD* pain/discomfort, *SC* self-care, *UA* usual activities

The mathematical representation of the model for health state X is:

$$V(X) = 1 - 0.069\,MO_2 - 0.079\,MO_3 - 0.206\,MO_4 - 0.376\,MO_5 - 0.043$$
$$SC_2 - 0.046\,SC_3 - 0.147\,SC_4 - 0.231\,SC_5 - 0.046\,UA_2 - 0.059\,UA_3 - 0.174$$
$$UA_4 - 0.299\,UA_5 - 0.084\,PD_2 - 0.152\,PD_3 - 0.270\,PD_4 - 0.367\,PD_5 - 0.064$$
$$AD_2 - 0.113\,AD_3 - 0.171\,AD_4 - 0.239\,AD_5$$

(i) **Date/wave of study**

Data were collected in the third wave of EQ-5D-5L valuation studies using the EQ-5D-5L valuation protocol 2.1. The following two adjustments were made to the EQ-VT: (1) the respondent was asked to answer the cTTO tasks for someone like them ("third person") instead of themselves as per protocol, (2) additional use of printed coloured DCE cards as visual aid. Interviews were conducted between November and December 2017.

(ii) **Sample size; sample frame**

1200 interviews with the general population were conducted in six provinces, representing different geographical regions: Northern mountains, the Red River delta, the Highlands, Central Coast, the South-East and the Mekong river delta. Multi-stage stratified cluster sampling with respect to region (stage 1) and residential area (stage 2), and a probabilistic quota-based method (stage 3) with respect to age (over 18 years) and gender was applied (Vietnam General Statistic Office 2017). Of the 1200 respondents included in the final value set, 51% were female and 49% were male. The age distribution of the respondents was:

18–24 years	18.4%
25–29 years	15.8%
30–39 years	22.9%
40–49 years	17.1%
50–64 years	19.4%
65–74 years	4.8%
75+ years	1.7%

(iii) **Representativeness of achieved sample**

The study sample was largely representative for the Vietnamese general population in terms of age, gender, and residential area (Table 4.98).

Table 4.98 Representativeness of the sample in the Vietnamese valuation study

		Study sample (N=1200)	Vietnamese general population[a]
Sampling characteristics			
Age, n (%)	18–29	410 (34.2%)	33.5%
	30–44	389 (32.4%)	32.5%
	45–59	257 (21.4%)	21.6%
	≥ 65	144 (12.0%)	12.5%
Gender, n (%)	Female	612 (51.0%)	50.7%
	Male	588 (49.0%)	49.3%
Socio-economic region, n (%)	Central Highland	80 (6.7%)	6.1%
	Mekong River Delta	230 (19.2%)	19.1%
	Northern Midland and Mountainous	146 (12.2%)	12.9%
	North Central and Central Coastal	259 (21.6%)	21.4%
	Red River Delta	270 (22.5%)	22.8%
	South-East	215 (17.9%)	17.7%
Residential area, n (%)	Urban	425 (35.4%)	34.5%
	Rural	775 (64.68%)	65.5%

(continued)

Table 4.98 (continued)

		Study sample (N=1200)	Vietnamese general population[a]
Marital status, n (%)	Currently married	873 (72.8%)	68.2%
	Others	326 (27.2%)	31.8%
	Missing	1 (0.1%)	-
Poverty, n (%)	Poor and near poor[b]	77 (6.4%)	7.0%
	Non-poor	1123 (93.6%)	93.0%

Reproduced from Mai et al. (2020)
[a]Vietnam General Statistic Book 2017
[b]Poverty level was based on Vietnam official poverty line

(iv)   **Mean observed cTTO values of EQ-5D-5L states** (Table 4.99)

Table 4.99 Mean observed cTTO values by health state

State	Mean	SE	State	Mean	SE	State	Mean	SE
11112	0.937	0.006	21345	0.429	0.034	43315	0.397	0.039
11121	0.916	0.007	21444	0.264	0.042	43514	0.368	0.033
11122	0.826	0.019	22434	0.412	0.043	43542	0.120	0.049
11211	0.906	0.007	23152	0.497	0.034	43555	−0.067	0.046
11212	0.851	0.011	23242	0.430	0.045	44125	0.344	0.034
11221	0.859	0.010	23514	0.445	0.041	44345	0.011	0.049
11235	0.535	0.034	24342	0.344	0.041	44553	−0.105	0.043
11414	0.591	0.029	24443	0.217	0.046	45133	0.308	0.048
11421	0.697	0.018	24445	0.068	0.048	45144	0.159	0.049
11425	0.516	0.033	24553	0.002	0.050	45233	0.309	0.043
12111	0.909	0.009	25122	0.576	0.038	45413	0.300	0.038
12112	0.866	0.012	25222	0.563	0.031	51152	0.168	0.049
12121	0.820	0.017	25331	0.507	0.032	51451	0.132	0.049
12244	0.467	0.039	31514	0.462	0.038	52215	0.316	0.048
12334	0.539	0.035	31524	0.471	0.034	52335	0.191	0.049
12344	0.446	0.039	31525	0.389	0.042	52431	0.271	0.041
12513	0.615	0.021	32314	0.640	0.026	52455	−0.114	0.047
12514	0.466	0.042	32443	0.332	0.048	53221	0.533	0.025
12543	0.223	0.054	33253	0.319	0.045	53243	0.139	0.050
13122	0.755	0.014	34155	0.159	0.047	53244	0.061	0.049
13224	0.597	0.039	34232	0.504	0.034	53412	0.322	0.044
13313	0.726	0.019	34244	0.302	0.040	54153	−0.011	0.048
14113	0.726	0.023	34515	0.272	0.047	54231	0.334	0.045
14554	0.038	0.048	35143	0.313	0.047	54342	0.172	0.042
15151	0.340	0.047	35245	0.170	0.047	55225	0.069	0.045
21111	0.925	0.008	35311	0.535	0.040	55233	0.148	0.049
21112	0.863	0.014	35332	0.440	0.038	55424	0.117	0.041
21315	0.643	0.028	42115	0.439	0.042	55555	−0.515	0.012
21334	0.564	0.029	42321	0.558	0.035			

SE standard error

(v) **Proportions choosing A in the DCE based on relative severities of A and B** (Fig. 4.50)

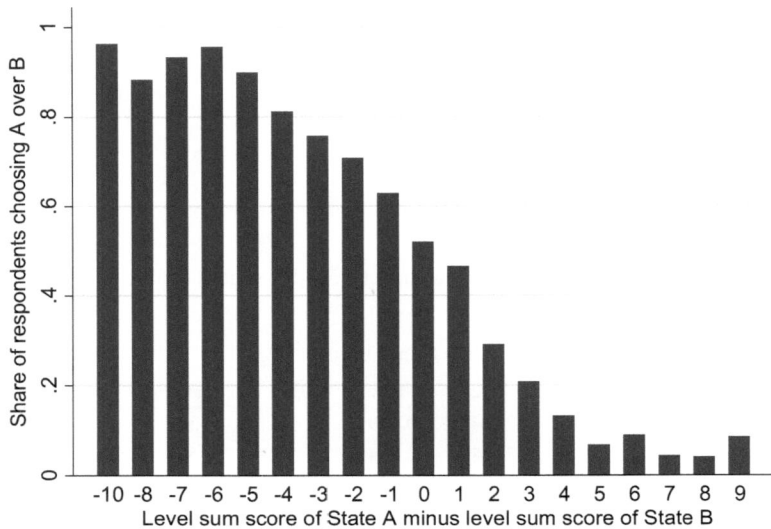

Fig. 4.50 Proportions choosing A based on relative severities of A and B

(vi) **Exclusion criteria**
A total of 8.9% of cTTO responses (n = 1068) were removed following the feedback module; but no respondent's entire cTTO responses were excluded. The observations of the ten manually added DCE pairs were excluded from the data analysis (details on the DCE design are provided in Chap. 3).

(vii) **Number of interviewers; Interviewer effects**
In total, 1200 interviews were conducted by 10 interviewers. The variance of the responses can be partitioned into variance related to differences between interviewers (4.0%), respondents (13.7%), and responses (82.3%).

(viii) **Description of modelling choices**
The Vietnamese EQ-5D-5L value set was based on a hybrid model combining a conditional logit model for the DCE data and a censored at -1 tobit model for the cTTO data. The intercept was constrained in the final model.

(ix)   **Value Set** (Table 4.100 and Fig. 4.51)

Table 4.100 Key characteristics of the Vietnamese value set

Characteristics	Vietnamese EQ-5D-5L value set
% states with negative values	8.3% (260 out of 3125)
Rank order of dimensions (from most to least relative importance)	Pain/discomfort Mobility Anxiety/depression Usual activities Self-care
Coefficient with highest weight	0.376 (level 5 of mobility)
Range of values	Maximum value: 1 Minimum value: −0.512
Max value < 1:	0.957 (value of health state 12111)
Linearity/non-linearity of value decrements by level	Value decrements for self-care, usual activities and mobility were similar for levels 2 and 3, and kinked around level 3, having much higher value decrements for levels 4 and 5, particularly in the case of mobility (Fig. 4.51). Value decrements for pain/discomfort and anxiety/depression increased almost linearly over levels 2–5, with sharper falls in value for pain/discomfort for worse problems.

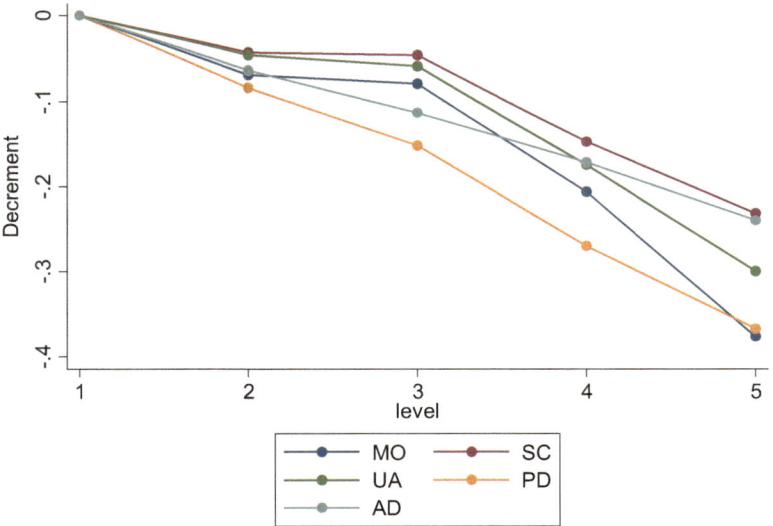

Fig. 4.51 Value decrements across dimensions (*AD* anxiety/depression, *MO* mobility, *PD* pain/discomfort, *SC* self-care, *UA* usual activities)

(x) **Uptake by local HTA/health care decision makers**

Vietnam's Ministry of Health (MOH) has taken a first step toward applying evidence-based medicine to health policy making process by enacting the national HTA guidelines and upgrading the health insurance package with cost-effective drugs based on HTA evidence (Ministry of Health 2017). The MOH has applied evidence-based HTA to produce well-informed healthcare decisions, initially in health insurance. According to the national guideline on HTA submissions, QALY is a required index. QALY estimates can either be sourced from related literature or measured directly using the suggested instrument, EQ-5D-5L. In Vietnam, the EQ-5D-5L is presently the only HRQoL instrument that can produce values which are based on the preferences of the Vietnamese general population (Mai et al. 2020).

(xi) **Reference(s) for this value set**

Mai VQ, Sun S, Minh HV, Luo N, Giang KB, Lindholm L, Sahlen KG (2020) An EQ-5D-5L Value Set for Vietnam. Qual Life Res 29(7):1923–1933

Further Literature

Ministry of Health (2017) Decision 2701/QD-BYT on promulgating the working regulation of drafting committee, editing team and specialized teams, and rules and criteria for formulation of the circular promulgating the list, ratio and payment conditions for modern medicines covered by health insurance. Appendix 2: Rules and criteria for compilation of the list of modern medicines covered by health insurance. https://thuvienphapluat.vn/van-ban/Bao-hiem/Quyet-dinh-2701-QD-BYT-2017-Quy-che-lam-viec-xay-dung-Thong-tu-thuoc-tan-duoc-bao-hiem-y-te-353139.aspx. Accessed 13 July 2021

Vietnam General Statistic Office (2017) Statistic Yearbook of Vietnam 2017. GSO, Hanoi. https://www.gso.gov.vn/en/data-and-statistics/2019/10/7559/. Accessed 13 July 2021

Chapter 5
Guidance to Users of EQ-5D-5L Value Sets

Nancy Devlin, Aureliano Paolo Finch, and David Parkin

Abstract One of the most common questions that the EuroQol Group is asked by users of the EQ-5D-5L is: 'Which value set should I use?'. The aim of this chapter is to provide guidance on this issue for users. There are two principal ways that EQ-5D-5L value sets are applied and used. The first is for summarising health-related quality of life to estimate quality-adjusted life-years (QALYs) and changes in QALYs that result from the health care use. This kind of evidence is often part of health technology assessment (HTA). The second category of use is when value sets are employed as a way of summarising and statistically analysing EQ-5D-5L profile data without the aim of estimating QALYs. In each case, the stated requirements of those who use this evidence in decision making is a key consideration. This chapter summarises the relevant considerations to be taken into account when choosing a value set for QALY estimation purposes; and the considerations which are relevant to choosing a value set to use in other, 'non-QALY' applications.

5.1 Introduction

One of the most common questions that the EuroQol Group is asked by users of the EQ-5D-5L is: '*Which value set should I use?*'. There is no simple answer to this, as it depends on the user's objectives in using the instrument, the decisions that it informs, and the context in which the information will be used. Selecting an EQ-5D-5L value set will also be affected by the availability of value sets and their acceptability to users. Which value set to use is straightforward under two

N. Devlin (✉)
Centre for Health Policy, University of Melbourne, Melbourne, VIC, Australia
e-mail: nancy.devlin@unimelb.edu.au

A. P. Finch
EuroQol Research Foundation, Rotterdam, The Netherlands

D. Parkin
Office of Health Economics, London, UK

City, University of London, London, UK

N. Devlin et al. (eds.), *Value Sets for EQ-5D-5L*,
https://doi.org/10.1007/978-3-030-89289-0_5
213

conditions: (a) an EQ-5D-5L value set, based on the EQ-VT protocol described in Chap. 2, is available for the country to which the data to be analysed refer; and (b) that value set is acceptable to those who will make decisions based on it.

However, in many countries a local EQ-VT-generated EQ-5D-5L value set is not available; and even if there is one there is no guarantee that local decision-makers will accept it. In these circumstances, alternatives include using another country's value set that was generated using the EQ-VT protocol; using a value set generated by an alternative valuation method; and mapping from the EQ-5D-5L to the EQ-5D-3L, where a local value set exists for the latter.

This chapter guides potential users through these and other issues that arise when choosing an EQ-5D-5L value set. Sections 5.2 and 5.3 present an overview of the principal considerations relevant to users, providing an easy access guide. Section 5.4 discusses some more technical and theoretical issues.

The first and most important question for any user of an EQ-5D-5L value set is: *'What is the purpose of representing EQ-5D-5L profile data as a single number?'*. There are broadly two main categories of use that can be identified. A first important category is when the EQ-5D-5L is used for summarising health-related quality of life (HRQoL) to estimate Quality Adjusted Life Years (QALYs) and changes in QALYs that result from the health care use. This kind of evidence is often part of health technology assessment (HTA). Section 5.2 discusses relevant considerations about choosing a value set for QALY estimation.

The second important category of use is when value sets are employed as a way of summarising and statistically analysing EQ-5D-5L profile data without the aim of estimating QALYs. Section 5.3 summarises the considerations relevant to choosing which value set to use in these 'non-QALY' applications.

5.2   Which Value Set Should Be Used to Estimate QALYs? – An Overview

The use of EQ-5D-5L values to estimate QALYs imposes requirements on the characteristics of those values. This specific use of values is of such importance that these requirements are largely built into the methods for eliciting and modelling them. Unfortunately, there is no consensus about the theoretical properties that the values used to estimate QALYs should have, as reflected in ongoing debates about which valuation methods best meet those properties. However, some principles are widely adopted, and requirements that meet these, detailed in Box 5.1, underlie all of the value sets produced using the EQ-VT protocol (see Chap. 4). Other valuation protocols may not. For example, value sets that rely exclusively on Discrete Choice Experiments (DCE) without a duration attribute or any other means of anchoring the DCE responses do not meet these requirements, largely ruling them out for use for QALY estimation.

Box 5.1: What Properties do EQ-5D-5L Values Need to Have to Be Suitable for Use in Estimating QALYs for Economic Evaluation?

For use in economic evaluation, QALYs must have some basic properties, for example that they can be used as an *unambiguous* measure of the *value* of *every* health care intervention (Morris et al. 2012). How this translates into requirements for the health state values that form the 'Q' element of QALYs is less clear and subject to debates over both economic and psychometric theory and practice. Possibly the only universally agreed property for these values derives from the definition of a QALY; full health maintained over one year will generate one QALY, implying that the value attached to full health should be equal to 1. Current practice underlying the value sets described in this book is therefore open to debate but does meet the basic requirements for measuring QALYs. It assumes that, at a minimum, values should be:

- measured on a scale anchored at 1 = full health and 0 = dead. States considered worse than dead are assigned a value < 0.
- obtained using stated preference methods from patients or a general population, rather than using external judgements by, for example, health care experts.
- obtained by forcing respondents to make explicit choices between mutually exclusive options that describe health states.

These requirements contributed to the EuroQol Group's decision to use time trade-off (TTO) and Discrete Choice Experiments (DCE) in the EQ-VT protocol for EQ-5D-5L valuation studies (See Chap. 2). Section 5.4.2 briefly discusses these issues further, with suggested further reading.

Values are sometimes referred to as 'utilities', but the value sets described in this book do not claim to measure utility according to any of its conventional technical definitions (see Drummond et al. 2015, Chapter 5, Section 5.4.2). For example, they may not conform to the axioms underlying von Neuman-Morgenstern measurable utility under conditions of uncertainty based on expected utility theory (EUT). The Standard Gamble (SG) method aims to elicit such utilities but is not widely used because of concerns about the validity of EUT and the ability of respondents to judge probabilities. Other value set properties required for estimating QALYs, such as constant proportionality and additive independence, are assumed to be satisfied, as is the case with all HRQoL instruments accompanied by values.

Figure 5.1 presents a summary of the main considerations in choosing an EQ-5D-5L value set when the main aim is QALY estimation. First, users should assess whether the QALY analysis is for use in HTA or other purposes, and who will be informed by it. HTA bodies and other decision-makers using QALY evidence may have specific recommendations about their preferred value set, which in most

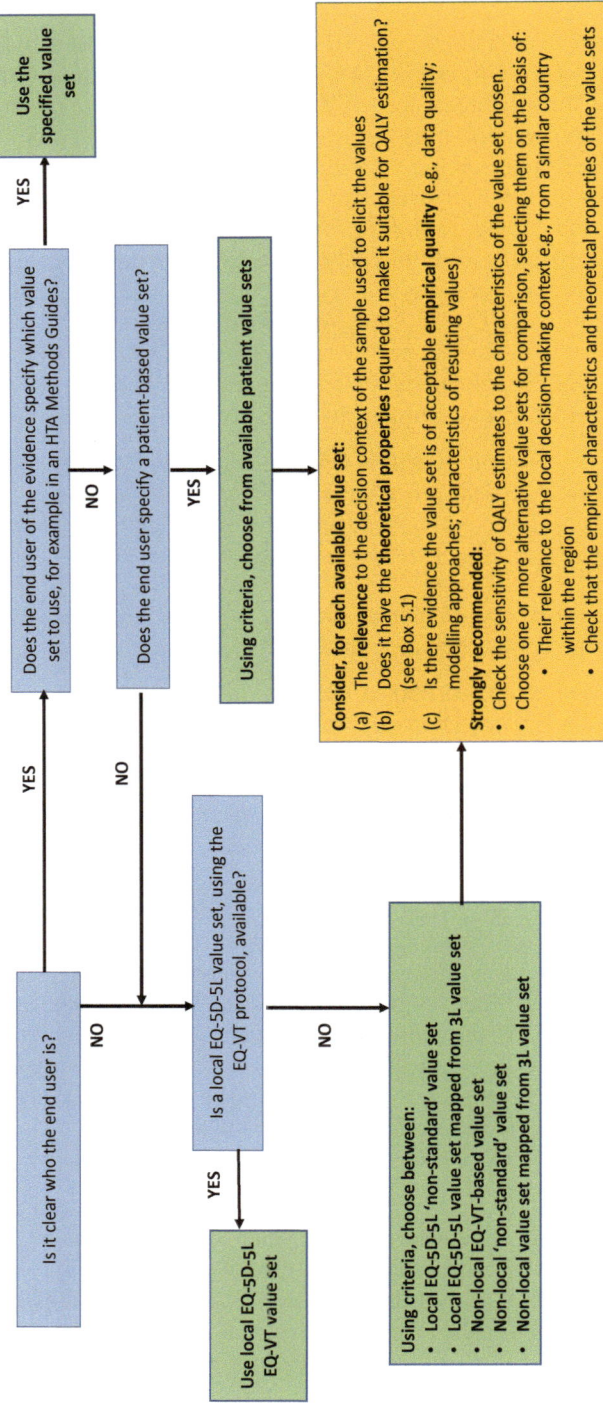

Fig. 5.1 Choosing which EQ-5D-5L value set to use in estimating QALYs

cases would be the first choice for the base case. If not, the choice to be made depends on factors such as the local availability of value sets, the relevance of available non-local value sets and, in either case, their empirical characteristics and their theoretical properties. These issues are discussed in more detail in the following sections.

5.2.1 End Users' Requirements and Recommendations

'End users' refers to whoever the analysis of EQ-5D-5L data is intended to inform. This could be national or local government bodies, HTA organisations, local health care budget holders, health care providers and insurers, health care professionals, patients or the general public. In practice, it is likely that the only end users who will specify a preferred or accepted value set are HTA organisations. Hence, when EQ-5D-5L data are analysed to generate estimates of QALYs for cost-effectiveness analysis, we recommend first consulting whether the relevant HTA body or other stakeholder has published a 'methods guide' or provide guidance stating their requirements for value sets selection.

Kennedy-Martin et al. (2020) provide a summary of stated requirements of health care decision-making bodies internationally regarding the valuation of health states. For example, the National Institute for Health and Care Excellence (NICE) in the UK (NICE 2013; currently being updated), Zorginstituut in the Netherlands (Zoorginatituut Nederlands 2016) and Haute Authorité de Santé in France (HAS 2020) each provide HTA methods guides on how EQ-5D-5L data should be valued for submissions to them. The Pharmaceutical Benefits Advisory Committee (PBAC) in Australia, in contrast to European agencies, is less prescriptive about which HRQoL instrument to use, and which value set to employ in conjunction with them (PBAC 2016). In most cases, HTA authorities' methods guides state that a value set based on the stated preferences of that country's general public is recommended. There are exceptions, for example, Sweden's Dental and Pharmaceutical Benefits Agency (TLV) indicates that the values used in submissions to them should reflect Swedish patients' experienced values, i.e. 'appraisals of persons in the health condition in question' (TLV 2003, 2017), rather than stated preferences of the Swedish general public.

There may be cases in which there is no end user guidance about value sets, or the guidance provided is too broad to assist in choosing between alternative value sets. This is a particular problem when QALY estimates are derived from multi-country trial data, or are used as evidence in multiple HTA submissions, or both. The choice of value set may be made even more difficult if the end user is a global organisation making recommendations that affect multiple countries. In these instances, the choice of value set is left to the user. In Sects. 5.2.2 to 5.2.4 we describe the criteria that users should consider in such cases.

5.2.2   Relevance to the Population to Whom the Analysis Refers

To our knowledge, most HTA methods guides recommend that QALY estimates should ideally be based on values obtained locally, that is from the area over which that HTA body has jurisdiction. This ensures that resource allocation decisions reflect that country's preferences about the relative importance of different health problems. There are more national EQ-5D value sets available than for any other generic measure of HRQoL. The availability of EQ-5D-5L value sets will continue to expand, as further countries undertake valuation studies to support the development and expansion of HTA worldwide. However, there will inevitably remain countries where no local value sets are available.

For a country that does not have an EQ-5D-5L value set but does have an EQ-5D-3L value set, mapping between the two descriptive systems provides one means of valuing the EQ-5D-5L – see Box 5.2 below. Mapping methods have also been used to estimate a link between the EQ-5D and other condition-specific measures of HRQoL, but these will not be discussed here as they do not produce a value set for the EQ-5D-5L. The use of mapping methods may meet HTA requirements; for example, current NICE guidance recommends mapping EQ-5D-5L to the EQ-5D-3L (NICE 2019) thereby allowing use of values from the York MVH 'A1 Tariff' EQ-5D-3L value set (MVH Group 1995).

Analysts are therefore recommended to consult relevant local HTA methods guides before choosing whether to use a mapping method, and which one to use. Box 5.2 provides further details on mapping.

If there are no local value sets for either the EQ-5D-5L *or* EQ-5D-3L, an obvious suggestion is to use a value set from a country that has a similar population, considering socio-demographic, cultural and linguistic characteristics that might be expected to influence health preferences (evidence about how such characteristics influence values is presented in Chap. 6). That is straightforward if there is only one such country, and their value set satisfies the other criteria detailed below. Where there is more than one value set which may be considered relevant and acceptable, the choice of value set should be subject to sensitivity analysis.

A special case is where a study is undertaken in more than one distinct population, as may be the case with, for example, a multi-country or multi-region clinical trial. While it has been proposed to use a single value set to represent the preferences for a region or continent when available (e.g., Greiner et al. 2003; Łaszewska et al. 2020), this solution is currently not widely applied. The possibility of developing regional value sets for EQ-5D-5L is explored in Chap. 6. If the results of the clinical study are to be used in different HTA jurisdictions, each of which makes recommendations about the use of value sets, these should be followed - which might result in more than one value set applied to the same data.

There are advantages to having a single value set that could be used in cases where there is no local alternative, or the values are required to cover more than one locality – for example, in enabling comparison of results in such cases. The EQ-5D

Box 5.2: Mapping Between 3L and 5L to Create Value Sets

The most notable example of the application of mapping methods to create value sets for the EQ-5D-5L that may be used when no valuation studies are available is van Hout et al. (2011). In this response mapping study, data from 3691 patients in six European countries who completed both the EQ-5D-3L and EQ-5D-5L were analysed using four different statistical methods. The chosen method was the 'indirect non-parametric method', which assumed independence of each EQ-5D dimension and removed inconsistent responses such as choosing level 1 on the 3L and level 5 on the 5L. This generates transition probabilities: the probability that a person would have recorded a particular response to the EQ-5D-3L given the response they gave to the EQ-5D-5L. The resulting 243 x 3125 table of transition probabilities can be applied to any EQ-5D-3L value set to generate a 5L 'crosswalk' value set.

At the time when the van Hout et al. (2011) mapping was developed, EQ-5D-5L value set studies had not yet been initiated, which made it impossible to develop a bi-directional crosswalk. More recently, following users' demand and due to the availability of EQ-5D-5L value sets, the same data used in the original van Hout et al. (2011) crosswalk were employed for mapping the EQ-5D-3L to the EQ-5D-5L, using indirect non-parametric and ordinal logistic regression methods (van Hout and Shaw 2021).

An alternative response mapping approach for deriving EQ-5D-5L or EQ-5D-3L values has been proposed by Hernández-Alava and Pudney (2017), but it currently remains less used. This mapping was re-estimated on multiple samples, with the most recent estimation being based on a large dataset of English responders (Hernández-Alava et al. 2020). Its statistical performance is similar to that of the van Hout crosswalk for mapping the EQ-5D-3L to the EQ-5D-5L (Hernández-Alava et al. 2020). The van Hout and Shaw (2021) mapping, using ordinal logistic regression including regressors coding for other EQ-5D-3L dimensions, show a slightly better performance than that of Hernández-Alava and Pudney (2017) for mapping the EQ-5D-3L to the EQ-5D-5L. It is notable that the current iteration of the Hernández-Alava and Pudney (2017) crosswalk only allows mapping to UK/English value sets, while the models developed in van Hout and Shaw (2021) are freely accessible in R, and are easily adapted to other value sets.

As there is currently no consensus about which of these approaches should be used, users are encouraged to check the latest recommendations from the scientific advisers in the EuroQol office and the relevant HTA body. The analysis tools section of the EuroQol website reports generic and country-specific algorithms for both the van Hout et al. (2011) EQ-5D-5L to EQ-5D-3L and the van Hout and Shaw (2021) EQ-5D-3L to EQ-5D-5L crosswalks, as well as syntax for the value sets for some countries.

These are available at: https://euroqol.org/support/analysis-tools/

value sets for the UK and the USA have sometimes been used for this purpose. However, there is no scientific rationale for choosing any value set as a default option.

5.2.3 Empirical Characteristics of the Value Sets

For most analysts, it is likely that the above considerations will suffice to choose a value set. However, there may remain cases where a choice between value sets must be made. In such cases, it is helpful to examine the quality of the study that generated the value set. This includes the quality of the valuation data and modelling choices made by the study authors and how the particular properties and characteristics of the value sets compare. Analysts who do not feel able to make judgements using the criteria discussed below are encouraged to contact the EuroQol office, whose scientific officers are well placed to advise.

A check list for assessing value sets, such as the one provided by Xie et al. (2015) (Checklist for REporting VAluaTion studiEs – CREATE) provides a structured way of approaching the assessment of study quality – see Box 5.3. However, this checklist focuses on the quality of the *reporting* of the studies and does not directly address considerations of the quality of collected data upon which models are based (other than where these lead to exclusions). Obvious questions to ask about the quality of the data collected in the value set study include: Was the sample size appropriate and was a reasonable response rate achieved? Is the sample representative of the general public? Is there any cause for concern about data quality - for example, were there high rates of missing or implausible valuations? Were there interviewer effects? Were the interviews conducted in a manner that was compliant with the protocol? These issues are addressed in Chap. 2 and are reported for each of the value sets summarised in Chap. 4.

With respect to the modelling methods used to produce value sets from the valuation data, quality may be judged both by the statistical methods used and also by conformity of the value set to properties that are essential or desirable for the way that they will be used. What criteria were used in selecting the specific model used to produce the value set?

In the case of the value sets reported in Chap. 4, many of these issues relating to data quality, though not subsequent modelling of the data, are dealt with by the rigorous quality control (QC) process applied to EQ-VT-generated data from wave 2 onwards (see Chap. 2). Users of the resulting value sets can therefore have greater confidence in their use. The value sets reported in Chap. 4 follow the EQ-VT protocol and study designs[1] set out in Chaps. 2 and 3. They have also been published in peer-reviewed journals, and therefore meet the scientific standards of those journals. However, the EuroQol Group does not currently have a formal process for

---

[1] With exceptions - for example, Peru used a 'Lite' version of the EQ-VT protocol, and Vietnam also used an adapted design. See Chap. 4 for further information.

Box 5.3: The CREATE Checklist (Reproduced from Xie et al. 2015)

Descriptive systems

1. The attributes of the instrument are described
2. The number of levels in each attribute of the instrument is described

Health states valued

3. The approach to selecting health states to be valued directly is explained
4. The number of health states valued per respondent is stated
5. Method(s) of assigning the health states to respondents is stated

Sampling

6. Sample size/power calculations are stated and rationalised
7. Target population is described
8. Sampling method is stated and rationalised
9. Recruitment strategies are described
10. Response rate is reported

Preference data collection

11. Mode of data collection is stated
12. Preference elicitation technique(s) are described

Study sample

13. Reasons for excluding any respondents or observations are provided
14. Characteristics of respondents included in the analysis are described

Modelling

15. The dependent variable for each model is stated
16. Independent variables for each model are explained
17. Model specifications are provided
18. Model estimators are described
19. Goodness of fit statistics for each model are reported

Scoring algorithm

20. Criteria for selecting the preferred model are stated
21. The scoring algorithm is presented

endorsing value sets, an issue which is discussed in Chap. 7. Furthermore, the QC processes used in the first wave of studies were not standardised and did not always satisfy the requirements of users; an example is the concerns expressed by NICE about the first EQ-5D-5L value set for England (see Hernandez-Alava et al. 2020 and van Hout et al. 2020). This issue was addressed via strengthened QC in subsequent waves, as detailed in Chap. 2.

There are also 'non-standard' EQ-5D-5L value sets available that do not follow the EQ-VT protocol and were undertaken independently of the EuroQol Group, for example, Craig and Rand (2018) for the USA and Sullivan et al. (2020) for New Zealand. Other 'non-EQ-VT' value sets may be produced in future. Researchers have employed different methods, using different protocols, and analysed their data using different econometric procedures, and the resulting value sets will reflect this. The EuroQol Group encourages the use of its EQ-VT protocol in studies aiming to produce national value sets for the EQ-5D-5L, to enhance consistency and comparability. The EuroQol Group does not aim to prevent or discourage improvement or innovation in methods for valuing the EQ-5D family of instruments, indeed it actively supports methodological studies.

Users should be aware of and familiarise themselves with the characteristics of the EQ-5D-5L value sets they choose, whether generated by the EQ-VT protocol or not. Are there important differences in preferences between dimensions? Are there any interaction effects in the values that apply when there are particular combinations of health problems? These characteristics of the value sets combine with the properties of the patients' EQ-5D-5L profile data to which they are applied with important implications for QALY estimates (Parkin et al. 2016).

In general, users should be aware of the characteristics of value sets, such as the overall range of values, how these are distributed and whether there are interaction terms, as these will all exert an influence on their use in statistical analysis (Parkin et al. 2010). For example, if the health condition under consideration involves very severe states, the way in which values for states considered 'worse than dead' have been calculated, rescaled or bounded in the value set will be of particular relevance. If the health states are experienced for long durations, it will be relevant to examine how this relates to the duration of states described in the valuation exercise given the possible effect of "maximum endurable time" on valuations (Sutherland et al. 1982) and the assumption of "constant proportionality" (Dolan and Stalmeier 2003). If the treatment under consideration involves marginal improvements from very good health states to full health, the way in which the constant term has been handled in modelling will affect the estimated change in QALYs.

5.2.4   Transparency and Uncertainty

The most important decision about which value set to use is for the 'base case' for analysis, but it is also recommended that where possible and appropriate analysts also undertake sensitivity analysis using alternative value sets.

The choice of a base case value set should be carefully considered before undertaking analyses, as well as which sensitivity analyses are required given the decision context. For a prospective study, it is important that both the choice of base case and alternative value sets and the rationale for choosing them are clearly set out in the project protocol and statistical analysis plan, and that these are adhered to.

It may be that, considering the factors discussed in the previous sections, there is no value set which is unequivocally 'the best'. In such cases, the analyst's choice of base case value set should be carefully justified; it is essential that analysts are transparent about the reasons for their choice of base case value set. Usual good practice for such decisions is to choose the value set that is likely to generate the most conservative set of results for the base case. For example, if used in a trial of a new treatment over an established alternative, the principle should be to choose the value set that will generate the results least favourable to it. It would clearly be unethical and contrary to principles of good scientific practices to choose a value set on the basis that it will generate results most favourable to the analyst's preferred outcome for the study.

In cases where there remain doubts about which value set to use, analysing and reporting the sensitivity of results and conclusions to alternative value sets will increase the value of the information generated. If results are not substantially affected by the choice of value set, this increases confidence in the findings. Where results and conclusions are contingent on which value set is used, it is very important to convey this information to those who will use this evidence in health care decisions. However, it is important that this recommendation is not interpreted as meaning that users should simply undertake their analyses using different value sets.

In these cases, the EQ-5D-5L values used in an economic appraisal are appropriately considered as part of the uncertainty around the variables that form the economic appraisal model. The analyst should treat the values in an economic appraisal as uncertain parameters and subject them to sensitivity analysis, as with other non-stochastic uncertain variables such as the discount rate. Currently this is not common practice, but it is readily done and would improve confidence in results.

5.3 Which Value Set to Use in 'Non-QALY' Applications – An Overview

Cost-effectiveness analyses is an obvious application for which a single number summary of EQ-5D-5L profile data is essential, but there are other contexts in which this may be useful. Examples of these kinds of applications include:

(a) Population health studies:

- Describing population norms. For example, Szende et al. (2014) published EQ-5D-3L data for 24 countries.
- Comparing population health between different regions, countries or other populations; or over time. For example, the Annual Health Survey for England (NatCen 2021) periodically includes the EQ-5D-3L, including the EQ VAS.
- Setting a baseline for measuring the impact of a population health care intervention. For example, Lubetkin et al. (2020) use the EQ-5D-5L to examine

the effect on the New York population of the 2020 lockdown during the COVID-19 pandemic.

- Measuring the impact of events that affect population health. For example, Andrade et al. (2021) estimated the impact on the local population's health of a technological disaster in a region of Brazil using the EQ-5D-3L.
- Measuring inequalities in population health (Franks et al. 2006; Lubetkin et al. 2005).

(b) Patient condition studies:

- Describing the severity of illness amongst patients. For example, van Wilder et al. (2019) published EQ-5D-3L values for many chronic conditions, disaggregated by patient characteristics.
- Waiting list management. For example, Derrett et al. (2003) applied EQ-5D-3L valuations to patients' EQ-5D-3L profiles as a means of creating a ranking of patients on elective surgery waiting lists in terms of the severity of their condition and their suggested priority for treatment.
- Summarising the performance of hospitals in achieving improved health outcomes for patients as a result of surgery. For example, the National Health Service (NHS) in England publishes hospital-specific data from its Patient Reported Outcome Measures (PROMS) programme using EQ-5D values from the UK population as a whole, rather than from patients who use the hospital, reflecting the fact that the NHS is a national service (Appleby et al. 2015).

Many of the considerations for choosing which value set to use in QALY estimation are also relevant in the context of 'non-QALY' applications, in particular the applicability of the value set to the population to whom the analysis refers (Sect. 5.2.2) and the value sets' empirical characteristics (Sect. 5.2.3).

A further essential consideration in this context is that the values used should be appropriate to the proposed application and context. As values are not neutral, they should reflect the views of those population and groups that count in judging importance given the decision context in which they are applied.

Figure 5.2 provides an overview of the considerations concerning whether a value set is appropriate to use in applications where the principal aim is not to estimate QALYs, and which value set should be chosen in such applications.

As indicated at the start of this chapter, the first and most important question for *any* user of *any* value set is: *'What is the purpose of representing EQ-5D-5L profile data as a single number?'*. Value sets are often used to provide a convenient means of summarising EQ-5D data as a 'single number' for the purposes of statistical analysis (Devlin et al. 2020).

There are important advantages in being able to summarise and represent an EQ-5D-5L profile by a single number – for example, it simplifies statistical analysis. However, it is important to note that there is no "neutral" set of values that can be used for this purpose. Any value set for the EQ-5D-5L explicitly or implicitly compares each level of each dimension with every other and attaches relative

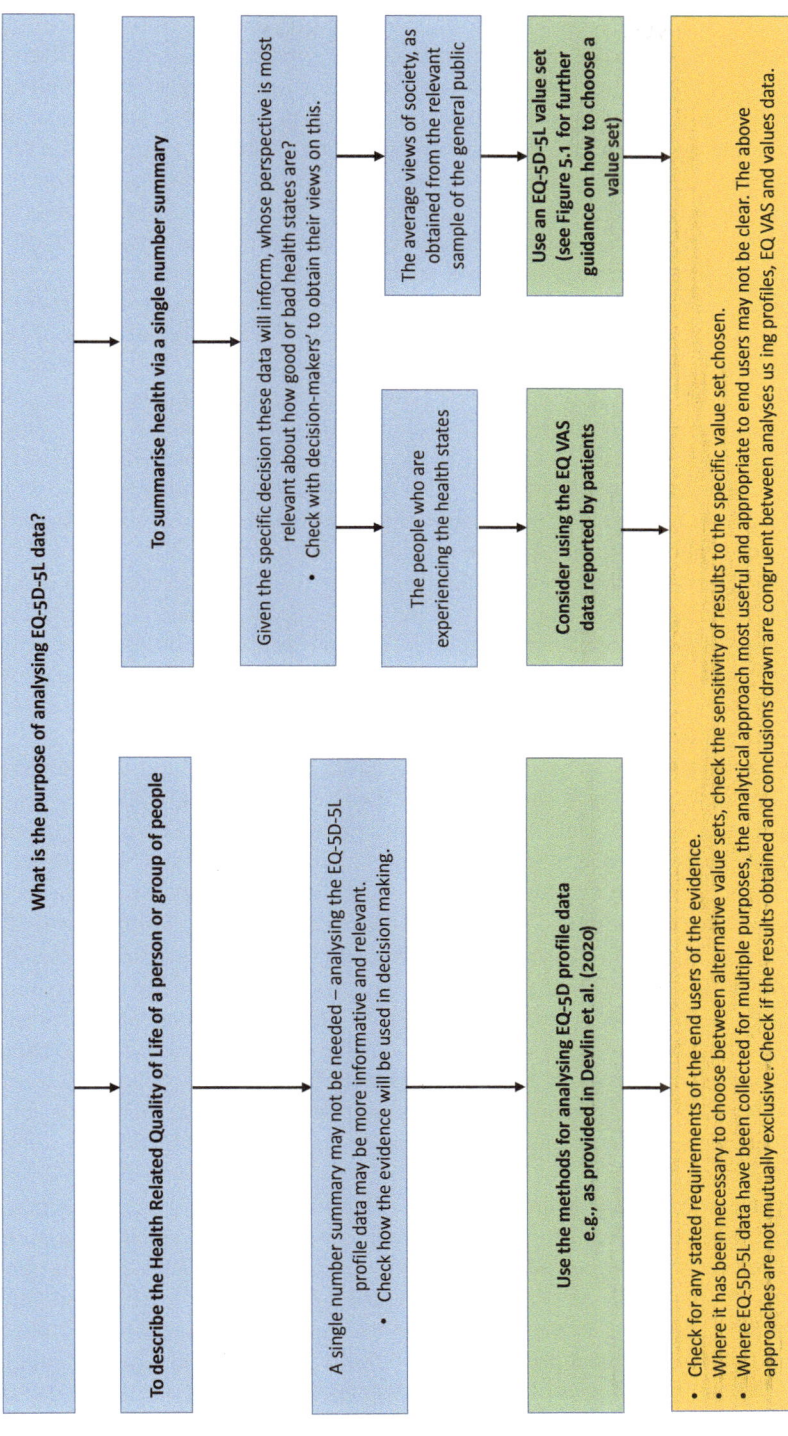

Fig. 5.2 Overview of considerations for using EQ-5D-5L value sets in 'non-QALY' applications

importance to them. No set of values is "objective": they all embody judgements about both what is meant by importance and the appropriate source of information for assessing it. It is therefore not possible to offer generalised guidance about *which* value set to use if the sole purpose is summarising profiles for descriptive or inferential statistical analysis. However, users should be aware that using a value set can introduce an exogenous source of variance that may bias statistical inference. For example, using one value set rather than another may make a difference to conclusions about whether there are statistically significant differences between EQ-5D-5L responses between arms of a clinical trial, two groups of patients, or two regions (Parkin et al. 2010; Wilke et al. 2010). Of course, where the purpose of analysis is to reflect a society's view about the relative importance of different kinds of health problems, this may be considered a desirable feature.

Users should consider the wider purpose for which the summary will be used. If there is no one purpose, rather just a desire to provide information, then it may not to be necessary to apply a value set to the data, but rather to report the EQ-5D-5L profiles themselves in some detail. This may also be preferable because EQ-5D values provide less detailed information than a profile. A range of methods for analysing and reporting profile data are provided in Devlin et al. (2020).

Further, in some cases where a single number is required to represent health, it may be more appropriate to focus on the EQ VAS data provided directly by the relevant patients or populations themselves, rather than using profile-based values. Whether the EQ VAS or value set-weighted profiles are most relevant will depends on the nature of the analysis, and its purpose, and whether it is patients or society's perspective that is most important.

An alternative to applying EQ-5D-5L values sets of the kind reported in this book, or to focussing analysis just on EQ-5D-5L profiles or EQ VAS data provided by patients, is to apply a different means of aggregating profile data. One approach which has been explored is to develop a scoring algorithm based on predicted EQ VAS. Using a sample of patients' or population data, the responses to the EQ-5D profile are used to predict the EQ VAS via regression analysis (Hardman et al. 2002; Whynes and The TOMBOLA Group 2008; Feng et al. 2014; Burstrom et al. 2014; Gutacker et al. 2020). These provide, for any given EQ-5D profile the average EQ VAS on a 0–100 scale (representing worst to best health imaginable). As such a scale is not anchored at dead = 0, it is not suitable for estimating QALYs – but does represent an average view of how good or bad health states are. Where the relationship between the profile and EQ VAS is based on patient data, such value sets are also claimed to represent patients' experience. This use of VAS data is examined further in Sect. 5.4.1.

In contrast to the application of EQ-5D-5L data in QALY estimation, where the requirements of economic evaluation provide a broad theoretical foundation to guide the choice of value sets (see Box 5.1), the analysis of EQ-5D-5L data in other applications may lack an obvious theoretical foundation to guide how data are appropriately analysed or reported. For users concerned with choosing value sets with particular theoretical properties, Sect. 5.4.2 provides a brief discussion of the issues. Where the end user of analysis is known, and where the kinds of decisions that the analysis will inform is clear, the choice of approach should be guided by any requirements of the end user or, where none are provided, by considering what is most relevant to the decisions at stake.

Note that in many of these 'non-QALY' applications of EQ-5D data, analysis of EQ-5D-5L profiles, EQ VAS and EQ-5D values may *all* be relevant to decision makers, as each provides different and complementary information. Where this is the case, the use of value sets to summarise EQ-5D-5L profile data should be accompanied by analyses of EQ-5D-5L profile and EQ VAS data. An example of this is the use of the EQ-5D-3L in studies of the general population in different countries, including those designed to generate population norms. The key EuroQol Group publication on this (Szende et al. 2014) includes values based on value sets, but also reports comparative EQ VAS and dimension and level data for 24 countries using the EQ-5D-3L.

Finally, where there is a clear rationale for using value sets to weight EQ-5D-5L data for statistical analysis (for example, where society's rather than patients' preferences are considered paramount), the advice provided in Sect. 5.2 will be equally relevant. For example, the basis for choosing which value set is used should be clearly stated, ideally in advance of analysis, and sensitivity analysis undertaken to determine whether the characteristics of that value set exert an important effect on results and conclusions.

5.4   Choosing Value Sets – Some Further Considerations

This section complements the overview provided in Sects. 5.2 and 5.3 with a more detailed discussion of two issues: relevance to the decision-making context, and theoretical properties of value sets.

5.4.1   Relevance to the Decision-Making Context

We have already noted that, as a general principle, users should choose a value set which is relevant to the decision-making context. A first assessment of relevance relates to the country in which values were obtained, as described earlier. Yet, other more nuanced facets may need to be considered to deem a value set relevant, including whose values are relevant in the context of interest and what is the appropriate source of such values.

The question of whose values are relevant has been widely debated and there are different possible answers to that (Dolan et al. 2003). Most of the evidence and considerations presented in this chapter relate to "social" value sets (such as those reported in Chap. 4), which are meant to represent the average values of the general public. In essence, these "social" valuations for EQ-5D-5L are generated from members of the general public being asked to consider states that may be hypothetical to them, and to value them from the perspective of imagining being in those states.

There are normative arguments advanced for using social valuations in economic evaluation. Broadly speaking, the purpose of any economic evaluation is to assess the value for money of alternative uses of scarce health care resources. Where the context of these decisions is the public sector, it is generally argued that the valuation of health states used in the assessment of 'benefit' should reflect, as closely as possible, the preferences of the relevant general public. This is both because, in publicly-funded health care systems, it is the general public who are funding health care, e.g. via taxes; and because the general public are potential users of the health care system and can provide valuations 'behind a veil of ignorance'.

An alternative could be to create a "patient-based value set" consisting of values elicited from patients, using either the same stated preference methods used for the general population or revealed preferences based on self-reported EQ VAS values. Patient-based value sets are preferred in some countries, such as Germany and Sweden (Rowen et al. 2017). Proponents of this choice argue that "patient-based value sets" reflect the preferences of those who are actually experiencing the states, and for this reason are more well-informed. Differences between patients' and the general public's valuation of states are common and have been extensively observed. For example, members of the general public often give a lower value to health states than those who experience them, as they cannot predict what their experience in that state would be or how they would adapt to it (Brazier et al. 2005). Ogorevc et al. (2019) report significant differences between patients' and general public values, but these varied by dimension, with patients considering mobility and self-care problems as less problematic, but pain/discomfort and anxiety/depression more problematic. While it may be desirable to include an assessment of patients' values as an adjunct to the main analyses in most studies, there are theoretical concerns about using these values in the context of, for example, economic evaluation. For example, the fact that values for health states may be modified by adaptation could be an argument against their use for decision making based on *ex ante* judgements about the value of health care interventions. Moreover, it may be difficult to include patients in valuation studies given their impaired health and unethical to perform an intrusive valuation interview with them. These considerations and practical limitations have led most HTA bodies (with the notable exception of Sweden's TLV, as noted earlier) and end users to specify that it is general public values which are required, and this is reflected in the protocol for valuation of EQ-5D-5L. For this reason, this chapter assumes that a representative sample of the general public is preferred.

Nevertheless, it may be that, pragmatically, the only available source of values is from the patients whose health states are being analysed, or that in some applications these are regarded by the relevant decision-makers as being the most appropriate. There have also been some debates about whether or not it is appropriate to use the values from sub-groups of the population rather than the population as a whole – for example, the values of women or older people for conditions which only affect them (Sculpher and Gafni 2001, 2002; Robinson and Parkin 2002). Similarly, there are debates about whether the values of children and adolescents, who are generally excluded from sampling but are also members of the general public, are relevant to include in social values (Hill et al. 2020). There is currently no consensus on these issues.

A second relevant issue is the point in time that value sets were generated. Just as there are important differences in health state values between countries (as is evident in the value sets reported in Chap. 4, and compared in Chap. 6), it is possible there may be differences in the average values within a country, over time. This would arise if preferences regarding health are not stable, as is normally assumed in economics, but change over time (Bridges 2003), perhaps because of changing experience of and expectations about health. Further, the composition of the general public changes through time, as a result of ageing, changes in immigration and emigration, and sociodemographic shifts, and such changes may also affect the *average* preferences of society that value sets reflect. We currently have very little evidence on these matters for EQ-5D-5L valuations, because of the relative recency of these value sets, or for other HRQoL instruments, because differences in methods used limit the comparability of valuation data through time. However, as a general rule, a more recent value set is preferable to an older one, providing they are equally relevant in other ways, and are otherwise comparable on the empirical and theoretical grounds discussed below. This question of what the appropriate 'shelf-life' of a value sets is, is considered further in Chap. 7.

5.4.2   The Theoretical Properties of Values and Value Sets

As well as the TTO and DCE methods used in the EQ-VT, there are other methods for valuing health states including Standard Gamble (discussed in Box 5.1), Magnitude Estimation, Paired Comparisons (PC), Rating scales, Visual Analogue Scales (VAS), the Better than Dead approach (van Hoorn et al. 2014), Number Equivalence (also known as Person Trade-Off) and Personal Utility Functions (PUF) (Devlin et al. 2019). And, while the EQ-VT uses a specific type of TTO, composite TTO (cTTO) (see Chap. 2), there are other forms of TTO (such as lead time TTO and lag time TTO); similarly, there are still other types of DCE (such as DCE with duration; and best worst scaling). These other methods are not currently widely used for valuing the EQ-5D-5L and in many cases have only been used in smaller experimental studies, rather than the large-scale representative sample studies appropriate to the construction of value sets for practical use. However, they have been used to estimate value sets for other instruments – for example VAS for the EQ-5D-3L and PC to estimate disability weights for the World Bank / World Health Organisation Disability Adjusted Life Years project. It is possible that future non-standard value sets may be generated that have different properties to those generated by the TTO and the DCE, which may be an important factor in the choice of value sets.

Unfortunately, the theoretical and empirical case for favouring one method of health state valuation over another is far from clear-cut. In the context of QALY estimation, for example, it has been argued that the QALY is no more than a convenient device to combine length and quality of life into a single metric (Parkin and Devlin 2006) and does not need to conform to theoretical concepts such as 'utility' or measurable 'utility'. The theoretical foundations of QALYs therefore do not require that quality of life be valued using a particular measurement method. However, the current dominant practice of using TTO and DCE methods, following the rationale provided in Box 5.1, has the merit of imposing consistency between the resulting value sets and giving a relatively clear interpretation to them.

The recommendation is therefore to exercise caution when considering using value sets resulting from non-standard valuation methods and to examine closely the rationale used by their developers.

5.5   Concluding Remarks

There is no simple answer to the question of which value set to use: the answer depends on the specific nature of the research application, the sort of decisions it informs, and the context in which the evidence from your research will be used.

In some cases, which value set to use will be determined by the stated requirements of those using the evidence to inform decision-making. Where this is not the case, we encourage potential users of EQ-5D-5L value sets carefully to consider each of the practical and theoretical issues discussed in this chapter. We strongly recommend that users clearly justify their choice of value sets in a transparent manner. Where there remains uncertainty over which value set to use, we recommend that researchers should report the sensitivity of their results and conclusions to the use of alternative value sets. In applications where QALY estimation is not a goal, there may not be a clear rationale for using a value set as the focus of analysis, and users are encouraged to make full use of the EQ-5D-5L profile and EQ VAS data provided by respondents.

References

Andrade MV, Noronha KVMS, Santos AS, de Souza A, Guedes GR, Campolina B, Cavalcante A, Magalhães AS, Duarte D, Kind P (2021) Estimation of health-related quality of life losses owing to a technological disaster in Brazil using EQ-5D-3L: a cross-sectional study. Value Health Reg Issues 26:66–74

Appleby J, Devlin N, Parkin D (2015) Using patient reported outcomes to improve health care. Wiley Blackwell

Brazier J, Akehurst R, Brennan A, Dolan P, Claxton K, McCabe C, Sculpher M, Tsuchyia A (2005) Should patients have a greater role in valuing health states? Appl Health Econ Health Policy 4(4):201–208

Bridges J (2003) Stated preference methods in health care evaluation: an emerging methodological paradigm in health economics. Appl Health Econ Health Policy 2(4):213–224

Burstrom K, Sun S, Gerdtham U-G, Henriksson M, Johannesson M, Levin LA, Zethraeus N (2014) Swedish experience-based value sets for EQ-5D health states. Qual Life Res 23(2):431–442

Craig B, Rand K (2018) Choice defines QALYs: a US valuation of the EQ-5D-5L. Med Care 56(6):529–536

Derrett S, Devlin N, Hansen P, Herbison P (2003) Prioritising patients for elective surgery. A prospective study of clinical priority assessment criteria in New Zealand. Int J Technol Assess Health Care 19(1):91–105

Devlin N, Shah K, Mulhern B, van Hout B (2019) A new method for valuing health: directly eliciting personal utility functions. Eur J Health Econ 20(2):257–270

Devlin N, Parkin D, Janssen B (2020) Methods for analysing and reporting EQ-5D data. Springer

Dolan P, Stalmeier P (2003) The validity of time trade-off values in calculating QALYs: constant proportional time trade-off versus the proportional heuristic. J Health Econ 22(3):445–458

Dolan P, Olsen JA, Menzel P, Richardson J (2003) An inquiry into the different perspectives that can be used when eliciting preferences in health. Health Econ 12(7):545–551

Drummond MF, Sculpher M, Claxton K, Stoddart G, Torrance G (2015) Methods for the economic evaluation of health care programmes, 4th edn. Oxford University Press, Oxford

Feng Y, Parkin D, Devlin NJ (2014) Assessing the performance of the EQ-VAS in the NHS PROMs Programme. Qual Life Res 23(3):977–989

Franks P, Muennig P, Lubetkin E, Jia H (2006) The burden of disease associated with being African American in the US and the contribution of socio-economic status. Soc Sci Med 62(10):2469–2478

Greiner W, Weijnen T, Nieuwenhuizen M, Oppe S, Badia X, Busschbach J, Buxton M, Dolan P, Kind P, Krabbe P, Ohinmaa A, Parkin D, Roset M, Sintonen H, Tsuchiya A, de Charro F (2003) A single European currency for EQ-5D health states. Results from a six-country study. Eur J Health Econ 4(3):222–231

Gutacker N, Patton T, Shah K, Parkin D (2020) Using EQ-5D data to measure hospital performance: are general population values distorting patients' choices? Med Decis Mak 40(4):511–521

Hardman G, Kind P, Macran S (2002) Living with a VASectomy: Exploring the relationship between EQ-5D responses and the EQ-5D VAS? Paper presented at the 19th Plenary Meeting of the EuroQol Group, York. Available at www.euroqol.org/uploads/media/Proc02York24Hardman.pdf. Accessed 19 July 2021

Haute Authorité de Santé (2020) Choices in Methods for Economic Evaluation. https://www.has-sante.fr/jcms/r_1499251/en/choices-in-methods-for-economic-evaluation. Accessed 29 June 2021

Hernández-Alava M, Pudney S (2017) Econometric modelling of multiple self-reports of health states: the switch from EQ-5D-3L to EQ-5D-5L in evaluating drug therapies for rheumatoid arthritis. J Health Econ 55:139–152

Hernández-Alava M, Pudney S, Wailoo A (2020) Estimating the relationship between EQ-5D-5L and EQ-5D-3L: results from an English population study. EEPRU, Sheffield/York

Hill H, Rowen D, Pennington B, Wong R, Wailoo A (2020) A review of the methods used to generate utility values in NICE technology assessments for children and adolescents. Value Health 23(7):907–917

Kennedy-Martin M, Slaap B, Herdman M, van Reenen M, Kennedy-Martin T, Greiner W, Busschbach J, Boye KS (2020) Which multi-attribute utility instruments are recommended for use in cost-utility analysis? A review of national health technology assessment (HTA) guidelines. Eur J Health Econ 21(8):1245–1257

Łaszewska A, Sajjad A, Simon J, van Busschbach J, Hakkaart-van Roijen L (2020) Conceptualisation of SupraNational value sets for the EQ-5D. Presentation at ISPOR Europe 2020. https://www.pecunia-project.eu/results. Accessed 21 April 2021

Lubetkin E, Jia H, Franks P, Gold M (2005) Relationship among socioeconomic factors, clinical conditions, and health related quality of life: examining the EQ-5D in the US general population. Qual Life Res 14(10):2187–2196

Lubetkin A, Haagsma J, Janssen B, Lond D, Bonsel G (2020) The impact of COVID-19 on health inequities as measured by EQ-5D-5L: results from New York. Paper presented at EuroQol Scientific plenary 2020

MVH Group (1995) The measurement and valuation of health: final report on the modelling of valuation tariffs. MVH Group, Centre for Health Economics, University of York, UK

National Centre for Social Research (NatCen), University College London, Department of Epidemiology and Public Health (2021) Health Survey for England, 2018. [data collection]. UK Data Service. SN: 8649. https://doi.org/10.5255/UKDA-SN-8649-1

National Institute for Clinical Excellence (NICE) (2013) Guide to methods of technology appraisal 2013. Process and methods. https://wwwniceorguk/process/pmg9. Accessed 19 July 2021

National Institute for Clinical Excellence (NICE) (2019) Position statement on use of the EQ-5D-5L value set for England (updated October 2019). https://www.nice.org.uk/about/what-we-do/our-programmes/nice-guidance/technology-appraisal-guidance/eq-5d-5l. Accessed 29 June 2021

Morris S, Devlin N, Parkin D, Spencer A (2012) Economic analysis in health care. (2nd edition) Wiley.

Ogorevc M, Murovec N, Fernandez NB, Rupel VP (2019) Questioning the differences between general public vs. patient based preferences towards EQ-5D-5L defined hypothetical health states. Health Policy 123(2):166–172

Parkin D, Devlin N (2006) Is there a case for using visual analogue scale valuations in cost-utility analysis? Health Econ 15(7):653–664

Parkin D, Rice N, Devlin N (2010) Statistical analysis of EQ-5D profiles: does the use of value sets bias inference? Med Decis Mak 30(5):556–565

Parkin D, Devlin N, Feng Y (2016) What determines the shape of an EQ-5D index distribution? Med Decis Mak 36(8):941–951. https://doi.org/10.1177/0272989X16645581

Pharmaceutical Benefits Advisory Committee (PBAC) (2016) Guidelines for preparing a submission to the Pharmaceutical Benefits Advisory Committee. Version 5.0. https://pbac.pbs.gov.au/information/printable-version-of-guidelines.html. Accessed 20 July 2021

Robinson A, Parkin D (2002) Recognising diversity in public preferences: the use of preference sub-groups in cost-effectiveness analysis. A response to Sculpher and Gafni. Health Econ 11(7):649–651

Rowen D, Azzabi ZI, Chevrou-Severac H, van Hout B (2017) International regulations and recommendations for utility data for health technology assessment. PharmacoEconomics 35(Suppl 1):11–19

Sculpher M, Gafni A (2001) Recognising diversity in public preferences: the use of preference sub-groups in cost-effectiveness analysis. Health Econ 10(4):317–324

Sculpher M, Gafni A (2002) Recognising diversity in public preferences: the use of preference sub-groups in cost-effectiveness analysis. Authors reply. Health Econ 11(7):653

Sullivan T, Hansen P, Ombler F, Derrett S, Devlin N (2020) A new tool for creating personal and social EQ-5D-5L value sets, including valuing 'dead'. Soc Sci Med 246:112707. https://doi.org/10.1016/j.socscimed.2019.112707

Sutherland HJ, Llewellyn-Thomas H, Boyd NF, Till JE (1982) Attitudes toward quality of survival. The concept of "maximal endurable time". Med Decis Mak 2(3):299–309

Szende A, Janssen MF, Cabases J (2014) Self-reported population health: an international perspective based on EQ-5D. Springer, Dordrecht

The Dental and Pharmaceutical Benefits Agency (TLV) (2003) General guidelines for economic evaluations from the pharmaceutical benefits board LFNAR 2003:2. Stockholm: TLV. https://www.tlv.se/download/18.2e53241415e842ce95514e9/1510316396792/Guidelines-for-economic-evaluations-LFNAR-2003-2.pdf. Accessed 19 July 2021

The Dental and Pharmaceutical Benefits Agency (TLV) (2017) Ändring i Tandvårds- och läkemedelsförmånsverkets allmänna råd (TLVAR 2003:2) om ekonomiska utvärderingar. (In

Swedish). [Changes in the Dental and Pharmaceutical Benefits Agency's guidance for eco-nomic evaluations]. Stockholm: TLV. https://tlv.se/download/18.467926b615d084471 ac3230c/1510316374332/TLVAR_2017_1.pdf. Accessed 19 July 2021

van Hoorn RA, Donders AR, Oppe M, Stalmeier PF (2014) The better than dead method: feasibil-ity and interpretation of a valuation study. PharmacoEconomics 32(8):789–799

van Hout B, Shaw JW (2021) Mapping EQ-5D-3L to EQ-5D-5L. Value Health. https://doi.org/10.1016/j.jval.2021.03.009

van Hout B, Janssen MF, Feng YS, Kohlmann T, Busschbach J, Golicki D, Lloyd A, Scalone L, Kind P, Pickard AS (2011) Interim scoring for the EQ-5D-5L: mapping the EQ-5D-5L to EQ-5D-3L value sets. Value Health 15(5):708–715

van Hout B, Mulhern B, Feng Y, Shah K, Devlin N (2020) The EQ-5D-5L value set for England: response to the "quality assurance". Value Health 23(5):649–655

van Wilder L, Rammant E, Clays E, Devleesschauwer B, Pauwels N, De Smedt D (2019) A com-prehensive catalogue of EQ-5D scores in chronic disease: results of a systematic review. Qual Life Res 28(12):3153–3161

Whynes D, The TOMBOLA Group (2008) Correspondence between EQ-5D health state classifi-cations and EQ VAS scores. Health Qual Life Outcomes 6:94–103

Wilke CT, Pickard AS, Walton SM, Moock J, Kohlmann T, Lee TA (2010) Statistical implications of utility weighted and equally weighted HRQL measures: an empirical study. Health Econ 19(1):101–110

Xie F, Pickard AS, Krabbe PFM, Revicki D, Viney R, Devlin N, Feeny D (2015) A checklist for reporting valuation studies of multi-attribute utility-based instruments (CREATE). PharmacoEconomics 33(8):867–877

Zoorginatituut Nederlands (2016) Guidelines for economic evaluations in health care. https://english.zorginstituutnederland.nl/publications/reports/2016/06/16/guideline-for-economic-evaluations-in-healthcare. Accessed 12 May 2021

Chapter 6
How Do EQ-5D-5L Value Sets Differ?

Bram Roudijk, Bas Janssen, and Jan Abel Olsen

Abstract This chapter aims to explore the differences in EQ-5D-5L value sets between countries/areas, and to investigate whether common patterns can be identified between them. EQ-5D-5L value sets for 25 countries/areas were extracted from published literature. These national value sets were compared on key characteristics, such as: the relative importance of the EQ-5D-5L dimensions; the value scale length and the distribution of values over the value scale. Using these characteristics, distinct preference patterns were identified for Asian, Eastern European and Western countries/areas. The Asian countries/areas were split into East Asian and Southeast Asian countries/areas, as these subgroups shared similar characteristics. Using mean values for countries/areas with similar preference patterns, several aggregate value sets were generated. These aggregate value sets describe mean values for all 3125 health states described by the EQ-5D-5L for countries/areas with similar preference patterns. Applying these values to EQ-5D-5L profile data for 7933 respondents in an international survey showed that these aggregate value sets represent the individual national value sets relatively well. This chapter identified large differences between value sets, yet was able to identify common preference patterns between selected countries/areas.

B. Roudijk (✉) ·
EuroQol Research Foundation, Rotterdam, The Netherlands
e-mail: Roudijk@EuroQol.org

B. Janssen
EuroQol Research Foundation, Rotterdam, The Netherlands

Section of Medical Psychology, Department of Psychiatry, Erasmus MC,
Rotterdam, The Netherlands

J. A. Olsen
Department of Community Medicine, University of Tromsø – The Arctic University
of Norway, Tromsø, Norway

Division of Health Services, Norwegian Institute of Public Health, Oslo, Norway

© The Author(s) 2022
N. Devlin et al. (eds.), *Value Sets for EQ-5D-5L*,
https://doi.org/10.1007/978-3-030-89289-0_6

235

6.1 Introduction

Since 2012, 25 EQ-5D-5L value sets have been published using the EuroQol Valuation Technology (EQ-VT), a standardised valuation protocol, as described in Chap. 4 of this book (Oppe et al. 2014; Stolk et al. 2019). These value sets have been developed across the world, concentrated initially in Western Europe and Canada, subsequently including more North American and Asian/Pacific countries/areas and (more recently) including countries/areas from Latin America, the Middle East, Africa and Eastern Europe.

Value sets have been shown to differ between countries/areas in a number of aspects such as: the relative importance of the five dimensions and their associated levels; the length of the value scale; how many health states are given values worse than dead (WTD); the location of the descriptive midpoint (33333) on the scale and the shape of the distribution of the values for all 3125 health states. In principle, there are two reasons why we observe such cross-country/area differences in values: (1) methodological differences and (2) genuine differences in populations' health state preferences.

In contrast to valuations elicited for the EQ-5D-3L instrument, the EQ-VT protocol used for the EQ-5D-5L instrument provides a standardised method to collect valuation data using a combination of composite Time Trade-Off (cTTO) and Discrete Choice Experiment (DCE). Although the use of EQ-VT standardises a large part of the valuation methodology, some methodological differences may persist between countries/areas. These include the choice of valuation method used for the final dataset (Norman et al. 2009), modelling strategy, translation of the EQ-5D-5L (which may lead to different interpretations of health problems as described by the instrument) and any imbalance in the socio-demographic composition of the sample that might undermine the sample's representativeness. The EQ-VT protocol allows local research teams to choose a sampling strategy that is acceptable to the HTA bodies of their respective countries/areas (Stolk et al. 2019). It also allows local research teams to decide on the modelling strategy e.g., whether to use both the cTTO and DCE data or cTTO only (see Chap. 2 for more details). All of these aspects introduce heterogeneity due to methodological differences, which may be reflected in the value sets.

The differences in populations' health state preferences are assumed to be affected by a wide range of institutional and other country/area-specific circumstances that impact individuals' health opportunities and challenges and may shape health expectations and norms. Countries/areas differ along highly relevant factors such as: their healthcare system (e.g., whether universal coverage is in place or not), social insurance (including sickness benefit schemes), wealth measures such as Gross Domestic Product (GDP), governance, culture (norms and beliefs) and even climate and geography (e.g., the importance of mobility, which may be related to the infrastructure of a country/area).

The aim of this chapter is to identify in which ways currently published EQ-5D-5L value sets differ and whether we can establish distinctive preference patterns which are common across groups of countries/areas. Previous work (Olsen et al. 2018) analysed seven EQ-5D-5L value sets and identified a 'Western preference pattern' (WePP). This chapter extends the work of Olsen et al. (2018), using the value sets reported from all 25 countries/areas reported in Chap. 4. We hypothesise that countries/areas that are similar in terms of institutional settings and other country/area-specific circumstances will have similar value sets. As 21 additional value sets have been published since the four Western countries/areas included in the Olsen et al. (2018) study (Canada, England, Netherlands, Spain) (Xie et al. 2016; Devlin et al. 2018; Versteegh et al. 2016; Ramos-Goñi et al. 2017b, 2018), it may be possible to further validate and refine the suggested Western preference pattern identified by Olsen et al. (2018). We also investigate whether other preference patterns emerge for other groups of countries/areas, i.e., whether there are any similarities in the value sets for countries/areas in other regions of the world, that may share similar characteristics.

6.2 Methods

6.2.1 Analysing Differences Between Value Sets

To determine how the value sets may differ from each other, several important characteristics of the value sets are used. Olsen et al. (2018) previously identified: (1) the relative importance of the different EQ-5D-5L dimensions; (2) differences in scale length between countries/areas, which gives an indication of the willingness to trade-off quality for quantity of life; (3) the marginal effect of moving from one severity level to another severity level; and finally, (4) the location on the value scale of the descriptive midpoint in the EQ-5D-5L, state "33333". To compare the relative importance of the EQ-5D-5L dimensions, we compare (1) the relative importance of the functional dimensions (mobility (MO), self-care (SC) and usual activities (UA)) versus the symptom dimensions (pain/discomfort (PD), anxiety/depression (AD)); (2) the relative importance of pain; (3) the relative importance of anxiety/depression.

For the current chapter, all 25 value sets published at the time of writing were used. A database was created in which utilities of each value set were assigned to all possible 3125 EQ-5D-5L health states. These value sets include: ten from Europe (Ramos-Goñi et al. 2017b, 2018; Versteegh et al. 2016; Devlin et al. 2018; Andrade et al. 2020; Ludwig et al. 2018; Ferreira et al. 2019; Hobbins et al. 2018; Golicki et al. 2019; Rencz et al. 2020; Jensen et al. 2021); two from North America (Xie et al. 2016; Pickard et al. 2019); three from Latin America (Augustovski et al. 2016; Augustovski et al. 2020; Gutierrez-Delgado et al. 2021); one from Africa (Welie et al. 2020) and nine from Asia (Luo et al. 2017; Shiroiwa et al. 2016; Kim et al. 2016; Mai et al. 2020; Pattanaphesaj et al. 2018; Lin et al. 2018; Purba et al. 2017; Wong et al. 2018; Shafie et al. 2019). As a preliminary exploration of the value sets, the kernel density distributions of each value set were plotted and compared graphically.

The relative importance of the EQ-5D-5L dimensions was assessed by comparing the values for single dimension level 5 problems health states (51111, 15111, 11511, 11151, 11115) between countries/areas, encompassing the maximum value decrement for each dimension.[1] A further sub-analysis was carried out to determine the relative importance of PD and the relative importance of mental health (i.e., AD), and their ranking compared to the other dimensions.

Differences in scale length between countries/areas are inspected by subtracting the value for state "55555" (extreme problems/unable to on all dimensions) from the value for state "11111" (no problems on any of the dimensions) for each country/area. The location of descriptive midpoint in the value distribution is assessed by taking the difference between the value for state "11111" and state "33333" and dividing this value by the scale length.

Analysing the marginal effect of moving from one severity level to another on a dimension is trivial in cases where a 20-parameter main effects model is used as the preferred model for a value set, as the coefficients of the 20-parameter model can be used for this analysis (see Chap. 4 for a description of the modelling of valuation data). However, this is not the case for at least some of the value sets included in this analysis, such as value sets that included an intercept, or that were defined according to a constrained 8- or 9-parameter model, where the distance between the levels of the EQ-5D-5L is kept constant over the dimensions.[2] Therefore, we calculated the values for each health state with problems on a single dimension only (e.g. for AD 11111, 11112, 11113, 11114, 11115) and plotted these in a line plot for each dimension for each country/area separately. This allows for a comparison of the 20-parameter model value sets with all other value sets.

6.2.2 Defining Preference Patterns and the Performance of These Patterns

To test the performance of the identified preference patterns, data from the Multi Instrument Comparison (MIC) study (Richardson et al. 2012) were used, as in the Olsen et al. study (Olsen et al. 2018). In the MIC study, patients from seven disease areas (arthritis, asthma, cancer, depression, diabetes, hearing loss and heart disease) as well as a healthy respondent group, completed the EQ-5D-5L, as part of a larger international survey. In total, 7933 respondents from six Western countries/areas (Australia, Canada, Germany, Norway, United Kingdom, United States) completed

---

[1] Note that this is a different and less sophisticated way of assessing dimension importance compared to that reported in Chap. 4 for each value set.

[2] The results of 8- or 9-parameter models can be presented as 20-parameter models, without changing anything of substance relating to the model.

the EQ-5D-5L. The values for the 25 different value sets used in the current chapter were assigned to the health profiles of the respondents, as were the values generated by the identified preference patterns. Using line plots, we compared the distributions of the values between the countries/areas and identified preference patterns. The preference patterns, or *aggregate value sets*, will be defined based on the mean of the coefficients of sets of value sets that share common properties. The properties used for this purpose are: (1) the relative importance of the EQ-5D-5L dimensions (calculated as described above, four different sub-characteristics are compared); (2) the distribution over values over the scale (six different sub-characteristics are compared); and (3) geographic proximity and cultural similarity.

6.3 Differences Between Value Sets

6.3.1 Relative Importance of the Dimensions

Table 6.1 provides information on the geographical region and subregion of the countries/areas in which value set studies were conducted. Furthermore, it shows which protocol version was used for the data collection, which reflects some of the methodological choices made in each study, such as the use of the quality control (QC) procedure, practice health states, a feedback module and dynamic practice examples. More can be read about this elsewhere (Stolk et al. 2019) and in Chap. 2. Furthermore, Table 6.1 shows the order of importance of the dimensions, which differs between countries/areas. In each country/area either MO, PD or AD is identified as the most important dimension. The least important dimension is either SC, UA, AD in Uruguay, and PD in the Indonesian value set. MO is ranked as the most important dimension eleven times (including all of the nine Asian countries/areas), PD is ranked as the most important dimension ten times (including seven Western countries/areas) and AD is ranked as most important four times (including the remaining three Western countries/areas). In 16 value sets, UA is ranked as the least important or is tied as the least important dimension. SC is ranked seven times as the least important dimension, while AD is ranked least important once and PD once.

Table 6.2 reports the individual weights, or partial value decrement, for having a certain level of problems on a certain health dimension compared to not having any problems on that dimension. The table restricts itself to the maximum level, so only the weights for level 5 problems are reported. The smallest value decrement assigned to any dimension with level 5 problems is UA, in Spain, with a value of 0.153. In contrast, the largest value decrement in Spain is for PD, with a value of 0.381. The largest value decrement assigned to any dimension with level 5 problems is AD in Ireland, with a value of 0.646. In contrast, the smallest value decrement assigned to any dimension with level 5 problems in Ireland is 0.187, for UA. The size of the range of value decrements assigned to the dimensions differs substantially between countries/areas. The smallest difference is reported in Japan, where the largest

Table 6.1 Summary information by country/area

Country/ area	Region	Subregion	Protocol version	Method[a]	Order[a]
Canada	Western	NA	1.0	cTTO	PD>AD>SC>MO>UA
England	Western	WE	1.0	cTTO+DCE	PD>AD>MO>SC>UA
Netherlands	Western	WE	1.0	cTTO	AD>PD>MO>UA>SC
Spain	Western	WE	1.0	cTTO&DCE	PD>AD>MO>SC>UA
USA	Western	NA	2.1	cTTO	PD>MO>AD>SC>UA
Germany	Western	WE	2.0	cTTO&DCE	PD>AD>SC>MO>UA
France	Western	WE	2.1	cTTO&DCE	PD>MO>SC>AD>UA
Portugal	Western	WE	2.0	cTTO&DCE	PD>MO>SC>AD>UA
Ireland	Western	WE	2.0	cTTO&DCE	AD>PD>MO>SC>UA
Denmark	Western	WE	2.1	cTTO&DCE	AD>PD>MO>SC>UA
Poland	Eastern Europe	EE	2.0	cTTO&DCE	PD>MO>SC>AD>UA
Hungary	Eastern Europe	EE	2.1	cTTO	MO>PD>SC>AD>UA
Japan	Asia	EA	1.1	cTTO	MO>AD>PD>UA>SC
Korea	Asia	EA	1.1	cTTO	MO>PD>UA>AD>SC
China	Asia	EA	1.0	cTTO	MO>PD>AD>SC>UA
Vietnam	Asia	SEA	2.1	cTTO&DCE	MO>PD>UA>AD>SC
Thailand	Asia	SEA	1.1	cTTO&DCE	MO>AD>PD>SC>UA
Taiwan	Asia	EA	2.0	cTTO&DCE	MO>PD>AD>UA>SC
Hong Kong	Asia	EA	1.1	cTTO&DCE	MO>PD>SC>AD>UA
Indonesia	Asia	SEA	2.0	cTTO&DCE	MO>UA>SC>AD>PD
Malaysia	Asia	SEA	2.0	cTTO&DCE	MO>PD>AD>SC>UA
Mexico	Latin America and Africa	LA	2.0	cTTO	PD>AD>UA>MO>SC
Peru	Latin America and Africa	LA	2.1	cTTO	PD>MO>AD>SC>UA
Uruguay	Latin America and Africa	LA	1.1	cTTO	MO>SC>PD>UA>AD
Ethiopia	Latin America and Africa	AF	2.1	cTTO&DCE	AD>PD>MO>UA>SC

NA North America, *WE* Western Europe, *EE* Eastern Europe, *EA* East Asia, *SEA* Southeast Asia, *LA* Latin America, *AF* Africa

AD anxiety/depression, *MO* mobility, *PD* pain/discomfort, *SC* self-care, *UA* usual activities

[a]The order of importance of the dimensions is defined by the weights assigned to the states 51111, 15111, 11511, 11151, 11115

[b]Method is defined as the data used for the final model (i.e., a cTTO-only or a hybrid model was used, or another strategy)

weight (MO) is only 0.079 larger than the smallest weight (SC). The largest differences are reported in Ireland, where the largest weight (AD) is 0.459 larger than the smallest weight (UA). These results show that countries/areas can differ considerably in terms of which dimension is considered most important and the absolute difference in weight assigned to the different dimensions.

Table 6.2 Weights assigned to level 5 problems in each dimension

Country/area	MO	SC	UA	PD	AD
Canada	0.258	0.293	0.240	0.370	0.330
England	0.274	0.203	0.184	0.335	0.289
Netherlands	0.250	0.215	0.239	0.462	0.468
Spain	0.337	0.196	0.153	0.381	0.348
USA	0.322	0.261	0.255	0.414	0.321
Germany	0.224	0.260	0.209	0.612	0.356
France	0.323	0.257	0.239	0.442	0.256
Portugal	0.356	0.294	0.263	0.406	0.284
Ireland	0.344	0.287	0.187	0.510	0.646
Denmark	0.220	0.209	0.174	0.537	0.618
Poland	0.314	0.264	0.205	0.575	0.232
Hungary	0.455	0.366	0.276	0.411	0.340
Japan	0.302	0.223	0.235	0.255	0.259
Korea	0.425	0.296	0.349	0.381	0.311
China	0.424	0.343	0.326	0.387	0.348
Vietnam	0.376	0.231	0.299	0.367	0.239
Thailand	0.371	0.250	0.248	0.256	0.295
Taiwan	0.477	0.323	0.351	0.453	0.421
Hong Kong	0.529	0.352	0.282	0.354	0.348
Indonesia	0.613	0.316	0.385	0.246	0.305
Malaysia	0.340	0.261	0.202	0.338	0.300
Mexico	0.270	0.259	0.276	0.458	0.334
Peru	0.473	0.355	0.347	0.476	0.422
Uruguay	0.312	0.286	0.245	0.284	0.190
Ethiopia	0.360	0.222	0.272	0.406	0.458

AD anxiety/depression, *MO* mobility, *PD* pain/discomfort, *SC* self-care, *UA* usual activities

6.3.2 Marginal Value Decrements of Moving from One Level to Another

Figures 6.1a and 6.1b report the marginal effect of moving from one level to another, by dimension. For some countries/areas, such as Canada and Japan, the marginal value decrement of moving to another level of problems is relatively similar between the dimensions. However, in countries/areas such as Indonesia, Ireland, Germany, the Netherlands and Poland, the marginal effects for one or two dimensions are significantly more negative. Furthermore, the slopes of the graphs in Figs. 6.1a and 6.1b differ between countries/areas, indicating different marginal value decrements. For example, in Japan the decrements in value by level seem to be relatively linear, while in several Western countries/areas (including Canada, England, Netherlands), there seems to be a "kink" when moving from level 3 to 4 on any dimension, and a "reverse kink" when moving from level 4 to 5.

These findings are supported by Table 6.3, which reports values for specific health states, representing the same level of problems on all dimensions; 11111, 22222, 33333, 44444, 55555. Table 6.3 shows how these important health states in

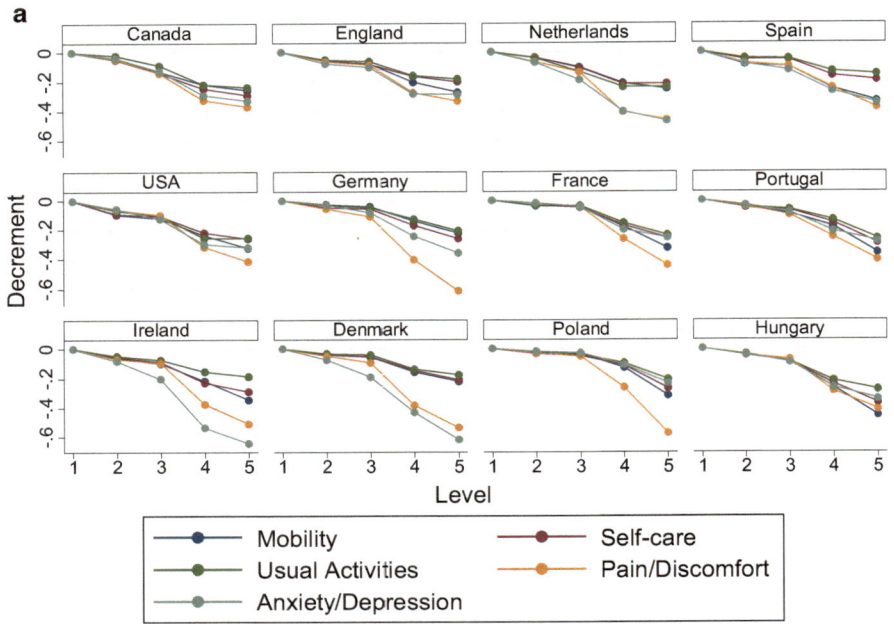

Fig. 6.1a Value decrements by level and dimension, by country/area for Eastern European and Western countries/areas

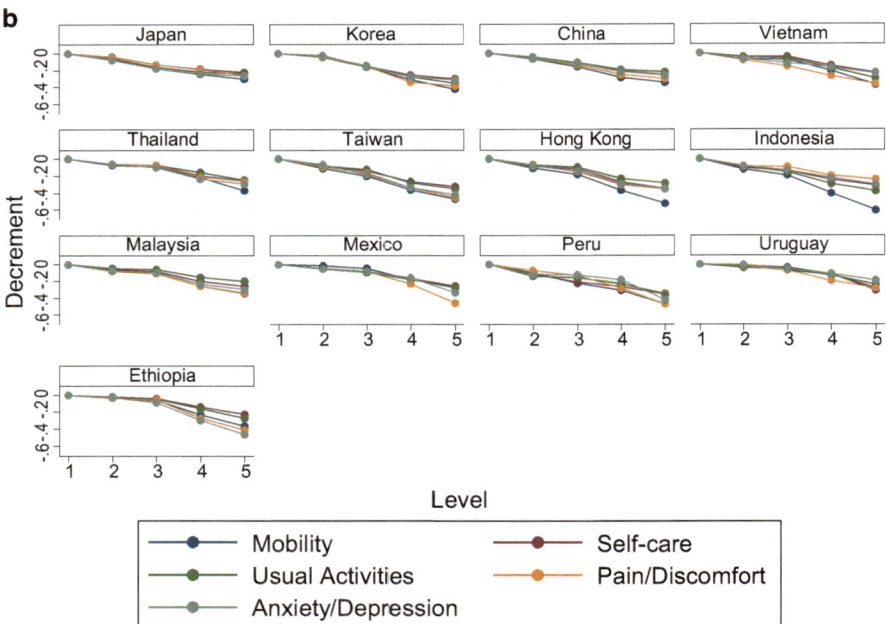

Fig. 6.1b Value decrements by level and dimension, by country/area for Asian, African and Latin American countries/areas

Table 6.3 Values for health states where all dimensions have identical level of severity, including the length of the scale (i.e. 55555-value minus 11111-value)

Country/area	Region	U(11111)	U(22222)	U(33333)	U(44444)	U(55555)	Scale length	Midpoint
Canada	Western	0.948	0.762	0.576	0.379	−0.148	1.096	38.69%
England	Western	1.000	0.701	0.593	−0.094	−0.285	1.285	31.67%
Netherlands	Western	1.000	0.705	0.511	−0.289	−0.446	1.446	34.95%
Spain	Western	1.000	0.663	0.570	−0.064	−0.415	1.415	30.39%
USA	Western	1.000	0.630	0.449	−0.329	−0.573	1.573	35.03%
Germany	Western	1.000	0.801	0.662	−0.085	−0.661	1.661	20.35%
France	Western	1.000	0.853	0.772	0.034	−0.517	1.517	15.03%
Portugal	Western	1.000	0.783	0.589	0.061	−0.603	1.603	25.64%
Ireland	Western	1.000	0.685	0.448	−0.506	−0.974	1.974	27.96%
Denmark	Western	1.000	0.771	0.571	−0.251	−0.757	1.757	24.41%
Poland	Eastern Europe	1.000	0.873	0.800	0.297	−0.590	1.590	12.58%
Hungary	Eastern Europe	1.000	0.802	0.571	−0.270	−0.848	1.848	23.21%
Japan	Asia/EA	1.000	0.659	0.484	0.189	−0.026	1.026	53.53%
Korea	Asia/EA	1.000	0.730	0.646	0.247	−0.066	1.066	36.49%
China	Asia/EA	1.000	0.734	0.363	−0.290	−0.391	1.391	45.79%
Vietnam	Asia/SEA	1.000	0.694	0.551	0.032	−0.512	1.512	29.70%
Thailand	Asia/SEA	1.000	0.704	0.608	0.002	−0.420	1.420	27.61%
Taiwan	Asia/SEA	1.000	0.592	0.204	−0.589	−1.025	2.025	39.31%
Hong Kong	Asia/SEA	1.000	0.581	0.324	−0.476	−0.865	1.865	36.25%
Indonesia	Asia/SEA	1.000	0.525	0.283	−0.384	−0.865	1.865	38.45%
Malaysia	Asia/SEA	1.000	0.656	0.543	−0.105	−0.441	1.441	31.71%
Mexico	Latin America and Africa	1.000	0.773	0.612	0.083	−0.596	1.596	24.31%
Peru	Latin America and Africa	1.000	0.441	0.148	−0.282	−1.073	2.073	41.10%
Uruguay	Latin America and Africa	1.000	0.879	0.743	0.353	−0.265	1.265	20.53%
Ethiopia	Latin America and Africa	1.000	0.848	0.711	−0.096	−0.718	1.718	16.82%

AD anxiety/depression, *MO* mobility, *PD* pain/discomfort, *SC* self-care, *UA* usual activities

the descriptive system are spread over the value scale. For example, in China the values assigned to these states correspond well with their location in the descriptive system, with state 33333 being roughly halfway on the value scale between state 11111 and 55555. For other countries/areas, such as France, this is not so: the difference between 11111 and 33333 represents only 15% of the scale, with the remaining 85% representing the difference between 33333 and 55555.

6.3.3 Scale Length and Location of the Descriptive Midpoint on the Health Utility Scale

Figure 6.2 reports the kernel density distributions of each value set. The differences in scale length between countries/areas are reflected in these distributions. The scale length for a country/area can be thought of as an indicator of their willingness to give up life years to improve quality of life. The shape of the distributions also differs, although in addition to the scale length, this is also related to the relative importance of the domains and modelling decisions, which may lead to normally or non-normally distributed value sets.

Table 6.3 includes the location of the descriptive midpoint (33333) of the EQ-5D-5L on the value distribution, expressed as a percentage of the total scale length. For the Western European countries/areas, the descriptive midpoints are in

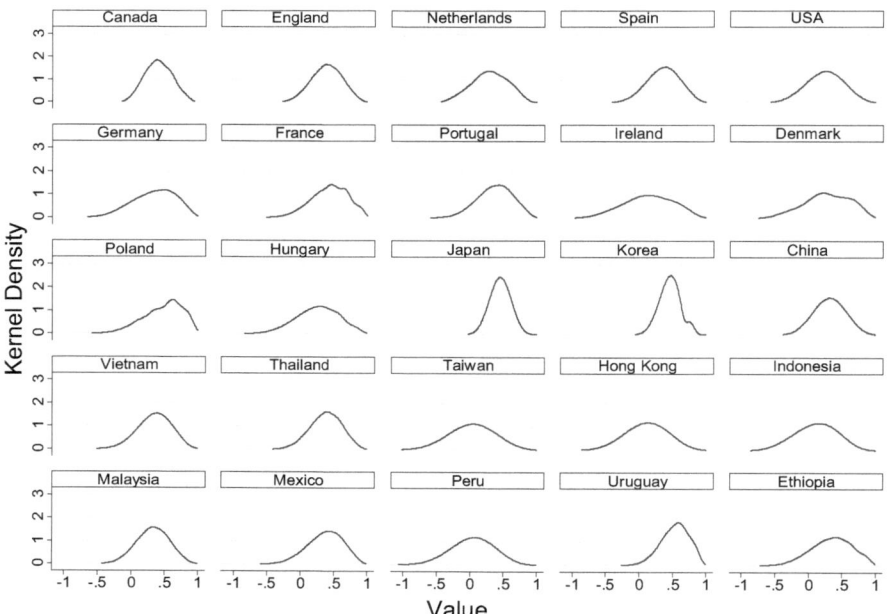

Fig. 6.2 Kernel density distribution plots by country/area

most cases assigned a higher value than the mathematical midpoint of the health value scale, indicating a relatively larger weights for severe and extreme health problems, compared to slight and moderate problems. For Asian countries/areas, this is the case as well, with the exception of Korea, where state 33333 is assigned a relatively low value compared to the scale range. Furthermore, Table 6.3 also reports the scale length for each value set. For Western countries/areas, these are relatively similar and are between 1.096 and 1.757. Ireland is an exception with a scale length of 1.974. For the Asian countries/areas, there is a clear distinction between East Asian and Southeast Asian countries/areas in terms of scale length; for East Asian countries/areas such as China, Japan and Korea, these are relatively small (between 1.026 and 1.391). For Southeast Asian countries/areas the scale lengths are much larger, with the lowest being reported in Thailand at 1.420 and the highest in Taiwan at 2.025.

6.4 Identifying Preference Patterns

Based on these findings, it appears that we can now differentiate between four regions: Asian, Western, Eastern European, Latin-American and African. Tables 6.4a and 6.4b provide more details on certain properties that are shared between the value sets for different countries/areas and by contrast also identifies differences. The Asian countries/areas can further be divided into the East Asian (Japan, Korea and China) and Southeast Asian (Vietnam, Thailand, Taiwan, Hong Kong, Indonesia and Malaysia) subgroups. The Latin-American (Mexico, Peru and Uruguay) and African (Ethiopia) regions are pooled due to the fact that there are few value sets available for that region and they do not fit into the other categories.

What can be seen from Tables 6.1, 6.2, 6.3, 6.4a and 6.4b, is that the relative importance of the dimensions differs fundamentally between Western countries/areas and Asian, Latin-American, African and Eastern European countries/areas. For the Asian value sets, MO is always the most important dimension, mostly followed by PD, with UA and SC being of least concern. In contrast, PD or AD is usually the most important dimension in Western countries/areas, followed by MO, SC and UA. Eastern European countries/areas show a high importance for PD and MO, followed by SC, AD and UA. For the Latin-American and African value sets, the orders of relative importance are more mixed. Other characteristics, such as a drop at the top of the scale, i.e., the drop in value associated to not being in state 11111 regardless of the health problems experienced and relative drops in value over the levels, seem mixed. Although Olsen et al. (2018) found substantial differences in the value sets from the first wave of valuation studies for the EQ-5D-5L, these differences are less apparent in the newer studies.

The scale length also differs substantially between countries/areas, as can be seen from Tables 6.4a and 6.4b. Western countries/areas seem more similar regarding how the values for some key points on the scale (states 22222, 33333, 44444 and 55555) are distributed over the value scale, as compared to other countries/areas.

Table 6.4a Key characteristics from each country's/area's value set, Western countries/areas and Eastern Europe

	Canada	England	Netherlands	Spain	USA	Germany	France	Portugal	Ireland	Denmark	Poland	Hungary
Dimensions; relative importance												
(PD + AD) ≈ (MO + SC + UA)	X	X	(X)	X		(X)	(X)	(X)	(X)		X	
PD ≈ AD	X	X	X	(X)					X	(X)		
MO ≈ SC	X	X	X		X		X	X	X	X		
UA < SC	X	X		X	X	X	X	X	X	X	X	X
Levels; characteristics of the scale												
Drop at the top (N1)			X									
Kink at level 3 in all dimensions	X	X	X	X	X	X	X	X	X	X	X	X
Reverse kink at level 4 in all dimensions	X	X	X	(X)	(X)							
Scale value ranges												
22222 < 0.7 – 0.8 >	X	X	X			(X)		X	(X)	X		(X)
33333 < 0.5 – 0.6 >	X	X	X	X				X	X	X		X
44444 < –0.1 – 0.1 >	X	X		X		X	X	X				
55555 < –0.2	X	X	X	X	X	X	X	X	X	X	X	X

AD anxiety/depression, *MO* mobility, *PD* pain/discomfort, *SC* self-care, *UA* usual activities

Table 6.4b Key characteristics from each country's/area's value set; Asia, Latin America and Africa

	Japan	Korea	China	Vietnam	Thailand	Taiwan	Hong Kong	Indonesia	Malaysia	Mexico	Peru	Uruguay	Ethiopia
Dimensions; relative importance													
(PD + AD) ≈ (MO + SC + UA)					(X)				(X)	(X)		(X)	X
PD ≈ AD			X			(X)	X	X	X				
MO ≈ SC										X			
UA < SC			X		X		X		X		(X)		
Levels; characteristics of the scale													
Drop at the top (N1)	X	X											
Kink at level 3 in all dimensions		X		X	X	X	X	X	X	X		X	X
Reverse kink at level 4 in all dimensions		X					X						
Scale value ranges													
22222 < 0.7 − 0.8 >		X	X	(X)	X				(X)	X			(X)
33333 < 0.5 − 0.6 >				X	(X)				X	(X)			
44444 < −0.1 − 0.1 >				X	X			(X)	X	X			X
55555 < −0.2			X	X	X	X	X	X	X	X	X		X

AD anxiety/depression, *MO* mobility, *PD* pain/discomfort, *SC* self-care, *UA* usual activities

Between the Asian countries/areas, there seems to be a distinction in scale length between Southeast Asian countries/areas and East Asian countries/areas, with East Asian countries/areas reporting shorter scale length than Southeast Asian countries/areas, indicating less willingness to trade life years for quality of life in East Asian countries/areas, compared to Southeast Asian countries/areas.

Olsen et al. (2018) found a Western preference pattern (WePP) in their previous study, which represented a hybrid of the value sets for England, Canada, Spain and the Netherlands. Of the ten key characteristics in their WePP-model (the characteristics in Tables 6.4a and 6.4b, except for the drop at the top/N1 term), Canada and England fulfilled all 10 characteristics, while the Netherlands and Spain met 9. The new value sets from other Western countries/areas appear to confirm the existence of this WePP, with Portugal and Ireland fulfilling 8 of the criteria, Denmark fulfilling 7, while France and Germany fulfilled 6 of the criteria. The US and the two Eastern European countries/areas are somewhat different from the Western preference patterns, as they only adhere to 4 or 5 of the criteria. Interestingly, the relative importance of AD is much lower in the Eastern European countries/areas, while MO and SC are more important, although this also applies to a lesser extent to France and Portugal.

Table 6.4b reveals more heterogeneous preferences behind the value sets. It seems that Asian countries/areas share similar characteristics, but can be subgrouped into East Asian and Southeast Asian preference patterns. The remaining countries/areas (Mexico, Peru, Uruguay and Ethiopia) are different in their characteristics from the (Southeast and East) Asian, Eastern European and Western value sets. As they also differ between each other, these are not grouped as another preference pattern. However, one common aspect of the value sets from Mexico, Peru, Uruguay and Ethiopia that can be clearly identified is that the value for state 55555 is lower than −0.2 in all these countries/areas.

Preference patterns and the aggregate value sets associated with them, are generated and defined as the means of the groups of value sets they represent. Taking the means of the values from several value sets that share similar characteristics ensures that the aggregate value sets broadly represent the value sets they should represent, without large variation. These aggregate value sets are reported in Table 6.5 and are presented as weights for the level dimension combinations (e.g., UA3 represents the weight for having moderate problems on UA).

6.5 How Do These Preference Patterns Perform?

Figure 6.3a-e show how these aggregate value sets perform compared to the national value sets they represent. These figures represent values assigned to the EQ-5D-5L health profiles of the respondents of the MIC study, based on the value sets for each country/area in the geographic region, and the aggregate value sets developed here, referred to with the prefix MN to each region. These values are plotted against the relative severity of the health profiles of those respondents, as defined by the level

Table 6.5 The aggregate value sets, presented as weights for level/dimension combinations (e.g., SC4 indicates level 4 problems with SC). N1 indicates a drop in value related to not being in full health/state 11111

State	MN-WePP	MN-EUR-E	MN-ASIA	MN-SEA	MN-EASIA
N1	0.010	0.000	0.018	0.000	0.053
MO2	0.058	0.030	0.081	0.092	0.059
MO3	0.082	0.062	0.131	0.141	0.110
MO4	0.195	0.195	0.278	0.304	0.226
MO5	0.286	0.385	0.402	0.451	0.305
SC2	0.055	0.038	0.061	0.071	0.039
SC3	0.076	0.068	0.091	0.098	0.079
SC4	0.183	0.176	0.201	0.221	0.161
SC5	0.243	0.315	0.261	0.289	0.205
UA2	0.047	0.029	0.056	0.064	0.041
UA3	0.065	0.063	0.091	0.095	0.083
UA4	0.168	0.157	0.203	0.216	0.176
UA5	0.210	0.241	0.270	0.295	0.220
PD2	0.060	0.037	0.068	0.078	0.047
PD3	0.096	0.062	0.109	0.121	0.086
PD4	0.320	0.275	0.245	0.264	0.207
PD5	0.442	0.493	0.310	0.336	0.260
AD2	0.061	0.029	0.064	0.070	0.053
AD3	0.123	0.061	0.115	0.127	0.092
AD4	0.312	0.185	0.229	0.249	0.189
AD5	0.387	0.286	0.286	0.318	0.223

AD anxiety/depression, *MO* mobility, *PD* pain/discomfort, *SC* self-care, *UA* usual activities

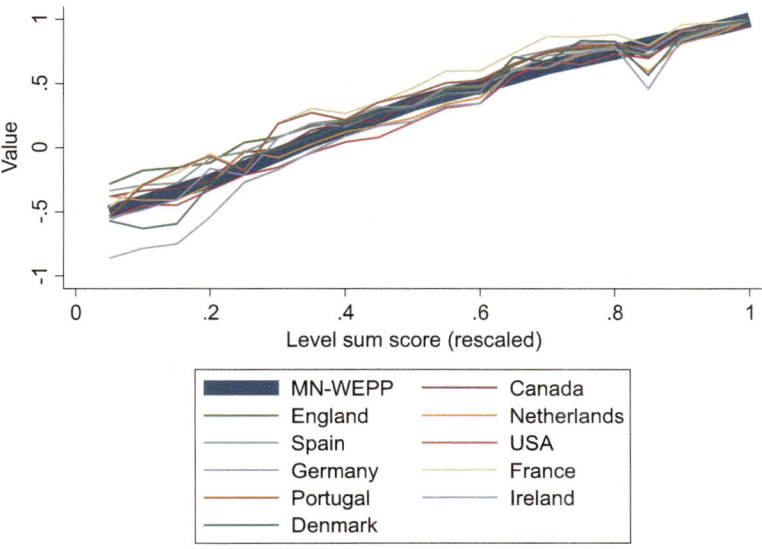

Fig. 6.3a Performance of the preference patterns: MN-WEPP

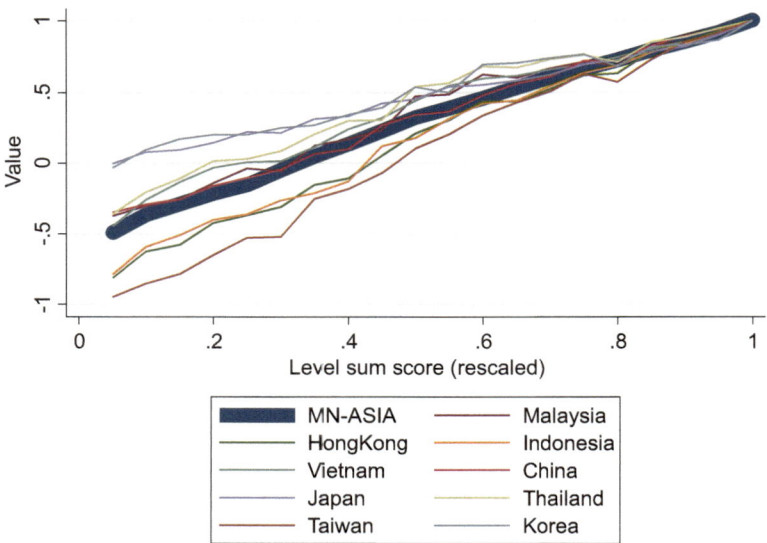

Fig. 6.3b Performance of the preference patterns: MN-ASIA

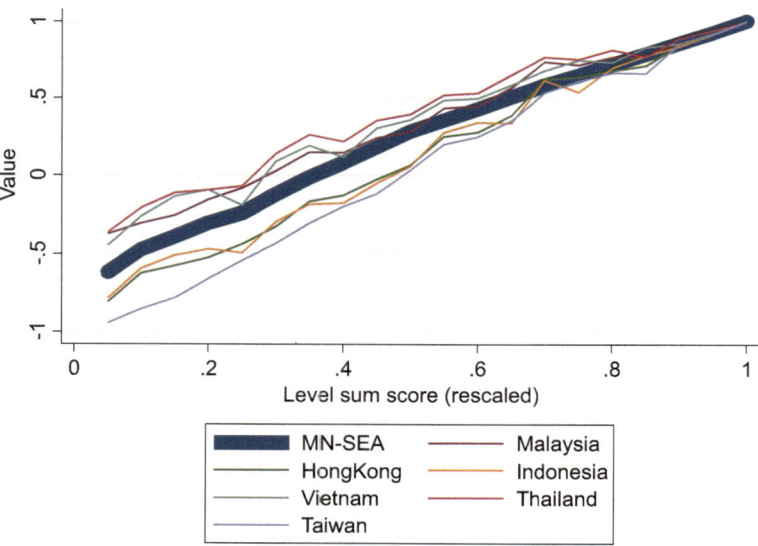

Fig. 6.3e Performance of the preference patterns: MN-SEA

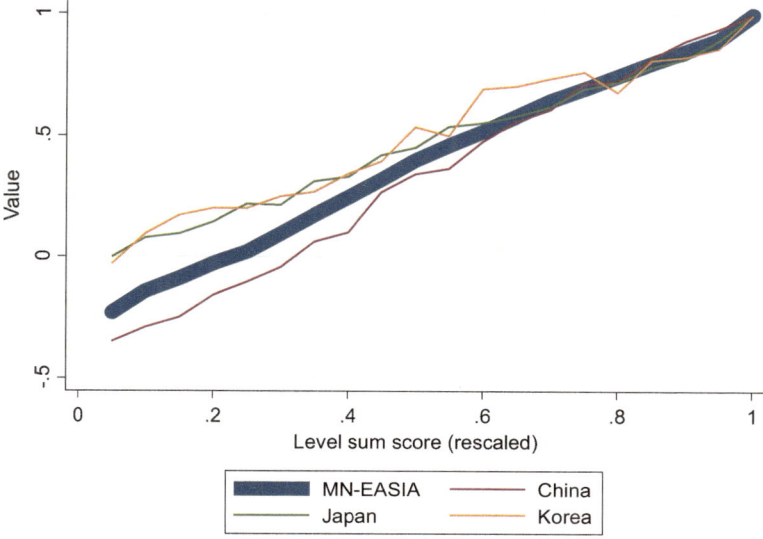

Fig. 6.3d Performance of the preference patterns: MN-EASIA

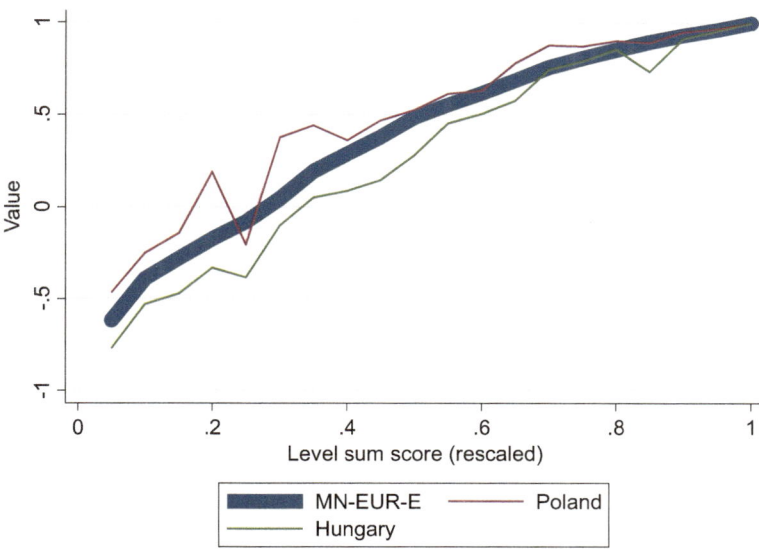

Fig. 6.3c Performance of the preference patterns: MN-EUR-E

sum score, calculated by taking the sum of the levels of problems for all dimensions of the EQ-5D-5L (e.g., for state 12315 this is $1 + 2 + 3 + 1 + 5 = 12$) and rescaled to a scale in which 0 is the worst health state and 1 is the best health state. This allows us to see whether the aggregate value sets could represent single country/area value sets well, when used in patient populations. If they perform well, these aggregate value sets may be useful to assess the quality of life in multi-country/area studies. What these figures show is that the Western aggregate value set based on means (MN-WEPP) performs relatively well and can be seen as an extension of the Western preference pattern ('WePP') model suggested by Olsen et al. (2018). However, this preference pattern may misrepresent the value sets of some countries/areas to some degree, such as Ireland and France. The values for Ireland are consistently lower than the MN-WEPP. The value set for France generates values that are frequently substantially higher than the other value sets for the mild and moderate states, yet the values for France become more comparable to the other European value sets and the aggregate value set for more severe states. Eastern European values (MN-EUR-E, Fig. 6.3c) are quite similar for the mild and moderate states, yet seem to diverge for the more severe states.

The results for the Asian aggregate value set (MN-ASIA, Fig. 6.3b) are mixed. The Southeast Asian aggregate value set (MN-SEA, Fig. 6.3e) performs relatively well for mild and moderate states, yet for severe states, there seems to be a split between two sets of 3 countries/areas. Taiwan, Hong Kong and Indonesia show substantially lower values than Thailand, Malaysia and Vietnam. For East Asia, Korea and Japan appear to have very similar preference patterns, yet China performs quite differently from those, leading to a misrepresentation of the East Asian aggregate value set (MN-EASIA, Fig. 6.3d). For the whole of Asia, there seems to be a lot of heterogeneity, with smaller groups of countries/areas being more alike, but no real pattern in values that is shared among all countries/areas.

6.6 Discussion

6.6.1 Main Findings

In this chapter we have identified several key differences between currently published value sets, by examining the distributions, scale lengths, relative importance of the dimensions, marginal differences in values between levels, and a focus on symptoms versus the functional dimensions. Furthermore, we were able to identify several preference patterns for countries/areas that share common characteristics in terms of geography and/or institutional settings.

6.6.2 Preference Patterns

We have identified five preference patterns; for Western countries/areas, Asian countries/areas, further subdivided into an East-Asian preference pattern and a Southeast Asian preference pattern and Eastern-European countries/areas. Our findings show that the countries/areas identified by Olsen et al. (2018) as having a similar pattern can be supplemented with other Western countries/areas as well, as they are also similar in value set characteristics.

Eastern European countries/areas differ substantially from the Western preference pattern, as MO is considered more important than in Western countries/areas, compared to PD or AD. Furthermore, AD is given low priority in general, compared to the Western preference pattern.

The Asian preference patterns are distinct from the Western preference pattern as MO is considered the most important dimension in all Asian value sets. Furthermore, a clear distinction between the Eastern European and Asian preference patterns is that on average, there is a higher importance for AD in the Asian value sets, compared to the Eastern European preference pattern. The scale lengths do not differ substantially from the Western and Eastern European preference patterns, yet differ substantially within the Asian preference pattern. Figures 6.3b, 6.3d and 6.3e illustrate this. The difference in scale length and divergence between the Eastern Asian and Southeast Asian countries/areas for the severe health states is the main difference between the two and leads us to distinguish two separate Asian preference patterns. This confirms findings by Xie et al. who concluded that there is less variation within Western value sets compared to Asian value sets (Xie et al. 2017).

6.6.3 Data Quality and Modelling Strategies

In addition to the factors discussed in the methods and results sections, there are two other key elements that may cause differences between value sets: (1) data quality and (2) modelling strategies. Especially in the first wave of valuation studies, some studies reported issues with data quality. Two key data issues identified were a lack of worse than dead (WTD) responses due to the fact that the WTD task of the cTTO was not explained to the respondents and satisficing by the respondents, leading to low values for very mild health states (Stolk et al. 2019; Ramos-Goñi et al. 2017a, b). Both of these are undesirable and may affect value sets, resulting in poor face validity. The lack of negative values may lead to a narrower value range than could have been found when genuine preferences had been captured, while low values for mild health states may lead to imprecision and underestimation at the top of the scale, resulting in low values for mild states in the value sets.

Modelling strategies may also affect some of the key aspects of a value set. These refer to: (1) whether cTTO data are combined with DCE data (hybrid modelling); (2) the assumptions on censoring at −1; (3) the way heteroskedasticity is dealt with; (4) accounting for preference heterogeneity; and (5) allowing for nonlinear terms.

Hybrid modelling combines the DCE and cTTO data into a single likelihood function, which allows the researcher to model both sets of data simultaneously (Ramos-Goñi et al. 2018). There is evidence that the scale length is somewhat longer in studies that use hybrid models when compared to cTTO models. For example, in the case of the US valuation study, the scale length differed by 0.126 between the cTTO and hybrid models, and the order of importance of the dimensions also differed (Pickard et al. 2019). Furthermore, there is an ongoing debate on whether hybrid modelling is an appropriate strategy when the DCE and cTTO data are not in agreement.

Taking into account the censored nature of cTTO data is another matter of concern that may affect value sets systematically. In the cTTO task, respondents are constrained by a minimum value of -1 that they can assign to health states. In practice, respondents may be willing to assign an even lower value to a health state. To account for this, assumptions can be made about the distribution of the responses at -1, which may be beyond this value. Tobit models are a way to deal with this and they may substantially lengthen the scale compared to models that make no assumptions about censored data. For example, in the Dutch study, the scale length differed by 0.119 between the Tobit and regular linear models (Versteegh et al. 2016). Furthermore, there may be consequences for the values at the top of the scale as well.

Models accounting for heteroskedasticity may be better at providing more exact estimates for cTTO data, as the standard errors are substantially smaller for the milder health states compared to the more severe states on the scale. Furthermore, accounting for preference heterogeneity by employing random intercept models may also account for differences between value sets. Finally, allowing for non-linear terms such as interactions in the models may cause differences between value sets, producing non-normal distributions.

6.6.4 Differences Between Value Sets Between and Within Preference Patterns

As identified in the introduction, there are many factors that may explain differences and similarities between value sets. Differences in genuine preferences may result from differences in cultural values, wealth, characteristics of health systems, whereas methodological differences can be caused by differences in measurement method, data quality and modelling strategies.

A study by Wang et al. investigated the results of seven Asian cTTO datasets, used for generating EQ-5D-5L value sets (Wang et al. 2019). They found substantial differences between value sets for Asian countries/areas and recommend developing value sets for each country/area independently, on the basis that a value set from one Asian country/area may not adequately represent the values from a neighbouring country/area. We also find some differences between Asian countries/areas, yet also some similarities that allow us to approximately group Asian value sets into two groups. One can speculate what may cause these differences between the two groups. It could be that some countries/areas are more similar in their preferences, as they share similar characteristics in terms of their wealth, healthcare systems, social insurance and culture. However, looking at the effect of culture, mixed results have been found. One study finds a relationship between the relative importance of the different attributes and differences in culture (Bailey and Kind 2010), while another study finds no relationship between scale length and differences in cultural values (Roudijk et al. 2019). Other factors such as study protocol and QC could also be an important factor in explaining differences between value sets. For example, the studies from the earlier waves of EQ-5D-5L valuation studies (Japan, China, Korea) report much smaller scale lengths than most of the other Asian value sets (Shiroiwa et al. 2016; Luo et al. 2017; Kim et al. 2016). This may partially explain differences between Asian countries/areas. A similar observation can be made for Western countries/areas, yet the difference seems to be smaller between Western value sets. More research, possibly in the form of a meta-analysis, is needed to assess key methodological differences between the value sets within geographical regions and to explore whether these methodological differences and macroeconomic determinants such as health systems may explain differences between the value sets.

6.6.5 Limitations

A limitation of this chapter is that the number of countries/areas included in each preference pattern differs substantially. For example, the Western aggregate value set includes value sets from ten countries/areas, while the Eastern European aggregate value set contains only two. Another limitation is that geographical/cultural regions such as Africa, the Middle East and Latin America are underrepresented in the number of available value sets. Once more value sets are available from these regions, it will become more feasible to determine if there are any preference patterns in these regions and compare them with the currently identified preference patterns. Finally, another limitation is that the patient data used to test the preference patterns was collected in Western countries/areas only. Therefore, the value sets from non-Western countries/areas (and subsequent aggregate value sets) may not adequately reflect the values for patients. Future research using patient data from non-Western countries/areas may improve our understanding of how well these aggregate value sets perform in non-Western countries/areas.

6.7 Conclusions

This chapter identified key differences between value sets and attempts to group value sets on similarities according to certain relevant characteristics. Five different preference patterns were identified. As differences between value sets for countries/

areas included within a preference pattern can still be substantial, we still recommend the development and use of national value sets rather than using a value set from a different country/area or from a composite of countries/areas. However, these aggregate value sets could be used for sensitivity analyses when applying foreign value sets.

References

Andrade LF, Ludwig K, Ramos-Goni JM, Oppe M, de Pouvourville G (2020) A French value set for the EQ-5D-5L. PharmacoEconomics 38(4):413–425

Augustovski F, Rey-Ares L, Irazola V, Garay OU, Gianneo O, Fernández G, Morales M, Gibbons L, Ramos-Goñi JM (2016) An EQ-5D-5L value set based on Uruguayan population preferences. Qual Life Res 25(2):323–333

Augustovski F, Belizán M, Gibbons L, Reyes N, Stolk E, Craig BM, Tejada RA (2020) Peruvian valuation of the EQ-5D-5L: a direct comparison of time trade-off and discrete choice experiments. Value Health 23(7):880–888

Bailey H, Kind P (2010) Preliminary findings of an investigation into the relationship between national culture and EQ-5D value sets. Qual Life Res 19(8):1145–1154

Devlin NJ, Shah KK, Feng Y, Mulhern B, van Hout B (2018) Valuing health-related quality of life: An EQ-5D-5L value set for England. Health Econ 27(1):7–22

Ferreira PL, Antunes P, Ferreira LN, Pereira LN, Ramos-Goñi JM (2019) A hybrid modelling approach for eliciting health state preferences: the Portuguese EQ-5D-5L value set. Qual Life Res 28(12):3163–3175

Golicki D, Jakubczyk M, Graczyk K, Niewada M (2019) Valuation of EQ-5D-5L health states in Poland: the first EQ-VT-based study in Central and Eastern Europe. PharmacoEconomics 37(9):1165–1176

Gutierrez-Delgado C, Galindo-Suárez RM, Cruz-Santiago C, Shah K, Papadimitropoulos M, Feng Y, Zamora B, Devlin N (2021) EQ-5D-5L health-state values for the Mexican population. Appl Health Econ Health Policy. https://doi.org/10.1007/s40258-021-00658-0

Hobbins A, Barry L, Kelleher D, Shah K, Devlin N, Ramos-Goni JMR, O'Neill C (2018) Utility values for health states in Ireland: a value set for the EQ-5D-5L. PharmacoEconomics 36(11):1345–1353

Jensen CE, Sørensen SS, Gudex C, Jensen MB, Pedersen KM, Ehlers LH (2021) The Danish EQ-5D-5L value set: a hybrid model using cTTO and DCE Data. Appl Health Econ Health Policy 19(4):579–591

Kim SH, Ahn J, Ock M, Shin S, Park J, Luo N, Jo MW (2016) The EQ-5D-5L valuation study in Korea. Qual Life Res 25(7):1845–1852

Lin HW, Li CI, Lin FJ, Chang JY, Gau CS, Luo N, Pickard AS, Ramos Goñi JM, Tang CH, Hsu CN (2018) Valuation of the EQ-5D-5L in Taiwan. PLoS One 13(12). https://doi.org/10.1371/journal.pone.0209344

Ludwig K, von der Schulenburg JMG, Greiner W (2018) German value set for the EQ-5D-5L. PharmacoEconomics 36(6):663–674

Luo N, Liu G, Li M, Guan H, Jin X, Rand-Hendriksen K (2017) Estimating an EQ-5D-5L value set for China. Value Health 20(4):662–669

Mai VQ, Sun S, Van Minh H, Luo N, Giang KB, Lindholm L, Sahlen KG (2020) An EQ-5D-5L value set for Vietnam. Q Life Res 29(7):1923–1933

Norman R, Cronin P, Viney R, King M, Street D, Ratcliffe J (2009) International comparisons in valuing EQ-5D health states: a review and analysis. Value Health 12(8):1194–1200

Olsen JA, Lamu AN, Cairns J (2018) In search of a common currency: a comparison of seven EQ-5D-5L value sets. Health Econ 27(1):39–49

Oppe M, Devlin NJ, van Hout B, Krabbe PF, de Charro F (2014) A program of methodological research to arrive at the new international EQ-5D-5L valuation protocol. Value Health
17(4):445–453

Pattanaphesaj J, Thavorncharoensap M, Ramos-Goñi JM, Tongsiri S, Ingsrisawang L,
Teerawattananon Y (2018) The EQ-5D-5L valuation study in Thailand. Expert Rev
Pharmacoecon Outcomes Res 18(5):551–558

Pickard AS, Law EH, Jiang R, Pullenayegum E, Shaw JW, Xie F, Oppe M, Boye KS, Chapman
RH, Gong CL, Balch A, Busschbach JJV (2019) United States valuation of EQ-5D-5L health
states using an international protocol. Value Health 2(8):931–941

Purba FD, Hunfeld JAM, Iskandarsyah A, Fitriana TS, Sadarjoen SS, Ramos-Goñi JM, Passchier
J, Busschbach JJV (2017) The Indonesian EQ-5D-5L value set. PharmacoEconomics
35(11):1153–1165

Ramos-Goñi JM, Oppe M, Slaap B, Busschbach JJ, Stolk E (2017a) Quality control process for
EQ-5D-5L valuation studies. Value Health 20(3):466–473

Ramos-Goñi JM, Pinto-Prades JL, Oppe M, Cabasés JM, Serrano-Aguilar P, Rivero-Arias O
(2017b) Valuation and modeling of EQ-5D-5L health states using a hybrid approach. Med
Care 55(7):51–58

Ramos-Goñi JM, Craig BM, Oppe M, Ramallo-Fariña Y, Pinto-Prades JL, Luo N, Rivero-Arias O
(2018) Handling data quality issues to estimate the Spanish EQ-5D-5L value set using a hybrid
interval regression approach. Value Health 21(5):596–604

Rencz F, Brodszky V, Gulácsi L, Golicki D, Ruzsa G, Pickard AS, Law EH, Péntek M (2020)
Parallel valuation of the EQ-5D-3L and EQ-5D-5L by time trade-off in Hungary. Value Health
23(9):1235–1245

Richardson J, Khan MA, Iezzi A, Maxwell A (2012) Cross-national comparison of twelve quality
of life instruments. MIC paper, 2. Monash University, Australia

Roudijk B, Donders ART, Stalmeier PF (2019) Cultural values: can they explain differences in
health utilities between countries? Med Decis Mak 39(5):605–616

Shafie AA, Vasan Thakumar A, Lim CJ, Luo N, Rand-Hendriksen K, Yusof FAM (2019) EQ-5D-5L
valuation for the Malaysian population. PharmacoEconomics 37(5):715–725

Shiroiwa T, Ikeda S, Noto S, Igarashi A, Fukuda T, Saito S, Shimozuma K (2016) Comparison of
value set based on DCE and/or TTO data: scoring for EQ-5D-5L health states in Japan. Value
Health 19(5):648–655

Stolk E, Ludwig K, Rand K, van Hout B, Ramos-Goñi JM (2019) Overview, update, and lessons
learned from the International EQ-5D-5L valuation work: version 2 of the EQ-5D-5L valuation
protocol. Value Health 22(1):23–30

Versteegh MM, Vermeulen KM, Evers SMAA, De Wit GA, Prenger R, Stolk EA (2016) Dutch
tariff for the five-level version of EQ-5D. Value Health 19(4):343–352

Wang P, Liu GG, Jo MW, Purba FD, Yang Z, Gandhi M, Pattanaphesaj J, Ahn J, Wong ELY, Shafie
AA, Busschbach JJV, Luo N (2019) Valuation of EQ-5D-5L health states: a comparison of
seven Asian populations. Expert Rev Pharmacoecon Outcomes Res 19(4):445–451

Welie AG, Gebretekle GB, Stolk E, Mukuria C, Krahn MD, Enquoselassie F, Fenta TG (2020)
Valuing health state: an EQ-5D-5L value set for Ethiopians. Value Health Reg Issues 22:7–14

Wong EL, Ramos-Goni JM, Cheung AW, Wong AY, Rivero-Arias O (2018) Assessing the use of a
feedback module to model EQ-5D-5L health states values in Hong Kong. Patient 11(2):235–247

Xie F, Pullenayegum E, Gaebel K, Bansback N, Bryan S, Ohinmaa A, Poissant L, Johnson JA
(2016) A time trade-off-derived value set of the EQ-5D-5L for Canada. Med Care 54(1):98–105

Xie F, Pullenayegum E, Pickard AS, Ramos Goñi JM, Jo MW, Igarashi A (2017) Transforming
latent utilities to health utilities: East does not meet west. Health Econ 26(12):1524–1533

Chapter 7
Where Next for EQ-5D-5L National Value Sets and the EQ-VT Protocol?

Richard Norman, Nancy Devlin, and Elly Stolk

Abstract The purpose of this chapter is to reflect on the future of EQ-5D-5L valuation studies, going beyond the value sets summarised in this book. This includes a number of linked themes. First, the EQ-5D-5L valuation research programme has allowed the continued evolution of methods, as methodological studies have demonstrated that aspects of the EQ-VT protocol could be strengthened or improved. This chapter describes some of the key candidates for future refinement of the methods for valuing EQ-5D-5L. Second, while the standardisation of valuation methodology is important, it is anticipated that many countries may require a less resource-intensive, but still rigorous version of the valuation protocol. This chapter outlines the progress towards developing a 'lite' version of the EQ-VT protocol, and considers the future possibility of valuation protocols based exclusively on discrete choice experiments, with accompanying strengths and weaknesses. Finally, the 'shelf-life' of value sets is considered, along with how demographic and other societal changes may manifest in how people value health, and the implications of that for the need to update EQ-5D-5L value sets.

7.1 Introduction

Previous chapters have provided an overview of the EQ-5D-5L value sets produced to date. Taken together, these value sets – and the methodological development which underpins them – constitute a very substantial body of work. The availability of EQ-5D-5L value sets has facilitated the use of EQ-5D-5L data collected from patients around the world for a variety of purposes. Primarily, these value sets are aimed at supporting the estimation of Quality Adjusted Life Years (QALYs) and QALY gains from health care for use in cost effectiveness and cost utility analysis,

R. Norman
School of Population Health, Curtin University, Bentley, Australia

N. Devlin (✉)
Centre for Health Policy, University of Melbourne, Melbourne, VIC, Australia
e-mail: nancy.devlin@unimelb.edu.au

E. Stolk
EuroQol Research Foundation, Rotterdam, The Netherlands

© The Author(s) 2022
N. Devlin et al. (eds.), *Value Sets for EQ-5D-5L*,
https://doi.org/10.1007/978-3-030-89289-0_7

providing evidence to inform health technology assessment (HTA) processes globally. Additionally, the value sets allow the use of EQ-5D-5L in other applications, such as monitoring population health (both in the general and patient population) where there is a requirement to summarise EQ-5D profile data, focussing on those aspects of health that are considered to be most important by society (see Chap. 5).

The production of these EQ-5D-5L value sets, coordinated by the EuroQol Group, represents a unique endeavour in scale and breadth, unprecedented in the preference-weighting of other measures of health-related quality of life (HRQoL). It has improved on the earlier EQ-5D-3L valuation efforts, which were largely researcher-driven, used protocols that were not always fully documented, and consequently had limited comparability because of differences in methods and protocols. In contrast, the EQ-5D-5L valuation studies have been based on a similar and well documented protocol for collecting data that is carefully managed in accordance with agreed metrics and includes a deliberate process for incremental improvement of the protocol. The high standards applied in developing the protocol and in the application of quality control in its use have resulted in a protocol (see Chap. 2) that has been successfully replicated in many different contexts. This suggests that a new level of maturity in valuation approach has been reached, and that the techniques used reflect modern best practice in the health valuation field.

While the EQ-5D-5L valuation effort already has significant global coverage, further EQ-5D-5L value sets are planned or underway (for example, in the Middle East and Africa where such studies are relatively few), reflecting continued growth in use of the instrument. The development of universal health care systems around the world (for example, in China and Mexico) will further reinforce the demand for evidence on 'value for money' to support the allocation of resources in publicly funded public health care systems. This is likely to result in continued demand for use of the EQ-5D-5L and its accompanying value sets in both existing and new contexts.

The purpose of this chapter is to reflect on the future of EQ-5D-5L valuation studies, beyond the value sets summarised in Chap. 4. This includes a number of linked themes.

First, the EQ-5D-5L valuation project has allowed continued evolution in methods, as methodological studies have demonstrated that aspects of the protocol could be strengthened or improved. This chapter will describe some of the key candidates for future refinement of the methods.

Second, while the standardisation of the methodology is important, it is anticipated that many countries may seek a less resource-intensive, but still rigorous version of the valuation protocol. We outline progress towards developing a 'lite' version of EQ-VT. This 'lite' version of EQ-VT will also include a description of the development of a stand-alone discrete choice experiment (DCE) protocol, with accompanying strengths and weaknesses relative to the 'gold-standard' approach described in previous chapters.

Finally, it is worthwhile considering the shelf-life of value sets. As time progresses, pre-existing studies become increasingly unreliable estimates of what a contemporary study would report as the 'average' preferences of a society, due to methodological improvements, changes in the demographic makeup of the population, and preference shifts caused by broader cultural trends that may manifest in how people consider HRQoL and its value relative to life extension. More broadly, there are questions about who should make judgements about value sets, e.g., who decides when a new value set is needed? Similarly, who decides whether it is the general public (however defined) or some other group whose preferences are relevant? And who should judge whether any given value set is acceptable for use? What is the role and responsibility of the EuroQol Group versus local HTA bodies or other bodies?

7.2 Future Directions for Improvements in the EQ-VT – An Overview

As has been demonstrated in Chap. 2, significant work has gone into ensuring that the EQ-VT protocol is a reliable and defensible method for the valuation of EQ-5D-5L health states. EQ-VT is a *living product* which will continue to evolve. Any concern that has been expressed or that will be expressed regarding the methods adopted in the EQ-VT protocol can act as a catalyst to further research and development and to inform and shape future methodological choices. Some key areas for future progress are described below. Before discussing these, it is important to point out that changing the EQ-VT protocol necessarily involves a balance between using the improvements in data that may arise from incorporating enhanced methods against the reduction in consistency and comparability between value sets. Each advance to the EQ-VT protocol needs to lead to demonstrably better data, ideally in multiple methodological studies in a multinational context. Given the level of existing work to refine the EQ-VT approach, as described in Chap. 2, this sets a high bar for change.

The principal questions concerning the future directions of EQ-VT are in effect the same questions that confront *any* stated preferences study for *any* HRQoL instrument, namely: (i) what method(s) to use to elicit stated preferences, using what mode of administration; (ii) what study design to use (what sample size is required; and what sub-sample of states to include in stated preference tasks); and (iii) what modelling approaches to use to interpolate values across the descriptive system for the HRQoL instrument.

7.2.1 What Methods to Use?

The choice to include both time trade-off (TTO) and DCE methods, made early on in the programme of work (see Chap. 2), reflected both the growing popularity of DCE methods in health economics and the long-standing role of TTO in providing evidence to support QALY estimation – and the lack of consensus in health economics about any one method being optimal.

Despite the widespread acceptance of TTO, and the leading place it has earned among EQ-5D valuation methods, there are nevertheless remaining issues with TTO and the variant of it used in EQ-VT, the composite TTO (cTTO). As with any TTO approach, the cTTO tasks in the EQ-VT protocol necessarily incorporate methodological choices e.g., about the iterative routing process used to achieve the point of indifference; and about the duration of the states being valued (see Chap. 2 for more detail). Each of these choices has the potential to exert a framing effect on the values which are produced and might be challenged. For example, the use of a ten-year duration for all states to be valued is very widely used and has come to be regarded as standard, but that duration might be considered as an arbitrary choice, and it is likely that the observed proportional trade-offs would differ if alternative durations were employed (Stalmeier et al. 2007; Craig et al. 2018; Jonker et al. 2018, Attema and Brouwer 2014). The use of a 10-year duration is known to encounter issues with violations of constant proportionality and with the difficulty of imagining states (especially severe ones) over such a long period, without relief. The use of cTTO also involves the use of different tasks for obtaining values > 0 (the conventional TTO) and < 0 (a lead time TTO task) (Devlin et al. 2011; Janssen et al. 2013). The use of different methods for obtaining values across the scale raises questions about the comparability of values above and below 0. The particular design of the task for states < 0 sets the minimum observable value at −1 by design, which has the appeal of avoiding the likely need for rescaling of values. However, it also raises the question of whether −1 is the lowest meaningful value possible and, if values less than that exist, how to reflect that (e.g., in modelling). These and other issues will remain the subject for future research.

DCE methods have the appeal of presenting respondents with a potentially simpler choice task, allowing the rapid collection of large quantities of stated preferences data via online self-completion. However, the DCE tasks as included in the EQ-VT protocol have the limitation that they produce values on a latent scale. When the protocol was initially established, DCE approaches that allow calibration of the values relative to 'dead' were still in an early stage of development and were rejected, mainly because results obtained when the methods were tested varied a lot for reasons that were poorly understood. However, research done in recent years has put these initial results into perspective, revealing a dependency of values derived from the DCE-duration approach on modelling choices, design specification and the interdependencies between the two (Lim et al. 2018; Jonker et al. 2018; Jonker and Bliemer 2019. This seems to have brought a future closer where DCE can reach more of its potential and have a larger role in valuation studies of EQ-5D instruments. To some extent, this can already be seen in the valuation protocol for EQ-5D-Y, where DCE plays a bigger role (Ramos-Goñi et al. 2020).

7.2.2 Procedural Aspects

Similarly, there is ongoing attention to various procedural aspects of valuation studies. A key one is the basis for decisions about the number of health states and choice tasks to be included in the valuation tasks. It is important to select health states and pairs which allow unbiased estimation of coefficients based on whichever functional form is required. Yang et al. (2018, 2019) advanced the field by showing just how much the statistical properties of the set of health states/pairs matter to the predictive performance of the designs, and demonstrated that many published ways to select health states were suboptimal (including popular designs used to value EQ-5D-3L) and that by contrast the design used in EQ-5D-5L valuation studies performed well in comparison to alternative approaches. In the statistical approach to create a design for valuing EQ-5D-5L, the functional form, design, and sample size were considered in parallel. A large number of candidate designs was created using random draws, and the performance of these designs was evaluated using a given model (main effect) and priors derived from pilot studies, and the best one was kept (Oppe and van Hout 2017) (see Chap. 3 for more details). However, scope for improvement may still exist as we do not yet know how larger designs perform, and what number of observations per state is optimal. Moreover, Yang et al. (2019) showed that accurate prediction of the value of mild states is especially challenging and that some designs that perform well overall, perform poorly with respect to the value of mild states. This in turn calls for more attention on the models too.

Questions also exist about the mode of data collection – debate over which was fuelled by the COVID-19 pandemic and the resulting disruption to face-to-face interviewer administration of EQ-VT, as described in Chap. 2, in countries which had been planning value set studies. This gave rise to the idea of conducting EQ-VT interviews online – i.e., interviewer-guided, rather than self-completed, but conducted via an online platform rather than face-to-face. Initial experimentation suggested online data collection to be feasible; to enable reasonable responder engagement; and to yield data that appears to be of acceptable quality (Lipman 2020). Online interviews may even have some advantages e.g., in reaching respondents from broader geographic areas; in reducing costs of interviewer travel; and allowing use of 'expert interviewers' who do not need to be based physically in the same region or even the same country as respondents. However, there are also potential disadvantages e.g., in accessing samples without access to internet. Further, caution is required as there may be important differences between the preferences obtained from each mode of administration. Further evidence is required to establish the equivalence of data obtained via online administration.

7.2.3 Analysis and Modelling

While the EuroQol Group has been prescriptive about the use of its protocol for study design and elicitation, local research teams have a choice about other analyses to undertake, which modelling methods to use and about the criteria to use when choosing which algorithm is regarded as the preferred one. As we have shown in Chap. 4, modelling practise varies widely, but the common underlying protocol nevertheless facilitates comparison of resulting values and value sets between countries.

In particular, value sets differ in regard to whether they base their preferred value set on cTTO data only (for example, China and US), or a hybrid of cTTO and DCE (for example, England and Denmark) (see Chap. 4). Such differences reflect both scientific and strategic issues. Strategically, in some countries HTA bodies have expressed a preference for TTO-based values, and this is reflected in the choice of modelling approach taken to value sets. Scientifically, as is the case when competing approaches are taken to measurement, there is ongoing uncertainty about whether the cTTO and DCE are measuring the same thing, and what should be made of inconsistency between them. For instance, recent work has suggested differing relative importance of dimensions between cTTO and DCE in Peru and Mexico (Augustovski et al. 2020; Gutierrez-Delgado et al. 2021). Going forward, any disagreement in values derived from DCE and cTTO tasks need to be reviewed carefully, in relation to the level of conceptual resemblance between cTTO and DCE, assumptions used in both methods (including modelling assumptions), and scope for implementation issues to arise.

As we survey the future of EQ-5D value set development, we are cognisant that there will *always* be methodological questions; this is part of the inquisitive nature of science and good science depends on scientific debate. Such questions can lead to different responses: either to strengthen the methods currently in the protocol or to investigate new methods. As long as no method exists that commands universal support – which is likely to be the case here since we have no external validation to judge – any methodological question will fuel debate and can lead to either type of response. The research and development investment of the EuroQol Group in recent years has mainly focussed on refinement of the methods included in EQ-VT, as described in Chap. 2. However, other methods development has also been supported and the EuroQol Group continues to be open to alternatives, both from within the membership and from the broader and vibrant community of health preference and valuation researchers.

The use of TTO over so many years means we have a considerable evidence base to support its use. This has raised the bar for other methods as well, requiring very considerable evidence on their performance and the properties of the preference data they yield, before they can be considered a candidate for use. This is particularly apparent in our cautious approach to DCE, where an ambitious programme of research is underway to yield a deep understanding of its use in valuing EQ-5D instruments. This is good scientific practise – but is also strategically important, as stakeholders have a lot riding on their use of EQ-5D data and value sets. No transition can be made lightly, and the level of maturity reached in the EQ-VT protocol is difficult to match. The EuroQol Group is committed to progressing the science around valuation and to ensure evidence supports a new generation of methods fit for purpose in the future.

7.3 Developing Alternative Approaches and Answering Different Questions

The EQ-5D-5L exists in a dynamic environment, both in terms of the methods that can be used to develop value sets, and the empirical questions it can help to solve. This ever-changing context we work in continues to also present new challenges. The development of a 'Lite' protocol, a lighter, less resource-intensive EQ-VT (as described in Chap. 3), is a good example of this. As we move into more resource-constrained settings, we need to reduce the cost of conducting valuation surveys, and to make the undertaking of such work more accessible to those who bring essential local knowledge, context and contacts, but relatively less experience in the more technical aspects of the work. But, if we progress down this path, it is unclear whether we yet know the impact of switching protocols, something which requires some caution and careful comparative evaluation.

Either as part of the Lite valuation or not, the configuration of the DCE is an important ongoing consideration. DCEs that include comparisons of states with 'dead' have the appeal of being simple; but DCE with duration arguably conceptually resembles TTO to a greater extent, which may be considered an advantage (Mulhern et al. 2014). This potential advantage was recognized when the EQ-VT protocol was developed, but it was coupled with concerns about the low values that were obtained in some initial applications. Stolk et al. (2019) suggest these results arise because of the difference between DCE with duration and cTTO: the latter observes values and uses lead time TTO to assess the strength of preferences for health states that are classified as worse than dead. In contrast, the DCE with duration task never indicates directly whether a health state has a value worse than dead. It also relies on extrapolation – and this comes with extra uncertainty and the potential for bias if the underlying assumptions are wrong. Evidence suggests estimates of values obtained by DCE with duration estimates are sensitive to model specification and in particular to assumptions made regarding time preferences. Models applied to cTTO rely on the assumption of constant proportionality, which may not hold. However, violations of this assumption can be a bigger problem for DCE with duration than for cTTO, because of the required extrapolation in the former. These issues with DCE with duration are an ongoing area of methodological research.

Quantitative approaches to valuing EQ-5D-5L are valuable and will always remain a centrepiece of value set development within the EuroQol Group. However, there is a growing literature focused on greater reflection and deliberation by respondents (Robinson and Bryan 2013; Devlin et al. 2019; Karimi et al. 2017, 2019). This line of enquiry is potentially extremely valuable in identifying *why* respondents place value on certain aspects of health, and also in minimising the risk from datasets being contaminated with ill-considered or hasty responses.

7.4   Making Scientific and Social Value Judgements About Value Sets

As discussed in Chap. 5, users of value sets should consider both the inherent scientific quality and the underlying social value judgements that value sets embody. Indeed, community decision makers are becoming more active in independently scrutinising value sets and applying their own quality assurance – for example, the England EQ-5D-5L value set, which was part of the first wave of studies, was subject to a formal review by the Department of Health for England (Hernández-Alava et al. 2020; van Hout et al. 2020) and ultimately rejected for use by the National Institute for Clinical Excellence (NICE) (NICE 2019). This has led to efforts (currently underway) to produce a new, UK-wide value set. More generally, the question remains of who is responsible for value set endorsement – is this a case of 'caveat emptor' i.e., is it ultimately the responsibility of users and decision-making bodies, or is there a role for the EuroQol Group? To date, other than allowing use of EQ-VT and monitoring data collection via quality control, the EuroQol Group has not imposed any process for approving (or not) the value sets modelled from EQ-VT data.

This question is particularly pertinent in settings where value sets have been developed using methods which are quite different from those recommended by the EuroQol Group at the time. For instance, EQ-5D-5L value set studies using different methods to elicit the state preferences of the general public have been conducted in the US (Craig and Rand 2018) and New Zealand (Sullivan et al. 2019). These value sets are not reported in this book, as our focus is on value sets produced using the EQ-VT protocol. Similarly, there is an emerging body of work examining the preferences of patients, rather than the general public – an example of a value set based on these 'experienced' values can be found in Burström et al. (2020) for Sweden. Such studies offer interesting methodological comparisons and can, under particular circumstances, be used in those countries. However, the differences in methods used in such cases means comparisons of the EQ-5D-5L values yielded by them with the value sets reported in Chap. 4 should be treated with caution, as these differences are attributable to both different local preferences and methodological differences, which are impossible to disentangle.

Moving away from scientific judgement of value sets, the social values that underpin the use of each are potentially important. While value sets are most commonly developed using the adult general population, this is defined differently in different countries – for example, in Japan and Taiwan this is considered to be those over 20 years of age; more commonly it is interpreted to be those over 18 years, while in some countries, such as Indonesia, this was set at 17 years and older (see Chap. 4 for details). The views of younger adolescents and children are typically excluded from such studies.[1] While the merits of such exclusion in the valuation population can be discussed, a key issue is how we define the age threshold. At what age do we define a person to have transitioned into adulthood and able to complete the cognitively challenging valuation tasks we use? And are we imposing age criteria for practical reasons (e.g., with respect to comprehension and data quality), ethical reasons (concerns about confronting younger people with life/death trade-offs) or philosophical/normative reasons about whose preferences should determine public policy – or a combination of all three? To the extent that age impacts on preferences, this can have significant implications for decision making in practice. It could be argued that such determinations are best made by the users of the value set themselves. The appropriate method for engagement on such topics is likely to be context-specific, and will yield different decisions, impacting the comparability of the value sets between nations. This trade-off between consistency and tailoring to the local context is an ongoing challenge.

7.5 Adapting to Change

Previous value sets for the EQ-5D-3L have remained in use and accepted by policy makers for long periods of time e.g., the UK MVH value set (Dolan 1997), data for which were collected in 1993/94, and NICE continues to recommend while awaiting a new EQ-5D-5L value set for the UK. This begs the question of what the shelf-life is of such value sets, and what factors might prompt the need for new value sets, bearing in mind both the potential benefits of updated values and the costs of producing them.

Samples are recruited to be representative of the general public at the point at which data are collected, and value sets represent the average preferences of society. Over time, the socio-demographic composition of populations changes due to population ageing, trends in fertility rates and patterns of immigration. These changes could be expected to lead to changes in the average preferences of the general public, if this means that the share of sub-groups in the population with different preferences changes. Perhaps less obviously, changes in the proportion of the population who are very elderly and more likely to be in residential care, or those incarcerated in prisons or are in other institutions may also be important, since these people often fall outside the sample frames used to recruit the general public. Such changes might indicate the need for a new value set. An alternative would be to use population weights to account for such changes, but this would rely on appropriate

---

[1] Child health status can be measured and increasingly valued using the EQ-5D-Y, but the value sets that accompany the EQ-5D-Y are typically based on the stated preferences of the adult general public, and not those of younger people.

demographic data collection during the initial value set development, which would be challenging as we do not know in advance the population demographics we would want to weight on.

Changes in preferences could provide another reason for updating value sets and may arise due to other factors influencing society. For example, over time living standards health and HRQoL have improved for many people, and this may increase our expectations about health and health care in ways that affect our preferences for HRQoL. There may also be specific health issues locally that exert an effect on preferences. One might speculate about whether the high-profile debates over euthanasia that have occurred in a number of countries might affect the trade-offs the general public were prepared to make against dead/duration. In Mexico, the relatively high importance placed on problems with mobility have been suggested to be linked to the widespread lack of support or social services for those with mobility problems (Gutierrez-Delgado et al. 2021). In general, increasing awareness of mental health issues may affect how people consider these health issues and their importance relative to other health problems. The COVID-19 pandemic, and its global impact, could also potentially exert an effect on how people value HRQoL. However, there is a lack of research on such factors and very little clear evidence on how they affect stated preferences.

These issues suggest a rationale for updating value sets from time to time – but there are currently no guidelines about this, and no consensus about what factors or *prima facie* evidence should trigger an update. One possibility may be to conduct a less expensive survey, such as a DCE, at regular intervals with updated sampling frames to monitor if there is evidence of preference shifts which might motivate conduct of a replication EQ-VT study to accurately capture the shift.

Further, the benefits of updating a value set need to be weighed up against the costs. These include not just the costs of producing a new value set but the costs and consequences for their use in decision making. For example, HTA bodies may be concerned about changes to the HRQoL values used in cost effectiveness evidence and the implications of these for consistency of their decisions. In economists' terms, these changes impose costs of their own, so updating may need to be balanced against these pragmatic and operational considerations.

7.6   Concluding Remarks

The national value sets for EQ-5D-5L summarised in this book play a vital role in supporting the use of EQ-5D-5L data, providing evidence for HTA and other health care decision making contexts. The EQ-VT protocol used to produce these value sets can now be considered to represent a mature and well-tested set of methods. However, there will *always* remain questions relating to which methods for eliciting and modelling values for HRQoL are best – and this is the case both for EQ-5D-5L and other HRQoL instruments. The EuroQol Group actively encourages and supports innovative research and development into valuation methods and is a leading investor in such research internationally. This ensures that there is scope for researchers to develop and explore potential new methods, and a process for assessing the case for their inclusion in the protocol in future. These efforts not only benefit studies to value EQ-5D-5L, but also inform the wider scientific agenda on valuation of HRQoL instruments.

References

Attema AE, Brouwer W (2014) Constant proportional trade-offs and health state evaluations. In: Michalos AC (ed) Encyclopedia of quality of life and well-being research. Springer, Dordrecht

Augustovski F, Belizán M, Gibbons L, Reyes N, Stolk E, Craig BM, Tejada RA (2020) Peruvian valuation of the EQ-5D-5L: a direct comparison of time trade-off and discrete choice experiments. Value Health 23(7):880–888

Burström K, Teni FS, Gerdtham UG, Leidl R, Helgesson G, Rolfson O, Henriksson M (2020) Experience-based Swedish TTO and VAS value sets for EQ-5D-5L health states. PharmacoEconomics 38(8):839–856

Craig BM, Rand K (2018) Choice defines QALYs: a US valuation of the EQ-5D-5L. Med Care 56(6):529–536

Craig BM, Rand K, Bailey H, Stalmeier PFM (2018) Quality-adjusted life-years without constant proportionality. Value Health 21(9):1124–1131

Devlin NJ, Tsuchiya A, Buckingham K, Tilling C (2011) A uniform time trade off method for states better and worse than dead: feasibility study of the 'lead time' approach. Health Econ 20(3):348–361

Devlin NJ, Shah KK, Mulhern BJ, Pantiri K, van Hout B (2019) A new method for valuing health: directly eliciting personal utility functions. Eur J Health Econ 20(2):257–270

Dolan P (1997) Modeling valuations for EuroQol health states. Med Care 35(11):1095–1108

Gutierrez-Delgado C, Galindo-Suárez RM, Cruz-Santiago C, Shah K, Papadimitropoulos M, Feng Y, Zamora B, Devlin N (2021) EQ-5D-5L health-state values for the Mexican population. Appl Health Econ Health Policy. https://doi.org/10.1007/s40258-021-00658-0. Online ahead of print

Hernández-Alava M, Pudney S, Wailoo A (2020) The EQ-5D-5L value set for England: findings of a quality assurance program. Value Health 23(5):642–648

Janssen BMF, Oppe M, Versteegh MM, Stolk EA (2013) Introducing the composite time trade-off: a test of feasibility and face validity. Eur J Health Econ 14(Suppl 1):S5–S13

Jonker MF, Bliemer MCJ (2019) On the optimization of Bayesian D-efficient discrete choice experiment designs for the estimation of QALY tariffs that are corrected for nonlinear time preferences. Value Health 22(10):1162–1169

Jonker MF, Donkers B, de Bekker-Grob EW, Stolk EA (2018) Advocating a paradigm shift in health-state valuations: the estimation of time-preference corrected QALY tariffs. Value Health 21(8):993–1001. Erratum in 2019: Value Health 22(3):383

Karimi M, Brazier J, Paisley S (2017) How do individuals value health states? A qualitative investigation. Soc Sci Med 172:80–88

Karimi M, Brazier J, Paisley S (2019) Effect of reflection and deliberation on health state values: a mixed-methods study. Value Health 22(11):1311–1317

Lim S, Jonker MF, Oppe M, Donkers B, Stolk E (2018) Severity-stratified discrete choice experiment designs for health state evaluations. PharmacoEconomics 36(11):1377–1389

Lipman SA (2020) Time for tele-TTO? Lessons Learned from Digital Interviewer-Assisted Time Trade-Off Data Collection Patient. https://doi.org/10.1007/s40271-020-00490-z. Online ahead of print

Mulhern B, Bansback N, Brazier J, Buckingham K, Cairns J, Devlin N, Dolan P, Hole AR, Kavetsos G, Longworth L, Rowen D, Tsuchiya A. (2014) Preparatory study for the revaluation of the

EQ-5D tariff: methodology report. Health Technol Assess 18(12):vii–xxvi, 1–191. https://doi.
org/10.3310/hta18120. PMID: 24568945; PMCID: PMC4781204

National Institute for Clinical Excellence (NICE) (2019) Position statement on use of the
EQ-5D-5L value set for England (updated October 2019) https://www.nice.org.uk/about/what-
we-do/our-programmes/nice-guidance/technology-appraisal-guidance/eq-5d-5l. Accessed 12
July 2021

Oppe M, van Hout B (2017) The "power" of eliciting EQ-5D-5L values: the experimental design of
the EQ-VT. EuroQol working paper 17003. https://euroqol.org/wp-content/uploads/2016/10/
EuroQol-Working-Paper-Series-Manuscript-17003-Mark-Oppe.pdf. Accessed 12 July 2021

Ramos-Goñi J, Oppe M, Stolk E, Shah K, Kreimeier S, Rivero-Arias O, Devlin N (2020)
International valuation protocol for the EQ-5D-Y-3L. PharmacoEconomics 38(7):653–663

Robinson S, Bryan S (2013) Does the process of deliberation change individuals' health state valuations? An exploratory study using the person trade-off technique. Value Health 16(5):806–813

Stalmeier PF, Lamers LM, Bussbach J, Krabbe P (2007) On the assessment of preferences for
health and duration: maximal endurable time and better than dead preferences. Med Care
45(9):835–841

Stolk E, Ludwig K, Rand K, van Hout B, Ramos-Goñi JM (2019) Overview, update, and lessons
learned from the international EQ-5D-5L valuation work: version 2 of the EQ-5D-5L valuation
protocol. Value Health 22(1):23–30

Sullivan T, Hansen P, Ombler F, Derrett S, Devlin N (2020) A new tool for creating personal and
social EQ-5D-5L value sets, including valuing 'dead'. Soc Sci Med 246:112707. https://doi.
org/10.1016/j.socscimed.2019.112707.

van Hout B, Mulhern B, Feng Y, Shah K, Devlin N (2020) The EQ-5D-5L value set for England:
response to the "quality assurance". Value Health 23(5):649–655

Yang Z, Luo N, Bonsel G, Busschbach J, Stolk E (2018) Selecting health states for EQ-5D-3L
valuation studies: statistical considerations matter. Value Health 21(4):456–461

Yang Z, Luo N, Bonsel G, Busschbach J, Stolk E (2019) Effect of health state sampling methods
on model predictions of EQ-5D-5L values: small designs can suffice. Value Health 22(1):38–44

Glossary of EQ-5D Terms

In this section, we set out the terms used in this book to describe specific aspects of the EQ-5D instruments and the methods used to develop and report their value sets. This glossary builds on that provided in Devlin et al. (2020), which has been reproduced here with permissions from the publishers and the authors and updated where necessary including adding terms relating to valuation of EQ-5D-5L which arise in this book. Further information on EQ-5D nomenclature is provided in Brooks et al. (2020).

Terms which appear in bold within each description indicate that to be a term which is also included and defined elsewhere in the glossary. Terms appear in alphabetical order.

Please note that general statistical terms used in this book which are not specific to the valuation of EQ-5D-5L are not defined in this glossary; readers who require clarification on methods used for analysing and modelling valuation data are encouraged to refer to relevant textbooks (e.g., Cameron and Trivedi 2005) and journal articles (e.g., Ramos-Goñi et al. 2017).

Term	Description
Better than dead (BTD)	A health state is considered BTD if the use of **stated preference methods** suggest it has a value >0.
Composite TTO (cTTO)	A form of **TTO** that makes use of two different tasks to elicit EQ-5D values across the value scale: the usual (conventional) TTO is used to obtain values >0, and a Lead Time TTO (LT-TTO) to obtain values <0 (see Oppe et al. 2014).
Crosswalk	See **Mapping**.
Discrete choice experiment (DCE)	DCEs are a quantitative technique for eliciting **stated preferences**. The method involves asking individuals to choose between hypothetical alternatives – in the case of valuing EQ-5D, this usually involves asking respondents to choose between pairs of EQ-5D profiles. Alternative variants of DCEs are also used – for example, introducing duration as an attribute of the profiles under consideration.

N. Devlin et al. (eds.), *Value Sets for EQ-5D-5L*,
https://doi.org/10.1007/978-3-030-89289-0

Term	Description
EQ VAS	A standard vertical 20 cm visual analogue scale, used in recording an individual's rating of their overall current health-related quality of life. The scale ranges from 100 ('the best imaginable health state' or 'the best health state you can imagine') to 0 ('the worst imaginable health state' or 'the worst health you can imagine'). There are different versions of these for the EQ-5D-3L, the EQ-5D-5L and the EQ-5D-Y; these are currently being harmonised. In the EQ-5D-5L, EQ-5D-Y and harmonised versions, the scale is accompanied by a box to record the rating.
EQ VAS score	Score between 0 and 100 recorded by an individual for their current overall health-related quality of life using the EQ VAS.
EQ-5D	The family of instruments developed and maintained by the EuroQol Group – for example, the EQ-5D-3L, the EQ-5D-5L and the EQ-5D-Y.
EQ-5D profile	A description of a health state defined by one of the EQ-5D descriptive systems. This may be summarised by a series of five sentences, one for each dimension and stating the level within that dimension; or a label consisting of five ordinal numbers, one for each dimension (by convention, in the order these appear in the questionnaire), defining the severity level, where 1 means no problems.
EQ-5D proxy questionnaires	A questionnaire that records a person's current health state as rated by a caregiver who knows the person well. Consists of a standard format for the proxy to record the person's health state according to the relevant EQ-5D descriptive system and the EQ VAS.
EQ-5D proxy-reported health state	A health state recorded by a proxy acting for the person experiencing it using any of the EQ-5D proxy questionnaires. This may be summarised in the same way as the EQ-5D profile.
EQ-5D self-reported health state	A health state recorded by a respondent using any of the EQ-5D questionnaires or by an interviewer recording their responses on the questionnaire. This may be summarised in the same way as the EQ-5D profile.
EQ-5D value set	A list of the values for every possible EQ-5D profile within a given descriptive system. For example, a value set for the EQ-5D-5L shows a value for each of the 3125 states that are described by it. These values are usually calculated using an algorithm that assigns a score to each level in each dimension, sometimes including adjustments for interactions between the dimensions. As value sets represent the average values of a sample of people, for example the general public of a particular country, it is important to state which value set is being used. Value sets are also sometimes referred to as 'tariffs'.
EQ-5D values	The value attached to an EQ-5D profile according to a set of weights that reflect, on average, people's preferences about how good or bad the state is. Values are anchored at 1 (full health) and 0 (dead) as required by their use in economic evaluation. Values less than 0 represent health states considered to be **worse than dead** (WTD). An EQ-5D value is also sometimes known as an 'index', 'score' or 'utility'.

Term	Description
EQ-5D-3L	Refers to either the **EQ-5D-3L descriptive system** or the **EQ-5D-3L questionnaire**. 'EQ-5D-3L' should always be referred to in full at first usage, but thereafter can be shortened to '3L'.
EQ-5D-3L descriptive system	Descriptive system for **health-related quality of life** states consisting of five dimensions (Mobility, Self-care, Usual activities, Pain/discomfort, Anxiety/depression), each of which has three severity levels that are described by statements appropriate to that dimension.
EQ-5D-3L questionnaire	Standard layout for recording a person's current self-reported health state. Consists of a standard format for respondents to record their health state according to the **EQ-5D-3L descriptive system** and the **EQ VAS.**
EQ-5D-5L	Refers to either the **EQ-5D-5L descriptive system** or the **EQ-5D-5L questionnaire.** 'EQ-5D-5L' should always be referred to in full at first usage, but thereafter can be shortened to '5L'.
EQ-5D-5L descriptive system	Descriptive system for **health-related quality of life** states consisting of five dimensions (Mobility, Self-care, Usual activities, Pain/discomfort, Anxiety/depression), each of which has five severity levels that are described by statements appropriate to that dimension.
EQ-5D-5L health state	See **EQ-5D profile.**
EQ-5D-5L questionnaire	Standard layout for recording a person's current self-reported health state. Consists of a standard format for respondents to record their health state according to the **EQ-5D-5L descriptive system** and the **EQ VAS.**
EQ-5D-Y	The version of the EQ-5D suitable for use with younger people. Refers either to the **EQ-5D-Y descriptive system** or the **EQ-5D-Y questionnaire.** The three level version of EQ-5D-Y is referred to as the EQ-5D-Y-3L. A five level version has also been developed, referred to as the EQ-5D-Y-5L.
EQ-5D-Y descriptive system	Descriptive system for young peoples' **health-related quality of life** states consisting of five dimensions (Mobility, Looking after myself, Doing usual activities, Having pain/discomfort, Feeling worried, sad or unhappy). In the EQ-5D-Y-3L each dimensions has 3 severity levels, described by the statements appropriate to that dimension; in the EQ-5D-Y-5L, each dimension has 5 severity levels.
EQ-5D-Y questionnaire	Standard layout for recording a young person's current self-reported health state. Consists of a standard format for respondents to record their health state according to the **EQ-5D-Y descriptive system** and the **EQ VAS.**
EQ-VT protocol	A standardised valuation study protocol (implemented using the **EQ-VT**) developed by the EuroQol Group to create standard value sets for the EQ-5D-5L. This protocol is based on the use of the **composite time trade-off** (cTTO) valuation technique, supplemented by a **discrete choice experiment** (DCE) (see EuroQol Group 2021).
EuroQol Portable Valuation Technology (EQ-PVT)	EQ-PVT is a portable version of **EuroQol Valuation Technology** (EQ-VT), which allows preference data to be collected without requiring direct links to the EuroQol Group software as is necessary for EQ-VT. It runs using similar algorithms to EQ-VT, but these are executed via Microsoft PowerPoint. Data are stored on the computer and can then be uploaded to secure sites when internet links are available. The first use of EQ-PVT in valuation of EQ-5D-5L is reported in Welie et al. (2020).

Term	Description
EuroQol Valuation Technology (EQ-VT)	Software developed by the EuroQol Group to obtain **values** for the EQ-5D in computer-assisted personal interviews. The methods currently used in **EQ-VT** to obtain stated preferences for EQ-5D health states are the **composite time trade-off** (cTTO) and **discrete choice experiments** (DCE).
Experimental design *or* **EQ-VT design**	Refers to methodological choices underlying the **EQ-VT protocol**, regarding the number of EQ-5D-5L health states for which values are to be elicited using either **DCE** or **cTTO**; which subset of states are selected for inclusion from the **EQ-5D-5L descriptive system**; how many respondents are included in the sample; and how many stated preference tasks and other questions each will be asked to complete. See Chapter 3 of this book.
Feedback module	The feedback module introduced in Version 2.0 of the **EQ-VT protocol** shows respondents what rank ordering of health states would be inferred from their **cTTO** responses. Respondents can indicate their disagreement with the implied rank ordering, allowing this information to be used by the study team. For further detail, see Chapter 2 and Stolk et al. (2019).
Health technology assessment (HTA)	'A multidisciplinary process that uses explicit methods to determine the value of a health technology at different points in its lifecycle. The purpose is to inform decision-making in order to promote an equitable, efficient, and high-quality health system' (O'Rourke et al. 2020).
Health-related quality of life (HRQoL)	Can be defined as 'how well a person functions in their life and his or her perceived wellbeing in physical, mental, and social domains of health' (Hays and Reeve 2010). However, there is a lack of consensus on what HRQoL is; readers are referred to Karimi and Brazier (2016) for a discussion of this issue.
Lead time TTO (LT-TTO)	A form of **TTO** that adds a fixed number of years in full health at the start (hence 'lead' time) of both profiles the respondent is asked to choose between. The LT-TTO was developed to allow a uniform approach to eliciting **EQ-5D values** < 0, = 0 and > 0 (see Devlin et al. 2011).
'Lite' protocol	An alternative version of the standard **EQ-VT protocol**, modified to reduce the overall cost or responder burden – such as by reducing the number of states to be valued via **TTO** overall, or by respondent. An example is provided in Yang et al. (2019).
Mapping	Mapping (sometimes also referred to as 'crosswalking') uses econometric methods to predict one measure of **HRQoL** using another outcome measure that is available. For example, in studies where EQ-5D data are unavailable, mapping is sometimes used to predict EQ-5D based on condition-specific measures of health (see Dakin et al. 2018). Mapping is also used to establish the relationship between the EQ-5D-3L and EQ-5D-5L – see van Hout et al. (2012) and van Hout and Shaw (2021). Mapping is discussed in Chapter 5 of this book.
Preference pattern	The properties of **value sets** observed within or between samples, with respect to, for example: the relative importance of EQ-5D dimensions, patterns of linearity or non-linearity in value across the levels in each dimension, the range of values and the shape of the overall distribution of values. Preference patterns in value sets are discussed in Chapter 6 of this book.

Term	Description
Quality control (QC)	From version 1.1 of the **EQ-VT protocol,** a QC procedure was introduced to review interviewer protocol compliance, identify interviewer effects and monitor face validity of the data while the study was ongoing. For further detail, see Chapter 2 and Stolk et al. (2019).
Quality-adjusted life year (QALY)	A measure of health that combines length of life and quality of life. The quality adjustment weight or **value** of each health state is multiplied by the time spent in the state and summed to calculate the number of **QALYs** (see Drummond et al. 2015).
Stated preference (SP) methods	The use of surveys or experiments to find out about people's preferences. SP relies on the assumption that 'the preferences obtained by offering people hypothetical choices are really those that underlie their choices in the everyday world and that the choices they make within the survey are those they would make if they were really faced with the alternatives offered' (Morris et al. 2012).
Time trade-off (TTO)	A **valuation** method commonly used to value EQ-5D. In its most common format, respondents are given a choice between two profiles – an EQ-5D profile for a given number of years, and full health for a shorter period of time – and asked which they prefer. The task then iterates to establish the number of years in full health at which respondents are indifferent between the two options. In effect, respondents are asked to trade between quality and length of life (Morris et al. 2012).
Valuation	The process of eliciting or otherwise assigning values to the health states defined by EQ-5D instruments, using **stated preference methods.**
Value set	Value sets provide a way of converting **EQ-5D profiles** into a single number that reflects how good or bad people think they are. The values are usually obtained using **stated preference methods,** and yield **values** that lie on a scale anchored by the value of 1 for full health, and 0 for dead. EQ-5D values cannot be higher than 1, but values <0 are possible, and indicate health states considered on average to be **worse than dead** (WTD). Value sets are generally intended to represent the average preferences of local/national populations. See **EQ-5D value set.**
Values	See **EQ-5D values.**
Worse than dead (WTD)	A health state is considered WTD if the use of **stated preference methods** suggest it has a value <0.

References

Brooks R, Boye K, Slaap B (2020) EQ-5D: a plea for accurate nomenclature. J Patient Rep Outcomes 4(1):52. https://doi.org/10.1186/s41687-020-00222-9

Cameron AC, Trivedi PK (2005) Microeconometrics: methods and applications. Cambridge University Press, New York

Dakin H, Abel L, Burns R, Yang Y (2018) Review and critical appraisal of studies mapping from quality of life or clinical measures to EQ-5D: an online database and application of the MAPS statement. Health Qual Life Outcomes 16(1):31. https://doi.org/10.1186/s12955-018-0857-3

Devlin NJ, Tsuchiya A, Buckingham K, Tilling C (2011) A uniform time trade off method for states better and worse than dead: feasibility study of the 'lead time' approach. Health Econ 20(3):348–361

Devlin N, Parkin D, Janssen B (2020) Methods for analysing and reporting EQ-5D data. Springer, New York

Drummond M, Sculpher M, Claxton K, Stoddart G, Torrance GW (2015) Methods for the economic evaluation of health care programmes. Oxford University Press, Oxford

EuroQol Group (2021) EQ-5D-5L. Standard value sets, Valuation. https://euroqol.org/eq-5d-instruments/eq-5d-5l-about/valuation-standard-value-sets/. Accessed 15 July 2021

Hays RD, Reeve BB (2010) Measurement and modeling of health-related quality of Life. In: Killewo J, Heggenhougen HK, Quah SR (eds) Epidemiology and demography in public health. Academic Press, San Diego, pp 195–205

Karimi M, Brazier J (2016) Health, health-related quality of life, and quality of life: What is the difference? Pharmacoeconomics 34(7):645–649

Morris S, Devlin N, Parkin D, Spencer A (2012) Economic analysis in health care, 2nd edn. Wiley, Chichester

O'Rourke B, Oortwijn W, Schuller T (2020) The new definition of health technology assessment: A milestone in international collaboration. Int J Technol Assess Health Care 36(3):187–190

Oppe M, Devlin NJ, van Hout B, Krabbe PF, de Charro F (2014) A program of methodological research to arrive at the new international EQ-5D-5L valuation protocol. Value Health 17(4):445–453

Ramos-Goñi JM, Pinto-Prades JL, Oppe M, Cabasés JM, Serrano-Aguilar R-AO (2017) Valuation and modeling of EQ-5D-5L health states using a hybrid approach. Med Care 55(7):e51

Stolk E, Ludwig K, Rand K, van Hout B, Ramos-Goñi J-M (2019) Overview, update, and lessons learned from the international EQ-5D-5L valuation work: Version 2 of the EQ-5D-5L valuation protocol. Value Health 22(1):23–30

van Hout B, Shaw JW (2021) Mapping EQ-5D-3L to EQ-5D-5L. Value Health. https://doi.org/10.1016/j.jval.2021.03.009

van Hout B, Janssen MF, Feng YS, Kohlmann T, Busschbach J, Golicki D, Lloyd A, Scalone L, Kind P, Pickard AS (2012) Interim scoring for the EQ-5D-5L: mapping the EQ-5D-5L to EQ-5D-3L value sets. Value Health 15(5):708–715

Welie AG, Gebretekle GB, Stolk E, Mukuria C, Krahn MD, Enquoselassie F, Fenta TG (2020) Valuing health state: An EQ-5D-5L value set for Ethiopians. Value Health Reg Issues 22:7–14

Yang Z, Luo N, Oppe M, Bonsel G, Busschbach J, Stolk E (2019) Toward a smaller design for EQ-5D-5L valuation studies. Value Health 22(11):1295–1302